after school

THEODOSSIS ISSAIAS
ALYSSA VELAZQUEZ

CARNEGIE MELLON —ARCHITECTURE

—in—otherwards—

Carnegie Museum of Art

CONTENTS

text book

counter index

lesson plans

FOREWORD

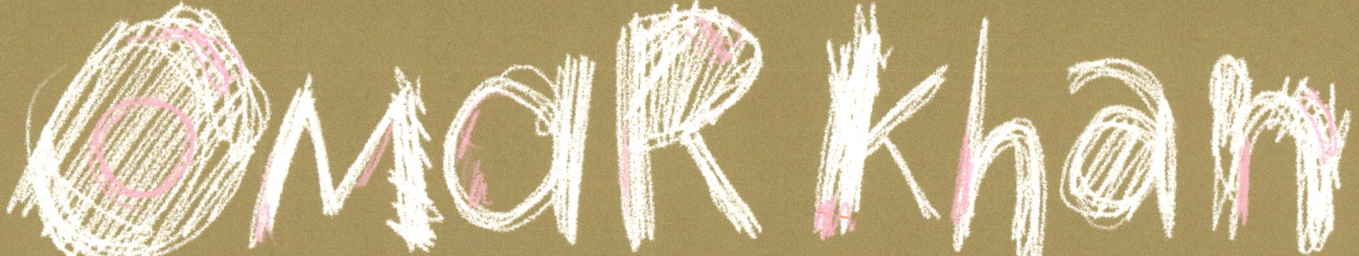

Eric Crosby
HENRY J. HEINZ II DIRECTOR, CARNEGIE MUSEUM OF ART
VICE PRESIDENT, CARNEGIE MUSEUMS OF PITTSBURGH

Omar Khan
PROFESSOR AND HEAD, SCHOOL OF ARCHITECTURE,
CARNEGIE MELLON UNIVERSITY

From classroom to hallway, from playground to neighborhood, from syllabus to floor plan, *after school* offers an in-depth reflection on the architecture of public education in the twentieth century. The exhibition and namesake publication emerged from a multiyear process of research and conversations co-led by Theodossis Issaias and Alyssa Velazquez. Together, they asked: how do educational spaces shape, and how are they shaped by, the struggles, desires, and imaginaries of their communities? This book is also the result of a collaboration between Carnegie Museum of Art and Carnegie Mellon University's School of Architecture (CMU SoA)—two civic institutions less than a mile apart and deeply rooted in Pittsburgh's urban fabric. More than a joint production, *after school* reflects a shared conviction that the museum and university are places where educational and spatial justice can be actively pursued—through critical inquiry, creative practice, and collective imagination.

CMU's School of Architecture has committed to engaging design as a cultural and political tool to address pressing social and ecological challenges through strategic initiatives such as the Pedagogies 2020 planning process. *after school* marks a significant milestone for the university: the first imprint in the School of Architecture's new publishing series, dedicated to expanding the public reach of design scholarship and research. Similarly, for decades, the Heinz Architectural Center—one of the few architecture centers embedded in a major art museum and soon undergoing a significant refurbishment—has bridged artistic inquiry with the politics of the built environment. Together, the SoA and HAC offer a cross-institutional framework for research and curatorial practice, foregrounding educational spaces and the social contracts they encode.

after school assembles a sustained architectural, archival, and testimonial history of Pittsburgh's public schools in relation to federal education policies and urban transformation. No such record previously existed. Many of the documents included here—located on the shelves of bureaucratic departments or shared by retired civil servants—are being exhibited or published for the first time. This book, like the exhibition, builds on Carnegie Museum of Art and CMU School of Architecture's commitments to cultivating cross-disciplinary research and advancing a pedagogical model that is civic, critical, and collaborative. *after school* invites us to stay after class—to reflect, imagine, and engage in the ongoing question: what might a more just, joyful, and critically engaged architecture of public education look like?

Anchored in Pittsburgh, *after school* brings forward figures and episodes that exemplify both the promises and contradictions of public education. Architect Walter Roberts—Carnegie Tech graduate and one of the few Black architects licensed in Pittsburgh—designed schools at a time when the city's desegregation plans were already failing. His story is interwoven with that of Raymond Saunders, whose departure from the Hill District as a student reflects longer legacies of displacement. Saunders—subject of a recent solo exhibition at Carnegie Museum of Art—draws our attention to the fact that schools are not only spaces of learning, but of artistic formation, memory, and political contestation. *after school* builds on these educational and architectural histories, bringing them into dialogue with newly commissioned works by contemporary artists, architects, collectives, and designers. They reimagine educational and spatial justice as a collective undertaking and remind us that the work never truly ends.

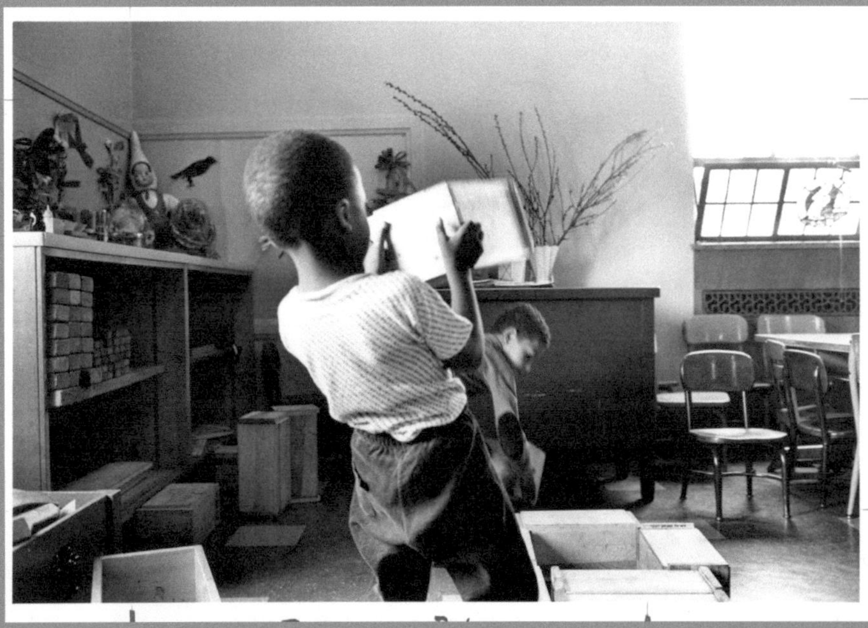

Student holding up a mask, ca. 1963, photograph; Detre Library & Archives, HHC

AN OPENING

THEODOSIS ISSAIAS

CURATOR, HEINZ ARCHITECTURAL CENTER

ALYSSA VELAZQUEZ

ASSISTANT CURATOR

Four years ago, we opened a folder in the archive marked 95.105.5 PPS. It had not been touched in decades. Inside were a series of watercolors, painted in meticulous washes of blue and brick red. One stood out: a pale sky shaded in precise gradations, offsetting figures in long coats standing beside idling motorcars before a monumental façade. Men and women in their outerwear gazed across Pittsburgh from this section of North Oakland, their bodies and machines arranged on the steps and parkway of Schenley High School. The drawing, dated 1915, was among several gifted from Pittsburgh Public Schools to Carnegie Museum of Art. But how and why? Who was the registrar at the time they were processed? Under what circumstances had they arrived?

The watercolors were instruments of persuasion, designed to show the promise of public education through the language of architecture. The symmetry of the façades, the carefully posed figures, the orderly streets: all visual arguments for the value of building schools, for the role of education in shaping a modern city. To encounter them in the quiet of the archive—when the city's classrooms themselves had fallen silent—was to glimpse how deeply education was once entwined with civic life and imagination.

When a school closes, its records often do not pass into district repositories but are instead dispersed: stashed in closets of the nearest operating school, occasionally finding their way to regional archives such as the Carnegie Library of Pittsburgh or the Heinz History Center, or carried away in the personal collections of teachers, principals, and students. Schenley was emblematic of this dislocation. After years of debate, the district closed the high school in the late 2000s, citing declining enrollment, costly maintenance, and the discovery of lead and asbestos. Within a few years, the building reopened as luxury apartments. The abruptness of this conversion—public infrastructure transformed into private profit—revealed in stark terms how the life of a school can be severed from its community, and how the traces of its memory are scattered. The closure of Schenley ruptured Pittsburgh's educational landscape: students and teachers were relocated, alumni protested, neighbors lost a landmark.

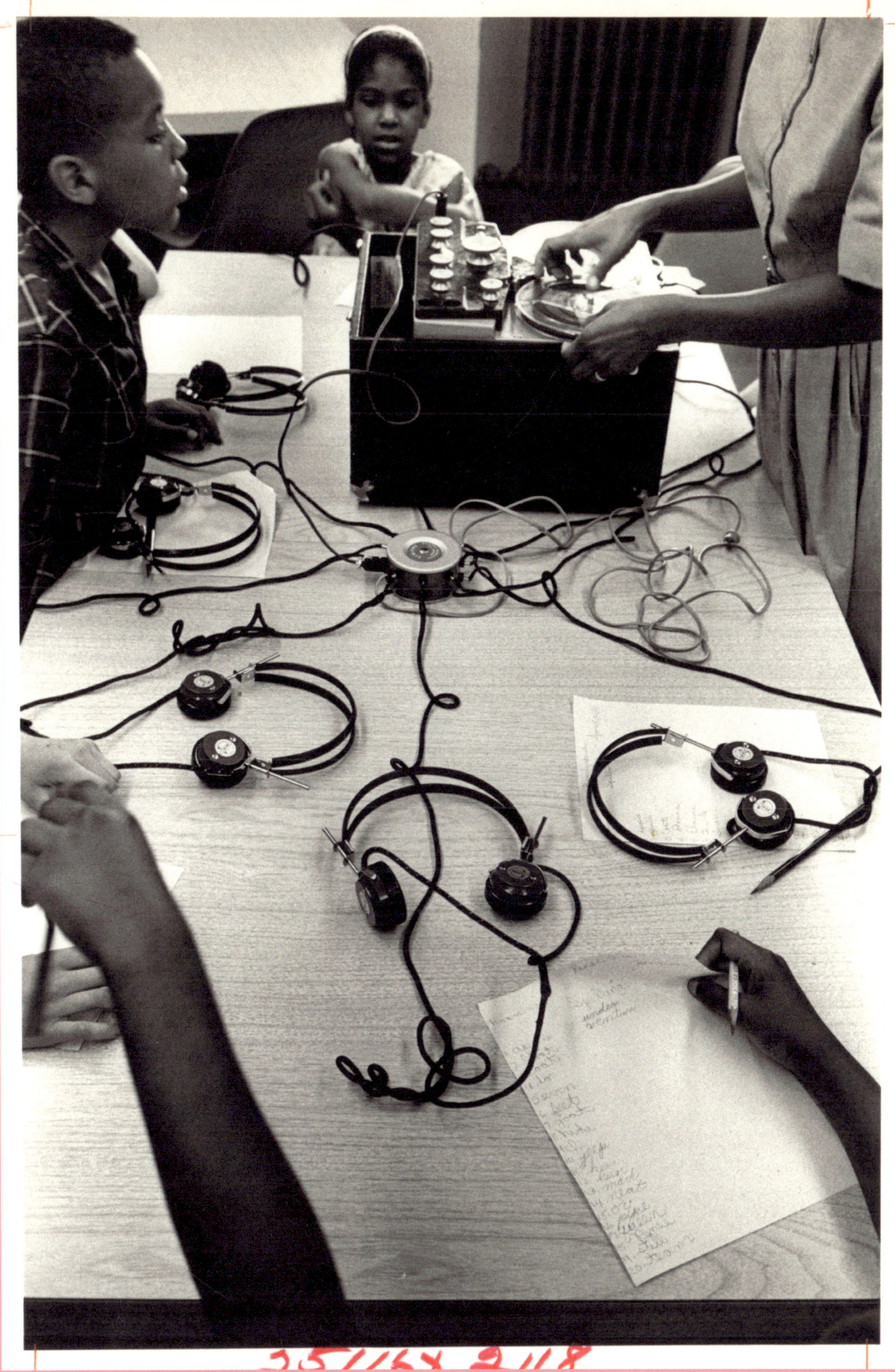

Table with audio equipment, 1963, photograph; Detre Library & Archives, HHC

This is where *after school* began—not as a fully-formed concept but as a set of questions and concerns attentive to the material, political, and affective conditions of public education. The right to free and public education—a right defended through generations of struggle—is once again precarious. Across the United States, public schools face intensifying assaults: waves of disinvestment and closures, mounting debt burdens, curricula narrowed and censored, and the steady march of privatization often cloaked in the language of "school choice." In Pittsburgh, as in many cities, the cycle is viciously familiar: diminished resources lead to reduced enrollment, which in turn justifies further cuts, consolidations, or closures. Students, teachers, and families bear the consequences, while the institutions meant to protect them grow fragile. As we witnessed during our research, each closure carries an afterlife—a community severed, an archive displaced, a building repurposed or left to decay. Demolished or renamed, the school persists in other forms: a landmark for directions, a memory shared among alumni, a presence folded into the city's fabric.

Schools are deeply contradictory places. They are where students are sorted, disciplined, and assimilated into prevailing norms; where difference is often repressed and histories redacted. Yet they are also where rights have been defended, where solidarities form, where play and discovery flourish against the odds. The school is an instrument of assimilation and a space of dreaming; it is a site of oppression and of collective care. These contradictions surface in the segregated bussing policies of the 1960s, in the grassroots Street Academies of the 1970s, in the everyday negotiations of classrooms today. *after school* tends to this tension, refusing to reduce the school to a single narrative. Instead, it asks how schools not only reflect broader social orders but actively shape the life of streets, neighborhoods, and cities. To study schools in this way requires a particular vantage point. Our entryway is architecture and design—understood not just as buildings and plans, but as the wider organization of space. The renderings of Schenley, the blueprints of unbuilt campuses, the plans for open classrooms are not neutral documents; they reveal pedagogical priorities, economic constraints, and political ideologies inscribed in brick and mortar. Equally important are the classroom rituals that dictate where students sit or how they move, the makeshift assemblies in church basements, the cooperative gardens and fugitive academies that arose when official institutions failed.

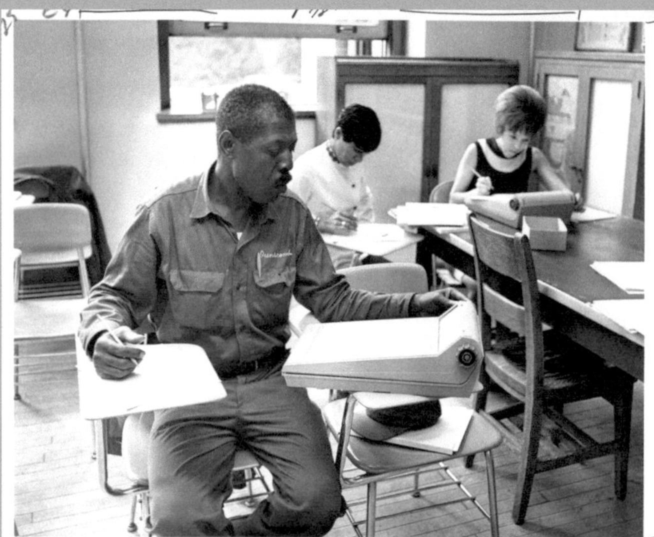

Robert Dunscomb enrolled in a summer tutoring program for GED applicants at Schenley High School, 1969, photograph; Detre Library & Archives, HHC

Taken together, these architectures offer a method of reading public education—its absences as much as its presences, its improvisations as much as its prescriptions.

This work has unfolded over years, in dialogue with peers, collaborators, and communities who have sustained and challenged it. Educators, parents, and students in Pittsburgh shared testimonies of closures and consolidations. Journalists traced the structural inequities embedded in policy decisions. Artists and architects tested new forms of lesson plans, playgrounds, and pedagogical tools. Scholars joined as co-travelers, offering conceptual languages—choice, fugitivity, compliance, responsibility—with which to parse our own findings. The project has never belonged to one author or institution. It has grown through a network of research, conversation, and practice. The exhibition at the Carnegie Museum of Art (August 23, 2025 – January 11, 2026), and the book you now hold, are moments within that ongoing process: partial, situated, and provisional, yet also collective and cumulative.

What follows, then, is not a comprehensive history nor a theory of public schooling. It is, instead, a set of propositions: fragments, case studies, and invitations to keep learning. The book is structured into three sections, each approaching the states and stakes of public education from a different angle—textual, archival, and speculative. Before turning to them, it is worth noting why we chose these three forms—text book, counter index, and lesson plans. Each carries a history of standardization: the textbook as the vessel of sanctioned knowledge, the index as the administrative ledger, the lesson plan as the tool of classroom management. Reworked here, these familiar forms might also become instruments of critique, memory, and imagination.

text book gathers essays and conversations that follow the infrastructures of public education—ceilings and contracts, classrooms and policies, memories and protests—searching how learning has been built, imagined, and reconfigured across time. Together they open different ways to read the histories and futures of public education. This first section begins with *A Plan for a Reflected Ceiling*, where a single architectural drawing becomes a prism for understanding schools as social infrastructures—systems in which ducts and wires are entangled with contracts, costs, and political imperatives. It traces how education itself takes form through these material and bureaucratic negotiations, continuously constructed and contested. Where the essay traces these negotiations in built form, Ujju Aggarwal's *Finding Each Other* examines them in policy. She shows how school choice was used to fracture publics while deepening racial and economic exclusions. Yet she also points to how communities mobilized choice to find one another and build alternative spaces of learning. Sister IAsia Thomas and members of the Equity Advisory Panel bring this insistence into the present, narrating three decades of speaking out against the mistreatment of Black students in Pittsburgh, and keeping an official complaint against Pittsburgh Public Schools alive. Their testimony demonstrates advocacy itself as a form of pedagogy—naming inequity, demanding accountability, and sustaining the fight for justice.

Extending this focus on how education structures belonging, *Modeling America in Van Dyke Brown* turns to the classroom, where civic myths can be quite literally modeled. The essay follows Works Progress Administration (WPA) plaster casts of Independence Hall and their role in patriotic pedagogy, revealing how national belonging is rehearsed through design objects, performances, and everyday rituals. Leigh Patel's *Life and Learning in the Practice of Fugitivity* attends to the ghosts of such classrooms. Public schooling, Patel argues, has long been structured by racial capitalism and settler colonialism, producing disparities that are both material and spectral. Yet within these gaps emerge fugitive practices: small refusals, lingering after-school gatherings, moments of joy that slip past enclosure. A conversation between Dana Bishop-Root and Dr. Sala Udin situates these struggles across institutions, where justice is pursued from both inside and outside formal structures—from school boards to museums to grassroots organizing.

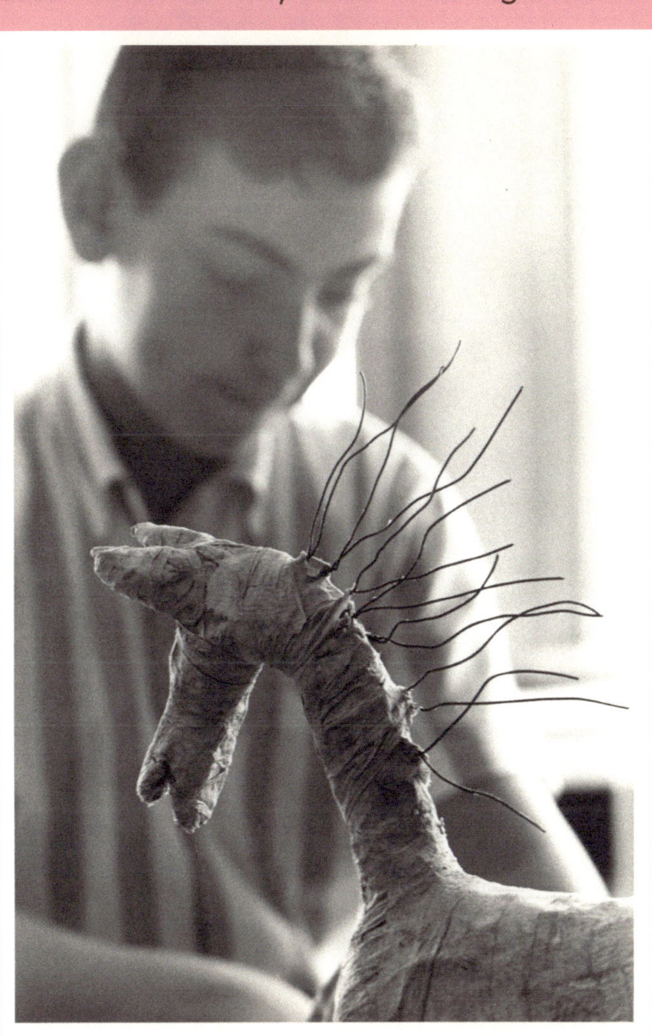

Student making a papier-mâché animal, ca. 1963, photograph; Detre Library & Archives, HHC

David Serlin's *Another Kind of Renaissance* begins with the story of Pittsburgh's Pioneer School, designed in 1960 for children with disabilities. From this case study, he opens a wider lens onto disability and design, inviting us to see architecture as a practice of care and civic imagination. Laura Nelson's *Media Study: Artmaking After School* revisits the California Labor School, where art and vocational training became tools of political imagination. At a time when vocational programs often restricted working-class and Black students to limited futures, the Labor School turned making into study, opening art as a practice of collective knowledge and political organizing. In dialogue with this history, Miguel Braceli and Stefan Gruber reflect on how art and collective making can generate new forms of commons. From porches to playgrounds, from public performances to participatory design, they describe how education expands outward, dissolving the boundaries of the school and cultivating solidarities in shared space. Read together, the essays of *text book* trace the layered infrastructures of public education—from ceilings and policies to ghosts, models, and playgrounds.

counter index takes its name from today's Facilities Condition Index (FCI), the capital-planning tool the Pittsburgh School Board uses to determine the fate of its buildings. The FCI weighs the cost of repairs against the cost of replacement, reducing schools to numerical scores that consultants present as the basis for closure. As of the publishing of this book, twelve schools in Pittsburgh are under review for immediate closure based on these metrics. It is within this context of disinvestment that Sarosh Anklesaria's essay frames the section, arguing for schools as vital forms of social infrastructure. Drawing on Pittsburgh's history of New Deal patronage, architectural ambition, and disinvestment, he shows how schools have functioned as civic anchors, even as decades of austerity have eroded their maintenance.

Across ten case studies, *counter index* proposes another way of reckoning with value by tracing Pittsburgh's schools through overlapping histories, where drawings and photographs show each building carrying multiple lives—established, relocated, renamed, remodeled, demolished, or abandoned. These are not linear chronologies but recursive ones, shaped by cycles of investment and disinvestment, expansion and closure, abandonment and reuse. They range from monumental complexes of the early twentieth century, sprawling modernist campuses of the postwar decades, and the everyday infrastructures of ventilation, heat, and light, each entangled with broader struggles over public education.

Alongside these architectural records, this section gathers testimonies of lived experiences: a student recalling the grandeur and contested closure of Schenley High; a teacher who returned to Peabody as an alum and witnessed its transformation into Obama Academy; families navigating promises and ruptures at Herron Hill/Milliones; children at Mifflin writing poems and drawing their school into being; a pastor reflecting on Burgwin as a neighborhood anchor lost to "realignment"; an archivist uncovering the fragile traces of Pittsburgh's demountables; a mother and daughter advocating for the survival of Pioneer; residents weighing the fraught reopening of Northview Heights; an educator and organizer reflecting on the legacy of street academies; and an architect in dialogue with his great-uncle, designer of Martin Luther King Jr. Elementary, on contextual design and open-plan classrooms.

lesson plans is framed by Rachel Delphia's essay *Life Lessons: Informal, Structured, and Subversive*, which reconsiders the history of pedagogy through toys, objects, and curricula preserved in the museum's collection. Lesson plans are typically instruments of standardization—designed to streamline instruction, regulate behavior, and enable oversight. Here, they are reimagined as propositions for learning otherwise.

Danielle Dean proposes a speculative syllabus titled *A Child Floating in Space: The American Dream of Education*. Through this lesson plan, she asks how the imagination has been industrialized by capital and technology, and how resistance might be mobilized in the face of corporate monopolies and data-driven futures. Ana Serrano, in dialogue with the WPA models of Americanization, turns to the materials of the everyday, asking students to construct cardboard models of places that shape their identity, to mark the erasures of gentrification, and to rebuild them in louder, more colorful forms—reclaiming architecture as a practice of presence and refusal. Gabo Camnitzer transforms the regimented "Lots of Dots" carpet into an environment of collective improvisation, where students are guided to move across the rug, take up forbidden postures, and redesign the carpet on their own. Leah Wulfman extends the geometries of play into inflatable architectures that expand and collapse with bodies in motion, offering collective movement as a curriculum in itself.

Toshiko Mori draws from her long-standing engagement with architectural pedagogy, contributing
a lesson plan that explores how design can be taught through material experimentation, cultural context, and collaborative practice. Estudio Teddy Cruz + Fonna Forman reimagine civic corridors across
the U.S.-Mexico border as Community Stations—distributed classrooms where resources and knowledges circulate reciprocally between institutions and neighborhoods. Soul Fire Farm offers a timeline
of Black, Latinx, and Indigenous struggles for land and food sovereignty, positioning agrarian practices
as both pedagogy and liberation. At Sankofa Village Community Garden and Farms, Ayanna Jones
with Vicky Achnani carry forward the legacy of the Black Panther Party's Free Breakfast Program,
teaching sovereignty and survival through soil, seeds, and shared meals.

Each of these contributions is a possible framework that can be tested, adapted, or enacted in practice.
Taken together, they propose education as play, as empowerment, as healing—an invitation to learn
through bodies, across generations, and beyond classrooms.

The three sections are threaded by a single insistence: that public education cannot be measured
only by balance sheets, blueprints, or test scores. It must also be read through the lives it shapes, the
communities it binds, and the futures it keeps open. *after school* is not an endpoint but a rehearsal—
an attempt to hold onto the fragile, embattled, and necessary institution of public education, while
also imagining a school unbound, not yet here.

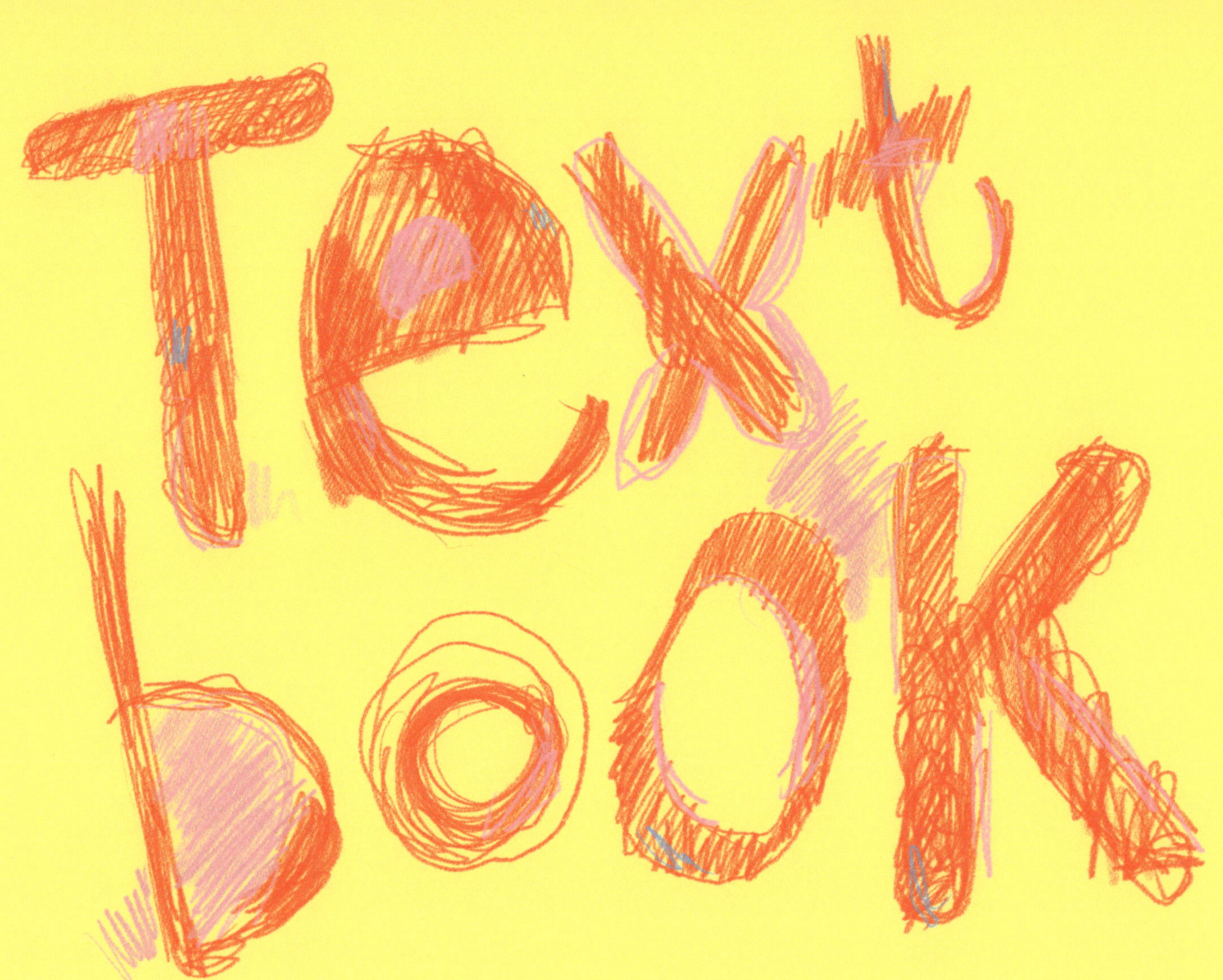

Text
book

A textbook is conventionally understood as a comprehensive resource of study within a given field, designed to instruct and standardize learning. Yet its etymology complicates this definition: derived from the Latin *textus* ("woven fabric") and the Old English *bōc* ("written document"), the term suggests more of an interlacing of knowledge. This section takes up that dual meaning. Rather than offering a totalizing account of public education, it presents a collection of interwoven narratives and perspectives that expose the contradictions at the heart of schooling. Attuned to these tensions, this section asks how schools both mirror and actively shape the social worlds that surround them, from the intimacy of neighborhoods to the life of cities.

THEODOSSIS ISSAIAS

14

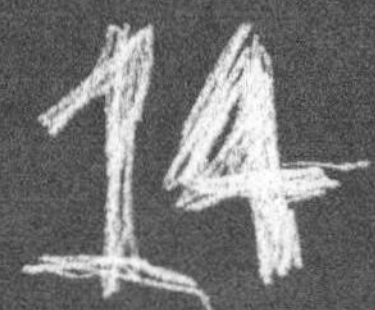

A PLAN FOR A
REFLECTED CEILING

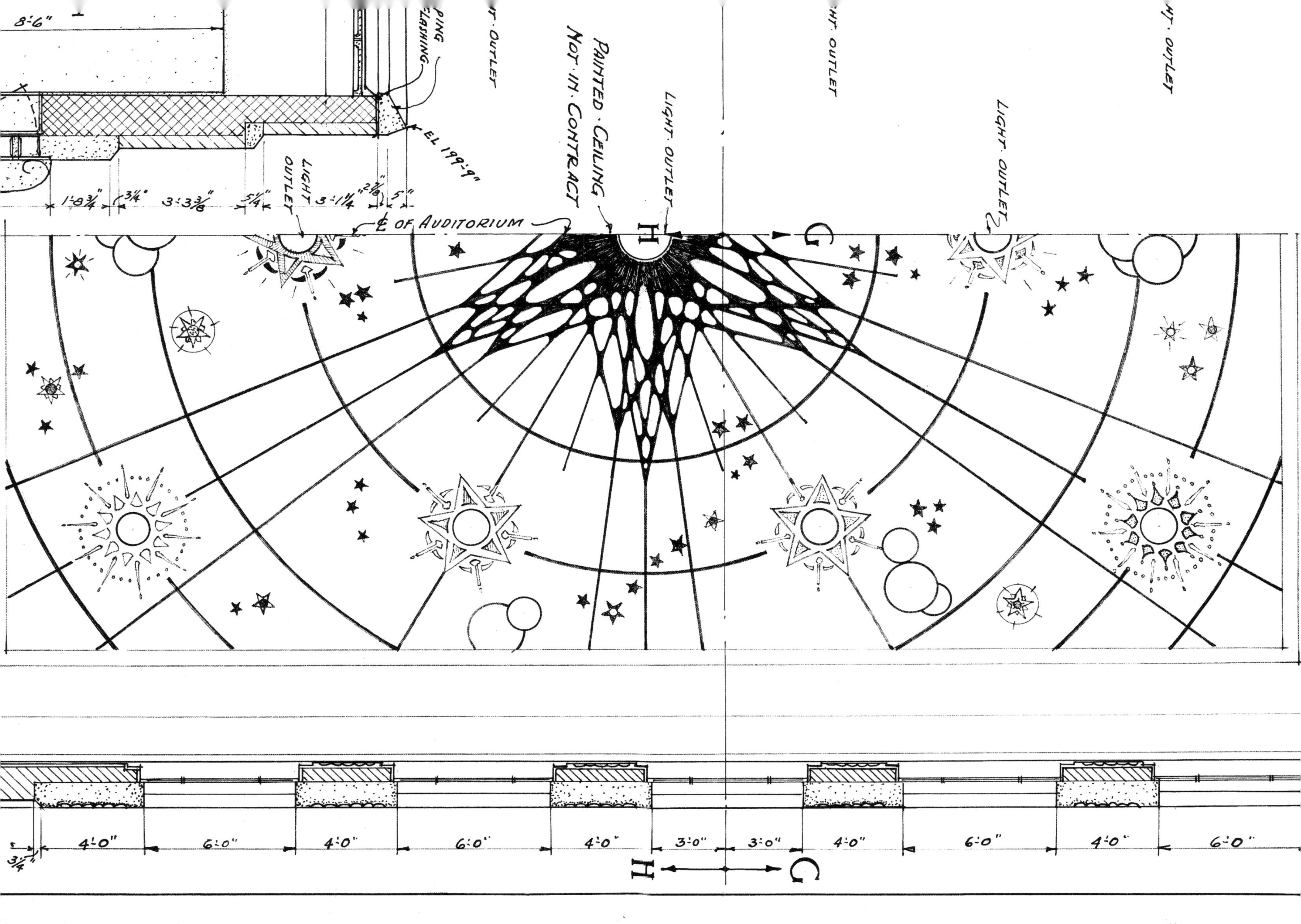
8'-6"
PING
FLASHING
HT. OUTLET
HT. OUTLET
HT. OUTLET
PAINTED. CEILING
NOT. IN. CONTRACT
LIGHT. OUTLET
LIGHT. OUTLET
LIGHT OUTLET
LIGHT
OUTLET
EL 199'-9"
℄ OF AUDITORIUM
1'-8¾"
¾"
3'-3⅜"
5¼"
3'-1¼"
2⅝"
5"
H
G
4'-0"
6'-0"
4'-0"
6'-0"
4'-0"
3'-0"
3'-0"
4'-0"
6'-0"
4'-0"
6'-0"
¾"
H
G

Previous page: Marion M. Steen, Zoomed-in segment of *Burgwin Elementary, Auditorium Details,* sheet no. 14, 1935, architectural drawing; PPBF

Constellations of glowing stars and scattered planets orbit a dense black core: a symmetrical, net-like pattern radiating from a sun—a central light fixture marked "H." From this nucleus, a spiderweb of lines refracts illumination, dilating toward the room below. The ceiling organizes itself around a cosmic diaphragm, expanding outward in concentric circles and calibrated sectors to incorporate the auditorium's infrastructure: ambient light fixtures, a projection port, intricate heating grilles, and footlights at the stage's edge.

Occupying the upper-right corner of a single sheet of paper, the plan for the reflected auditorium ceiling at Burgwin Elementary School completes a set of drawings—longitudinal and transverse sections, wall elevations, and details of cornices and curtain pockets. Yet an inscription on the drawing reads: "Painted Ceiling Not in Contract." The school, designed in 1935–1936 by Marion M. Steen, was funded by the Public Works Administration (PWA), a New Deal agency which financed public works to combat the Great Depression. Steen was the registered architect of record for Pittsburgh Public Schools and would soon be appointed its Superintendent of Buildings. Burgwin Elementary was one of many built during a period of municipal expansion, as Pittsburgh's population swelled. The school district, backed by federal funding and centralized oversight, pursued an ambitious building program across the city. In Hazelwood, where steel mills lined the Monongahela, Burgwin projected optimism despite an industrial economy still struggling to recover.

Burgwin Elementary's ceiling thickened. Dropped five feet below the roof line, it concealed thirty-six-inch steel I-beams that held the weight of the 325-seat auditorium roof. Through this dense section ran the electricity, heating, and lighting systems—a layered space where infrastructure gathered. Only a thin veneer of paint created the cosmic cartography—not as ornament, but as an organizing principle for making visible a public education infrastructure. The kind of ceiling students glance toward when lessons drag — heavens above! — or when the choir misses its cue, or when the principal pontificates. While the ceiling never materialized in its full glory, the care invested in its design was carried into more than twenty schools built across the city in those years. Yet for all this visible investment, the Superintendent of Buildings operated under persistent financial constraint. Steen was responsible not only for new construction, but for upgrading existing facilities, balancing operating costs, and managing a staff of 1041 employees across a city shaped by expanding populace, industry, and pollution.[1]

The skies of Pittsburgh were seldom clean or starry, darkened by smoke and soot from coal-fired furnaces and steel mills.[2] In the 1930s, the city annually recorded hundreds of hours of "heavy smoke," with visibility under half a mile. Industrial smog coated school interiors in an ever-renewing film.[3] As Steen observed, "Pittsburgh's atmosphere carries a higher percentage of dirt than most other cities, resulting in a cleaning problem in the schools which is very unusual."[4] Janitorial labor—also under his supervision—was the district's largest operating expense. To combat atmospheric pollution, the city continuously amended its anti-smoke laws, requiring buildings to reduce emissions by upgrading their facilities. The school district, in turn, had to replace manual stokers with mechanical ones, retrofitting 344 boilers across 132 schools—each under Steen's jurisdiction.

Electricity, too, became a source of budgetary strain. As enrollment increased, so did the physical footprint of the schools—and their energy demands. "The cost of artificial lighting and power current," Steen wrote, "shows a startling growth since 1925, and there is every reason to believe

1 **Marion M. Steen and the Department of Buildings,** *Progress 1911-1941* (The Board of Public Education Pittsburgh, PA, 1941), 15.

2 **Cliff I. Davidson,** "Air Pollution In Pittsburgh: A Historical Perspective," *Journal of the Air Pollution Control Association* 29, no. 10 (1979): 1038–39, https://doi.org/10.1080/00022470.1979. 10470892.

3 **Steen and the Department of Buildings,** *Progress 1911-1941,* 20.

4 **Steen and the Department of Buildings,** *Progress 1911-1941,* 14.

it will continue to increase unless there is a drastic reduction in rates."[5] Older classrooms had once been lit at four to six foot-candles—roughly the dimness of a cloudy day indoors. By the 1930s, new buildings were wired for twenty-five foot-candles, closer to the brightness of a well-lit shop floor, a six-fold increase in illumination. The power bill reflected the pedagogical ambitions of the day. "Our requirements for electric power have increased tremendously," Steen noted, "also by the fact that many schools are intensively used at night. Trade schools are on a twenty-four-hour, three-shift plan."[6] Year by year, the ceiling thickened with wiring and light.

Often overlooked, ceilings—like buildings themselves—bear the weight of more than mechanical systems: they condense networks of logistical, material, financial, and ideological demands. They register the unpredictable and deeply political choreography of school construction and operations—a negotiation between the architect's contractual obligations and the district's political ambitions, bureaucratic red tape and creative abundance, resource scarcity and infrastructural excess, the promise of social mobility and the persistence of structural barriers. As Gloria Ladson-Billings has argued, such inequities are part of an "education debt" built over generations—a debt visible not only in test scores and graduation rates, but also in the very spaces where learning takes place.[7] In Pittsburgh, a city shaped by waves of industrial investment and disinvestment, ecological degradation and cultural resistance, these tensions are embedded in the very ceilings under which children gather to learn. Thinning or thickening, suspended or exposed, ceilings are registers of shifting priorities which track the push and pull of pedagogical imperatives, politics, and maintenance cycles across decades.

Nearly a hundred years before the New Deal–era designs of Marion Steen, the city's educational landscape was already being reshaped by uneven waves of reform, beginning with the Commonwealth's Free Public School Act of 1834. The act established both the principle of free public education and the authority of municipalities to levy local taxes to sustain it. In Pittsburgh's civic mythology, this marked the beginning: in 1835, the first school opened with just five pupils under its roof. Within three years, the city operated twelve schools: ten for white students (divided evenly between boys and girls), one coeducational school for Black students, and one for infants. A second wave of reform came with an 1854 Act, which enforced statewide segregation, requiring separate schools for Black students in counties with more than twenty Black pupils. Pittsburgh readily complied with this racist mandate but was more reluctant when it came to secondary education. Although the act required the Central Board to establish two high schools, Pittsburgh opened only one—insisting, under the watchful eye of a rising industrial class, that one would suffice. This early ambivalence revealed a pattern: the city's approach to state mandates swung like a pendulum—readily enforcing those that preserved local hierarchies while evading those that threatened economic priorities and hierarchies based on race and class (see Dr Sister IAsia Thomas, p. 40).

In the decades leading into the early twentieth century, industrial expansion and population growth reshaped the city, triggering extensive yet fragmented school construction. Under a ward-based system, elected representatives oversaw local schools through a patchwork

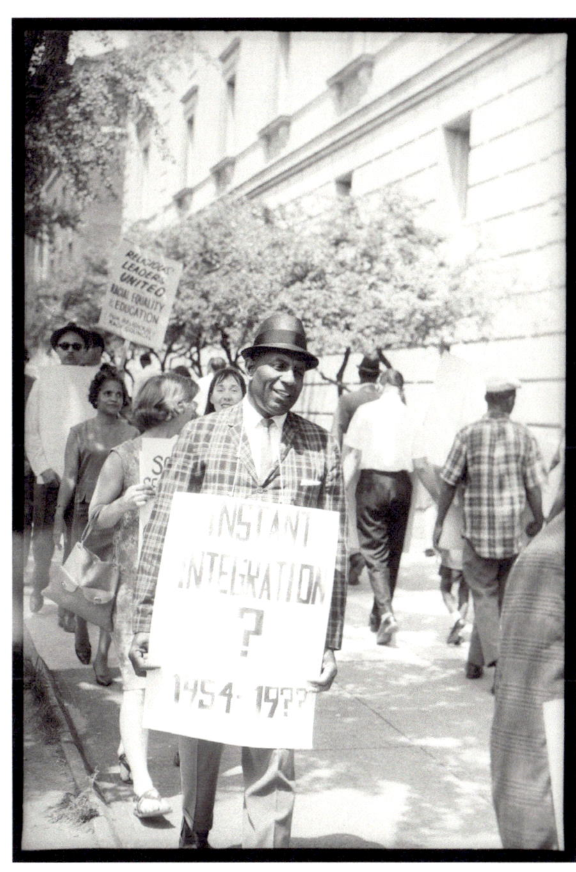

Charles "Teenie" Harris, Herbert Bean outside Pittsburgh School Board headquarters, 1966, photograph; Carnegie Museum of Art, HFF

5 Steen and the Department of Buildings, *Progress 1911–1941*, 17.

6 Steen and the Department of Buildings, *Progress 1911–1941*, 17.

7 Gloria Ladson-Billings, "From the Achievement Gap to the Education Debt: Understanding Achievement in U.S. Schools," *Educational Researcher* 35, no. 7 (2006): 3, https:// doi.org/10.3102/0013189X035007003.

of measures. Some schools were purpose-built, while others were adapted from vaulted churches, grand public halls, or dimly lit rented rooms. Responses were shaped more by local improvisation than coordinated planning, unevenly adjusting to shifting demographics, political pressures, and available resources. This organizational paradigm came to a halt in 1911, when Pennsylvania's School Code centralized authority under a single citywide district. A hallmark of the Progressive Era (ca. 1890–1920), the reform embodied irreconcilable contradictions.[8] While proclaiming education a democratic right and an instrument of civic uplift, the Code stripped constituents of the power to elect school representatives, transferring appointment authority to the district court. At the same time, it professionalized the system, introducing teacher certification, regulating qualifications, and enforcing compulsory attendance. These measures gave rise to a new administrative class of superintendents, inspectors, and specialists tasked with managing the school system through professed neutral expertise. Their claims of impartiality and scientificity often legitimized segregation and class-based educational stratification.[9]

NEW TEMPLES FOR LEARNING

Among this expanding administrative class, no figure embodied the spatial logic of the system more fully than the Superintendent of Buildings. Established to oversee the newly created Building Department, the 1911 Pennsylvania School Code specified that the superintendent "shall be an engineer or architect of good standing in the profession … responsible for the condition and care of all school buildings and premises."[10] What, exactly, did this role demand from the architect? And how did the evolving priorities of a profession increasingly defined by licensure, technical codes, and institutional prestige shape expectations for this position? What ceilings—protective, constraining, or aspirational—did these priorities construct for public education?

In numerical terms, the role oversaw 126 school buildings, inherited from the previous ward-based system, serving approximately twelve thousand students. Many students attended school in split shifts, owing to overcrowding and limited resources.[11] One district report described, "unfit cellar rooms used as classrooms," perhaps reflecting the rhetorical urgency driving reform more than actual conditions.[12] Beyond maintenance or expansion, the Building Department had to develop a "definite program incorporating all of the Board's [imperatives]."[13] These imperatives were grounded in a changing vision of schooling—one that extended beyond basic instruction to include moral development, physical health, public ceremony, and social order. Auditoria, gymnasia, vocational workshops, kitchens and dining halls, and medical inspection rooms became essential components of new school construction. In tandem, the department developed standards for classroom dimensions, ceiling heights, laboratory arrangements, desk arrangements, blackboard placement, heating systems, and maintenance protocols. What followed was a flurry of production: under Superintendent of Buildings C. L. Wooldridge, twenty-three school buildings were constructed in a single decade after 1911.[14] Design work was outsourced to private architects, while the Building Department retained responsibility for standard compliance, construction oversight, and maintenance. "In this way," the report noted, "the Board secured radically different types of architecture and uniformity

8 On the contradictions of Progressive Era reform initiatives in the United States, see **John Whiteclay Chambers II,** *The Tyranny of Change: America in the Progressive Era, 1890–1920* (Rutgers University Press, 2000); and **Michael McGerr,** *A Fierce Discontent: The Rise and Fall of the Progressive Movement in America, 1870–1920* (Oxford University Press, 2005).

9 **Jeannie Oakes,** *Keeping Track: How Schools Structure Inequality* (Yale University Press, 2005), 3–33, esp. 28–30.

10 **Nathan Christ Schaeffer,** *School Code of Pennsylvania and Other Laws: Act of May 18th, 1911,* 111.

11 **Marion M. Steen and the Department of Buildings,** *30 Years of History* (The Board of Public Education Pittsburgh, PA, 1941), 4–5.

12 **Steen and the Department of Buildings,** *30 Years of History,* 4.

13 **C. L. Wooldridge,** "Recent School Buildings in Pittsburgh, PA.: Erected under the Supervision of Mr. C. L. Wooldridge, Superintendent of Buildings," *School Board Journal* LIII, no. 6 (1916): 33.

14 Most thorough building documentation of the period can be found in the Archival Survey Project of the Pittsburgh Public Schools, 1981-1982 directed by Carolyn Schumacher.

of standards."[15] Most of the architects commissioned for this work were already embedded in elite professional and social networks, accustomed to designing private residences and commercial ventures for industrial magnates, as well as civic institutions funded through their philanthropic capital.

This architecture looked both inward—toward the formation and discipline of pupils—and outward, into the civic fabric of the city. The resulting complexes, while varying in stylistic invocation, were often monumental in scale: symmetrical, three or four stories in height, projecting authority, confidence, and the aesthetics of reform. This was the civic architecture of the City Beautiful movement (ca. 1890–1920), a nationwide aesthetic project—if not a crusade—to shape moral character through the proverbial beautification of the built environment, and to remake the urban populace in the image of the rising white bourgeoisie.[16] The anxieties driving this reform movement were both local and imperial. On the one hand, cities like Pittsburgh competed with industrial rivals such as Chicago, producing schools as markers of municipal power. As one district report declared, "Pittsburgh is a city richly blessed. … It could not hope to retain its own self-respect or the esteem of its neighbors if it did not protect in turn and develop the best life of its children."[17] On the other hand, these buildings participated in an imperial narrative of ascendance—expressing the ambitions of a country asserting itself on the international stage. As civic monuments, they solidified narrative through form: columned facades, neoclassical orders, ornamental friezes, patriotic inscriptions, and allegorical statuary conveyed ideals of national destiny, civic order, and civilizational progress.[18] Their columns and friezes rehearsed an old fiction: that the nation stood as heir to Greece and Rome, cradle of a so-called Western civilization, and thus the fulfillment of a universal destiny. Yet as buildings, they also remained sites of contradiction and potential.

Schenley High School is often cited as the fullest expression of these civic ambitions—"one of the finest high schools in the world," as the district proudly asserted.[19] Sitting on a steep triangular plot in North Oakland, the school replaced Pittsburgh's first high school, Central High, whose building had been deemed obsolete. Schenley's location was strategic, embedded within the dense academic ecology of the University of Pittsburgh, Carnegie Institute of Technology, and the Mellon Institute of Industrial Research. Designed by Edward Stotz Sr., the colossal limestone monolith known as "the Triangle" laid out the mass on the plot with cutting precision. Its plan arranged classrooms along three single-loaded corridors, forming a sharp triangular loop around two courtyards and a tiered auditorium with a seating capacity of sixteen hundred. Separate floors housed science laboratories and lecture halls, rooms for arts and crafts, and dedicated music studios. Here, the ceilings rose and dropped

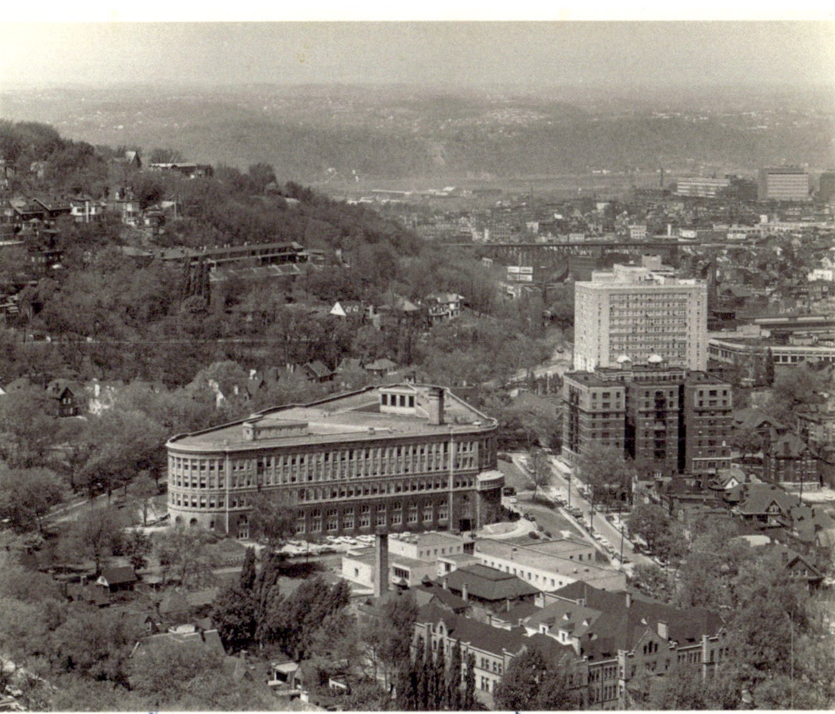

Bird's-eye view of Schenley High School and Bellefield Dwellings, ca. 1950, photograph; Detre Library & Archives, HHC

15 **Wooldridge**, "Recent School Buildings in Pittsburgh, PA.," 33.

16 **M. Christine Boyer**, *Dreaming the Rational City: The Myth of American City Planning* (MIT Press, 1986), 45; **Eric Mumford**, *Designing the Modern City: Urbanism Since 1850* (Yale University Press, 2018), 41–48.

17 **Wooldridge**, "Recent School Buildings in Pittsburgh, PA.," 32.

18 On the racialized language and practice of neoclassicism in the US see **Mabel O. Wilson**, "Notes on the Virginia Capitol: Nation, Race, and Slavery in Jefferson's America," in *Race and Modern Architecture: A Critical History from the Enlightenment to the Present*, edited by Irene Cheng et al. (University of Pittsburgh Press, 2020), 23–42.

19 **Wooldridge**, "Recent School Buildings in Pittsburgh, PA.," 33–34.

in response to the site's uneven topography and the building's intricate internal program. They followed the changing volumes of the educational cosmos: rising above the auditorium, descending into the pool, and adjusting to the fifteen-foot ceiling of classrooms, corridors, laboratories, and assembly spaces. These ceilings were massive steel-and-concrete slabs, engineered to carry immense loads and establish a clean datum, with all infrastructure left exposed beneath them, in the absence of dropped ceilings. In classrooms, pendant lights hung in measured rows; in workshops, a lattice of steam pipes stretched overhead. In the gymnasia, rings and climbing nets swung from beams, while in the kitchens the ceiling nearly vanished behind steam and a cloud of cooking pots, ladles, sieves, colanders, carving forks, and spatulas—shelves of utensils dangling from the ceiling itself.

These exposed infrastructures mirrored the educational multiplicity of the school itself. While college-track instruction was a central mission, the building also housed industrial education and adult learning programs, including vocational courses and, later, English language instruction and so-called 'Americanization' classes for new immigrants (see Alyssa Velazquez, p. 48). For nearly a century, Schenley remained a hub of secondary education in Pittsburgh, adapting to shifting demographics and curricular demands. Despite community opposition, the Pittsburgh Board of Public Education closed Schenley in 2008, leaving a scar on the city's educational landscape (see James Hill, p. 112). The closure was part of a decades-long cycle, beginning in the 1980s with the neoliberal dismantling of U.S. education. Underfunding drove enrollment down, and declining enrollment was subsequently used to justify additional cuts and closures.

ENGINES OF PUBLIC LIFE

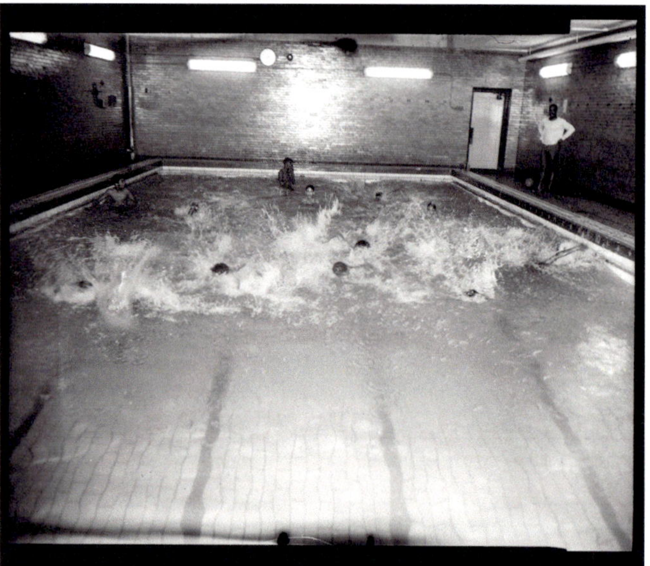

Charles "Teenie" Harris, Leo Woods supervising group of boys in Herron Hill Junior High School indoor swimming pool, 1954, photograph; Carnegie Museum of Art, HFF

If Schenley represents the architectural and administrative apex of the centralized Building Department, smaller projects like McKelvy Elementary (opened 1916, designed by Carleton Strong) and Herron Hill School (opened 1928, designed by James T. Steen and Sons) demonstrate how the department's expanded oversight could redistribute resources across an unequal urban landscape. In neighborhoods with limited tax bases—such as the Hill District, home to many Black residents and recent migrants—the department could channel public funds to build new schools. Both Herron and McKelvy were more modest in scale and materials than Schenley. And while detailing was simpler, with brick replacing Schenley's limestone facades, gymnasia, indoor pools, and other shared spaces remained integral to their design. This ability to extend public resources into underfunded neighborhoods was central to how Superintendent C. L. Wooldridge framed his work. To justify this redistributive role, he drew direct parallels between public schools and Pittsburgh's mills: "Just as Pittsburgh is happiest when her mills run double and treble turn, so the people … may receive greatly increased dividends upon their 135 schoolhouses … used by all of the people all the time."[20] He noted that while other cities first introduced industrial training in their high schools, "Pittsburgh recognized… the boy or girl of 13 or 14 [was] most in need of industrial training" and extended it in both directions—from kindergarten to adult education.[21] And he concluded: "A democracy … means that everyone has an inalienable right to that type of training or education which is suited to his ability or to his needs."[22] This line of reasoning, while a defense of the right to public education, also hints at a tension in a city defined by industrial labor. The distinction between vocational and academic instruction was a site of negotiation, if not contestation, particularly for working-class and Black students and parents. Or rather, the rhetoric of democratic access conditioned by this distinction, as James D. Anderson has shown, was often mobilized to limit the academic horizons of Black and migrant students.[23] At the same time, schools at every level were expected to serve as sites of adult education, industrial training, and neighborhood gathering. This expanded vision of civic utility, in which schools operate day and night as engines of public life, demanded infrastructural intensification. Ceilings continued to expand to accommodate new lighting grids, ventilation systems, projection booths, and acoustic treatments. Auditoria doubled as community halls; gymnasia were lit for evening recreation; classrooms were adapted for adult education and night schooling. Architecture had to perform across temporal rhythms, not just curricular ones.

By the mid-1930s, however, mounting public scrutiny and political pressure forced a re-evaluation of the district's building practices. In 1934, the Board of Education enacted a decisive policy shift: all architectural design was consolidated within the Building Department, where Steen was appointed to lead the in-house team. This reorganization was driven by two interrelated pressures. First, the Board faced growing public accusations of corruption and overspending, implicating both contractors and architects, and centralization promised greater transparency and institutional oversight. Second, the Great Depression had devastated Pittsburgh's industrial and construction sector, making public-sector employment one of the few reliable forms of work for architects, engineers, and contractors. Supported by federal initiatives like the Public Works Administration (PWA) and the Works Progress Administration (WPA), the district's Building Department expanded operations, hiring young architects, draftspeople, and engineers to meet its growing responsibilities. Architecture—from design to construction to daily use—became a vehicle for economic recovery.

The construction program continued apace, completing twenty-seven school building projects between 1935 and 1940. Under Steen, the distinction between management and design, architecture and infrastructure collapsed. His language, at times bureaucratic or managerial, may have eluded the antiquarian sensibilities of architectural historians in Pittsburgh, yet he proved a savvy administrator—at once capable of defending janitorial wages and advancing creative design strategies that exceeded mere efficiency or standardized operations. One of the most telling shifts during his tenure concerned how schools were assessed. Since 1912, the Superintendent of Buildings had conducted an annual facilities index, "The Physical Survey of the Pittsburgh School Buildings," rating each school's physical condition across a set of categories: efficiency of plan, construction and fireproofing, heating, ventilation,

20 C. L. Wooldridge, "Wider Use of Schools," *School Board Journal* LIII, no. 6 (1916): 32.

21 C. L. Wooldridge, "Industrial Education," *School Board Journal* LIII, no. 6 (1916): 32–33.

22 C. L. Wooldridge, "Industrial Education," 32–33.

23 James D. Anderson, *The Education of Blacks in the South, 1860–1935* (University of North Carolina Press, 1988).

sanitation, natural and artificial light, furniture, and playgrounds.[24] This report was updated each year as repairs and alterations were made, while anticipating those to come. But the survey, Steen argued, "considered only matters of safety, health, and comfort" without evaluating "what they offered in the way of facilities for obtaining a rounded education."[25] Schools lacking playrooms, auditoria, or toilets on every floor, he noted with frustration, often ranked lower than rudimentary facilities that simply met efficiency standards. The evaluative logic Steen critiqued nearly a century ago echoes in today's Facilities Condition Index (FCI), a system to determine which schools warrant investment or closure. Now calculated by private consultants, the FCI ranks buildings from "good" to "poor" based largely on the cost of repair relative to the cost of replacement. As Sarosh Anklesaria notes in this volume (see, p.102), such assessments obscure the underlying question: which kinds of educational space are being valued? Metrics of efficiency rarely account for the spaces that support collective life, play, or aspiration. In Steen's auditoria, beneath ceilings painted like a starry sky, a child could still look up, bored or dreaming, and imagine a world beyond the scarcity imposed on their schooling.

CLASSROOM IN A BOX

World War II marked a decisive rupture, diverting labor, materials, and political attention away from schools. Wartime priorities halted nearly all building projects, and deferred maintenance created a backlog that would haunt the district for the next two decades. By the early 1950s, the position of Superintendent of Buildings had been quietly dissolved, and the department reduced to the Division of Plant Operation and Maintenance. The timing was paradoxical: Pittsburgh's population reached a peak of 676,806 in 1950 and remained comparable to 1930s levels until 1960.[26] Yet only a handful of facilities were built during that decade—among them Pioneer School (1960) for students with disabilities (see David Serlin, p. 74). This disparity—between a boom in population and a bust in construction—belies the idea that demographic growth or decline alone explains school building cycles. As federal funds were redirected toward urban renewal, housing clearance, and highway infrastructure, school facilities were deprioritized, their deterioration normalized. What ultimately shaped school funding was not demographic pressure or educational need, but the absence of political will.

In 1960, the Board created an Advisory Committee of Architects, a move that coincided with the arrival of Sidney P. Marland Jr.—a staunch conservative and politically ambitious administrator—as superintendent of Pittsburgh Public Schools. Under Marland's tight grip, the committee hired outside architects and engineers by the hour on a project-by-project basis, producing reactive fixes rather than coordinated planning. The clearest expression of this shift was not a new generation of schools, but the rise of 'demountables'—prefabricated classrooms funded through the Educational Facilities Laboratory (EFL), established in 1958 by the Ford Foundation. Part of the Foundation's broader Cold War–era push to shape public education through design research, EFL positioned itself as a broker between architects, industry, and policymakers.[27] It launched national studies on new school typologies and coordinated the School Construction Systems Development (SCSD) project, standardizing components for mass production in partnership with manufacturers and school boards. Proliferating in the late 1960s as a spatial response to

24 **Marion M. Steen and the Department of Buildings,** *Progress 1911-1941* (The Board of Public Education Pittsburgh, PA, 1941), 11.

25 **Marion M. Steen and the Department of Buildings,** *Progress 1911-1941,* 11.

26 U.S. Census Bureau, *Population of the 100 Largest Cities and Other Urban Places in the United States: 1790 to 1990* (U.S. Government Printing Office, 1998).

27 **Amy F. Ogata,** "Educational Facilities Laboratories: Debating and Designing the Postwar American Schoolhouse," in *Designing Schools* (Routledge, 2016).

overcrowded schools and shifting metropolitan demographics, demountables embodied a new ethos of expediency and disposability.

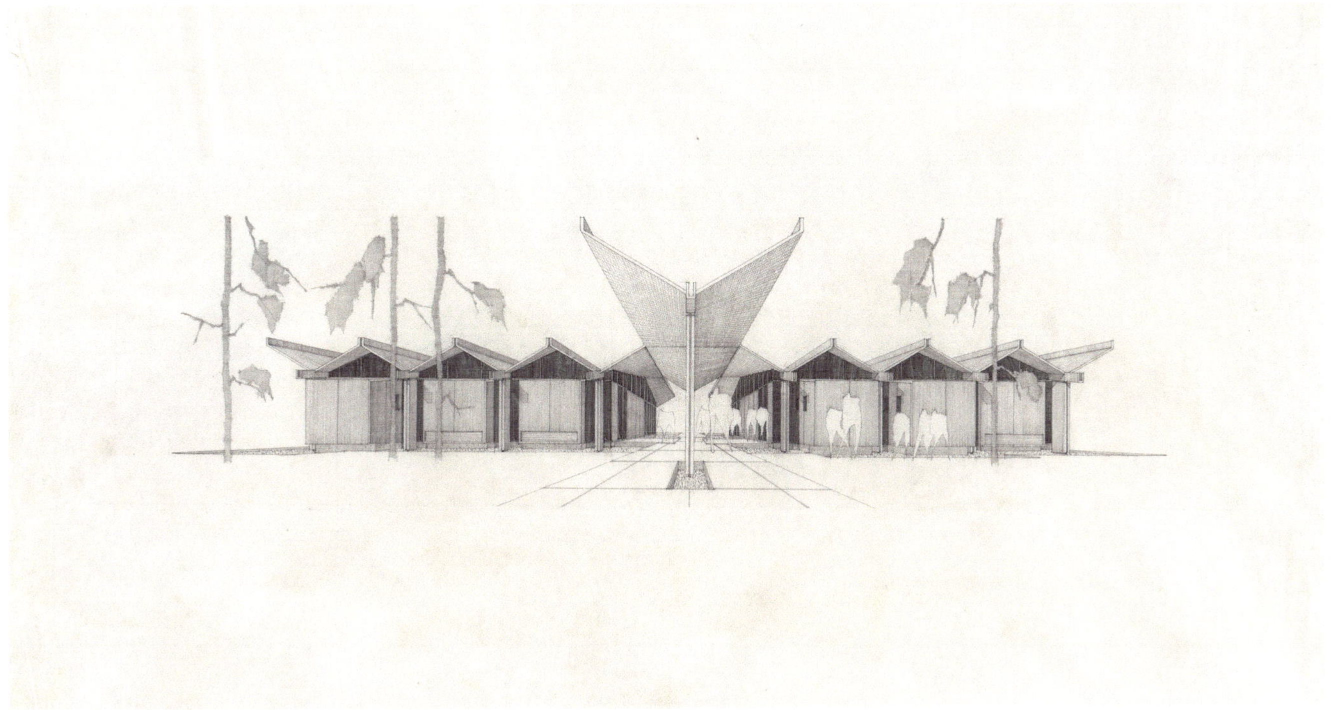

John Pekruhn, Lawrence Wolfe, Anthony Lee Wolfe, Russell Orrin Deeter, and Dahlen K. Ritchey, *Demountable School, Aluminum Study, Perspectival Elevation Drawing,* 1961–1962, pencil on tracing paper; CMUAA

Under the auspices of the EFL grant, Marland's Board appointed John Pekruhn to lead a committee of architects—Dahlen Ritchey (Deeter & Ritchey) and Lawrence Wolfe (Wolfe & Wolfe)—to test the economic and educational feasibility of demountable classrooms in Pittsburgh (see Lynn Kawaratani p. 148). "Facilities need to be as mobile and flexible as the population," Pekruhn proclaimed.[28] The design brief echoed this, demanding that each demountable be "completely self-contained and function as a unit separate from a permanent structure."[29] With a ceiling at seven feet six inches short, the module's dimensions followed the logic of freight. It replicated a standard trailer width of eight by forty feet—one quarter of a standard classroom. Because the aim was to create a unit capable of mass production by Pittsburgh's manufacturing sector, the study was organized into material tracks: steel, aluminum, and reinforced concrete, each corresponding to dominant regional industries. The steel prototype was developed in collaboration with the American Bridge Division of the U.S. Steel Corporation, translating postwar military technologies for mobile deployment into the domestic realm of school construction. Not coincidentally, the same design brief—couched in racialized terms—also demanded that urban classrooms "should be durable enough to withstand extremes of vandalism."[30] The logics converged: technologies designed for battlefields were redeployed to contain children already imagined as unruly, by default or by design.

Beyond its dimensions and materials, the design brief also returned to the skies—accounting for the environmental conditions in which these units would operate. By the 1960s, Pittsburgh's skies were nominally clearer thanks to the Smoke Control Act of 1946, yet as the architects observed, "artificial lighting tended to be in use an overwhelming percentage of the time," even "with the advent of smoke control and when

28 John Pekruhn, "Introduction," in *Demountable School Buildings: A Report Authorized by the Pittsburgh Board of Public Education Under a Grant from the Educational Facilities Laboratory* (Pittsburgh Board of Public Education Under a Grant from the Educational Facilities Laboratory, 1962), ii.

29 John Pekruhn, "Introduction," ii.

30 Richard L. Barrick, "Preface," in *Demountable School,* i.

adequate windows existed."[31] In other words, even after the city attempted to clean its air, classrooms still had to keep their lights on. Two prototypes emerged: six steel units installed at Philip Murray Elementary and four reinforced concrete units constructed at Homewood Elementary. Self-contained with their own lighting, ventilation, and heating systems, conforming carefully on the modules, the classrooms could be clustered, expanded, or disassembled as enrollment shifted. The ceilings carried none of the optimism of earlier schools. Corrugated sheets stretched taut and weightlessly across steel frames, their seams marked by relentless rows of fluorescent bands. These—often literally—paper-thin ceilings registered a shift in priorities: from permanence to disposability, from thermal comfort to construction speed, from long-term public commitment to stop-gap accommodation. These rudimentary amenities offered neglected and overcrowded schools a temporary fix at best—and a blunt reminder of the district's unwillingness to address structural inequities at worst. That same refusal echoed in the Board's uneven and reluctant compliance with federally mandated desegregation.

MEGASTRUCTURES OF CONTAINMENT

More than a decade after Brown v. Board of Education (1954), Pittsburgh had yet to pursue a comprehensive desegregation strategy. Reviews by the U.S. Office of Education and the Department of Health, Education, and Welfare (HEW) found that several schools in predominantly Black neighborhoods remained effectively segregated and underfunded. In response, local Black parents, the Pittsburgh branch of the Urban League, and the NAACP intensified their campaigns against the district's inaction—staging protests, compiling reports and statistical evidence, and drawing press attention to the disparities (see Ujju Aggarwal, p. 30). With mounting pressure across all levels—grassroots, state, and federal—Marland's Board, supported by another EFL grant, put forward a quixotic reform proposal known as the "Great High Schools." The plan called for consolidating all of the city's high school students into five enormous campuses, each accommodating five to six thousand students on forty-acre sites.[32] All existing high schools would be closed, repurposed, or converted into middle or elementary schools. Modeled on "educational park" schemes then being developed in New York, Los Angeles, and Washington, D.C., the proposal imagined these campuses as integrated complexes serving the city's entire secondary school population. Debated throughout the decade, the scheme was ultimately abandoned in 1970, leaving political fallout and public embarrassment for both the Board and the Mayor's office.

From the early studies to the end of the decade, the Board grew increasingly adamant that the Great High Schools were the only viable path forward—even as anticipated federal funding from the Great Society and War on Poverty programs failed to arrive.[33] As Black mobilization and civil rights groups pressed for substantive change, the Board hardened its commitment to the plan's scale and inevitability. Physical models and promotional materials for the proposed campuses began appearing in shopfronts and bank branches in a concerted persuasion campaign across the city. Against what Marland described as "the revolution for the poor," who demanded power and participation in decision making, he unabashedly proclaimed: "We have done much to remove smoke from our

31 John Pekruhn, "Introduction," ii.

32 "Five Sites Identified for Great H.S.'s," *The News from the Pittsburgh Public Schools* XXIII, no. 3 (1967): 1.

33 Sidney P. Marland Jr., "The View from Bellefield at Forbes," *Carnegie Magazine* (1964): 223–27.

city in revolutionary ways.[34] But there is still smoke in Pittsburgh, not visible. It rises from the long smouldering [sic] embers of deep discontent and hopelessness. This smoke too calls for revolutionary solutions."[35]

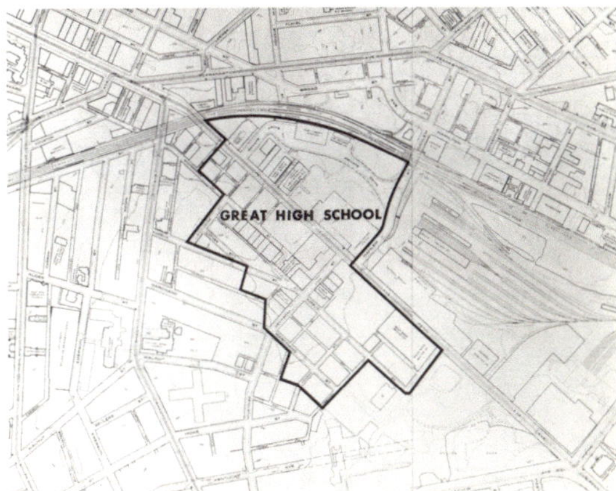

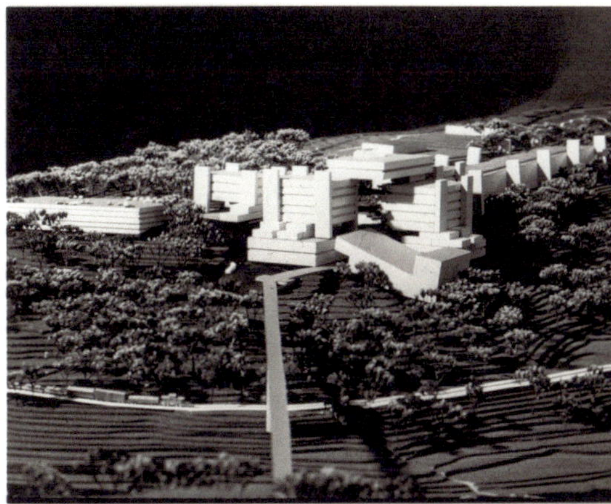

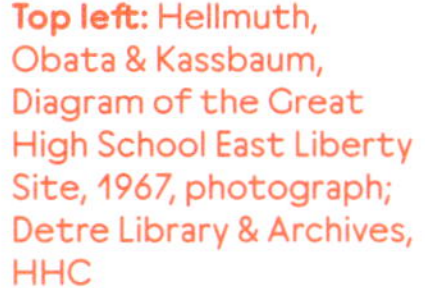

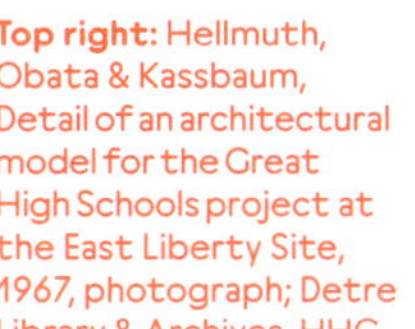

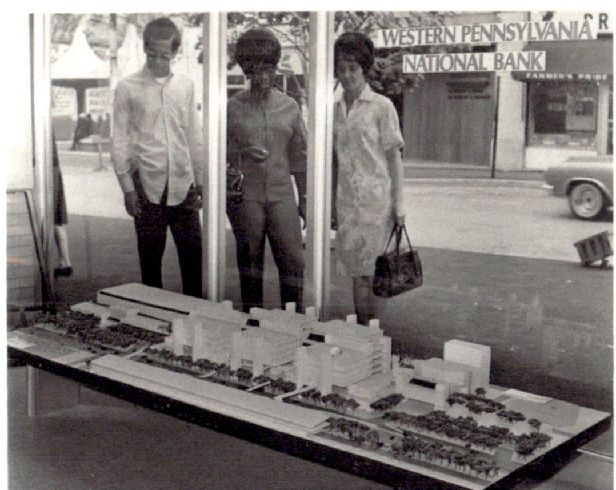

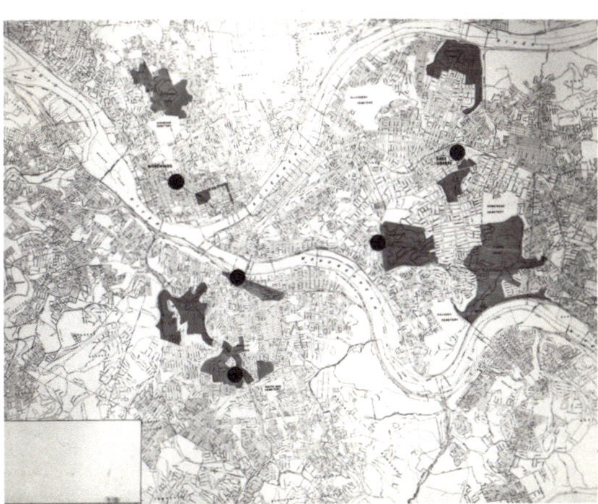

Top left: Hellmuth, Obata & Kassbaum, Diagram of the Great High School East Liberty Site, 1967, photograph; Detre Library & Archives, HHC

Top right: Hellmuth, Obata & Kassbaum, Detail of an architectural model for the Great High Schools project at the East Liberty Site, 1967, photograph; Detre Library & Archives, HHC

Bottom left: Three bystanders look at a model of the Great High Schools project in the window of a Western Pennsylvania National Bank, 1967, photograph; Detre Library & Archives, HHC

Bottom right: Drawing of map with planned locations for the Great High Schools project, 1967, photograph; Detre Library & Archives, HHC

Addressing the Pittsburgh Chamber of Commerce, he concluded, "If there is to be tranquility … and a wholesome life in the big cities of America, the schools must be given the freedom from harassment and tension."[36] What began as a proposal for school integration hardened into a strategy of containment.

The plan, however, was less revolutionary than it was hubristic. It mirrored the priorities of an architectural profession that was doubling down on its own ambition to reshape cities through large-scale interventions. In the 1960s, architects around the world embraced the idea of megastructures—vast, continuous buildings that combined housing, work, and public life within a single framework. Inspired by new technologies and a belief in design's transformative power, they imagined colossal structures into which entire neighborhoods could be plugged, replaced, or rearranged—urban machines meant to evolve endlessly with their inhabitants. While celebrated for their ambition, these visions often assumed that form and scale alone could produce new forms of community on a blank canvas—a quixotic optimism that faded by the 1970s as economic and political realities set in.

The rise and fall of the Great High Schools was no different: the project was led not by the city's own building department but by the corporate design firm Hellmuth, Obata + Kassabaum—then gaining national prominence for large-scale institutional and civic work.[37] The scheme envisioned five multi-story campuses rising from former industrial lands,

34 Sidney P. Marland Jr., "Renaissance in the Making – The Great High Schools of Pittsburgh," *Great Pittsburgh: Publication of the Chamber of Commerce of Greater Pittsburgh*, February 1968, 1–4.

35 Marland Jr., "Renaissance in the Making," 2.

36 Marland Jr., "Renaissance in the Making," 3.

37 "Name Architects for Great High Schools," *The News from the Pittsburgh Public Schools* XXIII, no. 3 (1967): 3.

their footprints replacing rail sidings and warehouse yards. Instead of a loose collection of facilities, the plan mapped students into a nested hierarchy of governance: advisory groups fed into counseling groups, counseling groups into houses, and houses into what the architects and the Board called the "Total School Society." Each campus was conceived as a dense machinery of school life organized into a single infrastructural system. Massive utility floors cantilevered over the brownfield sites, supported by vertical cores, with mechanical systems pushed to the periphery. The program extended beyond education to include housing development, transportation hubs, and links to major rail lines or arterial roads, embedding the campuses within metropolitan planning. But rather than serving as spaces of integration, they operated as self-contained enclaves whose scale and isolation deepened segregation and reinforced control. These educational factories resembled the vertical integration strategies of Pittsburgh's robber barons more than any effort to mix students equitably across neighborhoods. Like a monopoly absorbing every stage of production, the Great High Schools concentrated the city's entire secondary system into a handful of centralized and tightly managed sites. There was no ceiling here—only an unbroken and unbreakable lid of infrastructure, vast enough to enclose the city itself.

The Great High Schools scheme was abandoned in 1970, a year after Marland left for his next political post as U.S. Commissioner of Education in the Nixon Administration. Meanwhile, the projected budget swelled from $120 million to more than $250 million. Civil rights organizations, including the Pittsburgh NAACP and the Urban League, had long warned that the plan was a costly distraction from urgent integration measures. Not least, three of the proposed sites were located in white residential areas, requiring Black students to be transported across rivers, highways, and political boundaries. As historian Noliwe Rooks poignantly observes in her work on the persistence of educational apartheid, segregation in U.S. schools has consistently been reinforced "to keep those at both the top and the bottom of the social caste system so firmly anchored in their positions that, despite the (admittedly sporadic and episodic) efforts to integrate schools, we have been unable to significantly dislodge this inequity."[38] In what followed—new middle schools, redistricting, consolidations, and facility expansions—the dream of widespread integration became tepid desegregation.

INDEXES OF VALUE

The Great High School ruins emboldened a revamped Division of Facilities to oversee every aspect of school maintenance and to systematize the selection of private architectural firms for new school design, returning to an arrangement akin to the 1911 Building Department. At the same time, the district underwent major decentralization. New area assistant superintendents were appointed to operate from redrawn divisions of the city, bringing administrators closer to their constituents. Previously, the city's eighty-nine elementary schools and twenty-three high schools had been managed by associate superintendents working from the Board's headquarters in Oakland. The demographic picture of the city had also changed dramatically. After peaking in 1950, Pittsburgh's population had fallen below 540,000 by 1970—a loss of more than twenty percent in just two decades.[39] School closures seemed inevitable. Yet paradoxically, this was also a moment of concentrated building activity, particularly in

38 Noliwe Rooks, *Integrated: How American Schools Failed Black Children* (Pantheon, 2025), 4.

39 U.S. Census Bureau, *Population of the 100 Largest Cities*, 1998.

the North Side and East Hills: a final wave of new construction and facility upgrades before the long attrition of the 1980s and 1990s.

One of the most striking projects from this period was Martin Luther King Jr. Elementary, opened in 1973 along the edge of Allegheny Commons Park. Designed by Liff, Justh & Chetlin, the building was conceived as part of the park's landscape, its angled corners and pilotis softening the transition from city street to open green (see Noah Fritsch and Martin Chetlin, p. 180). The school departed decisively from the corridor-and-classroom model: six open "pods" were arranged within a matrix of interlocking half-hexagons, raised on columns above terraces. Movable partitions allowed teachers to merge or subdivide learning spaces, supporting both collaborative work and conventional lessons. To hold this constant movement and adaptation, the ceiling thickened again. A drawing of the school's ceiling plan reads like Burgwin's celestial cartography. Six hexagonal pods radiate from an indoor central square, each latticed with grids of lights and acoustic panels, their patterns angling and tapering to the geometry of the walls below. Lines and symbols drift across the page like constellations, mapping not only illumination but a choreography of air, sound, and play. The plan folds together the building's openness and precision—movable partitions below, adjustable atmospheres above. Every triangle and square denotes a fixture, a vent, a speaker, or a skylight, composing a kind of infrastructural star chart. In the central square, a small annotation—"basketball backstop shown in folded position"—marks the hinge between structure and action, between the stillness of the drawing and the kinetic life it anticipates.

Now one of twelve schools proposed for closure, Martin Luther King Jr. Elementary joins a list of buildings whose fates have been determined by the district's Facilities Condition Index—a tool that weighs repair costs against replacement costs to produce a score guiding investment or closures. Nearly a century after Marion Steen critiqued the narrow logic of his era's Physical Survey, today's Facilities Condition Index applies a similar metric, albeit in the language of consultants and capital planning. The result is a percentage score that can seal a school's fate, treating walls and ceilings as disposable once their upkeep exceeds a financial threshold. What these numbers capture is a calculus of decades of disinvestment—a self-reinforcing enclosure of public education, where defunding erodes enrollment and shrinking enrollment is then used to justify further cuts. What they omit are the ways the infrastructure of learning itself, the ceilings under which it unfolds, has sustained access and possibility.

To read these ceilings is to read the contracts of public life. Their grids of lights, vents, and annotations mark not only the terms of construction, but the conditions under which education itself has been built or dismantled. In this recursive, unfinished history, the fundamental right to free public education remains contested, under attack. From Burgwin's celestial cartography to MLK's geometric sky, the architecture of Pittsburgh's schools reveals less a history of permanence and more an unfinished record of ongoing struggles over resources, rights, and the meaning of the public.

Liff Justh and Chetlin, Martin Luther King Jr. Elementary School, Second Floor Plan of Reflected Ceiling, 1971, architectural drawing: PPBF

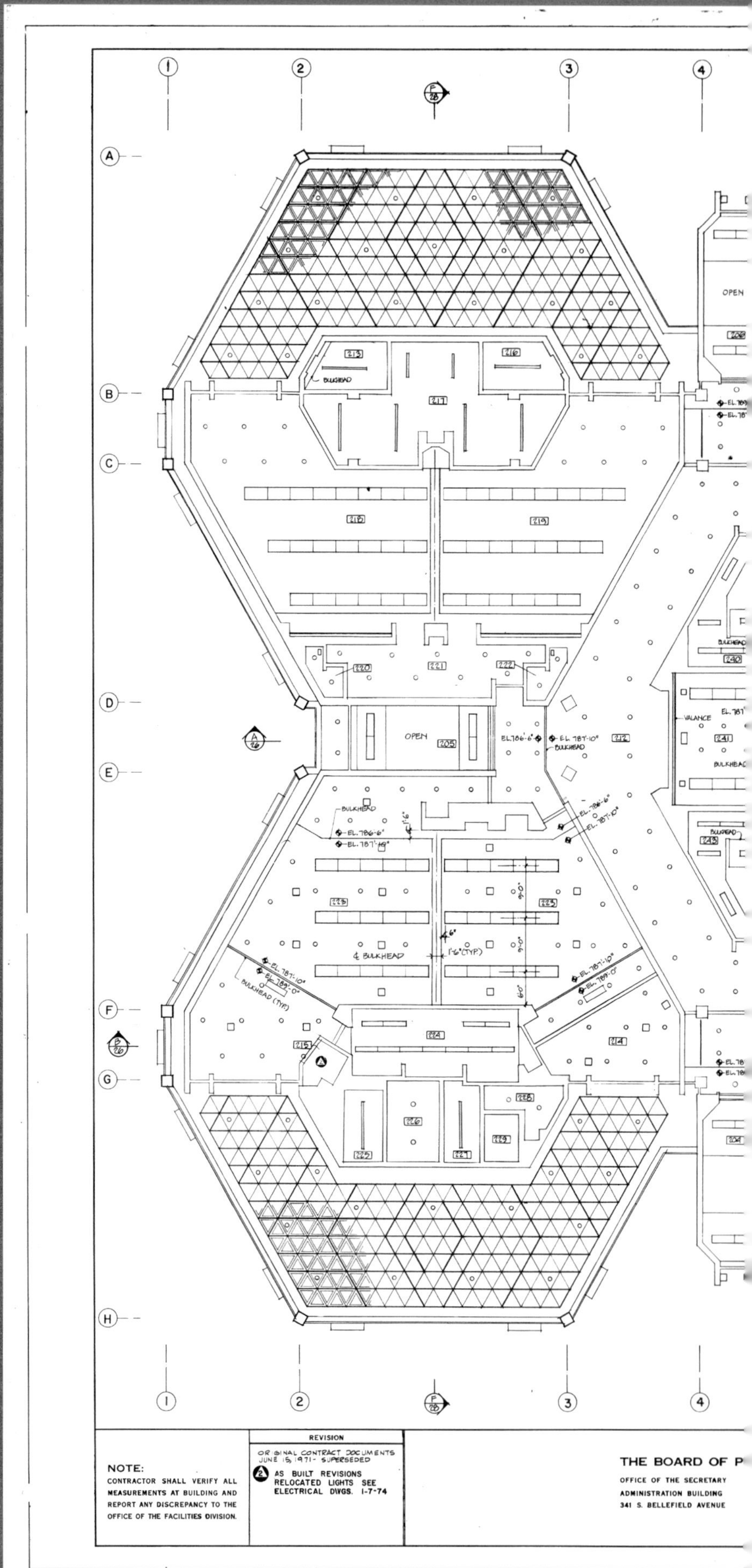

REVISION

ORIGINAL CONTRACT DOCUMENTS
JUNE 15, 1971- SUPERSEDED

AS BUILT REVISIONS
RELOCATED LIGHTS SEE
ELECTRICAL DWGS. 1-7-74

NOTE:
CONTRACTOR SHALL VERIFY ALL
MEASUREMENTS AT BUILDING AND
REPORT ANY DISCREPANCY TO THE
OFFICE OF THE FACILITIES DIVISION.

THE BOARD OF P

OFFICE OF THE SECRETARY
ADMINISTRATION BUILDING
341 S. BELLEFIELD AVENUE

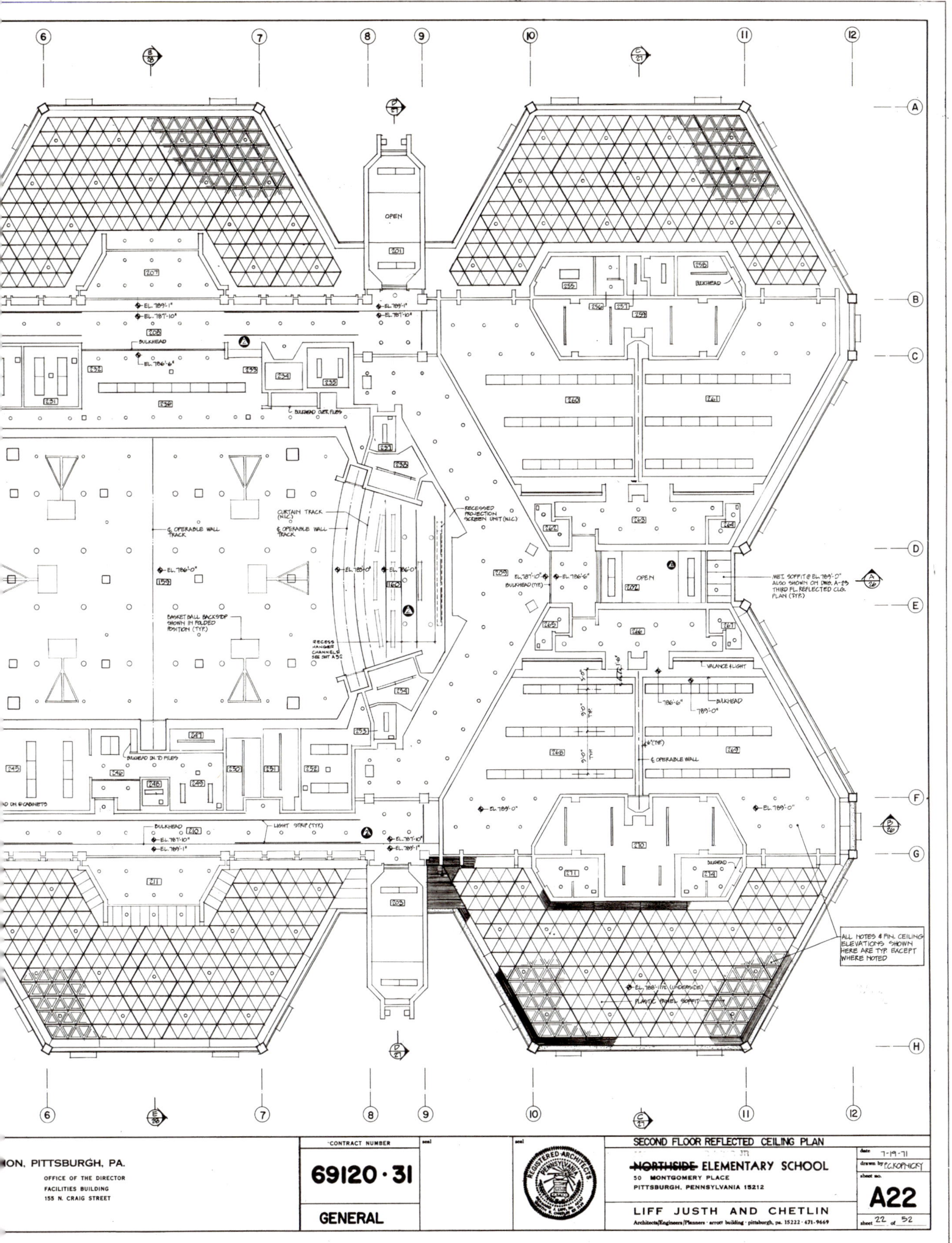
SECOND FLOOR REFLECTED CEILING PLAN
CONTRACT NUMBER
69120·31
GENERAL
NORTHSIDE ELEMENTARY SCHOOL
50 MONTGOMERY PLACE
PITTSBURGH, PENNSYLVANIA 15212
LIFF JUSTH AND CHETLIN
Architects/Engineers/Planners · arrott building · pittsburgh, pa. 15222 · 471-9669
date 7-19-71
drawn by P.G.KOPNICKY
sheet no.
A22
sheet 22 of 52
REGISTERED ARCHITECTS
PENNSYLVANIA
ION, PITTSBURGH, PA.
OFFICE OF THE DIRECTOR
FACILITIES BUILDING
155 N. CRAIG STREET
OPEN
BULKHEAD
CURTAIN TRACK (N.I.C.)
OPERABLE WALL TRACK
RECESSED PROJECTION SCREEN UNIT (N.I.C.)
BASKET BALL BACKSTOP SHOWN IN FOLDED POSITION (TYP.)
RECESS HANGER CHANNELS SEE SHT A52
LIGHT STRIP (TYP.)
VALANCE & LIGHT
OPERABLE WALL
MET. SOFFIT @ EL. 789'-0" ALSO SHOWN ON DWG. A-23 THIRD FL. REFLECTED CLG. PLAN (TYP.)
ALL NOTES & FIN. CEILING ELEVATIONS SHOWN HERE ARE TYP. EXCEPT WHERE NOTED
PLASTIC PANEL SOFFIT

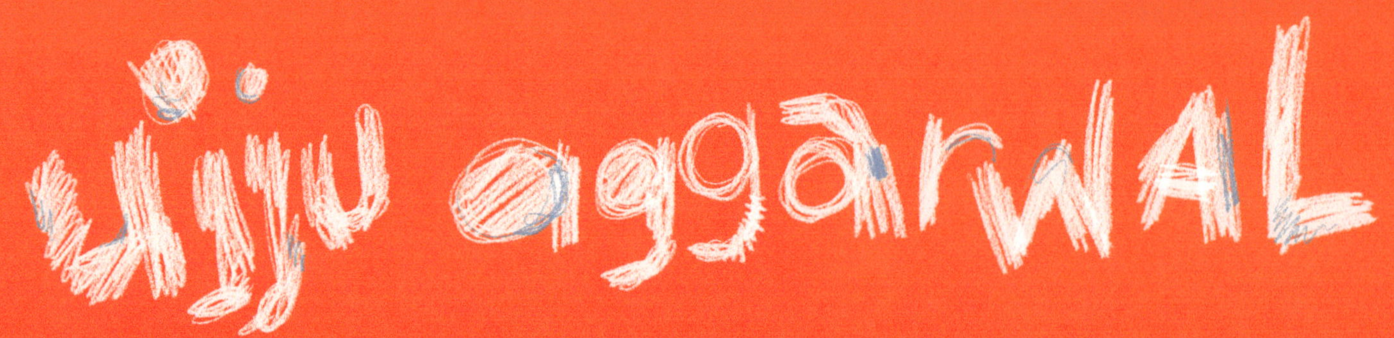

30

FINDING EACH OTHER: SCHOOL CHOICE AND MAPPING THE TERRAIN OF THE PUBLIC

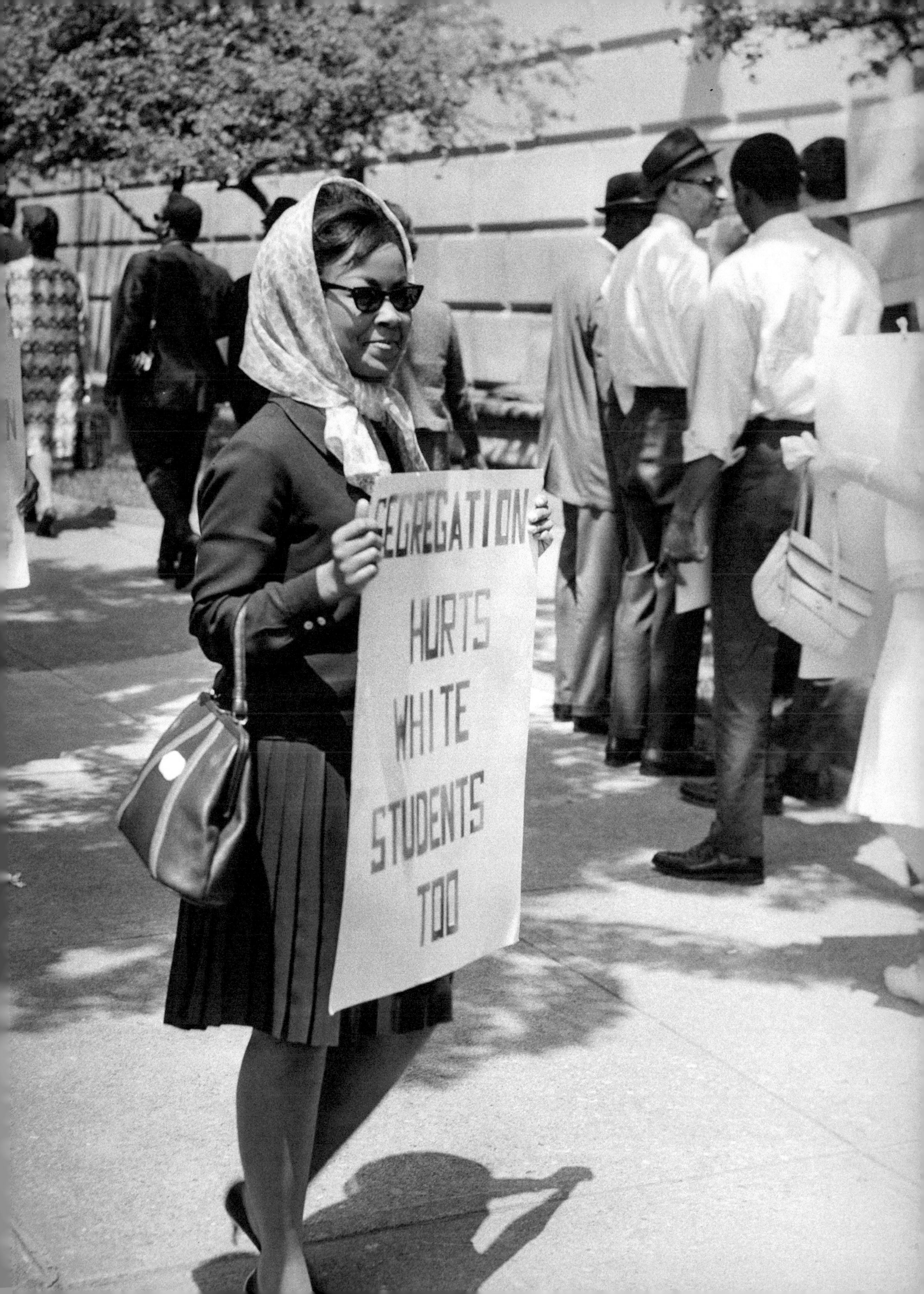

SEGREGATION
HURTS
WHITE
STUDENTS
TOO

"if they close the school, how will we find eachother?"

This question was posed years ago by a New York City public school student amidst aggressive waves of school closures not unlike those that have been proposed for Pittsburgh. The plan to systematically shrink public schools for the second time in just over a decade has occurred as the Appalachian city, once known for its steel industry, is growing. As indexical assessments—animated by market logics and enlivened by choice and standards—cut into the fabric of social relations and place-based histories of struggles bound up in public schools, it becomes ever more urgent to engage the pedagogy embedded in the question above. More generally, at a time when the last vestiges of the public are being aggressively dismantled, the question of how we will find each other propels us to ask: what kinds of relations might be made possible through public infrastructures, and what is sacrificed in their absence? In what follows, I consider this question through the lens of school choice. I trace the ways in which choice, as a key mechanism of reform and management that emerged in the aftermath of Brown v. Board of Education (1954), is integral to mapping the limits of the public we have and envisioning the public we might fight for.

Previous page: Charles "Teenie" Harris, Phyllis Moorman outside Pittsburgh School Board headquarters, May–June 1966, photograph; Carnegie Museum of Art, HFF

Below: The Urban League of Pittsburgh, Map of the Great High School Districts, December 10, 1969, report excerpt; Detre Library & Archives, HHC

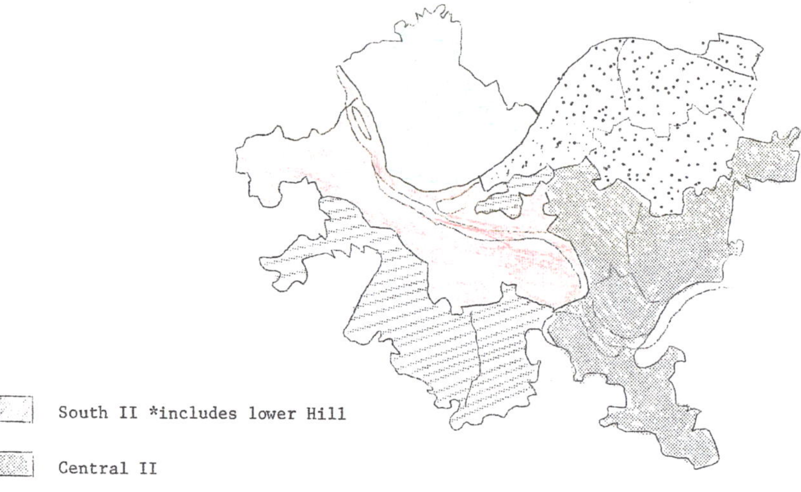

CHOICE AND A CIRCUMSCRIBED PUBLIC

At its most basic, school choice means options for parents, caregivers, and students regarding which school, or which type of school, they or their children might attend. As policy, it also provides school officials and administrators discretion in admissions processes: which students they will admit, include, and retain. In some instances, there can be state and non-state regulations regarding criteria for student selection, requiring, for example, a threshold for certain demographic representation. Practically, school choice can take shape through public, private, religious, charter, micro, or home schools—with overlap amongst these categories, mechanized by programs including vouchers, magnets, dual-language, and education savings accounts.

Increasingly recognized as a keyword and set of policies that threaten one of the last remaining "public goods" in the United States, school choice is often associated with privatization. Yet the reach and entanglements of choice are not always accounted for, requiring us to trouble what we assume to be binaries between public and private, consumer and citizen, the market and the state. Indeed, a critical genealogy of choice illuminates a contradictory public: one organized by market logics and racialized exclusion, and enlivened by a consumer citizenship entrenched in competition, scarcity, and precarity.

The landmark decision Brown v. Board of Education (1954) is central to mapping the contradictions of the public that choice reveals. While mainstream versions of U.S. history valorize Brown as a turning point—a moment when historical wrongs were finally made right, ushering in a new era of equality and rights—the decision might be better understood as a moment of realignment that provided for continuity amidst change.[1] To be sure, as critical race studies scholar Derrick Bell reminds us through what he terms "interest convergence": too often, though the demands made by marginalized racial groups may appear to be met or won, it is urgent to recognize that for dominant power, such instances are defined by strategic opportunism.[2] That is, the engagement of oppositional demands by the juridical state (representing white, elite, ruling class interests) must be understood as an instrumental part of a strategy to preserve, maintain, and reproduce, rather than transform, dominant power. In assessing the context that qualified Brown, Bell emphasizes the international visibility that U.S.-based Black freedom struggles had garnered, which drew attention to the fundamental contradictions inherent in U.S. claims of democracy, particularly in the context of the Cold War. Indeed, Bell demonstrates, with increased attention to U.S. racial apartheid as well as growing political consciousness among Black communities—particularly those who had served in the U.S. military and were returning "home"—it was to the benefit of the state to partially accommodate the demands of an increasingly radical Black freedom movement.

Considering Brown as a moment of interest convergence provides a way to map the realignment that took shape: to analyze the significance of not only what rights were won, but also how they came to be structured. Though SCOTUS's decision in Brown (1954) overturned Plessy v. Ferguson (1896), key questions remained: what would desegregation look like, and how would it be implemented? The following year, in its Brown II (1955) decision, SCOTUS determined that the shape and pace of desegregation would be left to the purview of states and carried out with "all

1 **Ruth Wilson Gilmore,** *Golden Gulag: Prisons, Surplus, Crisis, and Opposition in Globalizing California* (University of California Press, 2007); **Gloria Ladson-Billings,** "Landing on the Wrong Note: The Price We Paid for Brown," *Educational Researcher* 33, no. 7 (2004): 3–13.

2 **Derrick A. Bell,** "Brown v. Board of Education and the Interest-Convergence Dilemma," *Harvard Law Review* 93, no. 3 (1980): 518–533.

deliberate speed." As has been widely noted, devolution to the states ensured that "deliberate" was subjective and defined at the discretion of those who had already amassed political and economic power.

The same year, Milton Friedman, often referred to as one of the founding fathers of neoliberalism, put forward a vision of how to address what he understood to be the moral, political, and practical impasse presented by Brown. As he saw it, the question of how desegregation would take shape presented a conflict between the state, rights, and individual liberty. While Friedman understood state-sanctioned segregation to be morally wrong, he likewise qualified state-enforced desegregation as also problematic, as it impeded upon an individual's right to choose the best form of education for one's child. A "third alternative," he surmised, was necessary, and could be realized through the flexible structuring of rights as individual, private choices.[3] Such a structuring ensured that a family could pursue a range of educational options (private, public, religious, or segregated) based on their own priorities. Moreover, according to Friedman, an added benefit to structuring rights as choices scaled at the level of the individual was a competitive marketplace of schooling, one that would incentivize improvement and innovation.

Critical race studies scholar Cheryl Harris reminds us that the right to choose has historically been qualified by the right to exclude.[4] As she explains, the right to exclude has been the common nucleus that has consistently animated whiteness and private property, or what she terms whiteness as property. This has remained true even as the definitions of each have changed over time. Harris' clarity—regarding how the relationship between choice, exclusion, and the continued production of whiteness work through, rather than against, the expansion of "racially contingent rights"— put together with Freidman's "third alternative" helps illuminate the contours of the realignment that took place in the aftermath of Brown. In other words, if the structuring of rights as individual, private choices established a marketplace of education within the public realm, this marketplace, animated by the right to choose and the ability to exclude, guaranteed the continued production of inequity—that worked through race.

The years following Brown were marked by the development and implementation of choice-based programs and policies that would ensure the maintenance and continuity of schools governed by racial exclusion and joined to unevenness when it came to resources, facilities, curricula, and often, teachers. This unevenness, of course, was not happenstance. To be sure, school choice provided a consistent path for segregationists to advance local tactics which included informal yet structured practices as well as overt programs and policies. The latter ranged from what some have termed segregation academies and the development of voucher programs and charter schools to the partitioning of district boundaries. In other contexts, the right to choose informed how segregationists mobilized to oppose bussing programs—often undergirded by appeals to "parents' rights" or "neighborhood schools."

Tracing choice, thus, illuminates the temporal and spatial topographies through which the post-Brown realignment took shape—that are embedded in and yet stretch beyond local histories. As the histories engaged by *after school* demonstrate, these tactics unfolded in multiple ways in the City of Pittsburgh and choice also defined the discourse of organized white resistance that developed, and their use of boycotts in response to bussing and transfer programs.[5] In each of these instances, as well as others, the right to choose affirmed the continued production of whiteness as a material force, grounded in the protection of historically accumulated assets and resources.

3 For more on Friedman's "third alternative" argument, please see **Milton Friedman,** "The Role of Government in Education," *Economics and the Public Interest,* edited by Robert A. Solo (Rutgers University Press, 1955), 123–44.

4 **Cheryl I. Harris,** "Whiteness as Property," *Harvard Law Review* 106, no. 8 (1993): 1707–1791.

5 **Barbara A. Sizemore,** *Walking in Circles: The Black Struggle for School Reform* (Third World Press, 2008).

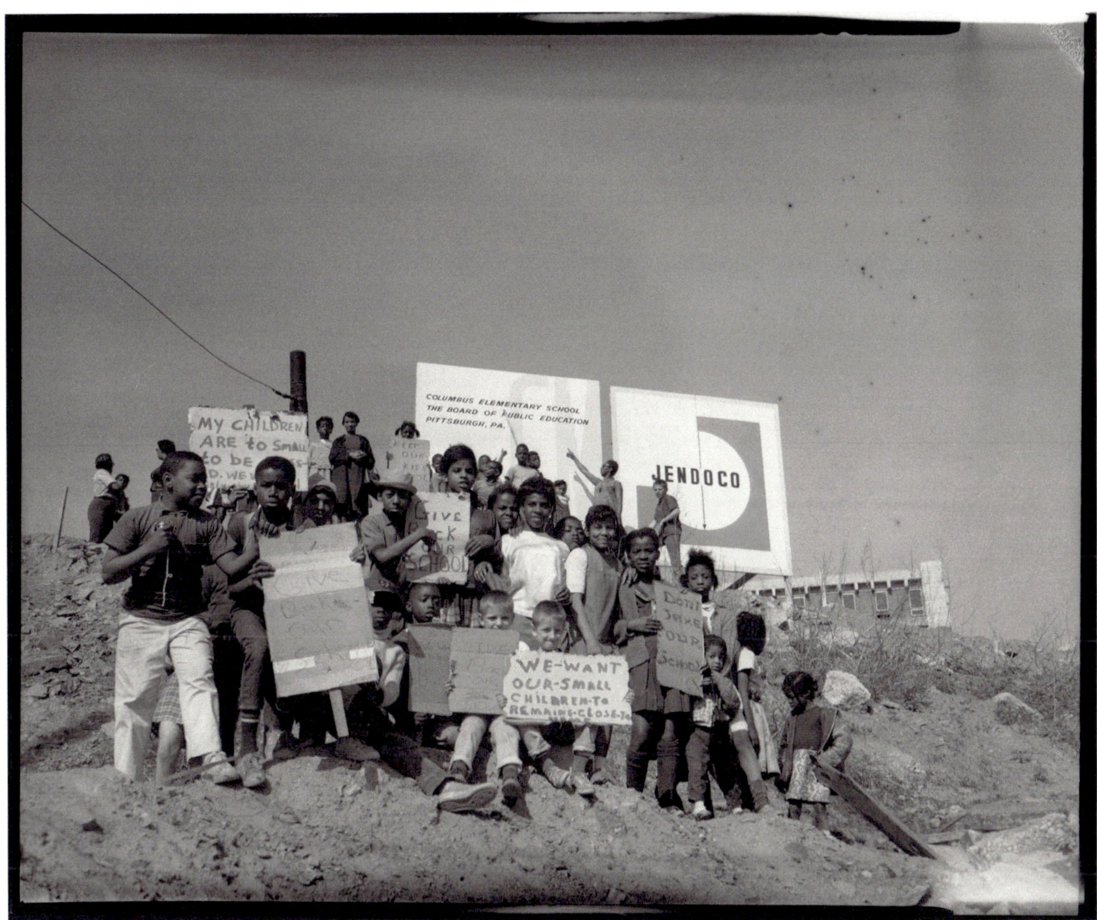

Charles "Teenie" Harris, Outside Columbus Middle School, North Side, Pittsburgh, PA, ca. 1967, photograph; Carnegie Museum of Art, HFF

FREEDOM STRUGGLES AND CHOICE AS STRATEGY

The post-Brown realignment, however, is not the only story of choice. The contradictions of the public also direct us towards instances in which Black, Indigenous, migrant, and other excluded communities have—in specific political-economic contexts—mobilized choice to advance desegregation as well as build autonomy and self-determination through education-based initiatives, projects, and experiments that worked against, outside, and through the state.[6] More than mere aberrations or footnotes, these efforts illuminate the structured unevenness of a public realm, giving us a clue about what rights have and have not meant to distinct communities.

They help us understand the assessments, made by some, that identified schools—infrastructures of social reproduction and everyday life—as sites of violence and control, where "local systems of public education [functioned] as colonial apparatuses designed to stultify children of color…of preparing youngsters for lives of marginality and servitude on the fringes of an opulent society."[7]

Charting what these efforts—exemplified by freedom schools, street academies, independent schools, the Movement for Community Control of Schools, and, at times, charter schools and voucher programs—looked like locally requires us to center the political subjectivities of

6 James Forman Jr., "The Secret History of School Choice: How Progressives Got There First," Georgetown Law Journal 93 (2004): 1287-1319; Kevin Lawrence Henry Jr., "Historicizing Black Educational 'Choice': Toward Black Educational Self-Determination," Educational Policy 38, no. 3 (2024): 741-767.

7 Russell Rickford, We Are an African People: Independent Education, Black Power, and the Radical Imagination (Oxford University Press, 2016), 7.

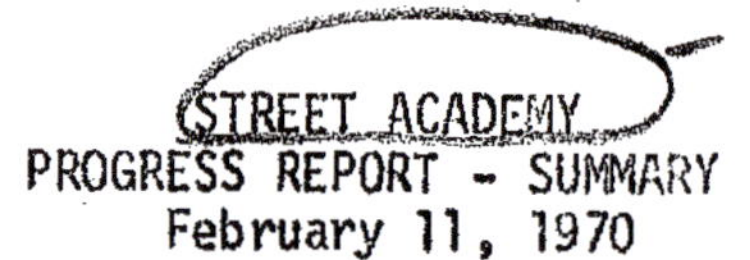

PROGRESS REPORT - SUMMARY
February 11, 1970

   The Street Academy Program began officially on September 15,
1969 when the staff was taken and the program was started. We
opened our doors for students on September 29, 1969 in the facilities located at 1252 Pennsylvania Avenue. The Academy of Transition opened in October, 1969 at 936 W. North Avenue.

I.   Staff - (Currently six (6) Teachers and one (1) Street Worker)

   Street Academy

      Ronald Green/Counselor - Math
      Judith Ralph (Miss) - English & Reading
      Phillip Washington - Black History & Personal Dynamics
      George Jones - Street Worker - Recruitment

   Academy of Transition

      Tommie Lewis (Mrs.) - English & Literature
      Harry Scott - Social Studies & Political Science
      David Worstell - Math & Social Studies
      Phillip Washington - Black History & American Histroy
      Eugene Bentley - Chemistry (Part-time)

II.   Curriculum, Activities, Programs

   Street Academy

      English/Reading
      Math (General Math & Algebra)
      Black History
      Personal Dynamics

   Academy of Transition

      English/Literature
      Math (Algebra, Advanced Algebra)
      American History
      Economics
      World Cultures
      Chemistry

   The schedule for classes at both buildings is:

      Day -   9:00 a.m. - 2:50 p.m.
      Evening -   6:30 p.m. - 9:00 p.m.
      Lunch -   11:20 a.m. -12:30 p.m.

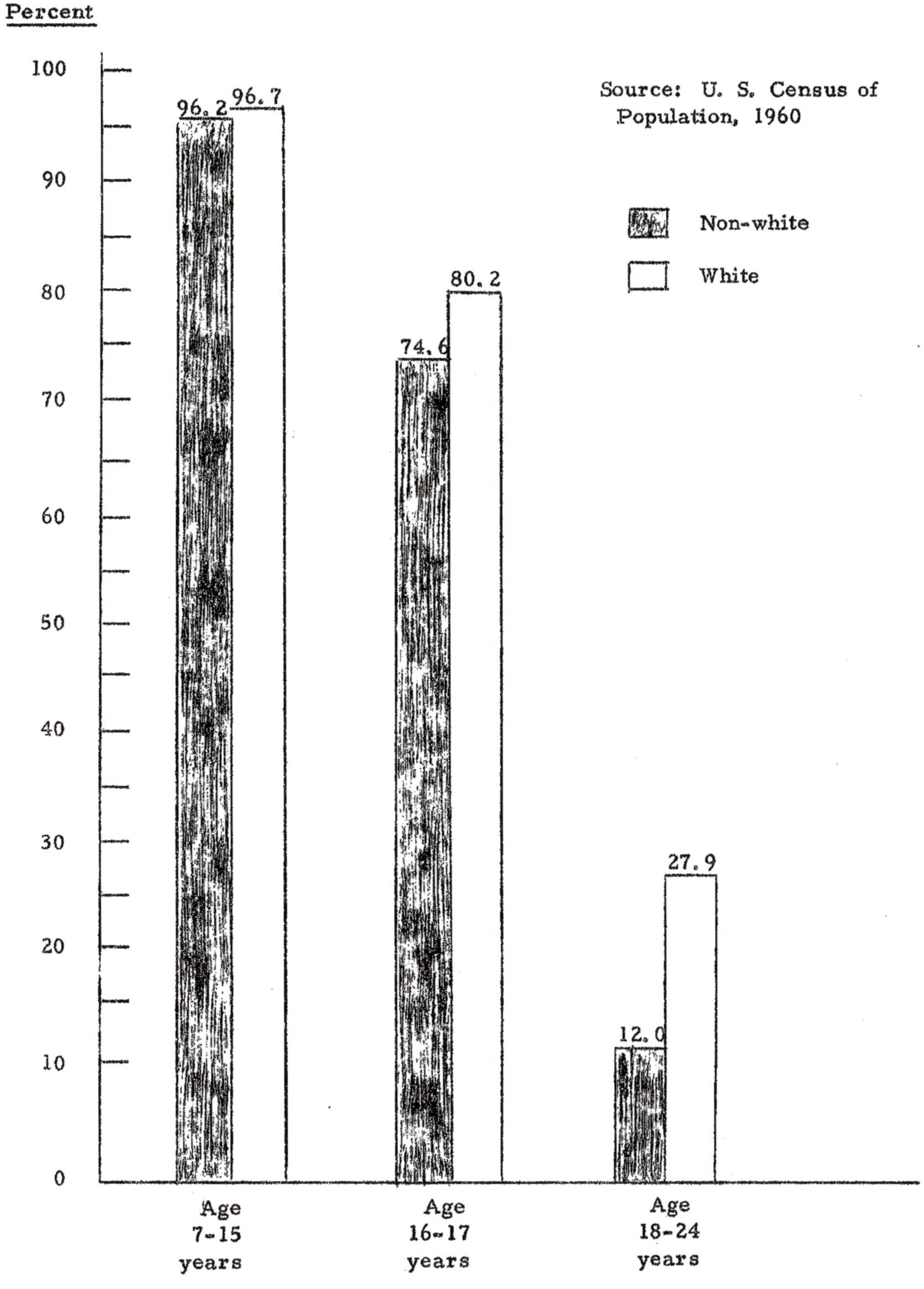

FIGURE 7
PROPORTION OF PERSONS ENROLLED IN SCHOOL
BY SELECT AGE GROUP AND BY COLOR, PITTSBURGH, 1960
Percent
100
90
80
70
60
50
40
30
20
10
0
96.2
96.7
74.6
80.2
12.0
27.9
Source: U. S. Census of
Population, 1960
Non-white
White
Age
7-15
years
Age
16-17
years
Age
18-24
years

excluded historical actors alongside place-based pedagogies of struggle, compelling us to ask: What were communities fighting for when they struggled over schools or through education? What do their efforts teach us about how they understood the post-Brown realignment, assessed their material conditions, understood power, and also about their implicit or explicit theories of the state, rights, and racial capitalism?

Considering these questions alongside Pittsburgh-specific histories brings into focus the significance of an observation made by Black Studies and education scholar-activist-practitioner Barbara A. Sizemore. She recalled that between the 1960s and 1980s "both the NAACP and the Urban League became more militant and aggressive in their demands for desegregation, equal educational opportunity and the inclusion of African American history and culture in the curricula of the [Pittsburgh Public Schools]."[8] Centering that the analyses of these, as well as other formations, were forged in dialectical relationship to specific political-economic contexts gives us insight about how and why such militancy grew a lens to locate the strategies that accompanied its development. Following the longitudinal pathways that activists, parents, students, and teachers paved through education-based initiatives reveals unrelenting organizing in place qualified by the creation (and re-creation) of spaces where people found each other practiced what education should be, and where political horizons and imaginations were expanded. In 1969, for example, the Urban League of Pittsburgh developed the Manchester Street Academy. The Urban League's Street Academies served as demonstrative projects, educating young people "who were branded as uneducable by a public school system whose responsibility it was to educate them […]"[9] The Manchester Street Academy was modeled in active dialogue with those that had been established in New York. Its curriculum, depicted in the previous spread, covered subjects such as the economics of slavery, welfare reform, and the origins of jazz, and its infrastructure included what we might define today as "wrap around services" such as counseling services that engaged students about their felt needs and goals.

If efforts like these remind us that, in specific instances, historical agents (parents, teachers, and students) understood that choice was neither a constant nor a given, but rather a strategy, then what was the potential of the strategy? Could choice actually be re-worked as antagonistic to Friedman's vision of competition and market rule? Insightfully, historian Russell Rickford, in his historiography of Pan African nationalist schools, finds that when part of larger political projects guided by principles of anti-imperialism and internationalism, education-based projects forged by Black communities employing choice presented potential for freedom. These projects often worked to address material needs while also cultivating radical relationalities and building collective capacity for struggle in and beyond education. However, when projects were not rooted accordingly, their engagement of choice—regardless of leadership—has, time and again, eventually (even if unintentionally) resulted in the advancement and expansion of the terrain of racial capitalist enclosure.[10]

---

8 Sizemore, *Walking in Circles,* 132.

9 Key Aspects of the Street Academies 1971, Box 7, Folder 32, New York Urban League Clippings, The Schomburg Center for Research in Black Culture, The New York Public Library.

10 Russell Rickford, *We Are an African People,* 2016; See also **Jack Dougherty,** *More Than One Struggle: The Evolution of Black School Reform in Milwaukee* (University of North Carolina Press, 2004); **Noelani Goodyear-Ka'opua,** *The Seeds We Planted: Portraits of a Native Hawaiian Charter School* (University of Minnesota Press, 2013); **Roseann Liu,** "Neoliberal Progressivism: Charter Schools as Claims to Urban Space, Asian American Self-Determination, and Multiracial Solidarity," *Journal of Urban History* 50, no. 6 (2024): 1276-1296.

CONCLUSION

The conflicting histories of school choice examined in this essay reveal a public in which whiteness as a structure and force of power has consistently been preserved and rearticulated, and where the structuring of rights fortified these processes, guaranteeing inequity and confirming a public realm where the scale of the individual came to be the "moral unit for political life."[11] As such, we might understand the significance of the post-Brown realignment as establishing the counter to the radical vision "born from colonized and racialized peoples' movements" that fought for such rights in the first place.[12] The problem, however, is not the expansion of rights. Rather, it is how rights came to be structured, what they do, and what kinds of social relations and political subjectivities they cultivate.

Bonnie Honig notes that public things like education represent the potential holding ground for what democracy, citizenship, and more generally our social relations might be.[13] Understood as such, the post-Brown realignment created a particular holding ground: one that worked to affirm and rearticulate racial hierarchy while also inscribing a myopia of consumer citizenship, marked by competition and a common sense of individual interest where inequity is anticipated and collective life foreclosed.

It was against this foreclosure that, in specific contexts, Black, Indigenous, migrant, and other excluded communities sought to rework choice. Their distinct efforts teach us about place-based strategies, inviting us to consider their assessments of power and theories of change. They also provide an entry to our present. At a time of expanding fascism accompanied by one of the most aggressive onslaughts to dismantle the last remaining public infrastructures in the United States, these conflicting histories of choice and the contradictions of the public that they reveal help us consider our own moment of realignment. They clarify the urgency to be precise in understanding not only what we are working to defend but also transform. They instruct us to evaluate what kinds of holding grounds we will construct and fight for, in dialogue with our political context and material conditions, to find each other—cultivating radical relationalities, teaching and learning our own histories, and practicing what education should be, while also extending the horizon of struggle for a public (and world) that is not yet.

11 Jodi Melamed and Chandan Reddy, "Using Liberal Rights to Enforce Racial Capitalism," *SSRC Race & Capitalism Series* 30 (2019).

12 Melamed and Reddy, "Using Liberal Rights to Enforce Racial Capitalism."

13 Bonnie Honig, *Public Things: Democracy in Disrepair* (Fordham University Press, 2017).

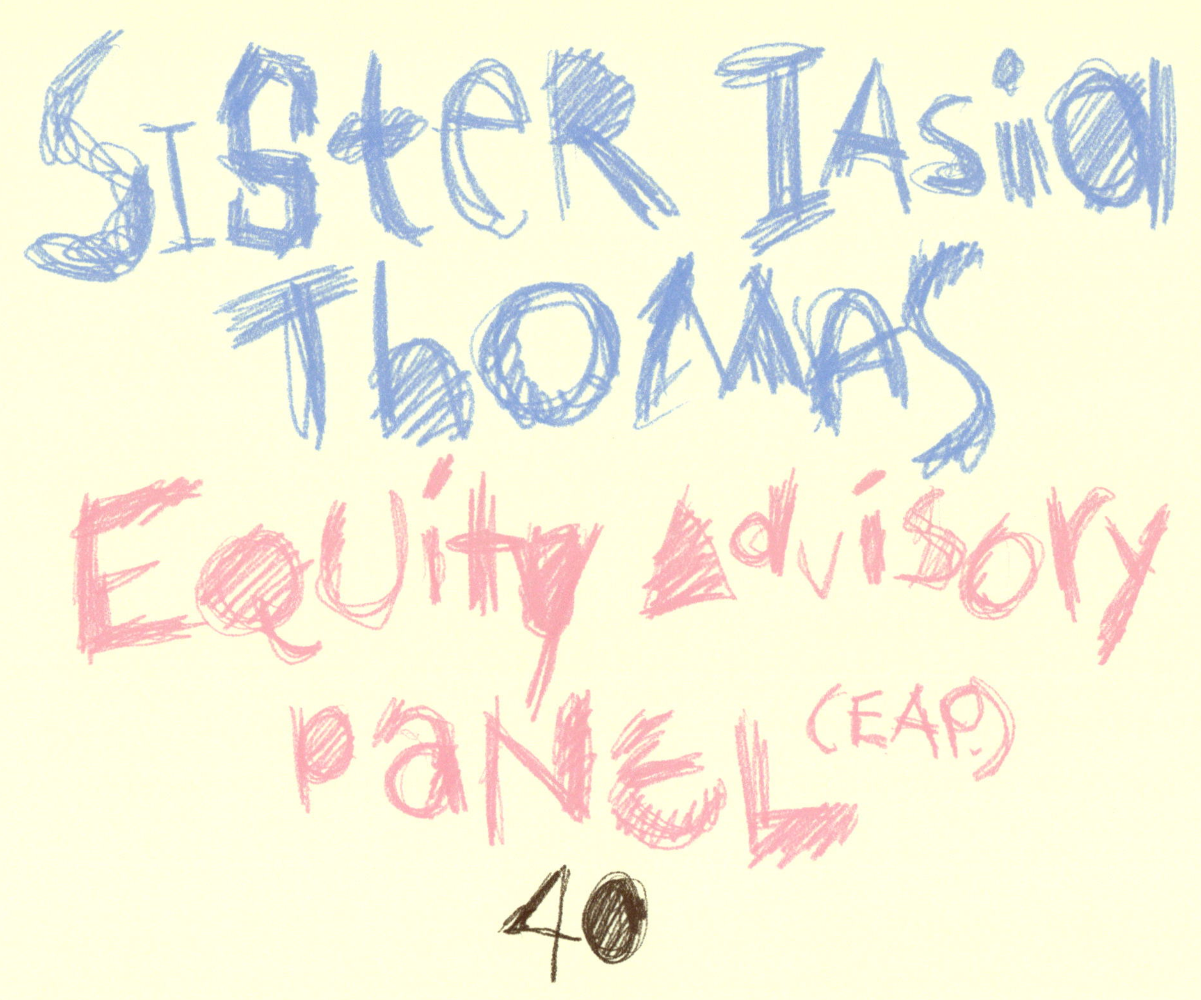

A COMPLAINT MUST BE KEPT ALIVE

A NOTE FROM DR. SISTER IASIA THOMAS

A complaint must be kept alive. For more than thirty years, the Equity Advisory Panel (EAP) has renewed its complaint before the Pittsburgh Public Schools. Now, we register the complaint with you. I, Dr. Sister IAsia Thomas, on behalf of the EAP, serve as the narrator and notetaker for this introduction. Let me enter into the record the stories of those who have organized and acted to make quality, equitable education a reality for the Black children of Pittsburgh.

DATE: MARCH 17, 2025
LOCATION: CARNEGIE MUSEUM OF ART
TIME: 5:00 P.M. TO 7:00 P.M.

IN THE AUDIENCE:

EAP MEMBERS—
Wanda Henderson
Regina Holley
Tamanika Howze
Anthony Mitchell
James Stewart
William Thompkins

CARNEGIE MUSEUM OF ART REPRESENTATIVES—
Dana Bishop-Root
Theodossis Issaias
Alyssa Velazquez

SIT Welcome to an introduction of those who seek to spiral understanding of the pathology of educational inequities impacting Black children as intolerable and deplorable in our own Pittsburgh. This introduction puts names and contexts to the relationships between the state, school district, and community vanguard. It reveres Dr. Barbara Sizemore as an embodiment of rectitude in Pittsburgh. It honors the Original Advocates for African American Students, founded in 1994, which eventually birthed the EAP—a movement that began in the eighties when Black communities responded to educational mistreatment towards Black children.

The EAP's contributions help move from lamentation to a celebration that "all the children are well," eventually and gradually. The Advocates' historical positions and oral histories are primary sources. In the EAP's Reports to the Community (August 25, 1992 through August 24, 2017), the reader is placed at the heart of Pittsburgh, traversing more than three decades—from the beginning of a complaint to its continuation today.

Learn about the parents of the movement who continue to work towards justice for Black children. Connect the cyclical and convergent stations of advocacy shared with a tenacious clutch by and from each altruist. Discern and behold what it takes to be enduring and steady with the project of education justice.

Presenting Our Equity Advisory Panel.

Chairwoman Wanda Henderson, Original Advocate for African American Students, Pittsburgh Public Schools. A regal and dedicated educational advocate who reminds us that the Advocates have been organizing for years, specifically more than three decades at the time of this writing.

Enter her narrative into the record:

Wanda Henderson says her work in advocacy was like "talking to a wall with little progress." She recalls that, in 1991, a search for a Pittsburgh Public Schools superintendent was funded by local philanthropy, in a community effort involving three potential candidates. One of the candidates, Dr. Loretta Webb from Virginia, was seen and held by Pittsburgh residents as the best. Nonetheless, the Board of Public Education chose not to hire her. Instead, they chose a less-qualified candidate named Mrs. Louise Brennan. Though Brennan had experience as an assistant superintendent, she did not have a doctorate like Webb, even though this credential was one of the criteria for superintendency.

This appointment disparity marked the proverbial straw that broke the camel's back. The education justice movement in Pittsburgh continued with its signature community mobilizing as a grassroots methodology. The planners and initiators, including community members, organized a mock funeral in protest of the Board of Public Education's appointment of an unqualified candidate. Protestors were equipped with a hearse, casket, and signage. As a catalyst for resistance and a frame for advocacy, a complaint was filed with the state of Pennsylvania's Human Relations Commission by the core voluntary group represented by William and Huberta Jackson-Lowman, Kim Jackson-Morris, Leroy Hodge (Esquire/Ancestor), Wanda Henderson, and Tamanika Howze. The Advocates prioritized five issues: hiring practices that resulted in a less-qualified candidate for superintendent; the suspension of African-American students at a higher rate than white students; class distribution disproportionately based on race; the exclusion of African-American students from special programs, including gifted and magnet programs. In essence, the Advocates were focused on these five points, and the overarching association of Black students with failure and discipline in the educational context.

After four years of the Advocates vacillating between the district's attorney, and upon filing various complaints with the Commission, the Commonwealth concluded in September 1996 that the Advocates lacked standing to file the complaint. Advocates Chairwoman Henderson remembered that:

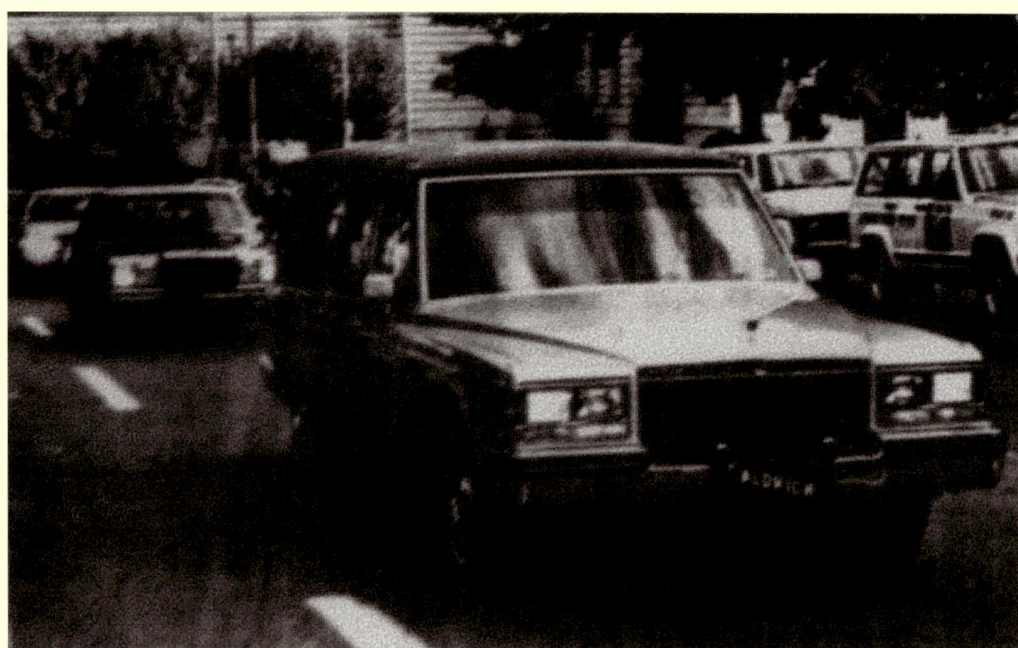

Detail of newspaper clipping from *Pittsburgh Courier*, "Education Advocates Stage 'Day of Mourning' for African-American Students," September 5, 1992, microfilm; New Pittsburgh Courier Collection, CLP

text book

"We met with people at the commission office in Downtown Pittsburgh, including attorneys, the investigator, and the regional director, and nothing happened. The Advocates were told that nobody in their right mind would take this case in Pittsburgh because it could be career-ending." Henderson and fellow Advocate Tamanika Howze forged onward, alerting and cautioning the community that the school-to-prison pipeline was in close proximity to the community's children, encouraging them to form as many circles of protection as attainable. Esquire Lane, advisor to Henderson, worked at State Correctional Institution—Muncy, so Henderson discerned a connection between the school-to-prison pipeline, seeing that mothers in prison were often described as having "no education." Henderson worked on the complaint, negotiating to see what the district would do. She recalled a case in Pennsylvania: a special education case (Gaskin v. Commonwealth of Pennsylvania) drawing statewide attention.[1] The group that filed the case won and created a Special Education Advisory Panel.

Inspired by this, and knowing that Pittsburgh Public Schools would not monitor itself, she founded the Equity Advisory Panel. The Advocates requested a nine-member panel. The Conciliation Consent Decree was signed on September 26, 2006, with ninety-four issues, according to Henderson. The school district was expected to strategize its efforts to ignite activity that would be deemed visible, actionable, and sustainable.[2] Notwithstanding, the EAP asserted that even one problem was too many when it came to Black students in the school district, and one problem was more than evident: the syndrome of discrimination and subsequent racism against Black students in the district.

SIT Grasp that Memoranda of Understandings (MoUs) have time stamps, expiration dates, of two to five years. In that time, substantial progress should be made. From 2006 to 2012, the district failed to make progress. From 2012 to 2014, the district failed again. In the pursuit of progress, another five-year term followed from 2015 to 2020.[3] Fathom that accountability with this body of ongoing educational advocacy is encircled by: answerability, liability, reporting, responsibility, and fulfillment. After 2020, with no substantial progress made with the PPS Board of Education, the EAP entered its current MoU from 2022 to 2027.

Now, let me present Tamanika Howze, Original Advocate for African American Students in the Pittsburgh Public Schools.

Enter her narrative into the record:

TAMANIKA HOWZE Tamanika Howze, Original Complainant and Advocate, is a proponent of holistic education and pedagogical enrichment, beginning with her own childhood experiences. As a young student, she entered Miller Elementary School, eager to learn from the first African American principal of Pittsburgh Public Schools, Mr. John Brewer, Sr. At eighteen, she came into her political, social, and cultural awareness. Her struggle, her fight for justice and liberation, began thrusting her into various causes.

During our conversation, Howze acknowledged an ancestor, a founding member of the Advocates: Dr. Barbara Sizemore. Having recently received a research grant on disparities present within PPS schools, Dr. Sizemore began to focus on three schools in particular: Vann Elementary, under the leadership of Doris Brevard; Madison Elementary, under the leadership of Vivian Williams; and Beltzhoozer Elementary, under the

1 Gaskin v. Commonwealth of Pennsylvania, 1994, U.S. District Court for the Eastern District of Pennsylvania.

2 Heather Thomas, "Towards Root Cause Inquiry: A Case Study for the Equity Advisory Panel (EAP)," (PhD diss., University of Pittsburgh, 2024) 196–218. https://d-scholarship.pitt.edu/46871/1/Sister%20I%20-%20ETD%20dissertation%20-%20finalized.pdf.

3 Thomas, "Towards Root Cause Inquiry," 124–153.

leadership of Lou Vincent. The first two schools, both located in the Hill District, featured a high-achieving, predominantly African American student body. The latter served students from Beltzhoover. The Advocates built upon Sizemore's findings channeling them to focus some of their work on principals leading Black schools. Let me enter into the record some of the accomplishments of the EAP, as guided by Howze and Sizemore:

Three executive Directors of Equity were instated.

An Equity Office (2012-present) was created.

An equity policy was instituted on the wings of foundational policy from 2012.[4]

The We Promise Program was created for Black male student mentorship (2012-2018).

The Promise of Sisterhood was created—an initiative to engage the district's Black and continental African girls in creative, academic, and cultural enrichment (2014-2023).

Drs. Molefi Asante and Ama Mazama led the Afrocentric Infusion Curricular Development.

The On Track To Equity Plan was written, serving as the EAP's plan to implement its MoU with PPS (2019).

Student Equity Advocates began serving select schools (2020-present).

Push for Ethnic Studies was launched, with origins in the African-American history curriculum (2020-2023).

Social workers, guidance counselors, learning specialists, and equity office staff participated in a two-year training led by the Association of Black Psychologists entitled "ABPSI-PPS Culturally Responsive & Trauma-Informed Practices for New Results" (2021-2023).

Tamanika also urged us to remember the important legacy of Leroy Hodge. In her words, "He was a member of the Advocates and was an attorney. And I mean, he was pushing hard for the advocates, and he was also one of the complainants. So, to these two ancestors—Dr. Sizemore and Leroy Hodge—I say: ashé."

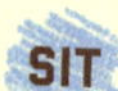

SIT And now, Dr. James Stewart, EAP Member and Earliest Chairman. **Enter his narrative into the record:**

DR. JAMES STEWART

The EAP's involvement with the district traditionally takes place in the form of meetings with district personnel. Dr. Stewart recounts that the EAP received three-inch binders of uninterpreted data from the school district, which district leaders would try to walk through during meetings.

4 School District of Pittsburgh, "Equity and Excellence in Education Procedures," no. 102-AR-1 of 1, 2019, https://resources.finalsite. net/images/v1721321978/pghschoolsorg/ segjsgexat4x0n6710vf/equitypolicy5-arv6.pdf.

Stewart recalls, "The MoU contains a lot of statistics. And the meetings did not end there. The meetings involving the EAP comprise trying to get behind the numbers, so to speak, and to pre-determine what sort of policy changes were being implemented. So, I used to have two shelves of these thick, statistical documents that really weren't generating any information, and that in my opinion were not that useful, in part because they didn't demonstrate any improvement. One of the things that EAP tried to do was to reduce the dependency on these large bodies of measures and come up with measures that they thought would enable them to really examine what was going on. So, there was an ongoing discussion about whether the mission, what they were proposing, was an alternative to whether it was going to complement the existing data collection."

Dr. Stewart made two changes to how the group dealt with all this data. First, he proposed a way of simplifying the data so the group could focus on the actual analysis and determine what the district had done to address issues. Secondly, in the original MoU containing ninety-four settlement items, the data was not required to be disaggregated by gender. "We proposed separating the data by Black males, Black females, white males, and white females." According to Dr. Stewart, the mission of the EAP was to determine whether or not any particular group was experiencing disproportionate disempowerment. The district was willing to acquiesce if the EAP agreed to lessen the perceived burden of producing voluminous data reports moving forward. The EAP did not agree as the intent and quest was and remains to report on data in areas of any disparity impacting Black learning identified in the complaint. Monitoring progress is an ongoing project that can allow the EAP to develop communications that focus on inequalities without deprioritizing analysis and subsequent root cause analysis.[5]

SIT Then, Dr. Anthony Mitchell, EAP Member.
Enter his narrative into the record:

DR. ANTHONY MITCHELL Dr. Mitchell established that some EAP members have come from clear African-centered education frameworks. There were a couple of members who brought clarity around the domain of multicultural education as well, and Mitchell affirmed that there is room for both of those strategies to coexist. However, there is a distinction concerning some of the critical issues that our community members face, specifically our parents and their historical experiences with educational trauma, which must be navigated deliberately. The bottom line is that through analysis and root cause inquiries, the reality of racism in Pittsburgh calls for clear action by PPS. Today, the EAP offers two primary roles to the District: monitoring progress and making recommendations.

Dr. Mitchell explains that, "The district has struggled to accept our recommendations and receive and validate us as an empowered community by the Pennsylvania Human Relations Commission."

SIT And let me also introduce Dr. Regina Holley, EAP Member.
Enter her narrative into the record:

5 Jacob Carruthers, "Science and Oppression," in African Psychology in Historical Perspective & Related Commentary, edited by D. Azibo (Africa World Press, 1996), 185-191.

6 "The Slave Experience: Education, Arts, and Culture," Slavery and the Making of America, *WNET New York*, Accessed September 12, 2025, https://www.thirteen.org/wnet/slavery/experience/education/docs2.html.

DR. REGINA HOLLEY When reflecting on the vision and leadership of Dr. Barbara Sizemore, Holley noted that, "Barbara just didn't talk about what needed to be done, she showed you how to do it. Barbara was a professor at the University of Pittsburgh in the Black Studies Department and researched schools that were doing well. Still, she wanted to show us how to do it within our schools when we had the opportunity." Dr. Holley was a mentee of Dr. Sizemore, working on behalf of families and boys. Holley learned that from Barbara, "to make sure that we give children as much time as possible to be in school. Because if school is a holistic place for them and a happy place for them, and it is a nurturing place for them, that's where kids want to be."

SIT And, finally, William Thompkins, EAP Member.
Let us enter his narrative into the record:

WILLIAM THOMPKINS "But what we've got to do is we've got to take a look at it all from the near future, in the far future," he says. Some things we will not realize immediately. But other things we will understand over time. Some of us will experience it. And some things, unfortunately, we will not be here to experience." Dr. Holley and Thompkins bring forward the ongoing prioritizations of literacies, student behaviors, and enrichments for students, such as Freedom Schools, often offered in the summer months. While there are bulleted and well-documented priorities, we perpetually and everlastingly have eyes and ears on: literacy, student behavior, impacting poverty, student career exploration, the Black family, and the quality of life. The EAP works with both the microscope and the telescope.

SIT In conclusion, consider the cyclical nature of history involving organizers and mobilizing. Would it be serendipitous that education justice legacies reclaim, recover, and remember by simulating the efforts of what learning has to do with liberating the minds of Black children? Would it be unthinkable that the remnants of prior endeavors continue to resound, and that their vestiges continue on? The struggle continues as the EAP persists in reaching back to consistently and tenaciously contribute to what has been in effect since 1830: a fight for quality education for Black children which involves families and communities, with representation from state authority.

The African Education Society (AES), formed on January 16, 1832, engraved in its constitution the idea that, "Ignorance will debase the mind and subject our followers to the lowest vices and most abject depravity."[6] Protesting the comparison between Black personhood and ignorance, the constitution directed the AES to invest in acquiring books, capital, and securing land to erect schools. Within a year, in 1833, Society members John Pick, Abraham Lewis, John Vashon, and Reverend Lewis Woodson opened The African School in the basement of the Bethel African Methodist Episcopal Church. Pittsburgh's own Martin Delaney served as one of its teachers. Delaney was a writer, abolitionist, and Black nationalist. During this time, Black children were excluded from receiving an education, resulting in community-led protests. Three years onward, in 1838, the school board subsidized the Miller Street School where Black children could attend. In the footsteps of Martin Delaney, John Templeton—a Black man—was assigned to teach there.

In 1867, the fight against educational apartheid once again rose. This time, the people demanded improved atmospheres and circumstances—transforming Pittsburgh's historic Hill District with a school at the cross-streets of Miller and Reeds. This site became the home of the Miller Street School, which was led by Jacob B. Taylor. Four plots of land were purchased, and a two-story building was erected on the site. In 1868, the Miller Street School for Black children was established, with Jacob B. Taylor as its principal. After the state of Pennsylvania officially abolished racial discrimination in the public school system in 1881, the Pittsburgh Board of Education allowed Black and white students to attend the same schools.

Pittsburgh's education justice history is extensive and protracted. In September of 2025, the Advocates will be celebrating over thirty years of contributions to the struggle. The work of the Advocates and the Equity Advisory Panel weeps for and grieves through activism and persistence, the casualties of an unkind and unjust multifarious history involving Black children. This work memorializes those who were trailblazers of the education justice movement in more extant times. They continue with unwavering tenacity and tenure, in service to the future of public education.

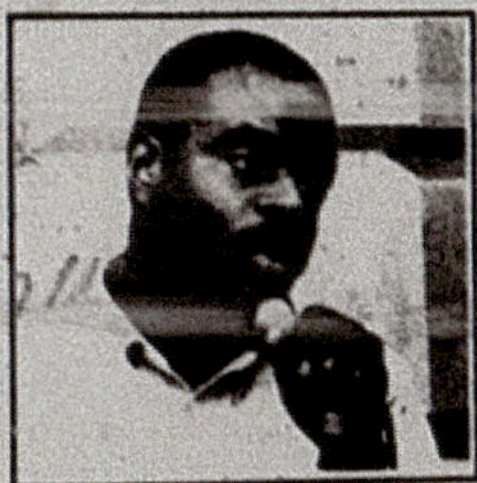

Education Advocates Stage 'Day Of Mourning' For African-American Students

By MARC HOPKINS
Courier Staff Writer

In a symbolic measure to illustrate the death of African-American students as a result of the election of Louise Brennen to the Pittsburgh Public School Board, parents gathered in front of the Board of Education building in Oakland, last Tuesday, to mourn the passing.

Approximately 70 parents, many wearing black, others with black arm bands, stood around a wood coffin bearing signs reading: "Improve Achievement of African-American students" and "Decrease the Drop Out Rate."

The "Day of Mourning" was sponsored by Advocates for African-American Students, the group that has lobbied in the past several months for the election of Dr. Loretta Webb to succeed outgoing Superintendent Dr. Richard Wallace.

During a school board vote on Aug. 19, former Deputy Superintendent Louise Brennen was chosen as the new head of city schools. Brennen's contract took effect on Sept. 1, the same day as the mock funeral.

"This (Brennen's election) means death to multiculturalism, to parent-teacher accountability...how many will we lose because of the direction of the school board..."
MARK BRENTLEY

The "Day of Mourning" is the latest in a series of events the Advocates have staged to draw attention to what they describe as the poor learning conditions African-American students face in public schools.

They cite the large achievement gap which exists between Black and white students on standardized tests, the disproportionate number of Black males suspended from school and the absence of a multicultural curriculum as the major issues of contention.

The group saw hope for the system with Webb as the superintendent. She has expertise in multicultural education and has demonstrated an ability to close the achievement gap in the Fairfax, Virginia, school system.

However, with the election of Brennen, who the group says is a less qualified candidate, the Advocates believe positive change for Black students cannot occur.

"This is the day the School Board takes the same old direction with nothing new for our kids," said Mark Brentley, who has led several of the prayer vigils in support for Webb.

"This (Brennen's election) means death to multiculturalism, to parent-teacher accountability...how many will we lose because

continued on A-4

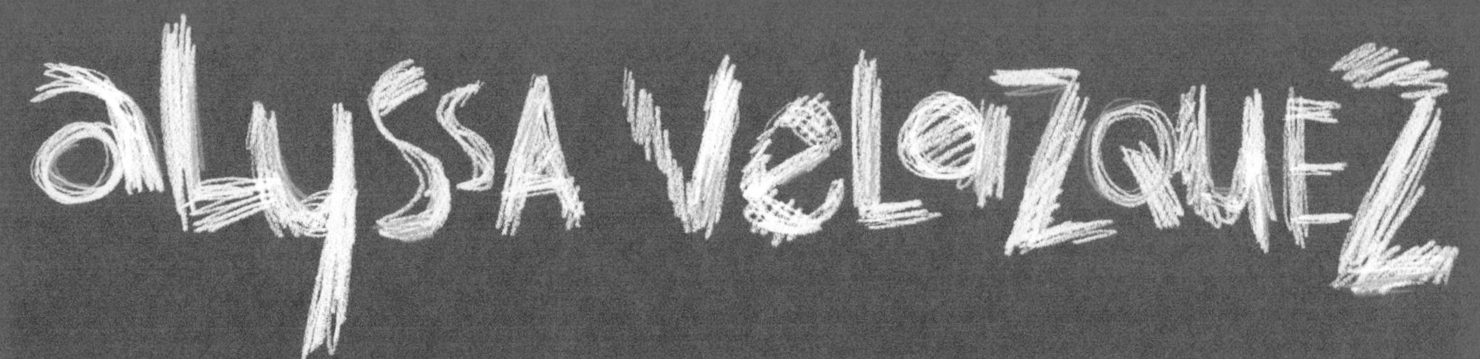

48

MODELING
AMERICA IN VAN
DYKE BROWN

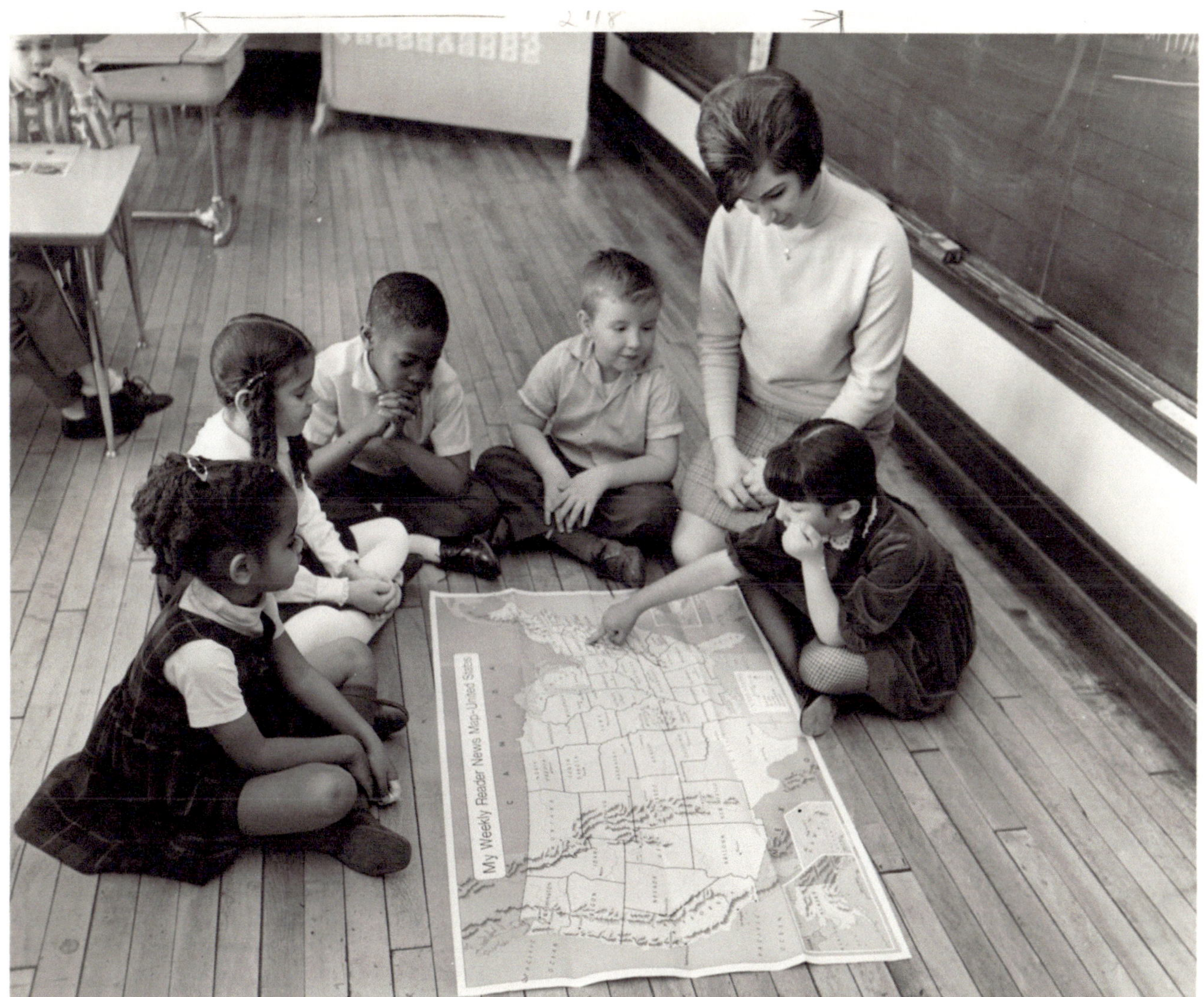

Students sitting on the floor with a teacher and US map, ca. 1950, photograph; Detre Library & Archives, HHC

I am in the tenth grade. My history teacher is on medical leave. They say they don't know when she will be back. They say settle down. They say for class today we're going to watch a movie starring Nicolas Cage.

A NATIONAL TREASURE

Benjamin (Ben) Franklin Gates believes there is a map to a legendary Freemason treasure on the back of the Declaration of Independence. Gates, played by Nicolas Cage in the 2004 American action-adventure film *National Treasure*, is joined in his quest by friend and codebreaker Riley Poole (Justin Bartha) and archivist and love interest Abigail Chase (Diane Kruger). To save the document from getting into the hands of people who would sell and barter off priceless artifacts, Ben steals the Declaration of Independence. An invisible cipher is cracked, leading this cast of characters to one of the most recognizable civic buildings in the United States: Independence Hall. Atop Philadelphia's Centennial Bell tower, Ben, Abigail, and Riley, wait to see the steeple's afternoon silhouette, directing them to their next clue. The timely shadow points to a particular section of Independence Hall where Ben discovers a Freemason-marked hollow brick that contains a pair of spectacles with "the vision to see the treasured past."[1]

During the month of September 1937, the Pennsylvania Historical Commission, in coopertion with the Museum Extension Project and Works Progress Administration (WPA), located at 3400 Forbes Street in Pittsburgh, distributed 2300 models of Independence Hall to schools and historical societies throughout the Commonwealth of Pennsylvania.[2] Presented as a gift from the Pennsylvania Historical Commission, every school was expected to organize assemblies and programs around the authentic scale model on September 17, 1937, marking the 150th Anniversary of the signing of the Constitution.

The Sesquicentennial Celebration of the Constitution brought together three branches of the Museum Extension Project, located in Pittsburgh, Harrisburg, and Philadelphia. The Pittsburgh project alone employed eight hundred people for a period of one year in order to distribute a scale model of Independence Hall to both public and private schools throughout Pennsylvania.[3]

Architects and artists from the Museum Extension Project visited Independence Hall to make measurements and authenticate coloring, and extensive research was conducted in the Carnegie Library of Pittsburgh regarding the history of the building for supplemental learning materials.[4]

School principals throughout the state received pamphlets from the Museum Extension Project which had been made to look like

WPA model of Independence Hall, 1937, photograph; PH and MCP State Archives

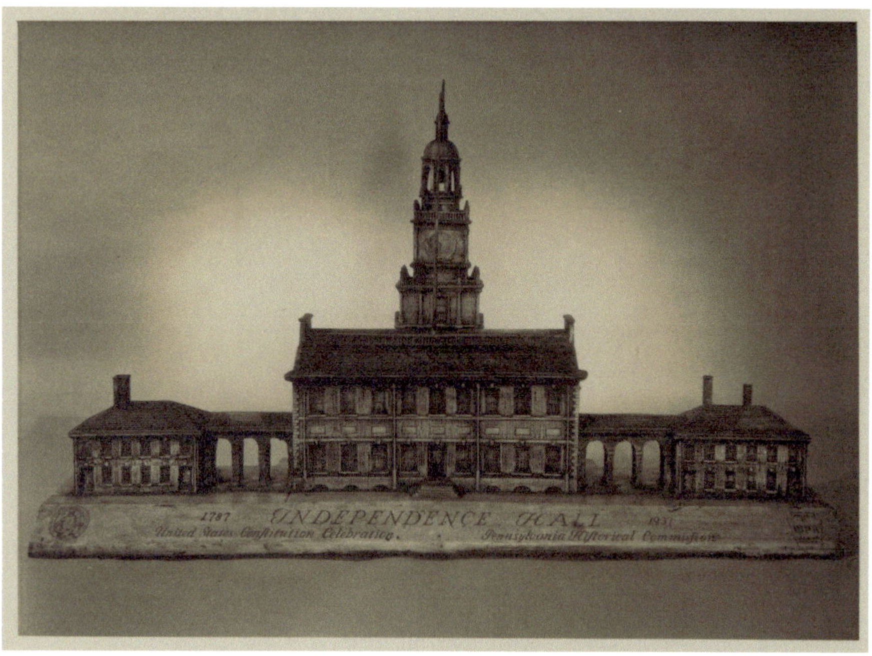

1 *National Treasure*, directed by Jon Turteltaub (2004; Walt Disney Pictures), DVD.

2 Report to the Governor from the Pennsylvania Historical Commission, October 5, 1937, Pennsylvania State Archives.

3 Governor's Bulletin, Pennsylvania Historical Commission, June 2, 1937, Pennsylvania State Archives.

4 United States Constitution Celebration 1787–1937: The Story of Independence Hall, Pennsylvania Historical Commission, Works Progress Administration, August 30, 1937, Pennsylvania State Archives.

parchment and printed with Colonial-Roman type that told the story of Independence Hall—including floor plans. The pamphlet was accompanied by a play titled "A Modern Newsboy at the Constitution Convention." The script was written with support from the research department of the Museum Extension Project and in collaboration with the National Theatre Project. The performative materials included costume plates, patterns, and sheet music should the high school, parochial school, or academy have an orchestra. Over the course of two days, 192 junior high schools and 1059 public senior high schools in Pennsylvania were sent copies of "A Modern Newsboy at the Constitution Convention," drawings, and a 1/8 inch-to-scale plaster-cast architectural model of Independence Hall.[5]

Twelve men and three die-makers wor-ked on the original Independence Hall model. In order to complete manufacturing in time for September 17, employees in the sculpture and casting department at the Museum Extension Project in Pittsburgh worked Saturdays, Sundays, and holidays. The models were cast in ten separate sections and left to dry for three days. Unlike the original, the central tower of the Hall was designed to be detachable, so as to better accommodate packing, shipping, and rail transit.

Originally, the models were to be painted red and white. However in a letter to Martha J. Bring (Executive Secretary at Pennsylvania Historical Commission), Florence H. Cochrane (Supervisor Women's and Professional Projects) shared that, "after a week's production it was learned that the models were being painted too slowly, and the workmanship, due to inexperienced painters, was rather poor."[6] In the interest of time and capacity, the color scheme changed to Van Dyke brown paint, with the exception of a selection of models painted in a more realistic fashion for high rank-ing government officials. Van Dyke brown was named after the Flemish painter Anthony Van Dyke. The color, a transparent brown, derived its warmth from organic matter such as soil or peat mixed with pigment. Manufacturers of watercolors and gouaches all offer a Van Dyke brown, each a different shade of brown reminiscent of Van Dyke's earthy pallet. Decades after the models' construction, television host Bob Ross would frequently use Van Dyke brown oil paint on *The Joy of Painting* as a color for trees, cabins, and basecoats. Thirteen of the more realistic models were sent as gifts from Pennsylvania's Governor George H. Earle to the governors of the original thirteen states. President Franklin D. Roosevelt received his very own model from Frank W. Melvin, Chairman of the Works Progress Administration's Historical Commission.

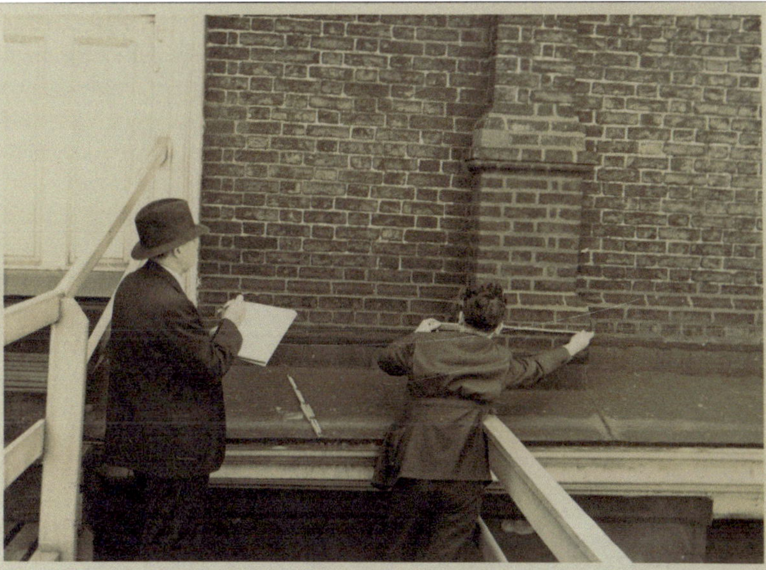

Top: WPA employees taking measurements of a tower plaster at Independence Hall, 1937, photograph; PH and MCP State Archives

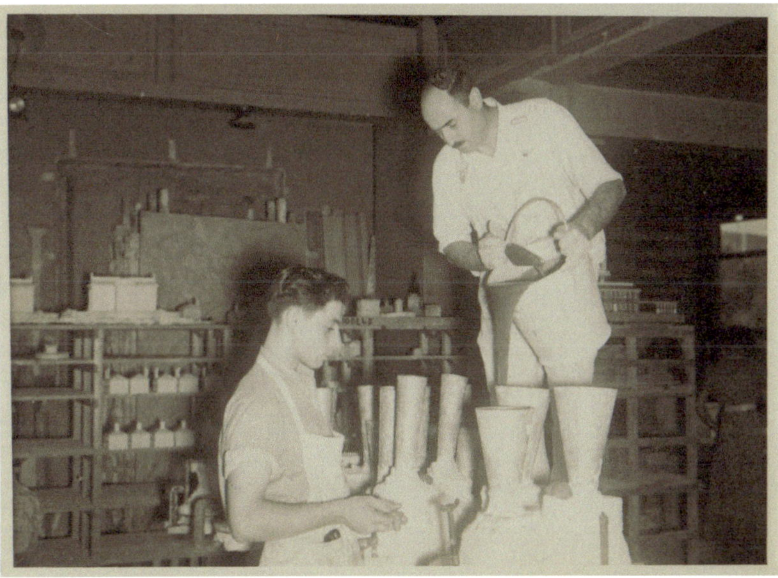

Bottom: WPA employees pouring and setting plaster molds of Independence Hall, 1937, photograph; PH and MCP State Archives

5 Listing of Schools, Colleges, Libraries, Committees, Societies, Mayors, etc., that received an Independence Hall Scale Model, September 17, 1937, Pennsylvania State Archives.

6 Letter to Miss Martha J. Bring, Executive Secretary at Pennsylvania Historical Commission, Harrisburg, PA, from Mrs. Florence H. Cochrane, Supervisor Women's and Professional Projects, District 15, October 14, 1937, Pennsylvania State Archives.

CONSCIOUS-RAISING CRAFT

When President Franklin D. Roosevelt created the Works Progress Administration by Executive Order in 1935, it provided opportunities for unemployed workers to apply their skills and training to public projects. After the establishment of the WPA, Pennsylvania began a Museum Extension Project also known as the State-Wide Museum Extension. The program divided its activities and employees into two general divisions: the production of visual aid devices and the financing of docent services to existing museums.[7] Through these expenditures, FDR's New Deal initiatives invested in increased staffing within artistic spaces and the teaching of arts and crafts. It changed how visitors saw and engaged with works of art in, often privatized and elitist, spaces.

This was different from programs that served a selective number of students through temporary loans from museum collections. One such example is the New York City Program of Circulating Exhibitions for High Schools of 1937, which selected ten schools to serve as sites for The Museum of Modern Art (MoMA)'s traveling exhibitions, teaching models, and visuals aids. Exhibitions included: *Objects Of Good Design: Which Do You Like?* and *Imagination In Architecture*. Unlike New York City's circulating exhibitions program, which focused on the few, the Museum Extension Project was financed with the broadest audience in mind. Rather than giving exposure, it prioritized continual access to arts education for all and the employment of skilled artisans.

District 15, the Pittsburgh office of the Museum Extension Project, was one of the most active in the state. It was sponsored by the Pittsburgh Board of Public Education and occupied a five-story building in the Oakland section of the city.[8]

In addition to the Independence Hall replicas, the Museum Extension Project catalog listed 110 plaster architectural dwellings, made to scale. A school could order up to fifteen of these economic and educational models, with each request supporting the art and architecture workforce during the Great Depression. Just like the models of Independence Hall, these objects were either distributed free of charge or—on occasion—sold for a nominal fee to tax-supported Pennsylvania school districts, libraries, and public institutions. Teachers, librarians, and museum curators were encouraged to use these visual aids to represent "the human race's evolutionary efforts to house itself."[9] Each built environment modeling the principles of democratic persuasion that were being articulated by American social scientists at the same moment."[10] A teaching tool that blurred the lines between information, art, and propaganda to inspire the next generation of artisans and laborers. Categories included:

Prehistoric dwellings	Byzantine	Pennsylvania Historic
Primitive dwellings	Romanesque	Late American
Egyptian	Gothic	Racial & Nationalistic[11]
Greek	Renaissance	
Roman	Early American	

Independence Hall, though made outside of these standard offerings, fit within an existing nationalist education. Each model then became the property of the educational entity that ordered or received them.

7 Works Progress Administration and Museum Extension Project, Pennsylvania: Handbooks Collection, 1935–1943, Pennsylvania: Museum Extension Project, 1935.

8 Works Progress Administration and Museum Extension Project, Pennsylvania, State Wide Museum Extension Project Catalog Number Three, Pennsylvania: Museum Extension Project, 1935.

9 State Wide Museum Extension Project Catalog Number Three, 1935.

10 Fred Turner, *The Democratic Surround: Multimedia and American Liberalism from World War II to the Psychedelic Sixties* (University Press of Chicago, 2013), 78.

11 State Wide Museum Extension Project Catalog Number Three, 1935.

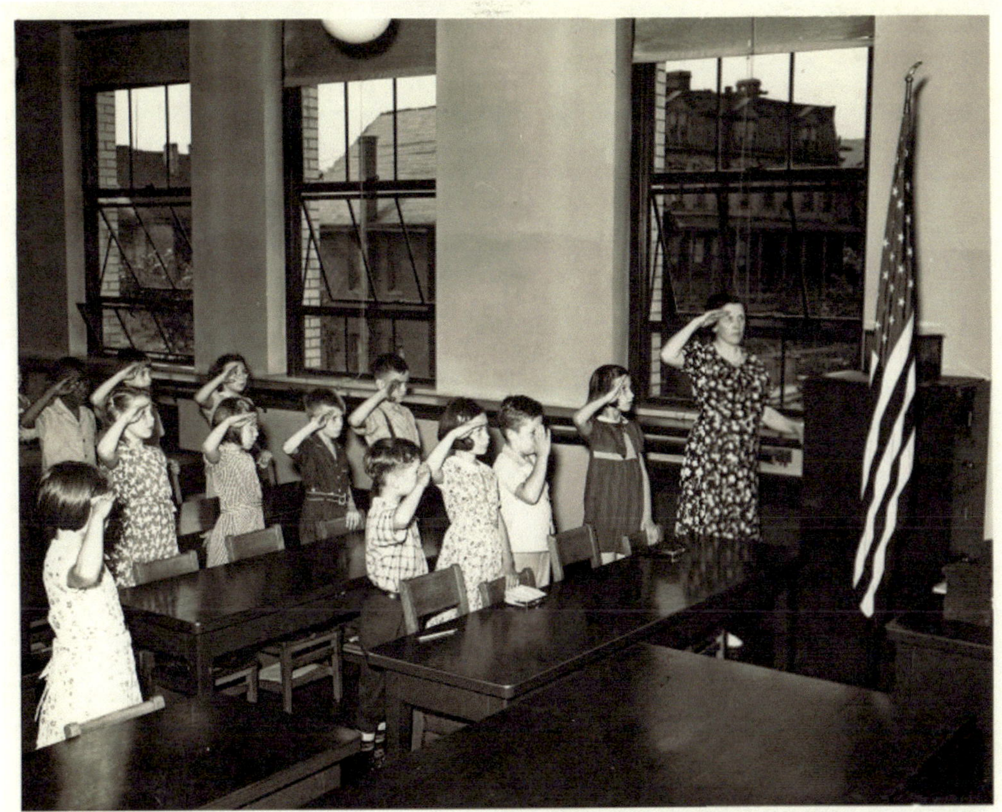

Flag salute at Burgwin Elementary School, 1944–1950, photograph; Library and Archives Division, HHC

THE VISION TO SEE THE TREASURED PAST

In the United States, the 1930s saw the advocacy of arts education with the publication of John Dewey's *Art as Experience*, emphasizing the relationship between art and everyday living— its ability to transcend barriers to create communal experiences; a medium for social unity. North American architectural models, unlike many of the buildings labeled by country or continent, were not examples of the everyday. Despite the egalitarian idealism associated with art projects sponsored through the Museum Extension Project, many models represented landed gentry estates or exemplary histories—noteworthy miniatures of historic landmarks renowned for their infamous occupants.

Independence Hall, for instance, was never intended to serve "the human race's evolutionary efforts to house itself."[12]

Designated a World Heritage Site in 1979, Independence Hall is a symbolic venue for political rallies and celebrations. Its replica performed a similar purpose—commemorating the United States' democratic spirit in library displays, trophy cases, and entryways. Albert Lindsay Rowland, President of the State Teachers College in Shippensburg, Pennsylvania, wrote to Dr. Lester K. Ade, Superintendent of Public Instruction, asking to receive an Independence Hall model for their college museum where it would be "worthily placed and will be an inspiration to our students."[13]

Dr. Ade's solicitation reveals another unique aspect to this Sesquicentennial-themed offering, as compared to the Museum Extension

[12] "Independence Hall," UNESCO World Heritage Centre, accessed December 14, 2020, https://whc.unesco.org/en/list/78/.

[13] Letter to Dr. Lester K. Ade, Superintendent of Public Instruction from Albert Lindsay Rowland, President of the State Teachers College in Shippensburg, Pennsylvania, September 8, 1937, Pennsylvania State Archives.

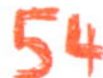

Magazine clipping from *The Schoolhouse Flag Movement*, 1909, advertisement; National Museum of American History

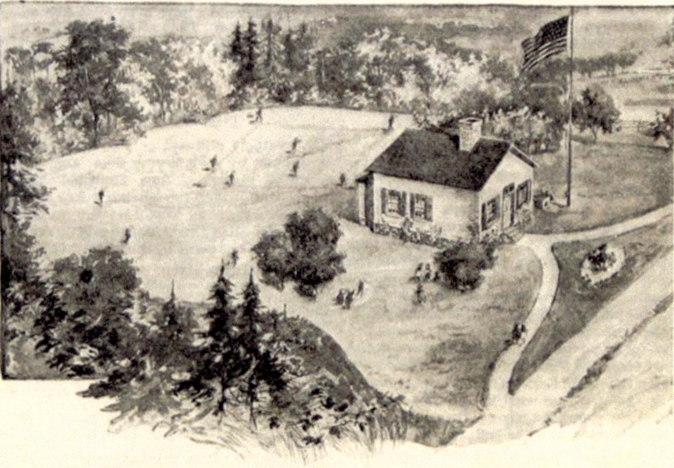

The Schoolhouse Flag Movement.

The "Schoolhouse Flag Movement" was organized by The Companion over twenty-one years ago. Though there are still many schools not provided with the flag, the time does not seem far distant when there shall be no public school too poor, too remote, or too indifferent to have the Stars and Stripes floating above its roof.

Many teachers report a distinct growth of real patriotism. Even the little children count the stars in the blue field of their flag, and learn what they mean. The older pupils ransack the books for the history of the flag itself, and in so doing are impressed with a new idea of its story, and of its relations to their own condition and privileges.

Thus the result in the cultivation of civic patriotism alone is richly worth all that has been expended upon it in money, time or effort.

It is the hope of The Companion that eventually every school in the land will have the Stars and Stripes floating above it. With this end in view, the publishers will be glad to send to any teacher a supply of Schoolhouse Flag Certificates and other special aids for securing the flag desired. These helps will be sent free of expense.

PERRY MASON COMPANY, 201 Columbus Ave., BOSTON, MASS.

Project's standard catalogue. Independence Hall models were distributed, not ordered. Interested public school officials who saw a model elsewhere had to solicit the Historical Commission for one of their own. And they did. Often cited in the distribution letters to principals is the lack of road access for a trucking service to personally deliver a model of Independence Hall to the school. This off-the-beaten-path rhetoric speaks to the intentional distribution of Independence Hall—a national symbol of freedom and democracy—to rural areas and their residents. Remote communities in the periphery of the Pennsylvania Railroad were steadily growing due to rising immigrant populations— foreign-born residents who were farmers in their homeland seeking opportunities as livestock workers, graders and sorters, equipment operators, and field managers. Schools in these areas offered the general populace literacy courses, adult English language classes, and citizenship test preparation (see Ujju Aggarwal, p.30).

Models of Independence Hall arrived to, and were viewed within, these programs of "Americanization." During the first half of the twentieth century, Americanization was a catch-all term for programs that U.S.-born citizens created in response to the influx of immigrants arriving between 1890 and 1925.[14] During that time, many educators, social activists, and intellectuals aimed to make immigrants into citizens through the creation of English language instruction, the securing of naturalization, and the promotion of patriotism within the nation's schools. In October 1892, children across the country recited the Pledge of Allegiance for the first time, coinciding with the four hundredth anniversary of Christopher Columbus's arrival in the New World.[15]

In 1937, Pennsylvania became the first state to establish June 14 as Flag Day—the same year the Museum Extension Project distributed Independence Hall models as visual-aid devices to large urban institutions and small rural schools.

Staff and administrators at educational facilities not along the train line were instructed to organize a pick-up of their Museum Extension Project models at the nearest depot. Driving along backroads, they might have passed extant nineteenth century structures, some of which were subsequently made into architectural models. The Nixon Tavern built in 1810 was part of a Historic American Buildings Survey in 1934 and, through the drafted elevations and detailed notes, was then made into a tactile teaching aid. Importantly, The Nixon Tavern and other models in the WPA's catalogue were based off governmental surveys that recorded and produced architectural drawings for the assessment and celebration of a white historical past. This Eurocentric take on the founding and expansion of the United States side-steps land grabs by settler-colonizers and the forced migration of enslaved Africans to North America

14 Jeffrey Mirel, *Patriotic Pluralism: Americanization Education and European Immigrants* (Harvard University Press, 2010), 6.

15 Scott Bomboy, The History of Legal Challenges to the Pledge of Allegiance," last modified June 14, 2023, https://constitutioncenter.org/blog/the-latest-controversy-about-under-god-in-the-pledge-of-allegiance.

in tandem with the systematic removal of Native American and Indigenous residents from entire regions of the United States. One such region is along the Rio Hondo near Taos, New Mexico. Pueblo houses in this area are multi-storied limestone structures characterized by a succession of flat roofs built in terraced tiers for the cultural ceremonies and everyday activities of present-day Pueblo Indian people in northern New Mexico. Tactically rendered by the Museum Extension Program, traditional Pueblo construction is cast to a base color-matched to the structures' walls, completely devoid of vegetation, despite the Pueblo Indians' rich agricultural knowledge and heritage. Around the same time, another government agency—the Farmers Security Administration—also took to creating depictions of Pueblo homes.

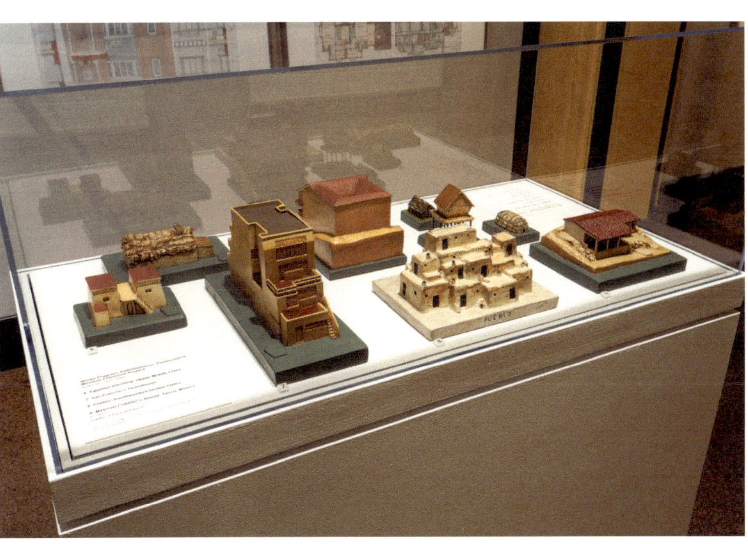

Museum display of WPA models, 2014, photograph; Carnegie Museum of Art

The Farmers Security Administration (FSA), created under the Department of Agriculture as part of the New Deal, helped generate and secure loans and credit for farmers. The FSA also hired photographers to document rural America in the process. In New Mexico, the Farmers Security Administration took pictures of Pueblo homes that the WPA models reductively depicted, alongside their Pueblo inhabitants, woodworking and metalsmithing at the Indian Service School (ISS). Founded with the intention of assimilating Native American children, service and boarding schools like the ISS emphasized training in the domestic and industrial arts. Students were not allowed to speak their native language or practice traditional customs, including pastoral culture.

Divorced from land and community through the slight lift and streamlined stabilization of a square base or pedestal, each plaster model platform bore the official emblem of the WPA and its district of origin. Whether it was a raised or impressed, a keystone on a model's base served as the Museum Extension Project's certificate of authenticity, asking its user to trust the accuracy of the miniature's construction. The WPA took their reputation very seriously, occasionally facing off against controversy about their product line and personnel.

Communists and other believers in "un-American ideologies" were accused of infiltrating the WPA. Projects for the restitution of a financially stable and culturally rich United States risked the continual employment of artists and supervisors who admitted to being members of the Communist party and Workers Alliance. Miss Margaret Lindsay, project lead of the WPA Museum Extension Project, received a letter dated July 31, 1940, that references a rumor traveling around to "the effect that you [Miss. Lindsay] are active in communistic circles."[16] The same letter asked for her to respond with her reaction. Miss Lindsay's response arrived on August 1st, stating, "the only academic interest in any form of Communism that I have ever had is in the communal life of the Harmony Society, which life I would never advocate either for myself or anyone else because of the sacrifices of personal liberty and democratic expression it entails."[17] Dr. Holland Roberts, head of The California Labor School 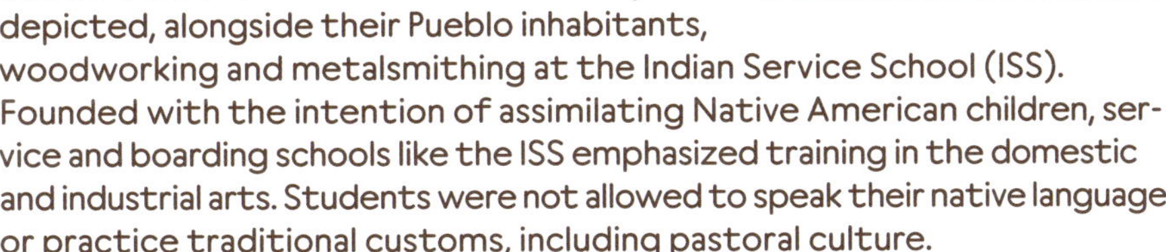 (see Laura Nelson, p.82), faced suspicion while running for office as Superintendent of Public Instruction in San Francisco. Roberts' opposition feared his network of suspected New Deal liberals, Communist Party members, and other leftist organizers teaching at the school. They also

16 Letter to Miss Margaret Lindsay, product head at WPA Museum Extension Project from Donald A. Cadzow, Executive Secretary of the Pennsylvania Historical Commission, July 31, 1940, Pennsylvania State Archives.

17 The Historical Commission and Museum Extension Project were involved in the rehabilitation of Old Economy Village in Ambridge, Pennsylvania, home to the Harmony Society, one of the most sucessful religious communal groups of the 19th century; Letter to Donald A. Cadzow, Executive Secretary of the Pennsylvania Historical Commission, from Miss Margaret Lindsay, product head at WPA Museum Extension Project, August 1, 1940, Pennsylvania State Archives.

feared the school's offerings to a student body of blue collar workers—the most popular being the California Labor School's arts program, including union song sing-alongs and mural classes "for the strengthening of democracy…in the war against fascism."[18]

PATRIOTIC EDUCATION

I am back in the tenth grade. My history teacher is still on medical leave. They say we're going to watch a movie, again. They have us watch National Treasure, again. They spend more than half the year lecturing on decades in North American; they cover centuries on other continents in a matter of weeks.

The year *National Treasure* was released on DVD, George W. Bush accepted a presidential nomination for a second term. In his speech at the Republican National Convention in New York City, he said, "I believe every child can learn and every school must teach, so we passed the most important Federal education reform in history. Because we acted, children are making sustained progress in reading and math; America's schools are getting better; and nothing will hold us back."[19] The federal education reform he referred to was the No Child Left Behind (NCLB) Act of 2002: a bipartisan bill that demanded curriculums of compliance and altered arts education. While the arts were identified as a "core academic subject," there remains a persistent decline in access to artistic programs in public schools.

Democratic expression, as Miss Lindsey called it, is an aesthetic of Americanization that appears implicitly and explicitly over time in public education. My substitute teacher was doing the best she could, given the circumstances and guidelines set out to prepare us for standardized intelligence tests that center nationalistic histories (see Leigh Patel, p.58). In Spring 2025, the conservative media organization PragerU partnered with Oklahoma's State Department of Education to develop "America First" assessment tests on the constitution and American exceptionalism. These assessments are not meant for students, but for school teachers relocating from what Superintendent Ryan Walter calls progressive states. Walter intends for the tests to evaluate teachers' abilities to "raise a generation of patriots."[20]

Was the model of Independence Hall a precursor to these assessment tests? Is it an instructive tale? Where is the national caution in these visual forms of democratic expression? In 1937, a model of Independence Hall was a welcome resource for educators across the country who sought to provide citizens and immigrants seeking citizenship with lessons around the Founding Fathers and celebration of the Declaration of Independence's adoption in 1776. Today, the President's Advisory 1776 Commission, established by Executive Order 13958 on November 2, 2020 and reinstated in 2025, is to "advise the President regarding how to better enable a rising generation to understand the history and principles of the founding of the United States in 1776."[21] However, the federal government does not have jurisdiction over school curriculum, and the initial 1776 Commission was housed under the Department of Education. Emergency rulings by the Supreme Court on July 15, 2025 resulted in mass layoffs from the Department, making it unclear just how and in what forms the 1776 Commission can or will be reinstated. But one of the initial promotions included in section 111(b) of title I of Division J of Public

18 California Labor School Catalogue, 1948, Labor Archives and Research Center, J. Paul Leonard Library, San Francisco State University.

19 George W. Bush, "Remarks Accepting the Presidential Nomination at the Republican National Convention in New York City" (speech, New York City, September 2, 2004), https://www.presidency.ucsb.edu/documents/remarks-accepting-the-presidential-nomination-the-republican-national-convention-new-york.

20 "Oklahoma schools are already struggling. Walters' 'wokeness test' doesn't help," The Oklahoman, accessed on July 20, 2025, https://www.oklahoman.com/story/opinion/editorials/2025/07/20/oklahoma-school-teacher-woke-test-walters/85204691007/?gnt-cfr=1&gca-cat=p&gca-uir=true&gca-epti=z114906p00045 0c000450e000900v114906b0061xxd006165&gca-ft=140&gca-ds=sophi.

21 The Secretary Of Education Washington, Charter The President's Advisory 1776 Commission, signed and established on December 14, 2020.

Law 108-447 stated that "each educational institution that receives Federal funds for a fiscal year shall hold an educational program on the United States Constitution on September 17 of such year for the students served by the educational institution."[22]

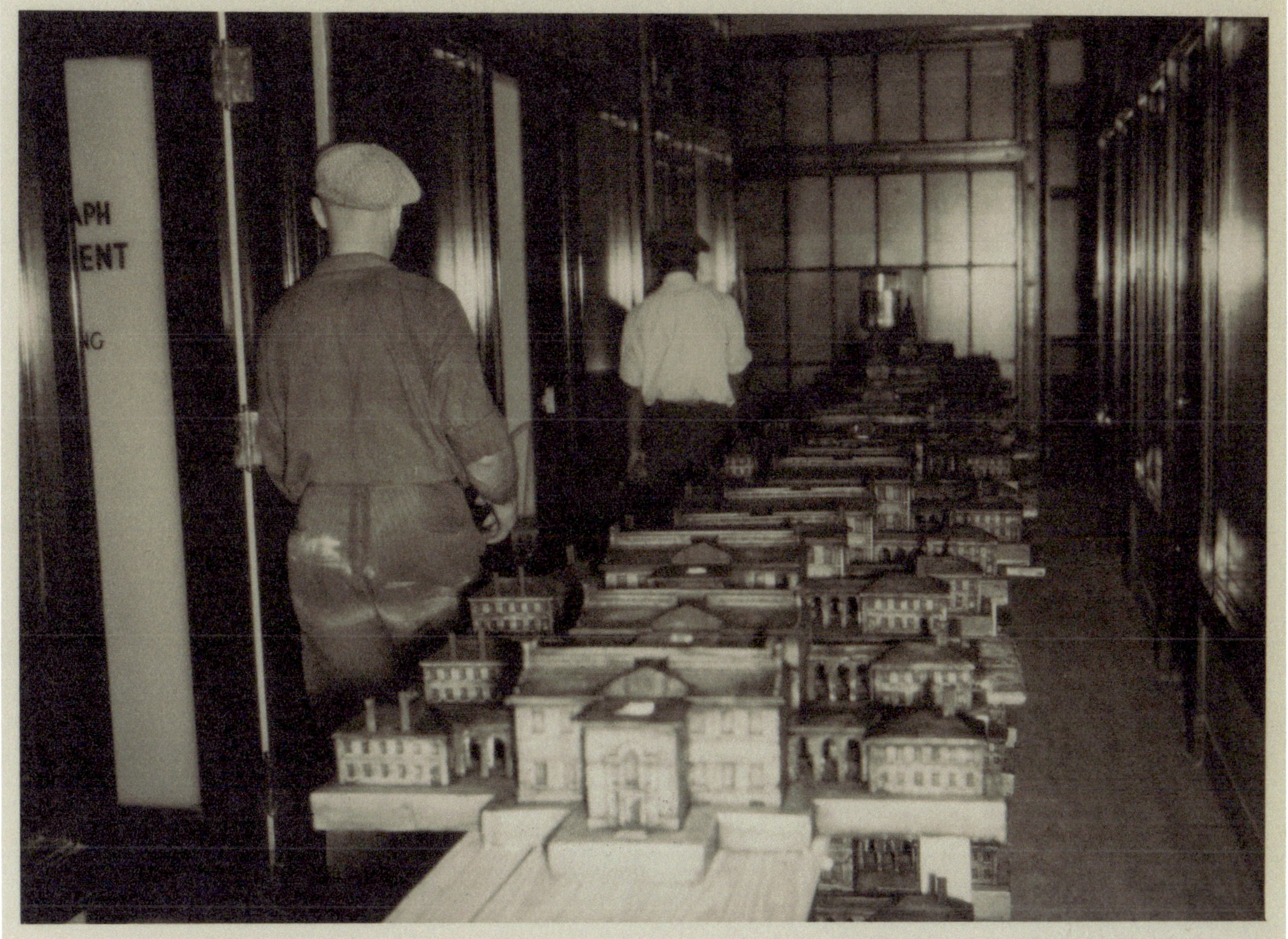

Painted WPA models on drying racks in Pittsburgh's Museum Extension Project office, 1937, photograph; PH and MCP State Archives

Modeling America in education through government and state-sponsored initiatives affirms the power of visual language or arts education to shape a nation. The replica of Independence Hall presents a structure of Americanism. And yet the state house and its unrealistic detachable bell tower, were painted in Van Dyke brown, a color indiscriminately used to paint thatched roofs, wooden shutters, and square pedestals. The practical decision to share a can of paint across these special projects unintentionally democratized the nation's view of the world and its place in it. At six-inches high, all civic amenities, cities, and countries, no matter where they are on Earth, can be brown. The wonder in these teaching aids resides in both their form and function as something both discernible and unrecognizable. An amusing sense of amateurishness in their point of view. Like the concept of a treasure map on the back of the Declaration of Independence. A physical trace of the creative liberties built for students in public schools.

22 "Ending Radical Indoctrination in K-12 Schooling," The White House, released on January 29, 2025, https://www.whitehouse. gov/presidential-actions/2025/01/ending-radical-indoctrination-in-k-12-schooling/.

LEIGH PATEL

58

LIFE AND LEARNING IN THE PRACTICE OF FUGITIVITY

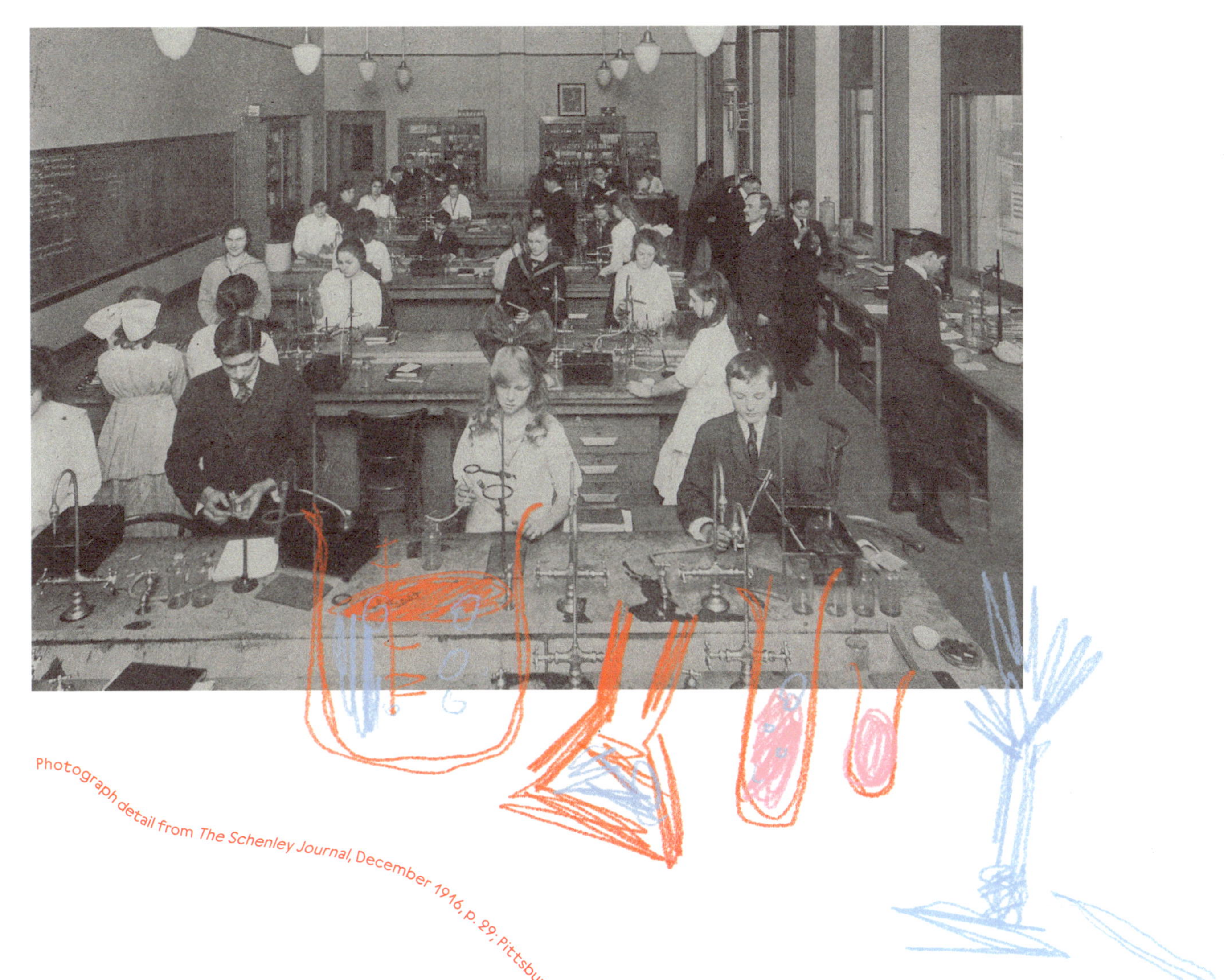

Photograph detail from *The Schenley Journal*, December 1916, p. 89; Pittsburgh Board of Education Archives, CLP

the plastic bin on the shelf held only beaker jars.

The jars were in excellent condition, each standing on its base, aligned equidistant from one another—clean, tidy, intact, and ready for use. Ms. Pickett, who once sat in this very school as a student and now teaches high school biology here, refused to let the school's underfunded infrastructure compromise the care she brought to her teaching. Her classroom had no lab, yet the beaker jars were kept in order—resisting decline through insistence on dignity. Across Pittsburgh, in another public high school, where income levels and funding were higher, Ms. Santiago's beaker jars occupied a science lab with bottles that could withstand heat and cold temperatures, sinks and protective eye wash stations, and a closet full of laboratory equipment for experiments required to pass the Advanced Placement College Board exam. The disparity between these two classrooms, with overlapping yet mismatched numbers and sizes of beakers, exposes a city-wide cartography of educational abandonment. The jars—objects of both presence and lack—become metaphors and accusations: quiet markers of what is withheld and what is endured.

Resources, beyond the stark contrast in their allocation and connected debt, can be used as a way to track the cartographies of racial capitalism. For schooling, which acts as a primary institution of long-standing, differential access to resources is shaped by control. Much like airports, prisons, military encampments, and even senior living facilities, schools are self-enclosed systems where almost all aspects of a person's life are carefully structured: when to eat, when to move, when to speak. Control of bodies, control of time, and control of content for the purposes of carcerality and extraction. Ms. Pickett's classroom can viewed as an unfortunate happenstance, an anomaly. And yet for Ms. Santiago, her supply of resources, fewer rules, more flexibility for students, and ample supplies made available to teachers, supplemented through fundraisers from upper middle-class families, allows for control to recede into the background. Mapped and read alongside each other, these two classrooms, while only miles apart, bring into vivid focus the social geographies of how poverty and wealth are linked through extraction that fuels property accumulation.

Social geographer Ruth Wilson Gilmore often speaks of organized abandonment of the systemic but locally experienced geographic localities where schools, public spaces, and gathering places have become marked more by the abandonment of these sites. Gilmore often invokes a grounding question, "I don't ask where is Nebraska, but why is Nebraska?"[1] Similarly, mapping the space, items, and remnants of peoples' uses of the resources at hand, we might ask more "why" questions about spaces and their uses, rather than stopping where excess and depletion exist. Within every specific social geography, the inventory, different than a cartography, brings attention to the resistance and undercurrents of agency that occur in and across varying forms of control. Defying the organized abandonment of her school and its predominantly Black neighborhood, Ms. Pickett's supply of beaker jars gesture to what should be expected in a high school biology laboratory space. The tidy, orderly jars beckon for respect both in spite of and in the face of

[1] For more on the intersection of carceral geography and abolition, see **Ruth Wilson Gilmore**, *Abolition Geography: Essays Towards Liberation.* (Verso Books, 2022).

systemic inequity. This inequity is not merely the unfortunate accumulation of good intentions but also reveals the little material change left of attempted, incremental reforms. As American scholar Charles Payne wrote, education is rife with change but with little change.[2] The reforms themselves are also found in this classroom as fragments and ghostly materials: a pamphlet about reading kits sits adrift from a similarly sparse English literature classroom and is used as a bookmarker in a textbook; a box containing safety eye masks with the educational supply company's name in raised letters on the top of the eye masks; an odd number of beakers; and in Ms. Picket's bottom desk drawer, the flyers that are a palimpsest of commercial education materials.

All of these classroom items and everyday objects haunt this purportedly democratic field. Although formal schooling has never been an entirely inclusive space, it looms large in the public imaginary as a democratic space, where the different playing fields can act as the great equalizer. If one works hard, follows the rules, and is classified as smart, the myth of meritocracy communicates that this combination in schooling will lead to an individuals' upward mobility, economic viability, and the freedom to buy a home. In other words, the American dream. Yet, this hologram of social stability through education, now including a college-for-all political platform, is intertwined with the reality of schools acting as one of the most efficient delivery systems of intertwined oppressions. Racism, ableism, heteropatriarchy, xenophobia, and whiteness as property are both explicitly and implicitly prescient and purposeful in the misalignment between public schools' imagined purpose as the great equalizer and the reality of their role in manifesting intertwined oppressions hourly, daily, and across generations. And yet the work of many social scientists, community-based educators, and artists compels us to lean into what we can learn from the remnants of public schools serving racial stratification rather than the public good.

The pamphlet used as bookmarker, the beakers existing without the company of laboratory stations equipped for complex experiments, are ghostly matters that sociologist Avery Gordon encourages us to sense and listen to their echoes of what has been lost and erased but which is still present.[3] Gordon reminds me that the banal statement, "life is complicated," only begins to scratch the surface of the perspectives and histories that whisper, gesture, and try to intimate our imaginations. Simply saying that life is complex potentially collapses our abilities to be with histories in the present: contradictions that somehow rely on each other and moreover, on how we make sense of ghostly matters and what we do with the legacies that have left imprinted. The chapter in which Gordon starts with "life is complex" is entitled "His Hand and Her Shape," and in those few words, Gordon invites us to not just imagine but to muster the courage to encounter the ghosts that have shaped how we are with each other as well as how physical spaces, like schools, are tangibly alive. Ghostly matters, in keeping with the complexity of many things being true at the same time, always keeps aloft the fugitivity in the actions that Ms. Pickett took to control and order the disorder and abandonment in her lesser-resourced or debt-addled school. The classroom numbers, the assembly spaces, and the rows of chairs with the teacher's desk at the front— all of these are traces of the ghosts of deservingness and racist, ableist capitalism that are coupled with compliance in school spaces.

An accumulation of research, including Chicago-based professor Erica Meiners' work on schools and prisons, teaches me that the design of public schooling has been carceral since the arrival of Europeans to

2 See Charles M. Payne, *So Much Reform, So Little Change: The Persistence of Failure in Urban Schools*, Vol. 8 (Harvard Educational Press, 2008).

3 Avery F. Gordon, *Ghostly Matters: Haunting and the Sociological Imagination* (University of Minnesota Press, 2008).

Turtle Island.[4] Authors Dolores Calderón and Leilani Sabzalian also offer necessary tracking and naming of the entrenched settler narratives in K–12 education and beyond.[5] The settler colony of the United States is an ongoing project whose social and political economic structure is manifested through settler colonialism. The structure of settler colonialism, in which land and property are primary, attempts to create Black lives as fungible chattel, Native lives as disappeared, and migrant lives as

4 E.R. Meiners, "Ending the School-to-Prison Pipeline/Building Abolition Futures," *The Urban Review* 43, no. 4 (2011): 574-565.

5 Dolores Calderón, "Uncovering Settler Grammars in Curriculum," *Educational Studies* 50, no. 4 (2014): 313-338; Leilani Sabzalian, "The Tensions Between Indigenous Sovereignty and Multicultural Citizenship Education: Toward an Anticolonial Approach to Civic Education," *Theory & Research in Social Education* 47, no. 3 (2019): 311-346.

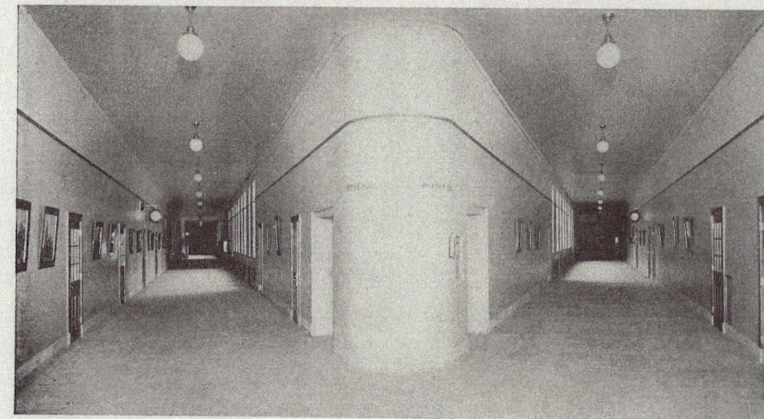

THE SCHENLEY JOURNAL

THE CORRIDORS

CLASSROOMS

On the outer side of the corridors are the classrooms and laboratories. In general, the classrooms are along the front of the building (the long side of the triangle) and the shops and laboratories along the two shorter sides. There are in all 40 classrooms, varying in capacity from 35 to 50 pupils. No desks are used, but all the rooms are furnished with school tablet arm chairs designed specially by the Building Department of the Board of Education under the direction of Dr. H. B. Burns, Director of the Department of Hygiene. This chair is so designed that the pupil is compelled to sit in the correct hygienic position. Each classroom is equipped with a teacher's desk, an office chair, two bookcases, a map and lantern screen case, the maximum amount of slate blackboard and a cork-covered bulletin board, and at least two pictures. Large windows and strong electric bulbs supply an abundance of light.

CHEMISTRY DEPARTMENT

The growing importance of chemistry in life to-day may be said to be reflected in the laboratory having for its motto "Chemistry is the intelligence department of industry." Here one hundred and sixty pupils working at slate-covered tables fitted with gas lines, hot and cold water, compressed air, vacuum, and electricity carry out all sorts of practical experiments in general chemistry. Such experiments as cause the generation of

26

disposable all for the purpose of property. Schooling is an essential extension to the settler nation, acting as an efficient delivery system of intertwined oppressions. Yet, Gordon also encourages her readers to a knowing that is more a sensing than a seeing, a practice of being attuned to the echoes and murmurs of that which have been lost but which remain present among us in the form of hints, suggestions, and tendrils from learning and teaching as part of a settler structure.

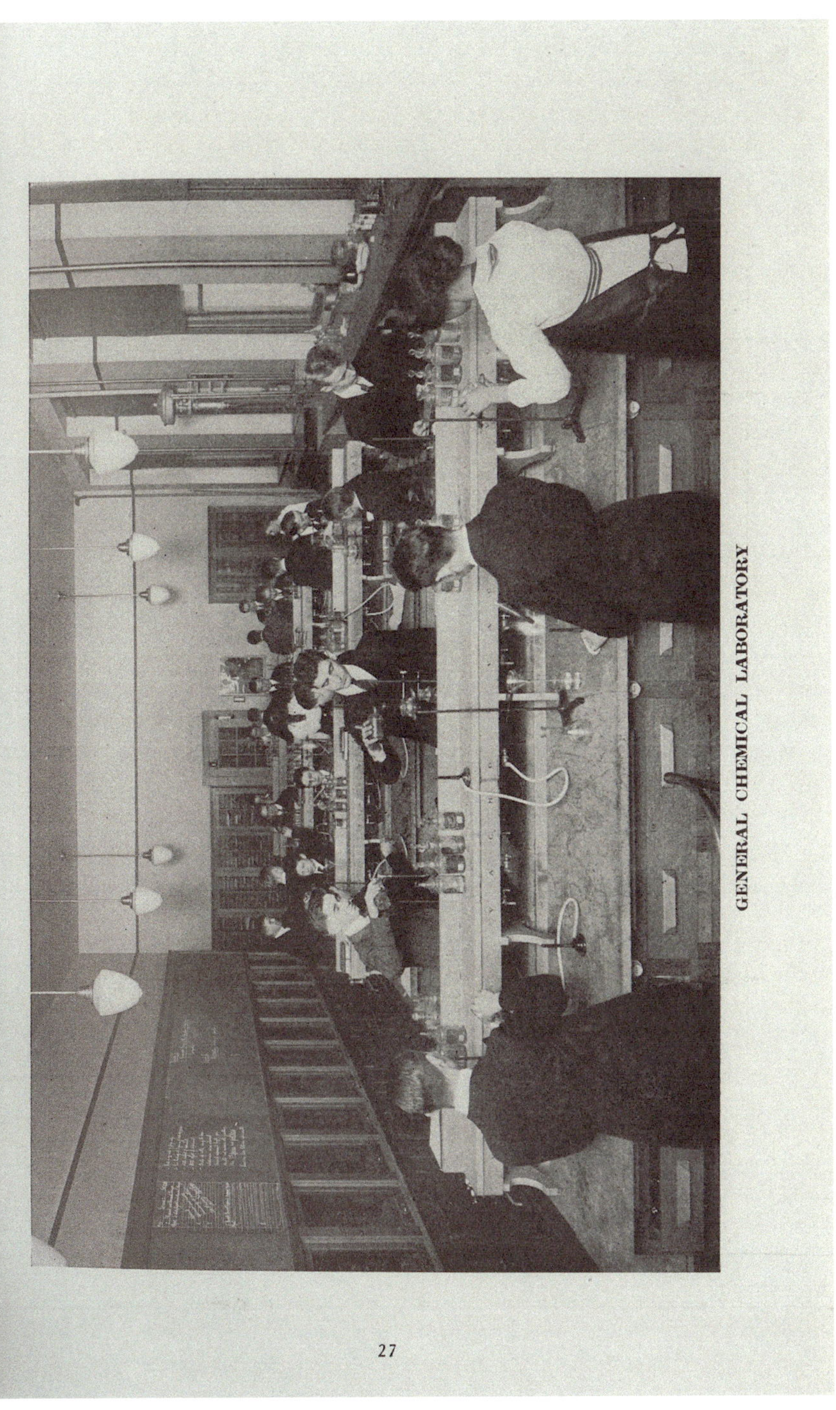

Interior folio of The Schenley Journal, December 1916, p. 26–27, Pittsburgh Board of Education Archives, CLP

But learning, as it turns out, is unpredictable, wily, and therefore often creates ruptures within and amidst the seeming order of organized abandonment. The ghostly materials in this one science classroom haunt the promise of equitable learning conditions. There should be an urgency to resource just this one classroom as part of the social contract that underlies public education. It is often referred to as the institution that can level the playing field for children and young people who are born into poverty and in neighborhoods that have long been sites of organized abandonment.[6] But the public imaginary seeks to maintain public school as, perhaps, one of the last holograms of the public good, even while it debates masking critical race theory, funding for charter schools, and masking policies from entirely individualistic instances. These debates, that have made school board meetings lightning rod geographies of individual versus collective well-being all share a common struggle between the public—the larger intertwined reality of all, and the fight for the individual, who can either embody meritocracy or bear the weight alone of public safety system failures. At its core, the public or the commons, means available to all, maintained and sustained by public funding that feeds back into the public for the purposes of community, connection, and free-will.

Sometimes the ghostly whispers of what public means are as loud as bombs. Formal schooling, specifically public schooling, re-creates the very logics of prisons through physical enclosure, control of bodies, created opportunities for discipline, and rampant ableism. Geographers and architects have mapped tracings of prison architecture with the architecture of schooling. Instead of prison guards, surveillance and enclosures are embodied in schools through metal detectors and the presence of designated 'safety' officers. But the pursuit of the public spaces where learning happens reaches far beyond public schools. The public is found in a Black parent tracing the letters of the alphabet in the palm of his child's hand, defying the state law that outlaws literacy for enslaved peoples. The public is found when a teacher reads from a text about Black reconstruction, nestled in the district-mandated textbook which has omitted any reference to Black education or civil rights.[7]

The public also is animated when a group of young people linger after school to read and argue about the school's removal of any text about the civil rights era. One says, "They already white-washed MLK… do they want him to look like Michael Jackson?!" and the group explodes into raucous laughter. And still their gathering, however fleeting, is connected to the incredible strength of fugitive learning happening in myriad locations and spaces. They are creating, just as Ms. Pickett did with her laboratory supplies, a fugitive practice of flight from abandonment to reliability and answerability. More simply put, fugitive spaces often hide in plain sight.

Historian Tina Campt defines fugitivity as a fundamental practice of refusing the terms of negotiation and dispossession.[8] Campt draws from anthropologist Audra Simpson's work on Indigenous refusal and applies it to the archived photographs of Black people engaging in quotidian refusal practices, such as a high school graduation.[9] While graduation is often taken for granted, the quotidian refusal can be found in the celebration of the Black graduate who was never supposed to graduate but meant to be enclosed in a school acting like a prison to only read what the district allows. And yet by simply graduating, that young Black person constructs a pluriversal connection across generations, time, and space. Whether they know it or not, they are connected to a pursuit of the idea of a public. For anyone who is not white, able-bodied,

6 See **Gordon,** *Ghostly Matters;* **Ruth Wilson Gilmore,** "Forgotten Places and the Seeds of Grassroots Planning," in *Engaging Contradictions: Theory, Politics, and Methods of Activist Scholarship,* edited by Charles R. Hale (University of California Press, 2008), 31–61.

7 **Jarvis R. Givens,** *Fugitive Pedagogy: Carter G. Woodson and the Art of Black Teaching* (Harvard University Press, 2021).

8 **Tina Campt,** *Listening to Images* (Duke University Press, 2017).

9 **Audra Simpson,** "On Ethnographic Refusal: Indigeneity, 'Voice' and Colonial Citizenship," *Junctures: The Journal for Thematic Dialogue* no. 9 (2007).

heteronormative, economically protected, and young, high school graduation, let alone simply being alive at the age of graduation is not always a given.

The seemingly quiet moments of fugitivity are all around us, if only we reach out and take the time to sense them. And they are anything but singular instances. The group of young people decrying and laughing at the feckless omission of a reference to Martin Luther King connects them to Claudia Jones (1915–1964), an Afro-Caribbean journalist, organizer, and target of the United States' surveillance for any communist activity. Her life and trajectory are, themselves, a study of fugitivity. Jones moved from Trinidad to New York City in 1924, when she was just eight years old. There, she found camaraderie and intellectual kinship in the Communist Party, participating in the everyday practices of reading and gathering. But in the era of McCarthyism, studying communism—to form a study group and create a space outside the state-sanctioned school—was considered subversive and dangerous. Jones was relentlessly surveilled and pursued by the state. In 1955, she was deported, yet she refused that designation, identifying instead as a refugee. This act of self-naming echoes the defiant order of Ms. Pickett's beaker jars: both assert autonomy and dignity amid systemic constraint. Both speak to the architectures of fugitive learning—of refusal, insistence, and survival. While being overtly communist put Jones into peril, it was also a determining factor for why and to whom she wrote about sociopolitical conditions. During what she called her exile in the United Kingdom, Jones founded not one but two newspapers, including the *West Indian Gazette*, where she embodied what schooling could be: the open sharing of information that links people to one another, to dialectical analysis, and to the making of worlds.

For over twenty years, I have been teaching in formal, public education spaces. I have also grown immensely in organizing spaces, learning to discern excitement from commitment. A vast amount of my learning is continually gifted from my students. They embody these words from bell hooks, "The academy is not paradise. But learning is a place where paradise can be created."[10] It is always the right time for freedom schools, for after school, and for fugitive schools. In the face of enclosure, this exhibition invites us into the possibility of schools.

10 bell hooks, *Teaching to Transgress: Education as the Practice of Freedom* (Routledge, 1994), 207.

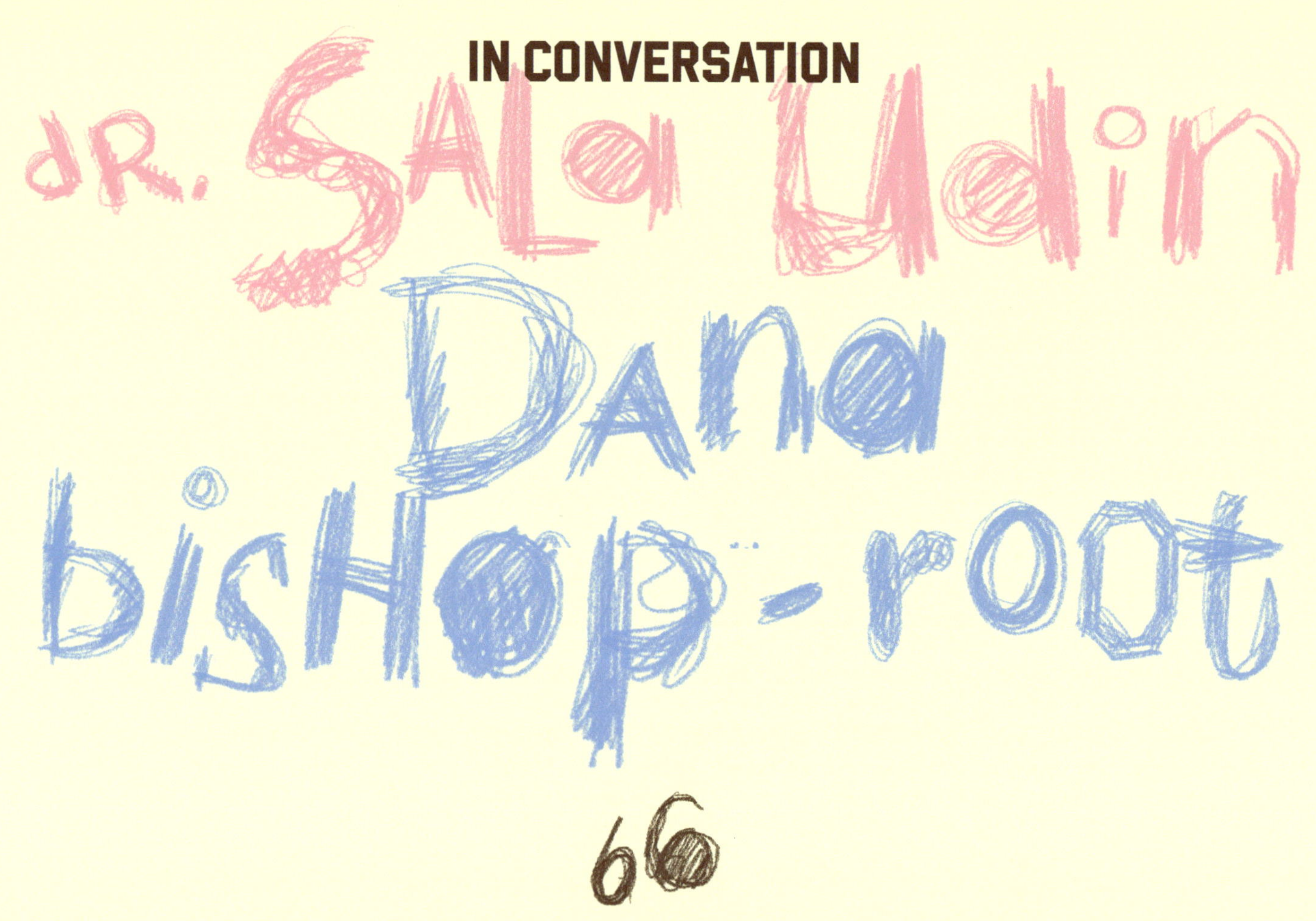

SEEKER OF KNOWLEDGE, A WAY TOWARD BEING

Your life's work, Dr. Udin, has been a direct response to the systemic denial of educational freedom for Black students and working-class communities—through underfunded schools, segregated structures, and policies that criminalize rather than support learning. Through organizing, activism, and public service—from civil disobedience to the Freedom School movement and African diasporic-centered education, to your current role on the Pittsburgh Public Schools Board of Directors—you've worked to create the conditions for Black children, families, and communities to reach forward and back while rooting in the present, to learn, imagine, grow, and flourish.

In one of your oral histories that I listened to, you spoke about your work in the South during Freedom Summers and the importance of organizing with people for people, outside of institutional or formal structures. You also named what was missing for you as a young organizer: a deep understanding that interracial solidarity and collective organizing are essential to liberation. I've been thinking about that in relation to how environmental and economic racism continue to produce segregated schools and to shape the very conditions for learning—the well-being of young people. With the life of learning you hold and share, what are you seeing now, in yet another cycle of school closures and community resistance, as a member of the Pittsburgh Public Schools Board?

The School Board is afraid to tackle the racial implications of a segregated education system. The fact that the segregated education system creates segregation in the academic performance of the students … so that when we look at the performance of white students in the third grade and find that, something like 67 to 70% of them are performing at grade level as opposed to only 30% of Black children who are performing at grade level, the school district looks at that difference and says: "Oh, well. That's what you will expect." Of course they would like to avoid the criticism of community groups like the Education Advocates of Pittsburgh, but there is an acceptance in placing the failure on the students and relying on racism as a way to accept the failure —racism is hard. We can hope that it changes. But hope doesn't change it.

Your use of the word fear … I think about how hard it is to learn when fear is nurtured and is present, it constrains and restricts. It prevents an active learning process; the absence of fear or contending with fear allows for a teaching and learning process.

It's not about learning.

We as adults, especially those in power, forget that we too must be the ones learning if we want students to learn. Without learning there is no way to imagine.

SU   Learning would require us to change. You've got to be willing to accept responsibility if you want to change it. The School Board only believes that they have a responsibility for continuing the status quo. It's hard to admit that the professionals—because they will deny this to the death, to their grave, even Black professionals in the school district—they accept this systemic low expectation of Black students learning. And therefore, they transfer that expectation to the children. And so, if we are measuring whether they are learning, third-grade learning is a good place to start, because if they haven't learned how to read by the third grade, they are unlikely to graduate from high school. They don't fix that from the third grade to the twelfth grade. It's locked in. If they cannot read by third grade, they are not going to learn how to read by twelfth grade.

DBR   It is strategically racial capital, it clicked for me during the Bush administration's No Child Left Behind (NCLB) Act, and the parallel proliferation of private prisons … people were paying close attention to third grade reading levels then …

SU   The penitentiaries. "How many beds are we going to need?" They had a stake in it—in ensuring those reading levels didn't improve.
The biggest difficulty, that I have learned both on City Council and on the School Board, is that institutions are structured to resist change. Even in education, as an example, our nine-member school board, which is majority African American, still resists change. Let's take reading. Until just a couple of years ago, we had been using incorrect, ineffective methods for how you teach children to read English. I became a member of the School Board in part for this reason. I continuously insist that the school district incorporate the most scientifically informed methods for how you teach children to read. Dr. Hamlet, the superintendent before our current one, openly confronted me, saying that he did not accept that the methods that they were using were antiquated and ineffective for teaching kids to read. Although all the information had been revealed and was in front of us, he denied publicly that the methods were devised and created by publishers. This communicated that he openly did not want to change. Now, a cynic like me would start to suggest, "Does he have a financial investment in the status quo?" Why would anybody refuse to use the most effective, most scientifically supported methods for how children's brains work when you're trying to teach them how to read English?

DBR   And this wasn't just happening in Pittsburgh. There were many others raising this at the same time.

SU   Across the country. It's financial. There's an economic investment. And they protect that investment by resisting change to the status quo.

DBR   And in that resistance to change is also comfort. As I am listening to you, I'm thinking a lot about … why we're so afraid of strategic change toward liberation, why we grip what we have been given. We settle into maintaining the oppressions and their impact. We learn to work with the oppression. In this moment of the Trump administration, we see our institutions doing a whole lot of changing, under threat of financial penalty, or to avoid notice of the government. Language and content are being controlled, policies are changing, and voices are silenced.

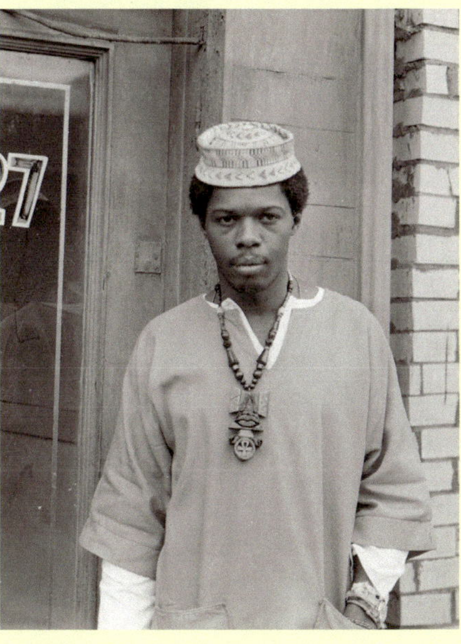

Charles "Teenie" Harris, Sala Udin, Hill District, Pittsburgh, PA, 1970, photograph; Carnegie Museum of Art, HFF

SU   That's easy.

DBR   That's easy, right? It has a whole system to click right into. That's why you see it and you're just like, "Wow, you can actually change how you are working. Look at that."
     Around Juneteenth, I was thinking a lot about the word "freedom," and how freedom is such a tricky word, because really, what it is, is the need to be. Without oppression, freedom is being. And so, Dr. Udin, whether you are working in movement-based work or within the City Council or non-profits or the School Board, you are devoted to creating the conditions where Black people can literally and expansively be through access to quality education. Was it a choice?

SU   No, it was the only thing that truly held my interest. Everything I'd done up to that point led me to center education. After the Civil War, Black leaders were offered land, money, and tools to start over in Liberia or Sierra Leone. The message was: "You can have everything you want—just not here." But they said, "No. You're offering land, but not schools. We've farmed for 300 years—we know how to do that. What we need is education. And the best education is here, in America. We've invested three hundred years in this country. We're not walking away from that. The road ahead is steep, but we'd rather climb it than start over."

DBR   So, what I'm hearing is that, for you, whether you're thinking about how the city is operating, housing, or about your family, education is where you land because it's root work through time. What is your vision of what can be for schools that hold the fullness of a young Black person? That hold the fullness of their humanity and cultivate it? What are the conditions necessary in that school?

SU   I'm thinking about the teacher. The teacher has to be resourced to create the space that centers our kids. The teacher has to have a high expectation that these children can reach that level of what you call "quality education." The teacher has to look at each child and see possibility. The teacher has to have curricula that has rigor and truth and cultural relevance. I think those are the most important ingredients. The teacher has to have the freedom and encouragement to go forward with expectations and preparedness to deliver the curriculum, along with evidence-based, scientifically supported reading. No matter the grade you are in, it all begins with reading—how to read English, how to read math problems, how to read science problems, how to read history, how to read.

DBR How to read stories, to find words for living, to read our world, to read other worlds, yes. You said that our teachers must feel supported and free. What conditions create this freedom?

SU The teacher has to want to incorporate their own learning to give it out. You can't give it unless you have it. You can't feel free without a desire to learn.

DBR What are we learning? What are we teaching? Dr. Udin, you have a life of learning, what is your learning history? How do you think of yourself as a student? How would you describe your life as a student?

SU Poor, but not as poor as some of the kids that I grew up with. My mother was a house cleaner for the Catholic school that was a block away down the street. And this school was primarily white, although whites were starting to move out of the Hill District, and the school population, the ethnic population, was churning.

My mother gave birth to twelve children. The Catholic school had a high tuition. She provided education to all of her children because of her relationship with the Diocese, for her to be a cleaning woman. I don't even know if they paid her or if it was just our school tuition. All her children were educated at that school. Holy Trinity was the name of it. And I had a painful experience. It was a good education; it was a better education than the public school system, but it was painful. Painful not because they had high expectations, but painful because the nuns who taught there were racist, and they couldn't prevent that racism from coming out in their teaching. So, they had a highly disciplined teaching style and method. They didn't even know that they were being racist, but I received and felt the discipline differently. When me and my siblings came to school with a haircut, it was a haircut we got from our father. I became a laughingstock from the other kids—laughing at me and my siblings and our haircuts. I would always have a close haircut, almost bald. The teachers used that opportunity to try to create some kind of rapport between me and the other students at my expense. My name was Sam. That's what everybody called me by the time I got to elementary school. So, in school, the lesson for reading became *Little Black Sambo*. And the teacher would rub my head, and the students would get a laugh and a great kick out of it.

DBR They would literally offer you as an object to the other students?

SU Yes, to create this story of *Little Black Sambo*. So, when you asked what my education experience was, it started there. That was too early for the school to know that they were using the wrong curriculum for teaching reading, but they did know that they could make the students laugh. And they probably also knew that the population of the school was changing, and they needed to create some rapport, some acceptance of the Black children by the white children, and one way of doing that was to make them laugh and make a joke out of *Little Black Sambo*. So, I guess I learned how to read *Little Black Sambo*. I read that story, and never learned, really, how *Little Black Sambo* got to become a laughing object.

DBR Right, but even without your own words at the time, you were experiencing it in every bone of your body.

SU Yes. The other students were also struggling with the racial dynamics of a community churning. They were not accustomed to Black students being students. That was a white thing. When Negro History Week came around, it was a joke to them and to the Brothers who taught. They were called Brothers; they weren't quite priests. And the white students were encouraged to make fun of other Black students, as if it were the only way to make sense of us—not quite human but a joke. And one day the white students decided to put a note on the table where Black students ate together in the cafeteria. There's a book called *Why Are All the Black Kids Sitting Together in the Cafeteria?*

DBR I know that book, Dr. Beverly Daniel Tatum.

SU So the note said, "Today is Black History Day. Invite your [N-word] to dinner today." And that was the culmination of all the abuse that we had been taking leading up to Black History Month, Black History Day. And that was all we could take. And the white students were over across the room looking at how we would receive this note. And of course, they were giggling, and we all decided that we had had enough. And we went, together, across the room to the other side of the cafeteria and turned it up.

DBR Yes, you did. There's only so long a person can intellectually and emotionally receive violence.

SU Absolutely. And that was the end of my Catholic education experience. They told me that I would fit in better in a public school. "This is not good for Catholic schools." "You weren't meant for Catholic schools." And so, we got a transfer to Schenley High School, a public school. At Catholic school I was getting a better education than some of the other kids on my block who were going to public school. But I also got this racial intimidation and oppressive

Charles "Teenie" Harris, Outside Schenley High School, Oakland, Pittsburgh, PA, ca. 1945, photograph; Carnegie Museum of Art, HFF

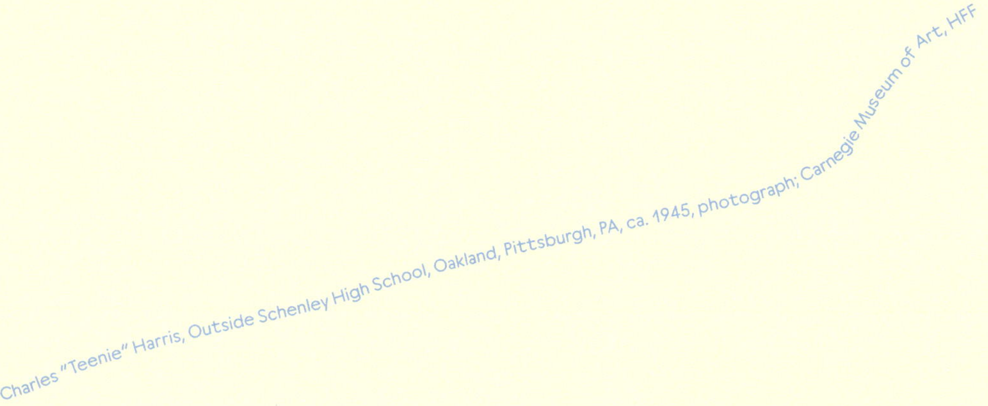

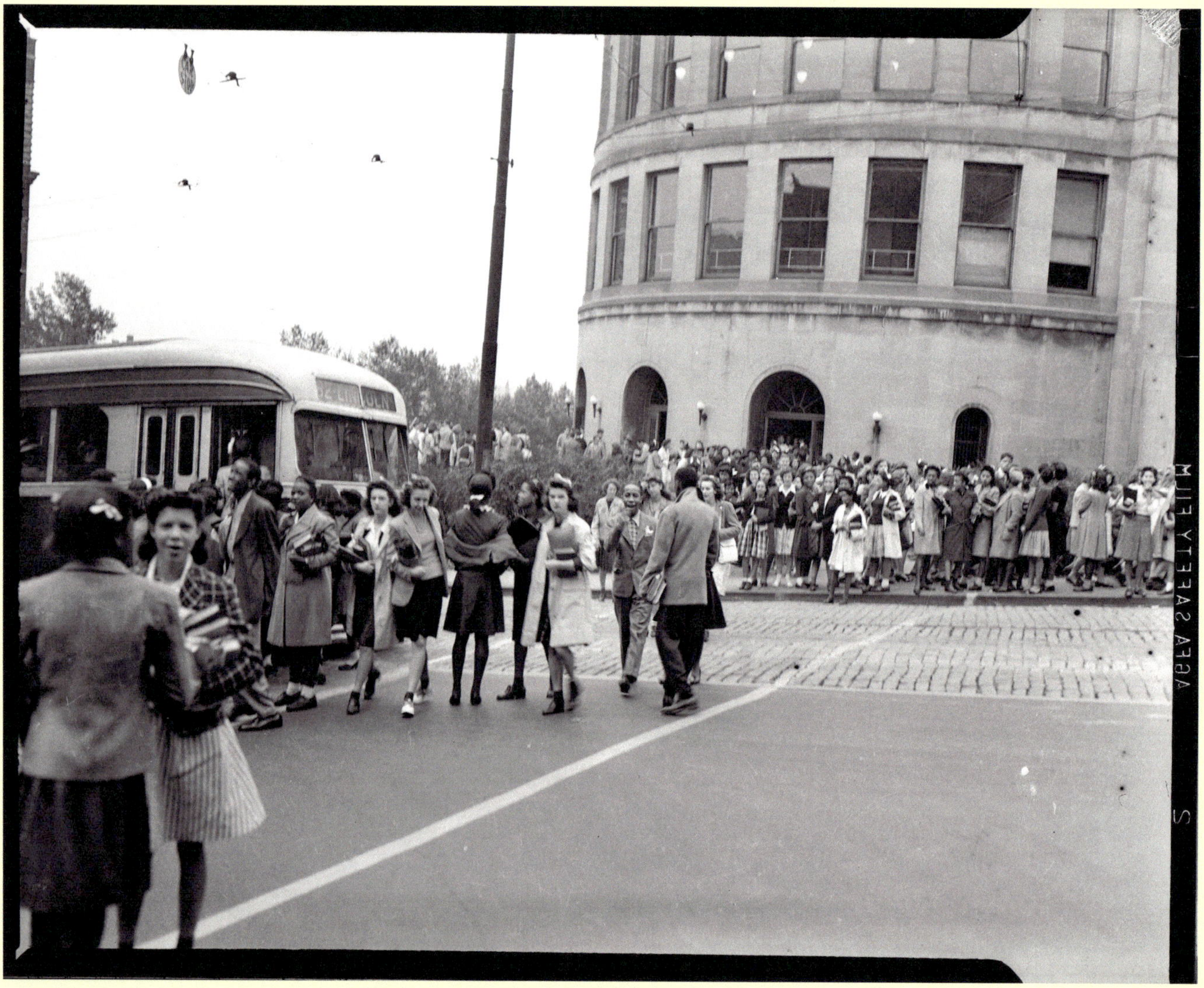

after school   text book

countenance from the teachers and, therefore, the students. You're getting a high-quality education and highly intense racial discrimination at the same time.

DBR   Right, how do you hold this dissonance and want to keep learning?

SU   Only with great difficulty.

DBR   Yes. And you have chosen to stay inside of learning, to continue to build a relationship to learning, curiosity, asking questions. Asking questions—a way to not just accept. Anytime I have heard you in interviews, you've talked about how you're known as someone who asks a lot of questions.

SU   That's my gifted name by my mentor: seeker of knowledge.

DBR   Dr. Sala Udin, even your "retirement" has been devoted to ensuring Black children and families, therefore all children and families, access education that is rigorous, up-to-date—education which sees, respects, and meets the high-quality education that your mother did everything to ensure you received, without the structural and enacted racism.

SU   That's right. For me, the priority of education in my life is real. Painful, but real. I was complete with my service on City Council, and the need to attack education as an institution was just sitting there waiting. I heard that the sitting representative for this district, District 3, within the Pittsburgh Public School Board had announced that he was no longer going to run for the next term. The seat was vacant. I looked for a younger person to support in doing the work, but here I am. I've been on the board for eight years now, and I speak up. I make people mad by all my speaking up. I stay focused on reading. It's one thing, but its everything. I think that's a good culmination of my time, my contribution. And now, I'm learning how to resign.

david serlin

74

ANOTHER KIND OF RENAISSANCE: BUILDING A FUTURE FOR DISABILITY AT PITTSBURGH'S PIONEER SCHOOL

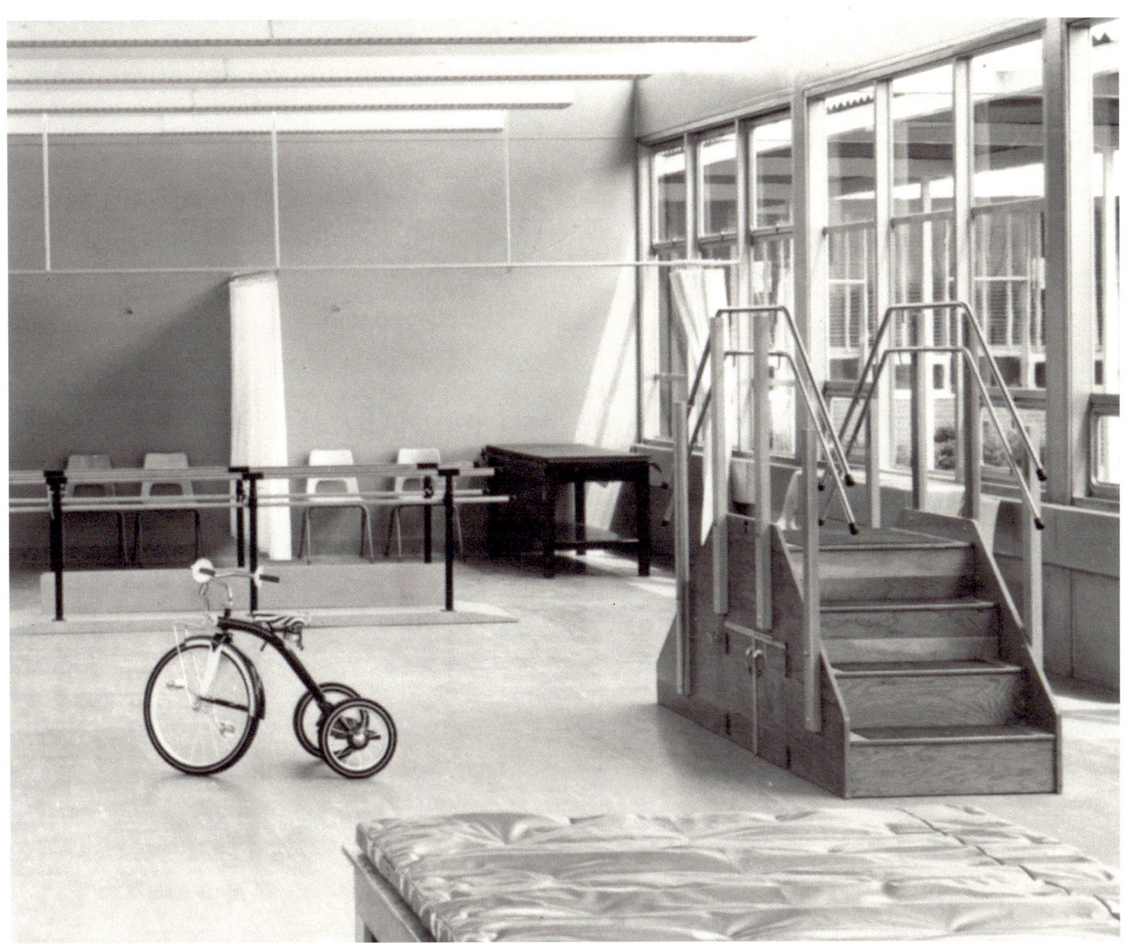

Detail of the Exercise Facility at the Pioneer School, ca. 1958, photograph; Detre Library & Archives, HHC

In 1958, the year of Pittsburgh's bicentennial, local media and urban boosters announced plans for two new innovative public projects, both of which tapped into the enthusiasm felt for the city's proverbial "architectural renaissance." The first building, the John J. Kane Hospital in Scott Township about three miles southwest of downtown Pittsburgh, was an ambitious new long-term public care facility intended for elderly patients and people with physical and cognitive disabilities. Sleek and modular, the hospital's architecture mirrored the articulated shape of internationally recognized structures like Le Corbusier's Unité d'Habitation in Marseilles, France, as well as the kinds of modern designs for public hospitals one might see in cities like New York, Chicago, and St. Louis. While there were already many private hospitals in and around the Pittsburgh area, the Kane Hospital was a public facility for which its distinctive modern architecture profile was intended to signal a new approach to civic care. The second building, announced the same year though it did not open officially until 1960, was the Pioneer School. Built on seven acres of city-owned property at the cross streets of Dunster and La Moine in the Brookline neighborhood, and broadly accessible via historic Pioneer Avenue, the school was designed for students with physical and developmental disabilities. The Pioneer School was realized through a partnership between the Pittsburgh public school system and private donors, who collectively raised the $850,000 (approximately $10 million today) required to build and furnish it. Years later, the school would formally change its name to the Pioneer Education Center, thereby confirming its focus on education as central, not supplementary, to its core mission.

In recent years, scholars have pointedly argued that the architectural renaissance of Pittsburgh in the 1950s and 1960s was not a renaissance for everyone. One of the most dramatic transformations, the building of the Civic Arena (1955), was only made possible through the displacement of over eight thousand black residents from the Lower Hill neighborhood.[1] The students at the Pioneer School were direct beneficiaries of an approach to both architecture and education as investments in a civic ideal and yet, the Pioneer School is often treated as an outlier, ignored by both historians and curators alike. The omission of the school from "Imagining the Modern: Architecture and Urbanism of the Pittsburgh Renaissance," an important 2015 exhibition and subsequent catalogue project, is telling, though not entirely unexpected.[2] Histories of people with disabilities, when they are recognized at all, tend to fly under the radar except in those instances when the experience of disability— being blind, deaf, or physically impaired—is something that has been fixed if not outright erased through medical interventions. Neglecting to highlight the history of the Pioneer School is a missed opportunity to consider a parallel type of architectural renaissance—one that is not only focused on massive infrastructural projects or glittering aluminum skyscrapers but on taxpayer-funded support for institutions that are essential structural components of the public good.

The Kane Hospital and the Pioneer School were hardly the first of their kind in Pittsburgh. Many institutions for adults and children with disabilities or chronic conditions, such as hospitals, asylums, and residential homes, first appeared in the mid-nineteenth century, when some of the first city and state facilities were established in Pennsylvania and across the United States. Some of these were private schools located far from the city center that were focused less on education and more on producing docile, well-behaved children with minimal practical skills. The Western Pennsylvania School for the Deaf, founded in the residential Edgewood Borough of Pittsburgh in 1884, was a notable

1 See Joe W. Trotter and Jared N. Day, *Race and Renaissance: African Americans in Pittsburgh since World War II* (University of Pittsburgh Press, 2010). See also **John F. Bauman and Edward K. Muller,** *Before Renaissance: Planning in Pittsburgh, 1889–1943* (University of Pittsburgh Press, 2006).

2 See **Chris Grimley, Michael Kubo, and Ramiel Samahy,** *Imagining the Modern: Architecture and Urbanism of the Pittsburgh Renaissance* (The Monacelli Press, 2016).

　　

exception—a public institution that has produced generations of educated students. Beginning in the late 1940s, however, many cities like Pittsburgh embraced the potential of modern architecture to address the types of outdated structures built in the nineteenth century, where students with disabilities had attended school for generations. This is because, whether public or private, these schools tended to emulate the kinds of bulky neoclassical or Romanesque institutional architectures in brick or granite that one observes in courthouses, libraries, auditoriums, community centers, and government buildings across the United States.[3] Until the arrival of the Pioneer School, many disabled students who wanted to receive a public school education were forced to navigate the Bedford Public School, an 1850s brick and marble Greek Revival building located on Bingham Street that is now a landmark on the National Register of Historic Places and was converted to residential lofts in 1997. Students who used wheelchairs, canes, or crutches would have spent their days challenged by the school's uneven surfaces and dark, unaccommodating rooms situated among the narrow streets and hulking steel mills of the city's South Side neighborhood.

The limitations of the Bedford Public School served as inspiration for Burton Kenneth Johnstone, the former dean of Carnegie Tech's College of Fine Arts (1945-53), who is best remembered for designing local academic spaces such as the Carnegie Tech's Graduate School of Industrial Administration (1951-52) and the Frick Fine Arts Building at the University of Pittsburgh (1962-65). For the Pioneer School, Johnstone imagined a non-commercial variation of the modern style seen throughout the city's architectural renaissance. He harnessed a spatial vocabulary that is still recognizable by any connoisseur of postwar architecture: large open communal spaces outfitted with double-height ceilings and enormous panel windows; classrooms in which accordion-style walls and doors could be adjusted to collapse or combine interiors rather than keeping them fixed and static; and intermediate spaces that were either lit by diffuse light coming through translucent panels or fully open to sunshine and blue sky.[4] Furthermore, Johnstone created different functional zones for teaching, eating, exercising, resting, and assembling, providing distinct environments for students, teachers, and administrators that did not shoehorn a superficial educational experience into what was essentially a medical institution—one of the conventions of schools or programs for young people with disabilities. Remarkably, the inverse was true: the Pioneer School made multiple forms of care available within what was essentially an educational institution. Pencil sketches made by Johnstone present a world where children in wheelchairs or on crutches cavort alongside young mothers, dutiful school administrators, and uniformed nurses in flexible spaces illuminated by natural light. In the literature developed to promote the project, members of the Pittsburgh school board and philanthropic groups used such sketches to solicit private funds to make the school a reality.

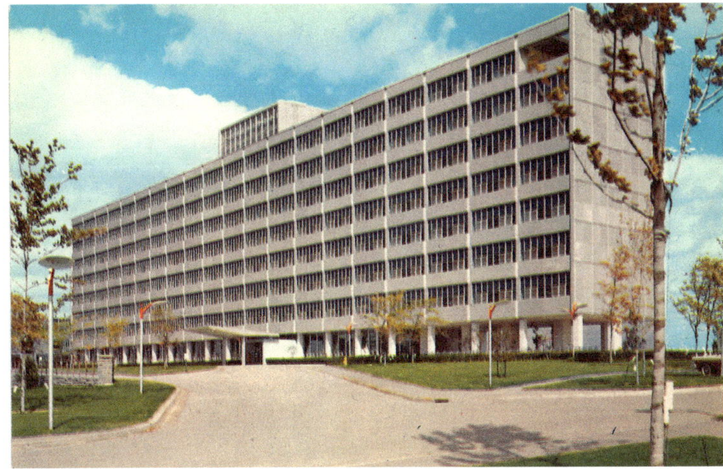

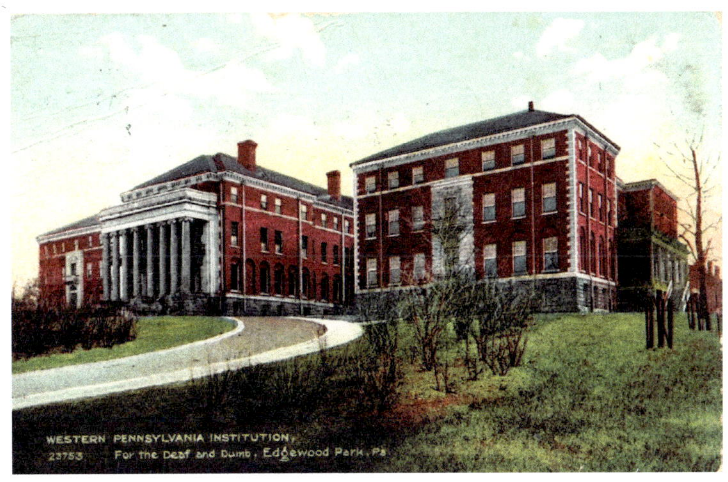

Top: Postcard of the John J. Kane Hospital, ca. 1960; Private collection

Bottom: Postcard of the Western Pennsylvania Institution for the Deaf, ca. 1910; Private collection

3 For more historical background about school architecture, see for example **Beatriz Colomina,** *X-Ray Architecture* (Lars Müller Publishers, 2019). See also **David Serlin,** "Disabling Modernism," *Places Journal* (May 2024): https://doi.org/10.22269/240501.

4 **Julliet Kinchin, Aidan O'Connor, Tanya Harrod, and Medea Hoch,** *Century of the Child: Growing by Design, 1900-2000* (Museum of Modern Art, 2012).

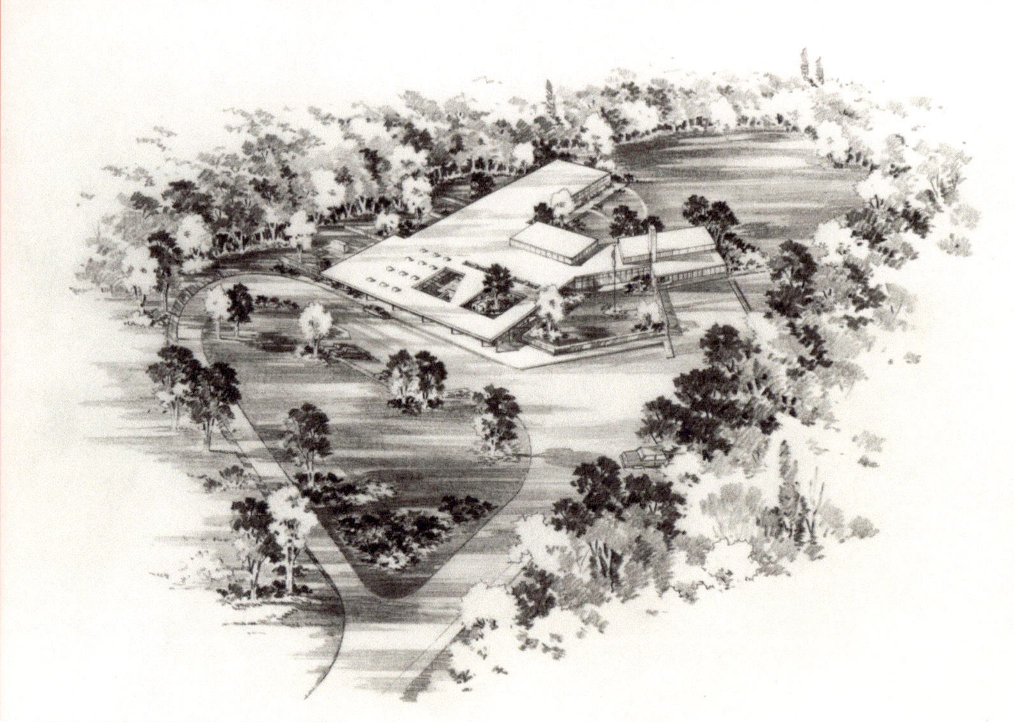

PERSPECTIVE OF SITE
A SCHOOL FOR PHYSICALLY HANDICAPPED CHILDREN

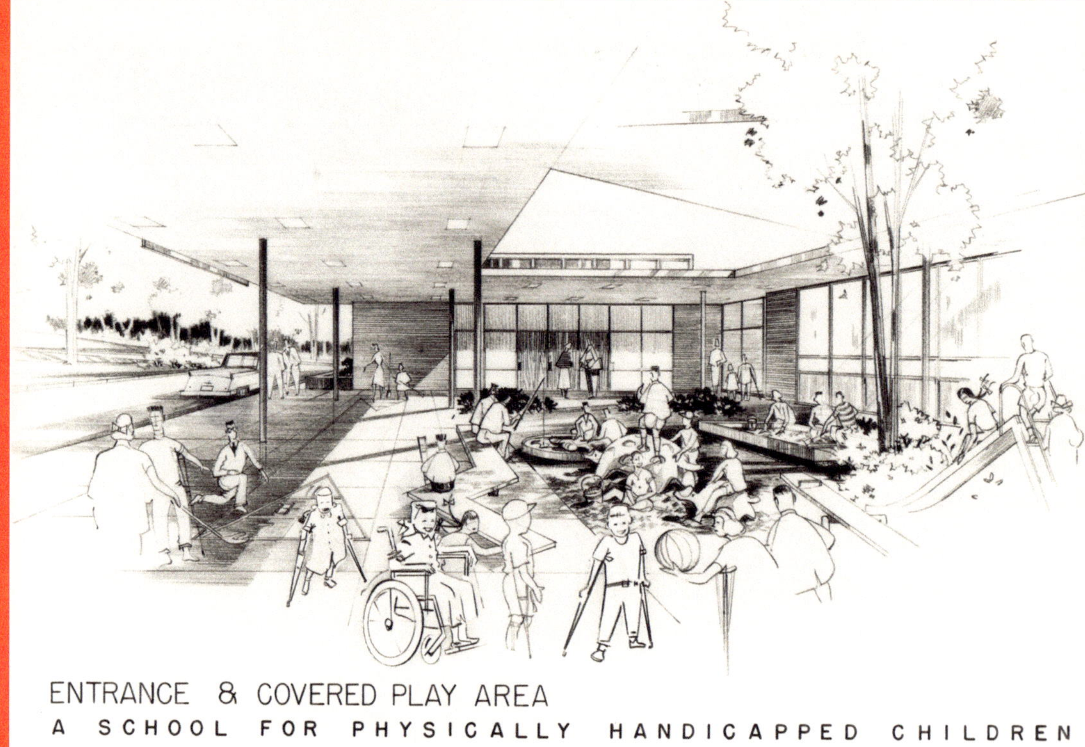

ENTRANCE & COVERED PLAY AREA
A SCHOOL FOR PHYSICALLY HANDICAPPED CHILDREN

Top: Burton Kenneth Johnstone, *Pioneer School, Perspective Drawing of Site*, 1957, pencil on paper; Detre Library & Archives, HHC

Bottom: Burton Kenneth Johnstone, *Pioneer School, Architectural Rendering of the Entrance and Covered Play Area*, 1957, pencil on paper; Detre Library & Archives, HHC

The architectural and pedagogical innovations imagined by Johnstone and his colleagues were not linked explicitly to Pittsburgh's fantasies of urban revitalization. Rather, they were imagined as ethical displays of care as well as spatial expressions of the city's status as a national center for groundbreaking research on children's educational and psychological development. In 1953, for instance, psychologists Erik Erikson, Mary McFarland, and Benjamin Spock co-founded the Arsenal Family and Children's Center at the University of Pittsburgh, one of the nation's premier research sites for studying children's behavior. Here, a young pastor named Fred Rogers, who was interested in the emergent technology of television, conducted clinical research towards a graduate degree.[5] A year later, Jonas Salk recruited over seven thousand children from the Pittsburgh school system for the second clinical trials of the polio vaccine before announcing its efficacy to the world in 1955. The design, funding, and construction of the Pioneer School demonstrates that dramatically improving the lives of vulnerable children was not the exclusive domain of university laboratories. It could also happen in the everyday space of the classroom, the cafeteria, and the playground.

The pedagogical ambitions of the Pioneer School were reflected as much in its built features as in its landscape design. Because it was sited on seven acres of land in Brookline and far from the city's historic industrial core, Johnstone did not have to deal with vertical designs typical of building in a densely packed urban neighborhood. Instead, the Pioneer School had the privilege of horizontal freedom to build on a single story, thereby communicating to students with mobility limitations that their engagement with the school would not be thwarted by navigating upper floors, platforms, or steps. The land adjacent to Pioneer was transformed into a sensory garden, an alternative recreational space featuring swings and slides. The space also included enclosures with flowers and fruit trees, intended to engage students' senses beyond those which required some kind of applied dexterity, such as putting one's legs into the narrow apertures of a swing seat. Designing gardens with a heady olfactory presence was not a new concept, but to foreground this feature at a public school funded by tax dollars and established for students with disabilities was an unexpected departure from convention. Most opportunities for meaning-making for disabled children were typically rerouted into practical activities like memorizing information and then regurgitating it back. In contrast, sensory pedagogy—using smell, touch, taste, and other subjective modes of encounter—would be adapted decades later into curricula across the Pittsburgh public school system, suggesting that the Pioneer School helped to expand conversations about how offering access to information, beyond its counterpart in providing access to space, could transform education.[6]

For all of its architectural and pedagogical innovations, in some ways, the Pioneer School was a product of its time and not without its limitations or constraints. While the school provided private areas with cots for students who easily fatigued or needed some form of rest from daily activities, the school was also invested in a medical model of disability that reinforced normative standards of physical or cognitive function. During the 1950s and 1960s, the use of surgeries, hormonal treatments, and corrective procedures were commonplace for disabled children in many day schools as well as in residential schools.[7] An early 1960s photograph of a Pioneer School classroom features a woodframe structure that was a common therapeutic technology. Students were made to stand inside the frame, sometimes for hours, to strengthen their leg muscles. These jail cells for the legs were by no means unique

5 For more of this background history, see **Lexis McCoy,** "Examining and Extending the Legacy of Fred Rogers's Influence on Contemporary Teacher-Student Relationships," (PhD diss., Northeastern University, 2022).

6 For more about the use of sensory pedagogy in the classroom, see **Claudia Soares,** "Emotions, Senses, Experience and the History of Education," *History of Education* 52, nos. 2–3 (2022), 516–38.

7 For more about this practice see, for example, **Rachel D. Elder,** "Safe Seizures, Schoolyard Stoics, and the Making of Contained Citizens at Detroit's School for Epileptic Children, 1935–1956," *Journal of the History of Childhood and Youth* 7, no.3 (2014), 430–461.

to the Pioneer School; they were intended to produce forms of bodily regimentation that were regarded as more socially productive and, therefore, more socially respectable. Yet such physical constraints, the residual effects of a medical model of treating disability, coexisted with forms of spatial accommodation, such as open classroom plans with flexible seating and table arrangements designed to accommodate different body types. What architectural historians now recognize as the emergence of the "open classroom" plan in public school designs in Pittsburgh and elsewhere was experimented with at places like the Pioneer School, where it made full use of a horizontal, single-story plan in order to be more directly attuned to students' experiences as well as the variety and pleasure of those experiences.

The Pioneer Education Center will celebrate its seventieth year of operation in 2028. Despite its longevity, the school is often overlooked—a survivor of Pittsburgh's postwar architectural renaissance that has successfully avoided the fate of many of its contemporaries. Much has been written about the rise and fall of the John J. Kane Hospital, for instance. In 1975, facing allegations of sustained abuse and neglect of its patients, Kane Hospital administrators were forced to close the hospital and admit their abject failure as public guardians entrusted with the care of the most vulnerable. The hospital was razed, and its core functions redistributed to existing hospitals and clinics across the city and region.[8] For many of its most vociferous critics, the hospital's architectural ambition was the shiny surface layer that distracted community members from the inevitable failure of publicly funded health care. This, they argued, was evidence that such services were best left to the private sector. Yet the neoliberal shift toward privatizing what were once understood to be essential public functions—caring for those with housing or food insecurity, or who are otherwise living precariously in the wider world—has not dimmed the bright light emanating from the Pioneer Education Center.

Like most hospitals and other care facilities, the number of schools for children with disabilities has grown exponentially since the 1970s, though the vast majority of these are managed through private, for-profit companies. This is a boon to families with the resources to use them, but it does maintain a seemingly irreconcilable divide between public and private ideas of care. Meanwhile, the footprint of the Pioneer Education Center, which has remained essentially the same since 1958, is now connected spatially to South Brook Middle School, a neighborhood public school that opened in 2001. Students from both schools overlap and interact in adjacent spaces in ways that students, teachers, and administrators at the Pioneer School could have never imagined in the 1950s and 1960s, when the movement to "mainstream" or integrate students with disabilities into local schools was still decades into the future. Creating a spatial as well as a social interface between the two schools to promote endless opportunities for students to empathize with one another is arguably one way to build inclusivity into the spatial fabric of education. More to the point, however, is the reality that both South Brook and Pioneer are taxpayer-funded public institutions, equally committed to forms of care in a local space made possible by Pioneer's original architects, planners, and educators. These are the kind of successful urban collaborations that remain the most reliable evidence for how innovative, empathic, and accessible architecture created with the public in mind is itself a public good.

8 For an overview of this shameful episode, see **Gabriel Winant,** "A Place to Die: Nursing Home Abuse and the Political Economy of the 1970s," *Journal of American History* 105, no. 1 (2018): 96–120.

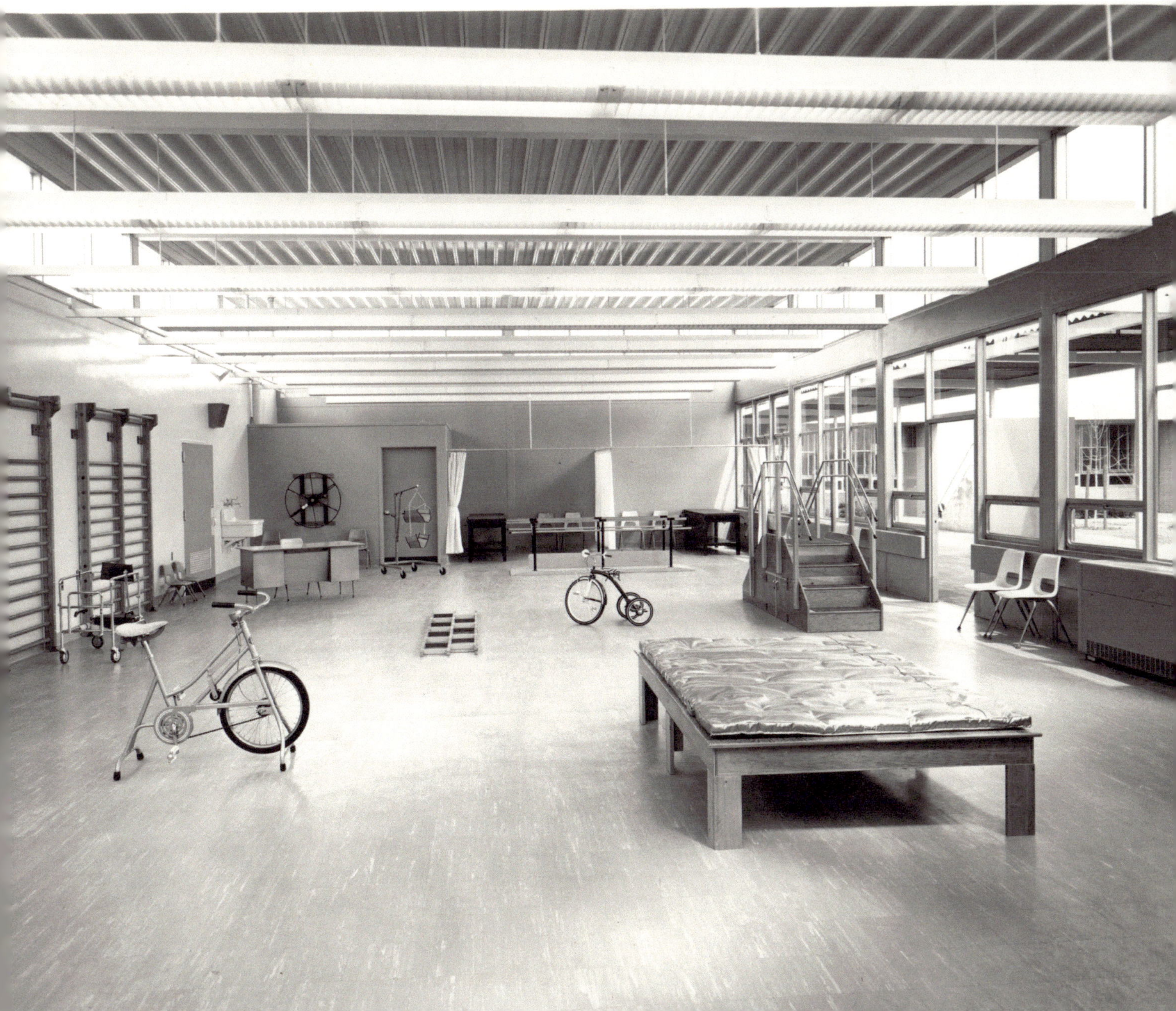

Exercise Facility at the Pioneer School, ca. 1958, photograph; Detre Library & Archives, HHC

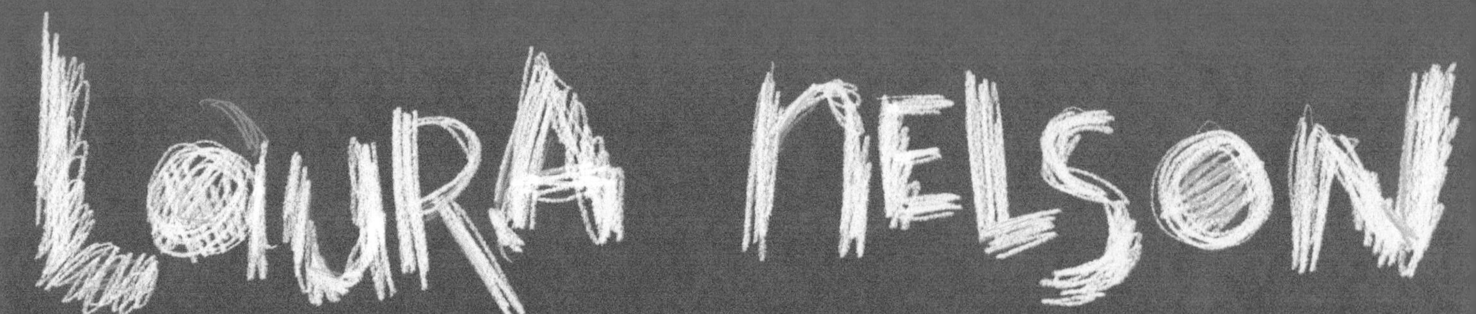

82

MEDIA STUDY: ARTMAKING AFTER SCHOOL

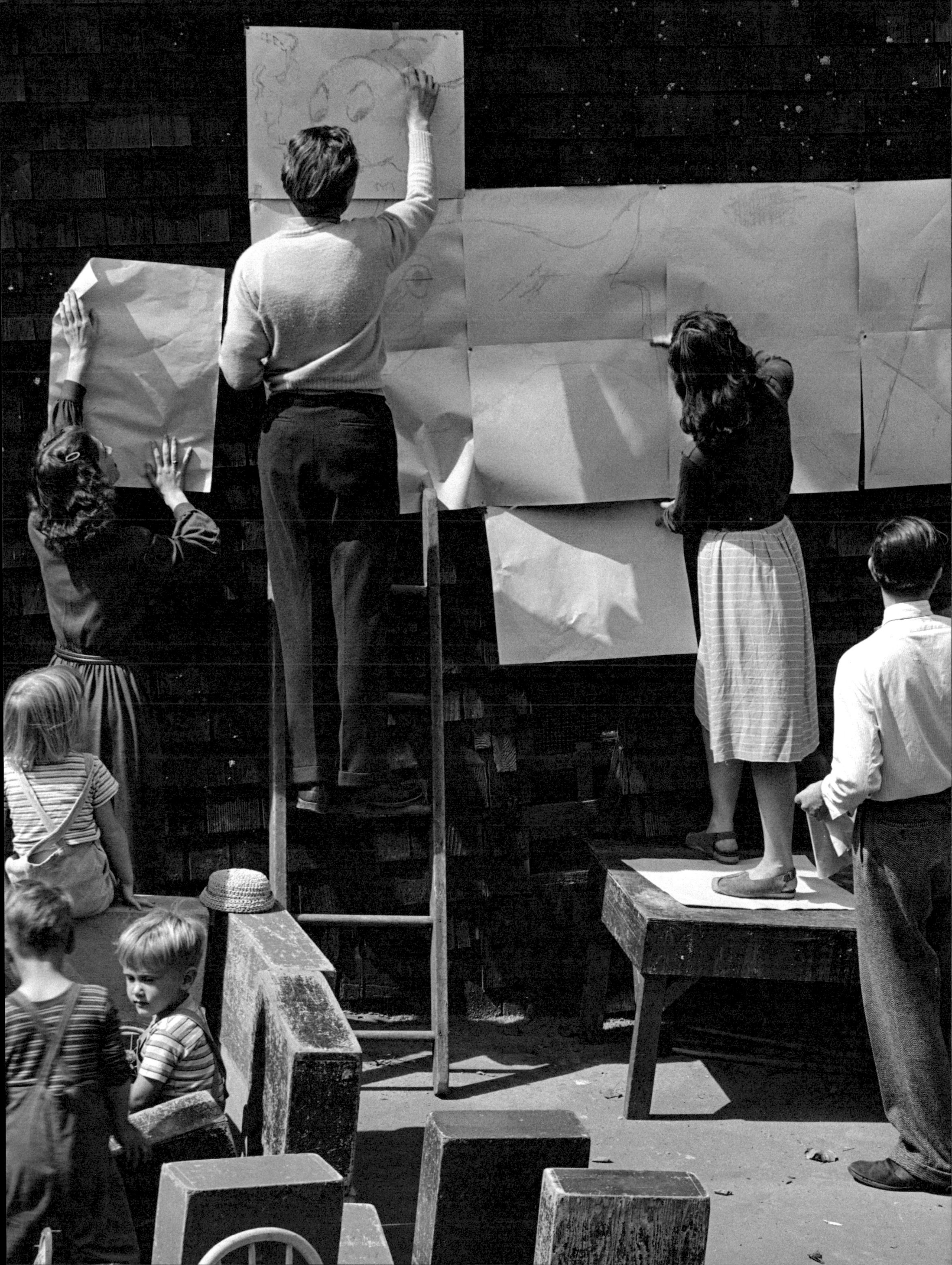

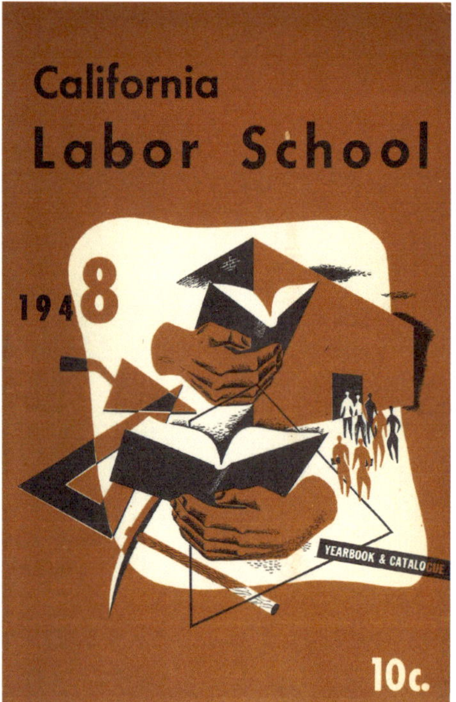

Above: Cover of the *California Labor School Yearbook & Catalogue,* 1948; Labor Archives and Research Center, JPLL

Previous page: Mural class at the California Labor School, ca. 1950, photograph; Labor Archives and Research Center, JPLL

1 **Maya Angelou,** *I Know Why the Caged Bird Sings* (Random House, 1969), 218–19.

2 **Angelou,** *I Know Why the Caged Bird Sings,* 218–19.

3 For more on study, see **Stefano Harney and Fred Moten,** *The Undercommons: Fugitive Planning and Black Study* (Minor Compositions, 2013); **Fred Moten et al.,** "Resonances: A Conversation on Formless Formation," *e-flux,* October 2021; **Tyson E. Lewis,** *Inoperative Learning: A Radical Rewriting of Educational Potentialities* (Routledge, 2018); and **Eli Meyerhoff,** *Beyond Education: Radical Studying for Another World* (University of Minnesota Press, 2019).

4 **Harney,** *The Undercommons,* 118.

5 **Harney,** *The Undercommons,* 118.

In her 1969 book, *I Know Why the Caged Bird Sings*, Maya Angelou recalls joining "white and black grownups" for dance and drama classes at the California Labor School as a fourteen-year-old in 1940s San Francisco: "I never knew why I was given a scholarship to the California Labor School. It was a college for adults, and many years later I found that it was on the House Un-American Activities list of subversive organizations."[1] Angelou vividly describes being with others in the dance studio—a site where she attended to her body and began to imagine new possibilities for creative movement:

> My shyness at moving clad in black tights around a large empty room did not last long. […] when the teacher floated across the floor and finished in an arabesque my fancy was taken. I would learn to move like that. I would learn to, in her words, "occupy space."[2]

This dance class was one of hundreds of arts courses offered at the California Labor School between 1942 and 1957. Over its fifteen years, the school was a site of artistic experimentation for thousands of people—trade union workers, veterans, children, and adults of many backgrounds—who came not only to study Marxism and union organizing but also to chisel, sing, sculpt, lithograph, design, and perform. At the Labor School, cultural production and artmaking were seen as inseparable from, and constitutive of, political education. Through its embrace of media and the arts, the Labor School enacted a labor-art-organizing praxis in which collective artmaking was critical to radically imagining and prefiguring other economic, social, and political forms. Through hosting art programs as well as informal sites of learning, the California Labor School created the scaffolding for after school "study."

The concept of "study" provides a generative lens for reading the artmaking in the Labor School as well as configurations of learning outside and on the edges of formal institutions. In recent years, Stefano Harney, Fred Moten, and other theorists have offered "study" as a counterpoint to more traditional modes of learning that are ends-oriented, market-driven, and focused on the individual.[3] While Harney and Moten don't offer a singular definition of study, they use it as a capacious term to describe the social and collective intellectual life beyond traditional schools and universities. Harney extends an invitation to consider this "whole other world where study is already going."[4] He reflects on how to enter and join this other world: "I felt I ought to have some way to be able to see that world, to feel that world, to sense it, and to enter into it, to join the study already going on in different informal ways, unforming, informing ways."[5]

Study is a way to name the social practices of learning that have always been taking place on the edges of schools. Study is ongoing, provisional, in process, and formed with others. It is enacted repeatedly as people gather to creatively refuse existing institutions and build small-scale, localized alternatives from where they are. As a theoretical concept and lens, study invites noticing and thinking alongside experimenting with forms of collaborative intellectual and artistic life outside (and often in opposition to) formal modes of education.

The California Labor School is part of a long tradition of artists and workers who have critiqued dominant modes of education and attempted to create new forms of learning. Within their artmaking classes and informal programs, they created the enabling conditions for "media study." Working with paint, film, wood, plastic, and other materials was both a form of shared knowledge formation and political study. Students analyzed

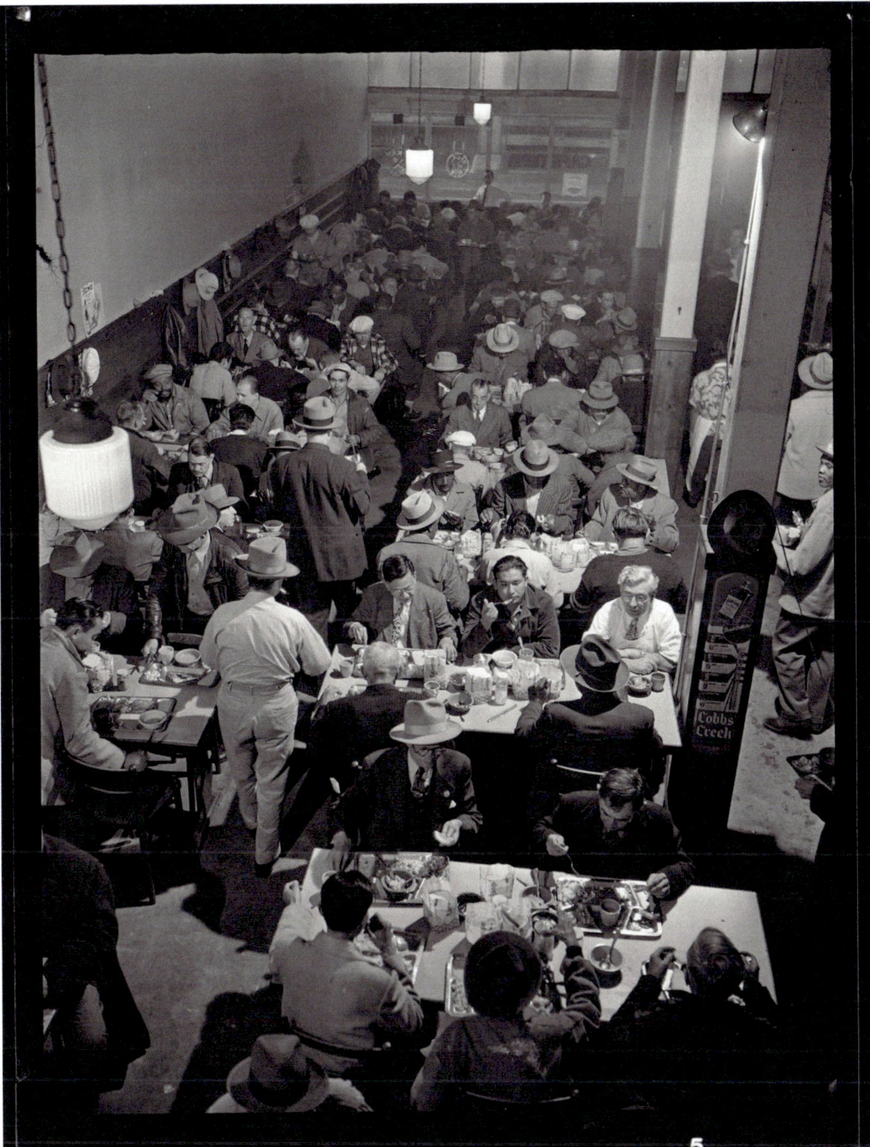

California Labor School Cafeteria, ca. 1950, photograph; Labor Archives and Research Center, JPLL

social conditions while learning skills and practices—mimeographing, designing, filmmaking, and more—that could support broader labor organizing. Experimenting with form at the small scale was also a way of considering larger forms—economic, political, social—that might organize society after capitalism. The school's "media study" was always social, and its art program was one of the school's biggest draws. As Carol Cuénod, a volunteer in the print studio who designed and printed the school's leaflets, put it: "Once I walked into the School, I didn't leave until they locked it up. It had that kind of vital attraction."[6]

The California Labor School opened in 1942 over an auto sales garage on Turk Street in San Francisco. The idea for the school was generated "on a ship at sea."[7] As one version of the story goes, a group of longshoremen, including the school's first director, David Jenkins, began talking about "the urgent need for a school" for workers.[8] They envisioned a learning environment with inclusive admissions, experimental pedagogies, and non-traditional courses for those "not reached by existing education."[9] It was the middle of World War II, and they saw a need for a school that could be a "democratic weapon" against fascism—a space for workers to study and imagine political, economic, and social possibilities for a

[6] Carol Cuénod Oral History, interview by Harvey Schwartz, 1994, SFSU Labor Archives.

[7] "Education for the People," California Labor School Term Catalogs, 1948, Box 1, Folder 6, California Labor School Collection, 1942-1957, Labor Archives and Research Center, J. Paul Leonard Library, San Francisco State University.

[8] "Education for the People," SFSU Labor Archives. The organizers described their school as "a part and a continuation" of a tradition of worker schools and labor colleges that were part of America's educational history. They were also part of a movement in the 1940s and 1950s of Communist Party-affiliated labor schools, including the Jefferson School of Social Science (New York) and the Abraham Lincoln School for Social Sciences (Chicago).

[9] "Education for the People," SFSU Labor Archives.

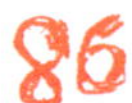

Painting Class at the California Labor School, ca. 1950, photograph; Labor Archives and Research Center, JPLL

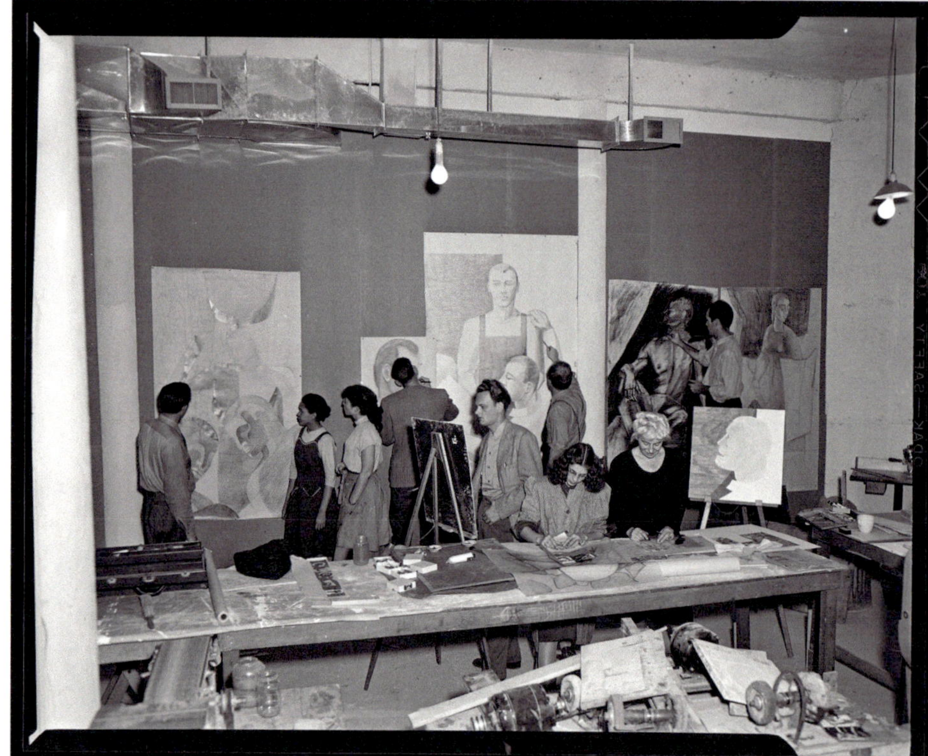

10 The school was originally called the Tom Mooney Labor School, named after the Socialist activist and labor organizer Tom Mooney, who was convicted of bombing the 1916 Preparedness Day Parade in San Francisco, leading to decades of imprisonment. In 1944, then director Dave Jenkins motioned to change the name to the California Labor School—a name he thought would appeal to a broader audience.

11 The California Labor School briefly qualified for G.I. Bill funding and was able to provide veterans free education and housing stipends. They were also committed to "eliminating all traces of discrimination against minority groups" and worked to specifically recruit Black instructors, lecturers, and participants.

12 "Filling the Vacuum," c. 1971, Box 1, Folder 7, Holland Roberts California Labor School Collection, SFSU Labor Archives.

13 Fredric Jameson, *Postmodernism, Or the Cultural Logic of Late Capitalism* (Duke University Press, 1991).

14 George Herman, quoted in "Letter from Allen Rosenfield," September 1946, California Labor School, Fundraising 1944-1957, Box 4, Folder 2, California Labor School Collection, SFSU Labor Archives.

15 "Education for the People," SFSU Labor Archives.

16 "David Jenkins: The Union Movement, the California Labor School, and San Francisco Politics, 1926-1988," 1993, interview by Lisa Rubens in 1987 and 1988, Oral History Center, The Bancroft Library, University of California, Berkeley.

17 California Labor School 1947, California Labor School Collection, 1942-1957, Labor Archives and Research Center, J. Paul Leonard Library, San Francisco State University.

18 "something new—" in *Education for Action: The Student Worker*, Winter 1944, Box 4, Folder 7, California Labor School Collection, SFSU Labor Archives.

postwar world. The school opened with a catalogue of night and weekend classes on economic theory, national liberation movements, race relations, and labor history.[10] Tuition was low; there were no grades or entry requirements.[11]

The School set out to "fill the vacuum" within the existing educational system, aiming to "help longshoremen, truck drivers, painters, steel workers, mechanics, students and the general public—businessmen and women, too, enlarge their concepts of living and advance the quality of their lives."[12] Through courses on race, gender, labor, and capitalism, they aimed to create an environment for what literary scholar Fredric Jameson might describe as "thinking the present historically."[13] Or, as one student put it, the Labor School was "an answer to understanding life in America and why things are the way they are."[14]

Over its first few years of operation, "classes overflowed" the small space as thousands of people showed up for seminars, lectures, workshops, and after school programs.[15] By its second year, the California Labor School was becoming a hub for the arts. According to David Jenkins, artists, dancers, and writers "started to flock to the school," saying "that they had an audience and they wanted to teach, and they wanted space."[16] Courses invited students to gather around the following questions: "What is art? Where does it come from? Does it affect your life?" and "What, in short, is the place of art in society?"[17]

These questions could be taken up in a range of courses that spanned media: typographical design, furniture making, documentary photography, printmaking, and more. Within these varied spaces of learning, instructors aimed to dismantle the hierarchies they saw in traditional classrooms. Refusing the rigid pedagogies of formal art schools, they aimed instead to convene in what one instructor called a "practical workshop atmosphere."[18] They eschewed grades, evaluation, and requirements in favor of learning that was social, ongoing, and provisional. They established spaces in which participants could collaboratively and creatively work with many kinds of materials. Put another way, they aimed to create the conditions for "study."

The "living force" of the Labor School can be glimpsed through its printmaking studios, photography labs, sculpture workshops, and typographical layout sessions, in which the investigation of media and forms was connected to understanding, and eventually shaping, the broader social world. The pedagogical vision of the arts program is perhaps most lucidly articulated in a 1944 description of a course called Arts and Crafts, which states that "all people have creative ability" and that the "function of education is to uncover it—to activize and develop it."[19] In this class, participants could join a collaborative hands-on process of "reexploring and rediscovering" materials: "[Testing], by means of experimentation and construction, [their] aesthetic and physical qualities and the functional possibilities."[20]

The materials at hand—plastics, metal, wood, stone, film, paper— regularly formed the basis of media study. In a course on Modern Design, instructor Margaret de Patta promised to introduce students to design through "the experimental approach to available materials."[21] By taking things apart, then putting them together, students could open "a world of discovery."[22] In a 1947 drawing class, Anton Refregier prompted students to draw an eclectic array of objects—"[a] bird skeleton, dry seaweed, fragments of machinery, laboratory equipment, etc.," emphasizing that that these objects should "not be studied in terms of the esoteric or unusual but rather in tangible investigation of material."[23] Media study involves assembling around and with the materials at hand and beginning to develop creative methods alongside those materials.

Media study reframed San Francisco and the surrounding area as a site for learning. In a 1947 mural class, Refregier describes bringing students on shared walks, paying attention to the emotions associated with specific areas of the city:

> Study will include analysis of the use of the area, the type of people and the emotional condition they are in while in the area…(night club, gay and frivolous…waiting room of a hospital, tense, etc.,) the time the people spend in the area… (subway station…library.)[24]

In this class, the city—its people, lights, energy—became the material for collective learning; study emerged in and through the social experience of walking and collaboratively reading San Francisco's social environments. As Refregier elaborates, "Study will be conducted on a collective basis with the whole class participating."[25]

At the California Labor School, the organization of lines, sentences, paint strokes, and more were seen as constitutive and critical to the work of organizing toward a world beyond capitalism. In *Politically Red* (2024), Eduardo Cadava and Sara Nadal-Melsió write that, "sentences belong to the possibility of mass formations, collective action, and insurrectionary politics."[26] Throughout the Labor School's art classes arose a chorus of voices articulating a similar conviction—that artistic and design choices were critical for collective action and political work. Courses provided students with the tools to learn how to design posters, leaflets, and other printed matter so they could make materials for their union and organizing projects. In Layout, "a practical course for workers," participants could study "modern techniques of all graphic media" such as mimeographing, lithography, offset, and montage to make publications for strikes and political actions.[27] In Composition, students could gather

19 "California Labor School Summer 1944," 1944, Box 1, Folder 2, California Labor School Collection, SFSU Labor Archives.

20 "California Labor School Summer 1944," 1944, Box 1, Folder 2, California Labor School Collection, SFSU Labor Archives.

21 "Modern Design for Arts and Crafts," 1942-1944, Box 1, Folder 1, California Labor School Collection, SFSU Labor Archives.

22 "Modern Design for Arts and Crafts," SFSU Labor School Archives.

23 "Plan of Study," Box 1, Folder 9, California Labor School Collection, SFSU Labor Archives.

24 "Plan of Study," Box 1, Folder 9, California Labor School Collection, SFSU Labor Archives.

25 "Plan of Study," Box 1, Folder 9, California Labor School Collection, SFSU Labor Archives.

26 **Eduardo Cadava and Sara Nadal-Melsió,** *Politically Red* (MIT Press, 2003), 26.

27 "Layout," 1942-1944, Box 1, Folder 1, California Labor School Collection, SFSU Labor Archives.

around visual elements, asking: "How can you organize lines, values or colors to express most effectively what you want to say in a poster, painting, a piece of sculpture, or a leaflet?"[28]

Media study was also social and ongoing. It often spilled beyond the formal classroom—into the cafeteria, the coffee shop, the bar, and even to ships at sea. In addition to formal classes, the Labor School offered lectures, ran a vacation school, and hosted elaborate parties and social events. As one participant and instructor, Isobel Cerney, put it, most of the learning took place "during informal interchanges, between classes, and late at night."[29] Instructors also thought imaginatively about how to create the scaffolding for experimentation that could continue beyond class. For example, they designed courses for longshoremen who couldn't attend courses while out at sea, giving them prompts with "wood, clay, metal, stone or plastics" that they could work with while on long voyages.[30] The hope was that by providing students with the materials and resources, they could continue to study after school.[31]

In March of 1957, at the height of McCarthyism, the California Labor School was labeled a "Communist front" after prolonged state and federal investigations, effectively leading to its closure.[32] Everything at the school, including its building, was sold at auction. According to one reporter, "it took seven minutes to sell its physical remains."[33] Watching the school reduced to itemized assets— "several typewriters, 141 reams of mimeograph paper, 92 upright wooden chairs and 24 folded, a mimeograph machine and accessories—stencils, ink, and a mimescope"—the same journalist reflected on the social and artistic life that had infused the school for fifteen years. "[It was a place] where singers had sung and actors had acted and lecturers had lectured, where the work of artists had been displayed, where occasions, great and little, had been celebrated or commemorated, where ideas had been expressed and exchanged, where thousands had come over the years for learning or for joy or for beauty."[34]

The legacy of the Labor School was always more than its physical objects—its books, chairs, its mimeographs. It was a living communal experiment in which people came together to think about what education could be. It was continuously made and re-made by the workers, union leaders, artists, and children who moved, sang, chiseled, painted, and studied within it.

The artists and students practicing media study extend an invitation to anyone interested in rethinking education today. They prompt us to pick up the materials at hand—seaweed, cloth, paper, clay, charcoal, books, the sites of the city—and begin to shape something with one another. They invite us to look around and, in the words of Harney, "join the study already going on" after school.[35]

after school study takes place anywhere that people gather to creatively refuse the commodified logics of education. It happens when people attempt to move beyond critiquing existing structures and begin imagining and trying out other (thought and learning) formations. It is a social and communal process of unmaking and remaking. Even when one experiment or project ends, practices of study remain open and ongoing. To sense, see, feel, and join this other world of study involves attending to the openings experiments like the California Labor School provide. So even though the school formally closed, it continues to offer an invitation to imagine—and study—*after school*.

28 California Labor School (Spring 1945), California Labor School, Term Catalogs, 1945, Box 1, Folder 3, California Labor School Collection, SFSU Labor Archives.

29 **Isobel Cerney,** "Teaching Workers at the California Labor School," in *The Cold War Against Labor*, vol. 1 (Meiklejohn Civil Liberties Institute, 1987), 145.

30 California Labor School (Spring 1945). California Labor School Collection, 1942–1957, Labor Archives and Research Center, J. Paul Leonard Library, San Francisco State University.

31 **Cerney,** "Teaching Workers at the California Labor School," 145.

32 The passage of the Internal Security Act of 1950, also called the McCarran Act, authorized the government to create a federal agency to identify and sanction "subversive organizations." When the Subversive Activities Control Board (SACB) labeled the Labor School a "Communist front," the organizers refused to accept this label. They were unable to pay the fines and legal fees necessary to fight the case.

33 **Al Richmond,** "Strange Auction on Divisadero Street: Government Sells 'Subversive' Books," *People's World*, June 1, 1957, Box 5, Folder 6, California Labor School Collection, SFSU Labor Archives.

34 **Al Richmond,** "Strange Auction on Divisadero Street."

35 **Harney,** *The Undercommons*, 118.

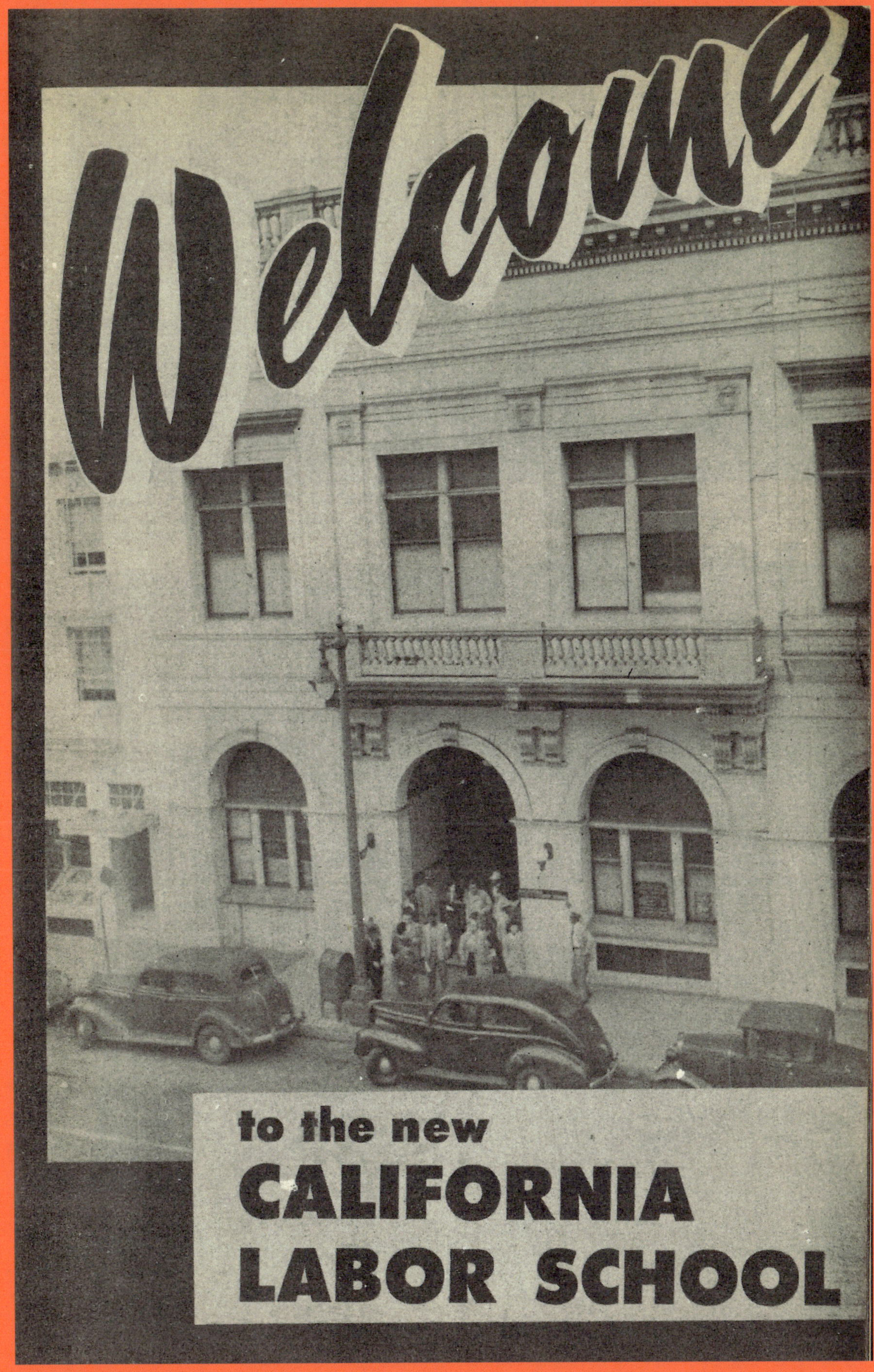

Interior cover of the *California Labor School Yearbook & Catalogue*, 1948; Labor Archives and Research Center, JPLL

SERVICES TO UNIONS

DURING 1947 over a thousand trade unionists from the AFL, CIO and Railroad Brotherhoods participated in over 500 class sessions conducted by the School in its extension work in San Francisco, Oakland, Richmond, Martinez Sacramento, Stockton, Fresno, San Jose, Santa Rosa, Redwood City, Los Angeles, San Pedro, Petaluma and other places.

These extension courses may take one of several forms:

EVENING CLASSES are held once a week or once in two weeks, either at the union hall or at the School and average ten sessions. The cost is $15.00 per session, reduced rates for longer courses.

DAYTIME CLASSES are organized on the same basis as above, but conducted during the day for the convenience of swing or night shift workers.

WEEK-END SCHOOLS are a new and especially successful method developed by the School. These schools are for one day or two, as desired. Sessions are held in the morning and afternoon, with an evening program of motion pictures, or an additional school session if requested.

FULL-TIME SCHOOLS are organized especially for the training of union leadership, with students released from work for the duration of the school. Average length of the school is one week; morning and afternoon sessions; evenings are devoted to special programs, supervised study, preparation of reports, and selected study projects.

A wide variety of subjects is offered for these extension courses. Principal titles follows:

What is Unionism? The general history of labor and the history of your international Union.
Stewards' Duties. Based on the union's problems.
Collective Bargaining in Your Industry.
Economics and Labor, Wages, prices, profits, unemployment crises, and imperialism.
Legislative and Political Action.

Full-time Los Angeles Labor School, September, 1947

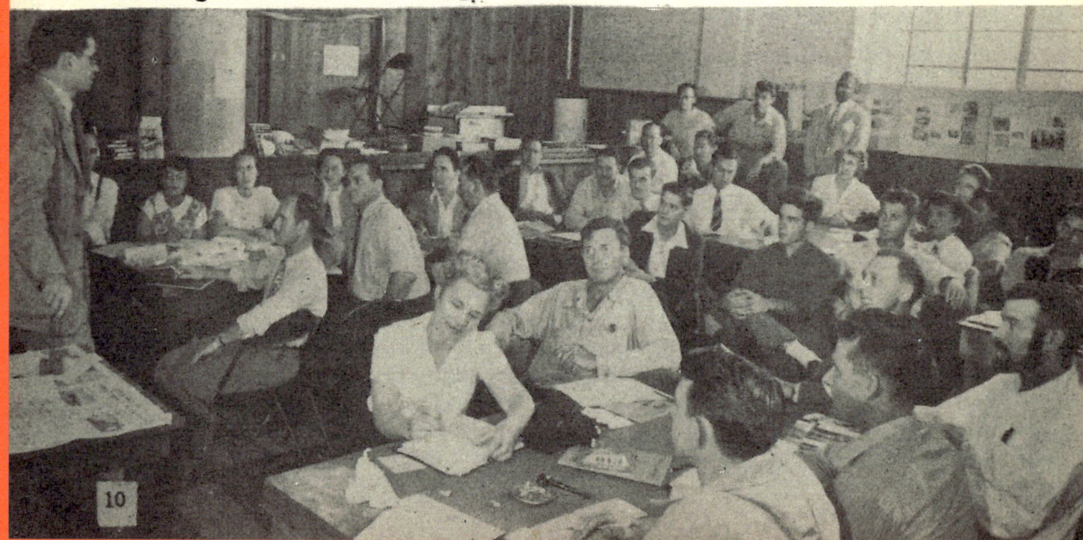

The Taft-Hartley Act and other anti-labor laws.
Public Speaking and Parliamentary Procedure.
Minority Groups' Contribution to Democracy.
Organizing Techniques.
New Members' Introduction to Labor.
Labor Laws. Unemployment Compensation, Disability Insurance, Workmen's Compensations, Old Age Pensions, and other laws.
The Role of Art in Support of Labor's Struggles. Cartooning, and other practical needs.
Recreational Art. Modeling, painting, drawing, leather tooling and general recreational classes.

INSTRUCTORS: Jules Carson, Irwin Elber, David Hedley, George Hitchcock David Jenkins, Giacomo Patri, Holland Roberts, Gordon Williams, Andrew Zirpoli, and selected trade union leaders.

AT THE 1947 CIO CONVENTION the School once again won unanimous endorsement for its work in union education. All affiliated locals were asked to use the services of the School in local educational work.

VISUAL EDUCATION

Our Visual Education and Information Service offers Labor unions and other organizations the following:

1--Help in setting up libraries and offering books and pamphlets for sale to members. Our book department carries a complete stock of popular trade union material.

2--Films for your union meetings. The School maintains a labor film library under the direction of Leo Nitzberg. Films, film strips, and projection equipment is available for rental.
Write for our complete film catalogue.

3--Publications. Special pamphlets can be written to order. The School's own publication include such successful pamphlets as: The Big Lie, Made In Berlin, Why Work for Nothing, and What is Philosophy.

LECTURES AND CONSULTATION SERVICE

The School is prepared to act as consultant to unions in setting up educational committees, stewards councils, etc. The School can also furnish speakers for union meetings on all labor topics.

EAST BAY LABOR SCHOOL: Many of the classes listed in the catalogue are offered in Oakland and Berkeley. Oakland offices of the School are at 178 Grand Ave., HIgate-4-1544, Gordon Williams, director. Unless otherwise indicated Berkeley classes are held at the American Veterans Committee clubrooms, 2114 Durant Ave., Berkeley.

LOS ANGELES SERVICES -- The School is now equipped to offer its full extension and trade union services to unions in Southern California. Communications should be addressed to David Hedley, Assistant Director. Regular programs are also being offered in Sacramento, Contra Costa, Santa Clara and Sonoma counties. Residents of those areas should write the School for details.

Miguel Braceli
Stefan Gruber

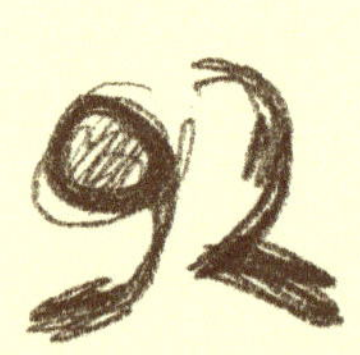

92

PORCHES, PLAYGROUNDS & OTHER SCHOOLS

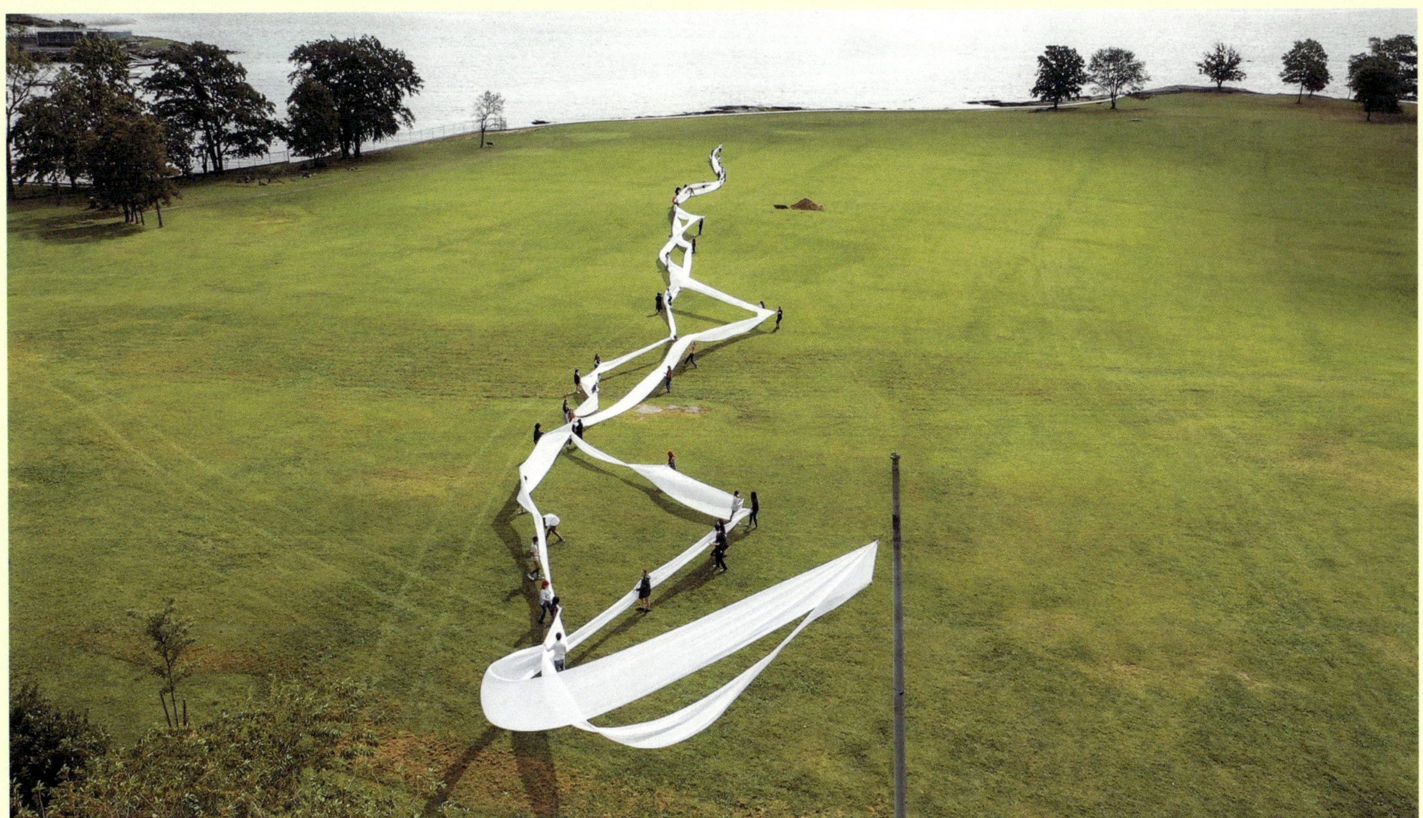

Miguel Braceli, *Here Lies a Flag*, 2021, photograph; Courtesy of the artist

MIGUEL BRACELI

I appreciate the opportunity to reflect on our shared backgrounds and practices in architecture, artmaking, education, and beyond. It's interesting to note that, while we both have similar educational foundations, our processes have diverged significantly. In my case, after I graduated from the Central University of Venezuela, I became actively involved in higher education and began noticing the limitations of traditional academic environments. They felt disconnected from real life and social realities, which motivated me to explore alternative learning practices. These experiences, informed by both historical and contemporary experimental art and pedagogical practices in Latin America, are crucial to understanding LA ESCUELA___ as it exists in public spaces, outside and apart from the conventional boundaries of university teaching.

In contrast, as I understand it, your path involves transitioning directly from architectural practice—juggling the complexities and tensions between power and architecture in influential firms —to university education and research. How has this trajectory shaped your current practice and project, *An Atlas of Commoning*, and what impact did higher education have on the development of this project?

STEFAN GRUBER In my experience, the university was initially a retreat from professional practice, a space for critical reflection. Architecture is expensive and often serves to perpetuate existing systems rather than challenge them. In turn, buildings quite literally cement social relations and habits in place, shaping society for generations. Education, too, can replicate these dynamics.

SG The 2008 financial crisis prompted me to interrogate the role of both the market and the state in shaping our lives. The prime mortgage collapse exposed how deeply housing—and architecture at large—was entangled in financialization, reducing architecture to a commodity. Academia provided me with the necessary distance to analyze these forces and consider alternative approaches. I began studying initiatives in which communities take collective action to shape their environment beyond the logics of profit-driven growth or top-down government control. These examples ultimately laid the groundwork for *An Atlas of Commoning.*

MB I think LA ESCUELA__ shares a similar experience, as it's deeply connected with another kind of crisis, specifically the global COVID-19 crisis. In 2020, as a graduate student at Maryland Institute College of Art (MICA), I wrote "The Naked School," a critique of art schools' tendency to replicate institutional norms, which became particularly evident during the pandemic. The text advocates for a curriculum that tangibly centers artistic production within social and political contexts. Employing the architectural metaphor of a "divested building," it proposes a kind of learning space where art and education are integrated within contemporary practices and active community engagement. Conceptualized as a post-COVID project, LA ESCUELA__ operates as an artist-run platform for collective learning, exploring new ways of relating and learning through hybrid online and on-site projects. Co-founded with the international non-profit Siemens Stiftung, LA ESCUELA__ partners with universities, institutions, and communities to produce educational art projects in public spaces, while continuing a long-standing practice of international exchange that has deep historical roots in Latin America. Similar to projects like Ciudad Abierta (Open City) in Chile and Parque Lague in Brazil, LA ESCUELA__ brings together artists and educators from across geographical divides to collaborate and co-create educational projects that, at once, respond to major global themes as well as specific challenges of our current socio-political contexts by working in public spaces.

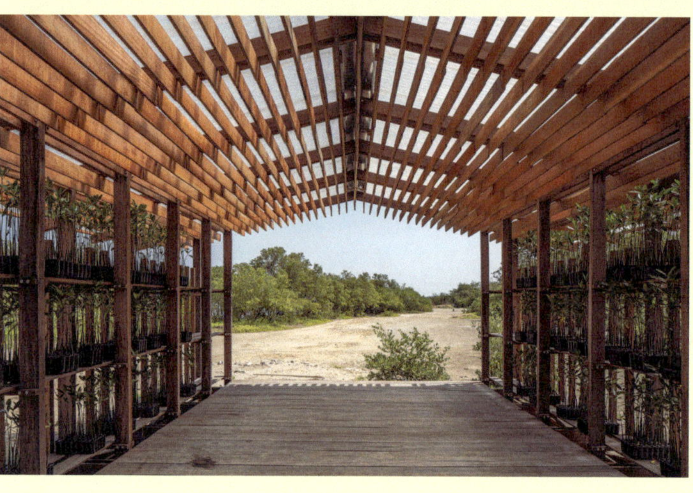

Top: Tom Little, *An Atlas of Commoning*, photograph; Courtesy of Stefan Gruber

Bottom: Miguel Braceli, *LA ESCUELA__ CLASSROOMS,* Building Schools__*Public Spaces, CUNA,* Porous School of Landscape Construction, photograph; Courtesy of the artist

SG When we speak of *public* space, *public* education, or *public* health, we often invoke the idea of "the public" as a unified and unquestioned good. As a result, discourses around "the public" risk obscuring the contested and constructed nature of the term. Public space, for instance, is typically state-controlled and regulated by authorities such as the police. What appears accessible to all can also be a highly codified form of exclusion. The commons, by contrast, are governed by their users, who collectively define shared values and steward resources through mutual responsibility and self-organization. The commons introduce a third sphere beyond the binaries of the public or private.

An Atlas of Commoning is an ongoing curatorial research project and traveling exhibition. In each host city, we add new case studies of commoning initiatives to the growing knowledge archive. At its core, the *Atlas* defines "commoning" as it refers to practices in which people come together, pool resources, and act as collective stewards of shared assets through self-governance. These commons—whether material, like grazing land or co-housing, or immaterial, like cultural knowledge—foster solidarity, self-determination, and community resilience. In times of crisis—when public institutions falter or collapse—people are often forced to invent new forms of collaboration to survive. These moments reveal that our systems are not natural or inevitable; they are designed and, therefore, also open to transformation. It is in such ruptures that we begin to see that other worlds are possible and already in the making.

MB   Because your work involves fields such as urban design and housing—forms of permanent architecture, so to speak—your project has to address questions of legal structures and ownership. Within LA ESCUELA_, on the other hand, we often engage in artistic interventions based in knowledge production that temporarily occupy and transform public spaces, thereby approaching the idea of *education as art*.

More recently, LA ESCUELA_ has also been incorporating architectural operations to offer more direct and permanent public interventions that keep community leadership at the forefront. For example, within our work with the AULAS (Classrooms) Program, we have been developing an architecture series. *Extramuros* is one of them, bringing together several elementary schools in Peru, Colombia, and Ecuador on a project led by architect Javier Vera Cubas. Each school participated in the transformation of their buildings, a process that dissolved boundaries between educational spaces and their surroundings. In certain cases, these efforts resulted in the demolition of school walls to create public playgrounds, generating dialogue between children and citizens, the public and the private. In other cases, temporary architectural devices were created to activate the classroom in different public spaces.

SG   That is fascinating! The participatory nature of *Extramuros* speaks a lot to a recent project called *Roaming Porches*, in which I collaborated with the Manchester Academic Charter School in Pittsburgh to help them reimagine vacant lots they had acquired. We engaged with the students in a course co-taught by university students, which offered an opportunity to explore the surrounding neighborhood and learn about the community members' everyday lives, their histories, and possible futures. The project yielded the design and construction of three mobile porch structures that could be used by teachers and their students to transform urban spaces into an outdoor classroom of sorts. Rather than prescribing solutions, the mobile classrooms prompted the students and teachers to experience the vacant lots and envision possibilities for their future on-site. In another collaboration, we worked with the non-profit organization Community Forge to transform a vacant elementary school in Wilkinsburg into a community center. After engaging the neighborhood in a visioning process, we ultimately focused on incremental transformations. Starting with small, tactical design interventions—what we sometimes call "urban acupuncture"—we created opportunities for the community to experience and respond to changes in real time. Their continuous feedback fostered a strong sense of agency and ownership throughout the process. One of my favorite aspects of Community Forge was their youth council, where neighborhood kids engaged in participatory budgeting.

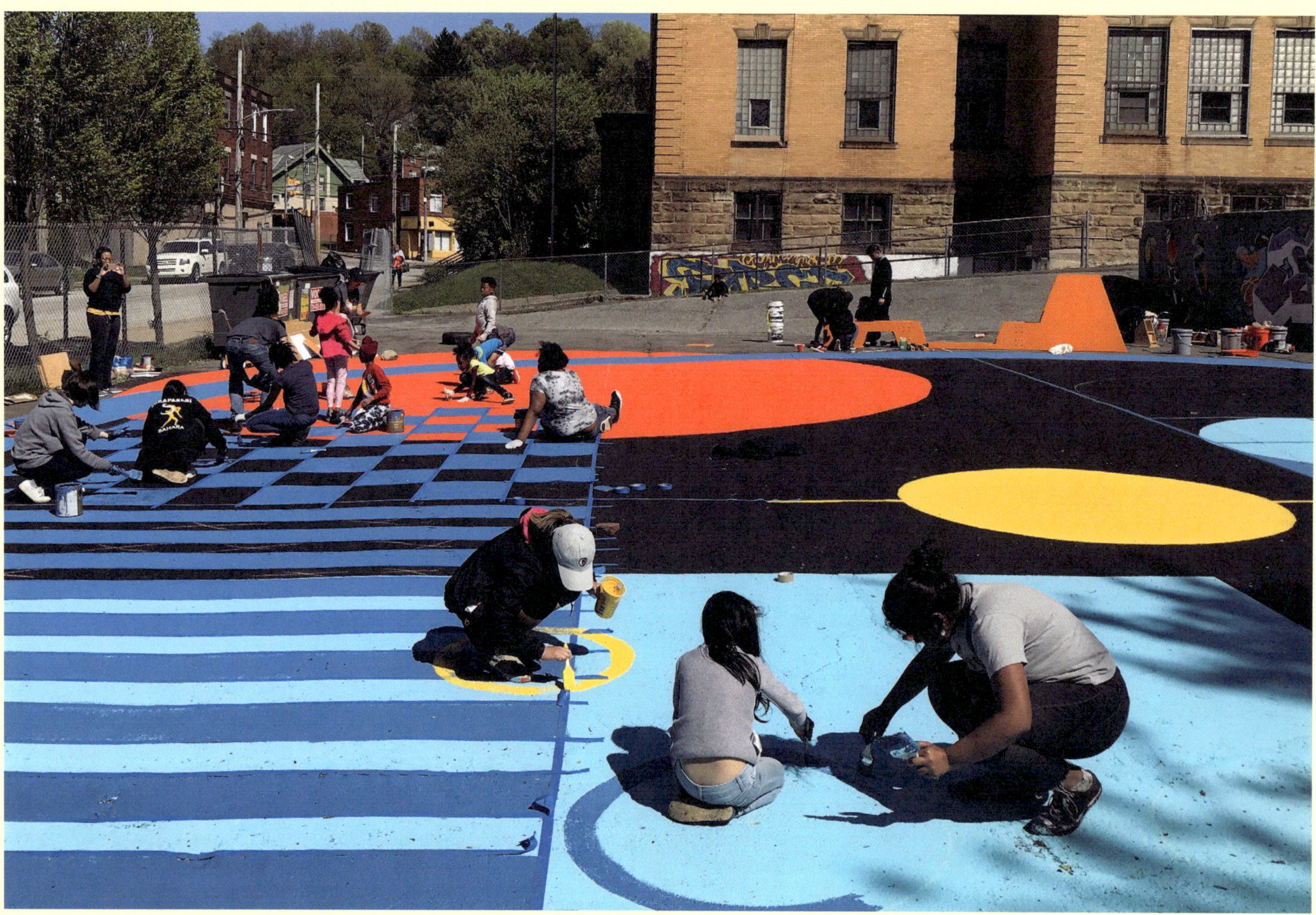

Stefan Gruber, The Urban Collaboratory *Studio, Community Forge*, Wilkinsburg, 2019, photograph; Courtesy of the artist

MB Those are such inspiring examples of community-based education. Your *Roaming Porches* project and collaboration with Community Forge remind me of LA ESCUELA__'s architectural competition, *Construir Escuelas__Espacios Públicos*, which organizes, designs, and builds a school as a public space. Then we would come in with the necessary funding and curatorial support for building and programming their proposals. This was another way we imagined shifting public space dynamics by empowering people to find and participate in the making of their own commons, to use your term.

SG I think it's really interesting how LA ESCUELA_ 's work encompasses such a wide range of practices. Through both ephemeral, as you say, and more architectural interventions, you seem to redirect attention, create new experiences, and open up ways of perceiving public space, monuments, and other conditions in the built environment that shape our communities. I'd love to hear more about the participatory performance projects you've done. How do you conceive of them, and how do they function as educational practices?

MB In my work, I aim to explore the possibilities that art offers to engage communities in interacting with and intervening in their own environments through collective and embodied learning experiences. This involves engaging with monuments, national symbols, urban semiotics, and other imagery within built environments to address complex subjects, such as migration, identity, and local or geopolitical issues. I develop performances or interventions presented in public spaces to evoke questions and responses that unfold collectively and bodily. Specifically, in my project *Horizontal Monuments*, I created a one-to-one replica of an existing monument—a massive obelisk honoring Benito Juárez—but displayed it horizontally next to the original one in Guadalajara, Mexico and changed its materiality from concrete to fabric. This alteration prompted questions about accessibility and engagement from the public, ultimately transforming the monument into a new, more accessible form as well as a site of assembly to discuss its destiny. We collectively decided that we would move it to a park nearby and, once the horizontal monument was placed in a different site, it evolved into a playground, reshaping our understanding of monuments, public art, and particularly the role of public space as a framework for free and open education. For me, this practice underscores the value of learning in public spaces. Knowledge transcends the dynamics and exchanges between professor and student; it becomes collective and community driven.

SG I'm drawn to this question as well: how do we build community and explore the role of place within a situated practice? For me, this implies no longer viewing the design as an endpoint but as an instigator of transformation. Instead of working towards the moment when a design is "completed" and users take over, I'm more interested in how design interventions, even modest and temporary ones, can act as catalysts; similar to the project you mentioned, *Construir Escuelas _ Espacios Públicos*, which brings community members together and engages them in a collaborative, incremental process of transformation. This approach also decentralizes expertise, aligning with LA ESCUELA_ 's model of dismantling intellectual hierarchies and fostering open-ended learning.

MB Indeed, I often describe LA ESCUELA_ as a platform of escuelas—a platform for thinking and practicing education in multiple ways. Within this dynamic interchange of knowledge, perspectives, and practices, we promote a rotation of power. An essential aspect of LA ESCUELA_ is the network we have developed, which has emerged as one of our most significant assets. The network encompasses art educators and community-based organizations and projects across Latin America. We view this network as a means to propel other initiatives that operate outside the confines of LA ESCUELA__ itself. The potential for collaboration and innovation lies within this fluidity and openness, enabling projects and individuals to connect without centralized control.

SG That is the project of *An Atlas of Commoning*. We seek to foster translocal networks of mutual learning and exchange, aiming to empower participants and help transform isolated struggles into a shared, collective experience. A central challenge, however, lies in cultivating these connections without imposing a totalizing or essentializing framework. What particularly interests me is how the traveling nature of the exhibition continually disrupts and reorients our understanding of commoning. But ultimately, there is a pressing need for a paradigm shift in which more communal, local, and decentralized approaches are recognized as standard practice. This aspiration encourages us to rethink our definitions of valid forms of art, architecture, and education. A crucial aspect of this transformation lies in fostering interconnections and establishing a networked system where all these practices can thrive and expand.

MB Those are all excellent points, particularly regarding the role of participatory architecture. The emphasis there is not merely on extracting aesthetic preferences or meeting specific needs; it's about embarking on a co-development process that begins at the outset and transcends traditional definitions of co-design. The challenge lies in moving these practices from the margins to the forefront of discourse and implementation within established systems.

SG Agreed. That's the challenge. But maybe the real question isn't how to bring these practices into the center, but whether we should accept the center's terms at all. In their 2013 book *The Undercommons: Fugitive Planning & Black Study*, Fred Moten and Stefano Harney describe "fugitive study" as a form of collaborative, subversive intellectual work that exists within and against the institution—not to reform it, but to refuse its logic.[1] The undercommons are not about shifting the center; they are about inhabiting its cracks, creating spaces of resistance that evade capture and resist professionalization. For me, this raises a broader question: how do we design institutions that don't reproduce power, but instead embed redistribution and collective governance into their structures? Much of what we consider legitimate knowledge has been defined by its exclusivity—a logic that upholds the cost of higher education and sustains the myth of meritocracy, especially in the United States, where scarcity is manufactured by design.

1 Fred Moten and Stefano Harney, *The Undercommons: Fugitive Planning & Black Study* (Minor Compositions, 2013).

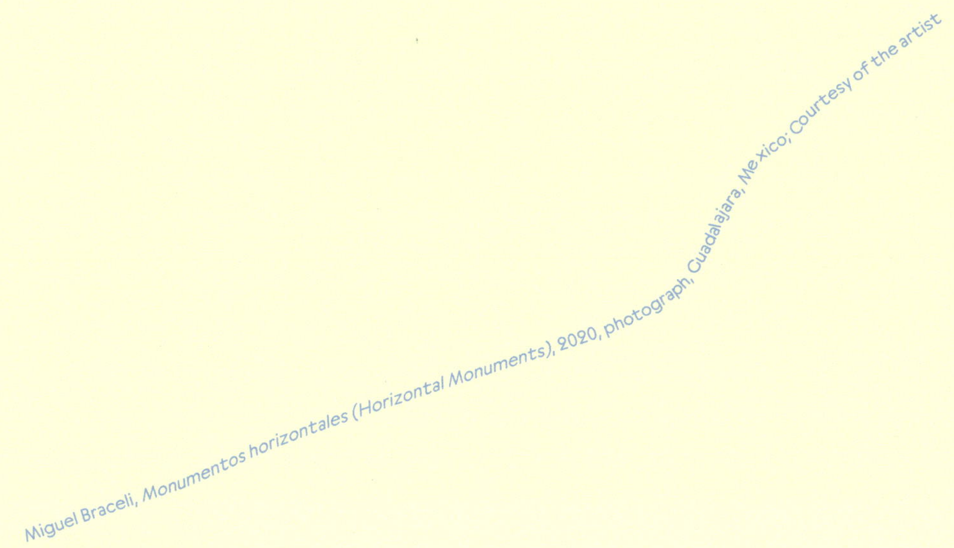

Miguel Braceli, *Monumentos horizontales (Horizontal Monuments)*, 2020, photograph, Guadalajara, Mexico; Courtesy of the artist

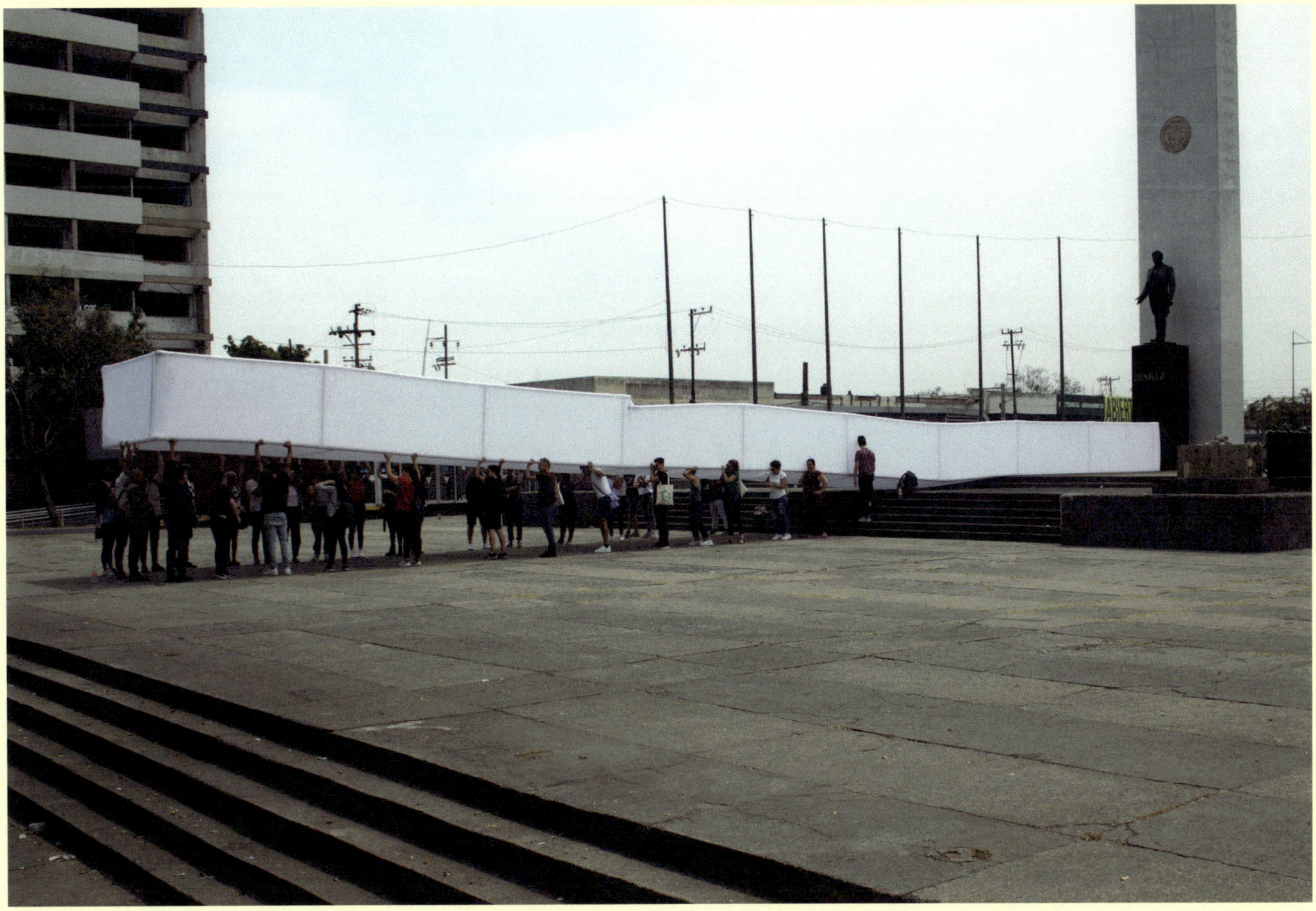

MIGUEL BRACELI & STEFAN GRUBER   Porches, Playgrounds & Others

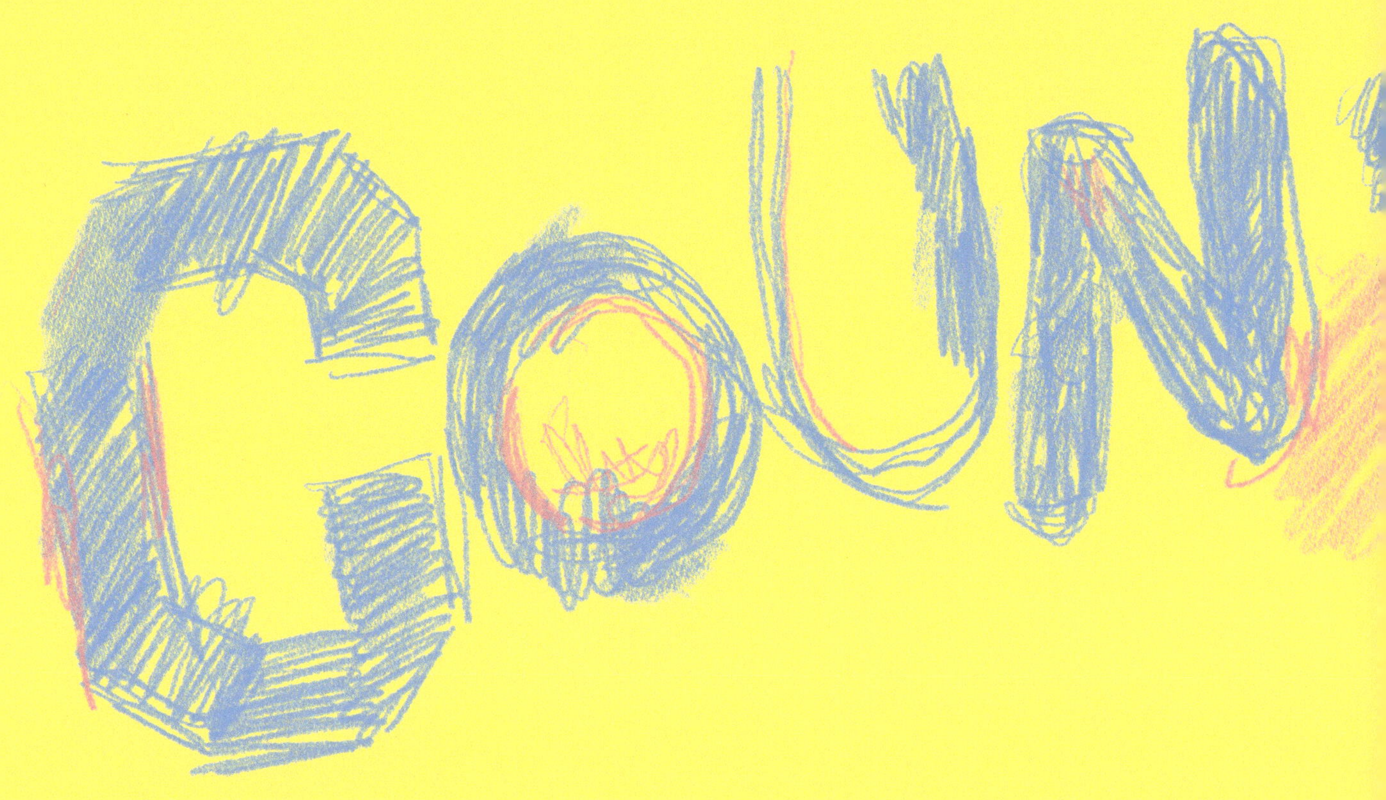
COUN

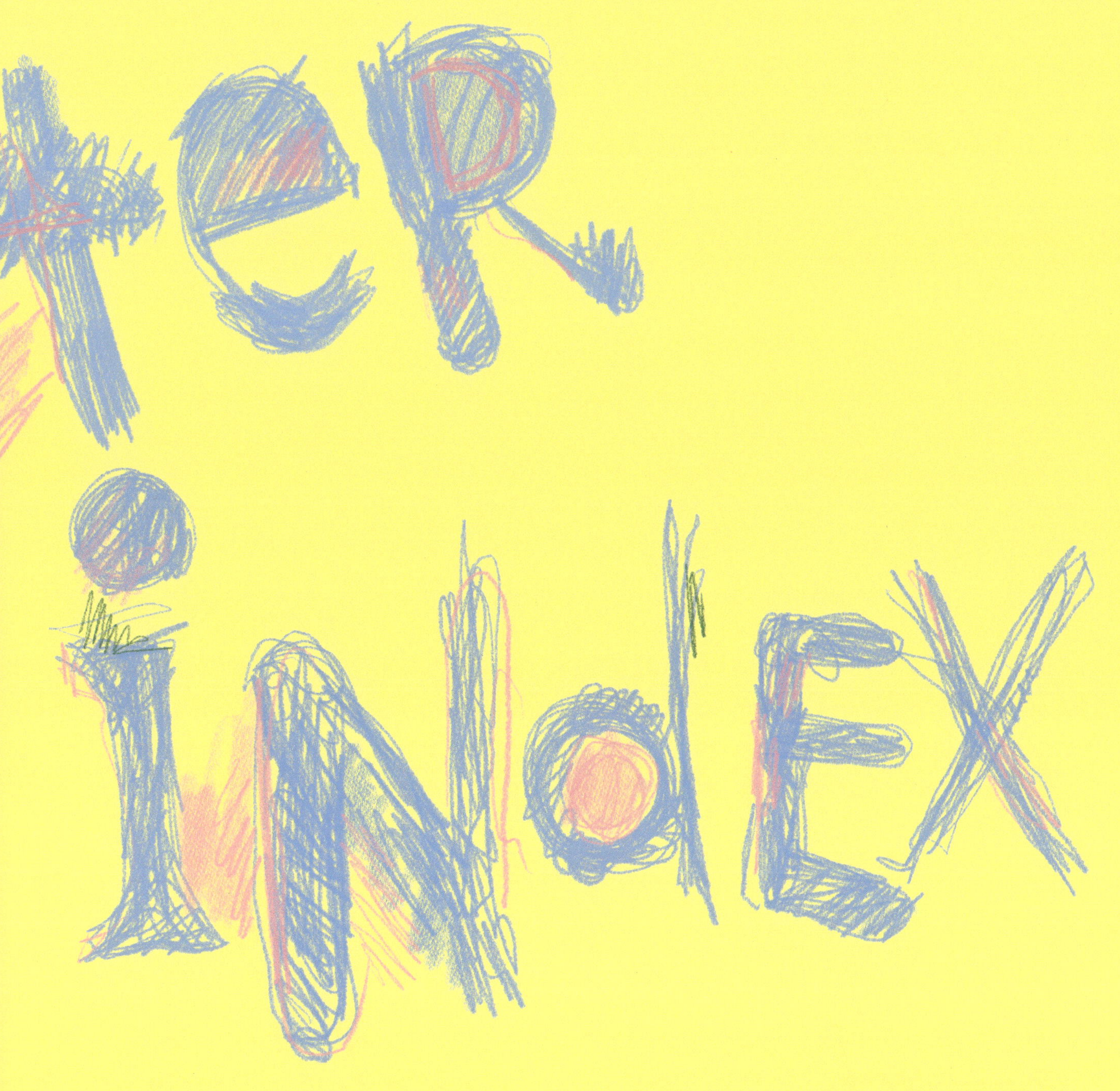

Pittsburgh Public Schools (PPS) assesses the state of its facilities through the Facilities Condition Index (FCI), a metric that measures the cost of repairs against the cost of replacement to determine which schools are renovated, consolidated, or closed. This section of *after school* proposes a "counter index"—one that looks beyond technical assessments to oral, written, and visual accounts of resistance, imagination, struggle, and care. Through ten Pittsburgh-based case studies, multivocal narratives and personal testimonies reveal how the educational landscape has been constructed and reconstructed—physically, politically, and emotionally—over time. Rather than assessing buildings, this index measures schools through the experiences they cultivate and the broader connections they enable. By bringing together stories and archival fragments, it offers an unfinished yet evolving record of collective and divergent encounters with public education, reminding us that a school's condition is shaped as much by communal memory and meaning as by its physical maintenance.

Axonometric Drawings by Sharvi Shah and Nicholas Thies, M.Arch Class of 2026, School of Architecture, Carnegie Mellon University.

EDUCATION AS A PRACTICE OF SOCIAL INFRASTRUCTURE

Sarosh Anklesaria

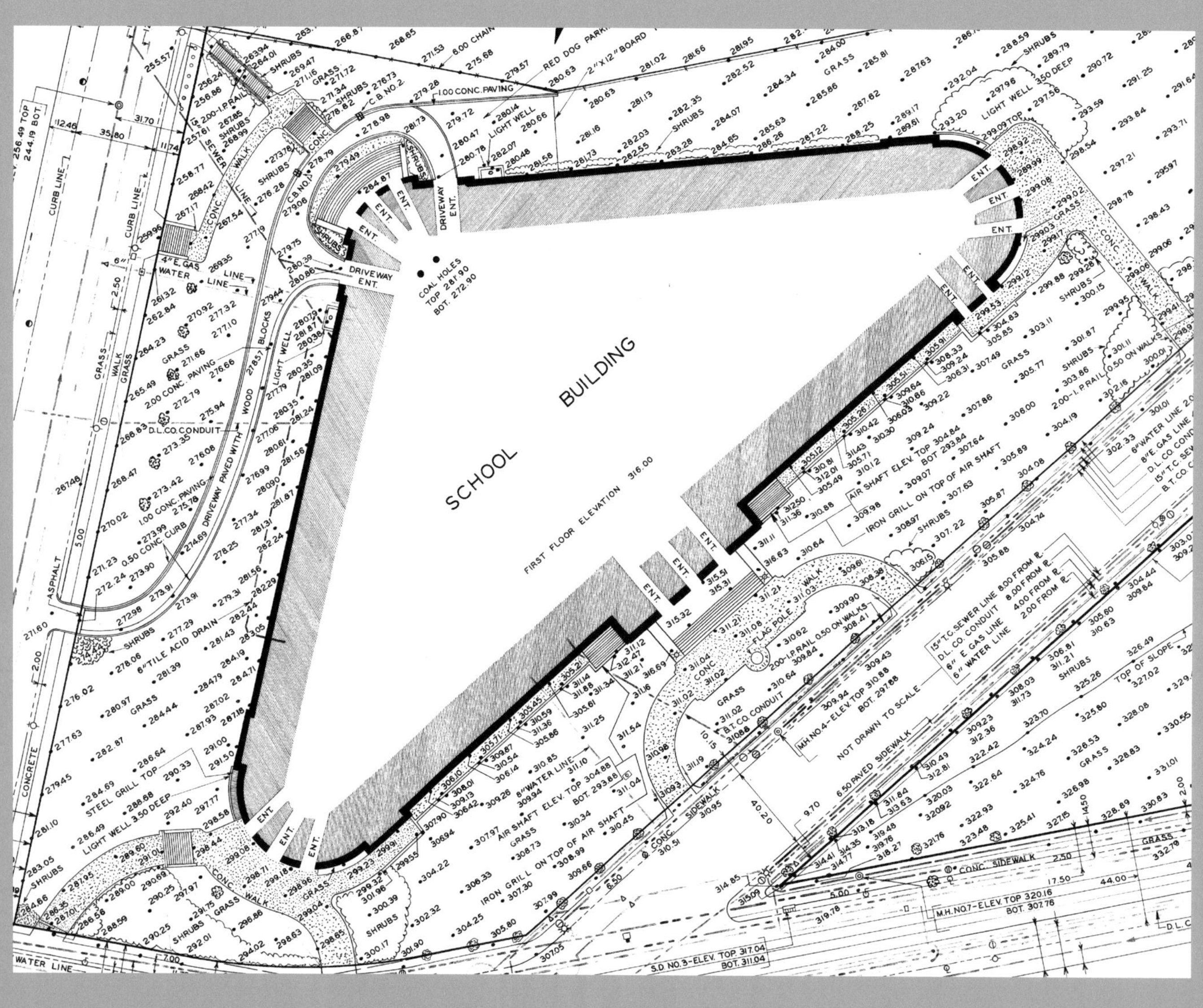

I write this essay at a watershed moment in the history of education in the United States, on the very day that the Federal Government has, through executive order of the President, called for the dismantling of the U.S. Department of Education (ED)—a move ostensibly aimed at granting the states full autonomy over matters of public education. Yet beneath the rhetoric of federalism lies a deliberate abdication of the federal government's responsibility to uphold education as essential social infrastructure. Although the net contribution of the ED to local district programs is minimal, it currently provides crucial resources to twenty-six million children living in high-poverty school districts, Pell Grants to over seven million students pursuing higher education, vital funding to millions of children with disabilities, and critical funding for initiatives like the National School Lunch Program.[1] The abrupt closure or even partial dismantling of the ED would disproportionately impact poor working-class families, unravel critical support systems, and significantly weaken education's capacity to serve as a public good and a foundation for democratic life. Recognizing these impacts, it is imperative to ask what are the critical infrastructures of citizenry and how is architecture entangled in their making and unmaking? In an era of disinformation and post-truth, what counts as "public goods"?

This essay argues that public schools must be recognized as critical forms of social infrastructure—central to practices of care, community-building, and democratic life. It foregrounds the role of architecture and architectural patronage in shaping civic public space and draws on Eric Klinenberg's concept of social infrastructure to position schools as foundational institutions rooted in care work and collective investment. Drawing on Pittsburgh Public Schools (PPS) as a case study, I demonstrate how many of the city's schools were conceived as social infrastructures through public funding and federally sponsored New Deal programs (1933–1945) that enlisted architects to create civic spaces for democratic education. This architectural legacy reflects a vision of schools not only as educational facilities but as integral to the social and democratic fabric of a city. The essay traces how that vision began to unravel in the 1970s and 80s with the rise of neoliberal ideologies and the ongoing consequences of that unraveling, namely the continued privatization and systematic disinvestment in public infrastructure. Today, the neglect and chronic underfunding of public schools—particularly regarding maintenance and repair—has led to widespread closures, often justified in technocratic terms. Paradoxically, many of the same buildings deemed unfit for public education have proven resilient enough to be converted into luxury condominiums and boutique hotels. The essay concludes by advocating for alternative ways of valuing public schools—not merely as deteriorating physical assets but as vital spaces of social reproduction, public care, and civic possibility.

Left: Marion M. Steen and S. A. Ollis (delineator), Detail of WPA Survey Project of Schenley High School, 1941, architectural survey; PPBF

1 See U.S. Department of Agriculture, Economic Research Service, "Food Security in the U.S.—Key Statistics & Graphs," last modified January 8 2025, https://www.ers.usda.gov/topics/food-nutrition-assistance/food-security-in-the-us/key-statistics-graphics; Feed the Children, "Five Facts About Hunger in America," accessed June 12 2025. Pell-Grant figures are from National College Attainment Network, "Double Pell," accessed June 12 2025; https://www.ncan.org/page.pell.

ARCHITECTURE AND PUBLIC PATRONAGE: NEW DEAL SCHOOLS AS SOCIAL INFRASTRUCTURE

Speaking of schools as indispensable civic anchors, as "a shared commitment to the common good," the American sociologist Eric Klinenberg has argued that:

> "Schools are organizations but they're also social infrastructures…. For students, teachers, parents, and entire communities, schools can either foster or inhibit trust, solidarity, and a shared commitment to the common good…. There is a considerable body of psychological research showing that peer groups and school environments affect child development far more than parents do."[2]

Schools as civic armatures emerged in the late nineteenth century, forged amid the sweeping public works experiments of modernity in the United States. Before the New Deal, public school construction was driven by a broad faith in universal education rather than federal policy. Nineteenth century reformers, such as Horace Mann in Massachusetts and Thaddeus Stevens in Pennsylvania, saw free common schools as a bedrock for democracy, a principle enshrined in Pennsylvania's 1834 Free Public Schools Act. Early teachers' unions echoed that ideal, calling for cooperative, self-managed schools under the banner "Democracy in Education; Education for Democracy."[3] In 1907, William Wirt, inspired by the philosophies of John Dewey and Frederick Taylor, put into place the "Work-Study-Play" plan or "Gary Plan," with "its emphasis on activity-based learning and the school's role in developing community."[4] Students rotated between workshops, classrooms, and playgrounds, allowing every space to stay active all day. This idea of the school as the microcosm for a community or "a city within a city" resonated with many modernist architects in later decades.[5] The architect William Ittner translated this idea into fire-proof, light-filled E-, U-, and H-shaped buildings with broad corridors, tall windows, gyms, pools, libraries, and workshops—amenities justified as social infrastructure despite their cost. Pittsburgh embraced Wirt's vision with projects like Schenley High School—a Beaux-Arts landmark funded by public and philanthropic sources and widely celebrated as the pride of Pittsburgh's public schools. The board extended this model with Greenfield Elementary (1922)—equipped with workshops, gyms, a pool, and a 660-seat auditorium—and later at Westinghouse, Allderdice, and several other schools.

Gaining prominence in military parlance of the Second World War and postwar years, the term "infrastructure" was first used to describe the relatively invisible systems of hard engineering—roadways, ports, bridges, tunnels, water, or sewage lines. While modernist paradigms of infrastructure privileged this idea of a concrete, literal, and figurative foundation necessary for civilization to thrive, the term "public works" only gained prominence during the New Deal era. There has been much scholarship and documentation on the astonishing scale of The New Deal projects as a form of "cultural infrastructure."[6] The Final Report on the WPA Program, 1935–1943 claims 45,000 new and 85,000 improved buildings. This includes 5,900 new schools; 9,300 new auditoriums, gyms, and

2 Eric Klinenberg, *Palaces for the People: How Social Infrastructure Can Help Fight Inequality, Polarization, and the Decline of Civic Life* (Crown, 2018).

3 Christopher Phelps, "Why Did Teachers Organize? Feminism and Socialism in the Making of New York City Teacher Unionism," *Modern American History* 4, no. 2 (2021): 131–58.

4 Kerry Ellard, "Gary, Indiana and the Complicated History of Education in America," Montessorium (blog), March 2, 2022, https://montessorium.com/blog/gary-indiana-and-the-complicated-history-of-education-in-america.

5 For more on the continued relevance of the Gary Plan see Kevin Kaluf and George Rogers, "The Gary Plan: A Model for Today's Education?" *Journal of STEM Teacher Education* 48, no. 1 (2011): 13–21. The idea of the school as a city-within-a-city inspired the school designs of many modernist architects—notably Aldo van Eyck and Herman Hertzberger.

6 For more on how the New Deal shaped the cultural landscape of the United States see Richard D. McKinzie, *The New Deal for Artists* (Princeton University Press, 1973); Victoria Grieve, *The Federal Art Project and the Creation of Middlebrow Culture* (University of Illinois Press, 2009); Jerre Mangione, *The Dream and the Deal: The Federal Writers' Project, 1935–1943* (University of Pennsylvania Press, 1983); and Robert D. Leighninger, "Cultural Infrastructure: The Legacy of New Deal Public Space," *Journal of Architectural Education* 49, no. 4 (1996): 226–36.

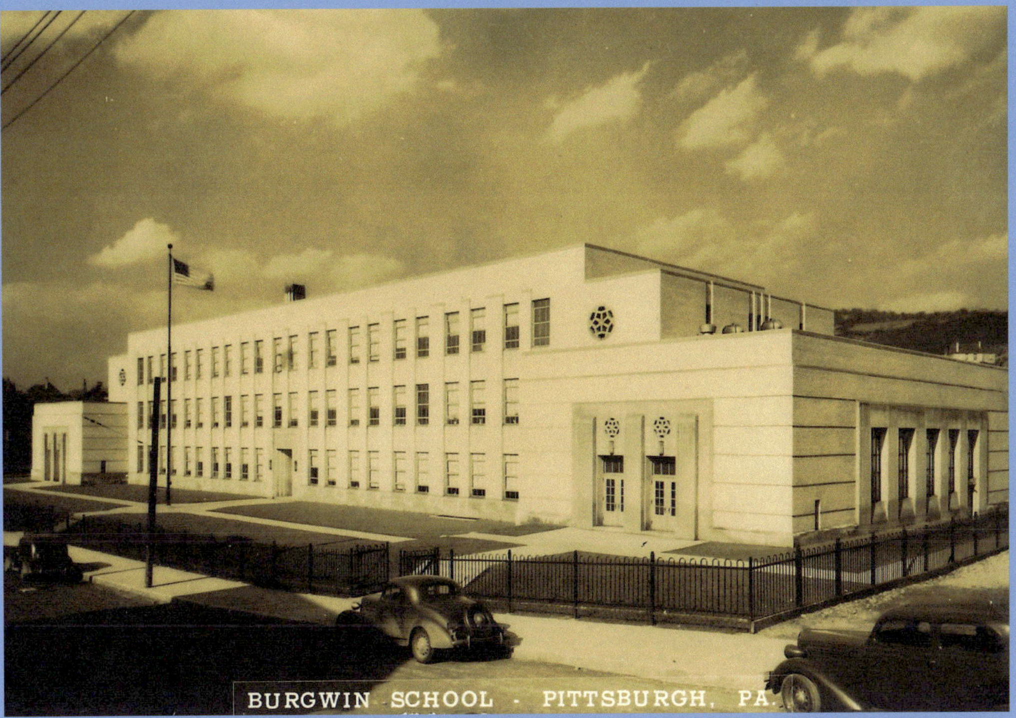

Postcard of Burgwin Elementary School, ca. 1940s; Carnegie Museum of Art

recreational buildings; 1,000 new libraries; 7,000 new dormitories; and 900 new armories.[7] In addition to the WPA, federal agencies like the Public Works Administration (PWA) funded the design and construction of thousands of public schools across the country.

Through a stupendous series of government programs, the Roosevelt administration not only aimed to create jobs in the wake of the Great Depression but also to catalyze a national leap in infrastructure development while cultivating a vision of democratic citizenship rooted in public investment.[8] Federal investment went beyond the building of roads and rural electrification to include aspects of social infrastructure, such as public buildings, parks, libraries, and—notably—public schools.[9] Public works projects as executed by various New Deal entities were instrumental in putting together much of the foundation for "a common good" that carried the promise of modernity and produced a prosperous and aspiring American middle class in the postwar years.[10] While officially championed as universal, such social infrastructures for the "common good" were often built on exclusion—particularly of communities of color and Indigenous peoples—and in many cases enabled or reinforced explicitly racist policies like redlining.[11] It was not until 1954 that segregation was outlawed in public schools across the country. These structural injustices notwithstanding, the New Deal framed public works as a democratic project of national recovery and civic life and even sponsored the construction and repair of public schools.

New Deal architecture funded directly by the PWA included the construction of Burgwin Elementary School (built 1937 and closed since 2006), Lemington Elementary School (built 1937 and on the National Register of Historic places as a significant Art-Deco building; closed and now operating as a charter school), Washington Trade School in Lawrenceville, (also known as the Washington Education Center; built 1936–1937, operational until 1969; a TRYP hotel since 2019), and extensions or improvements for several schools, including Perry Hill School,

7 Federal Works Administration, *Final Report on the WPA Program, 1935–1943*, (Government Printing Office, 1946), 52.

8 Borrowing from an unpublished thesis by **Jean Weir**, *WPA Experiment in Architecture and Crafts*, Robert Leighninger makes the interesting observation that while taking people off relief and job-creation was the initial goal of The Works Public Administration (WPA), it evolved to include infrastructural ambitions, and in the longer term "the social rather than the economic outlook became more and more pronounced." **Robert D. Leighninger,** "Cultural Infrastructure: The Legacy of New Deal Public Space," *Journal of Architectural Education* 49, no. 4 (1996): 226, https://doi.org/10.2307/1425295.

9 For an extensive documentation of The New Deal see "Living New Deal Map," *Living New Deal*, accessed June 12, 2025, https://livingnewdeal.org/map; see also "School Sites," *Living New Deal*, accessed June 12, 2025, https://livingnewdeal.org/new-deal-categories/education-health/schools/.

10 To name a few, the Civilian Conservation Corps (CCC), Federal Emergency Relief Administration (FERA), Civil Works Administration (CWA), Works Progress Administration (WPA), and National Youth Administration (NYA), the Public Works Administration (PWA), Tennessee Valley Authority (TVA), and the Virgin Islands Company.

11 Two key New Deal housing agencies—the Home Owners' Loan Corporation (HOLC, est. 1933) and the Federal Housing Administration (FHA, est. 1934)—formalized the practice of what came to be known as "red-lining" through mapping and underwriting rules. Those federal guidelines were created to revive the mortgage market during the Depression—racial segregation was long embedded into the country's housing system well before The New Deal. For a nuanced rendition of The New Deal's impact on African Americans see: "African Americans," Living New Deal, https://livingnewdeal.org/racism-and-beyond/new-deal-inclusion/african-americans-2/; and **Katie Rader,** "No, the New Deal Wasn't Racist," *Catalyst: A Journal of Theory and Strategy* 8, no.1 (2024).

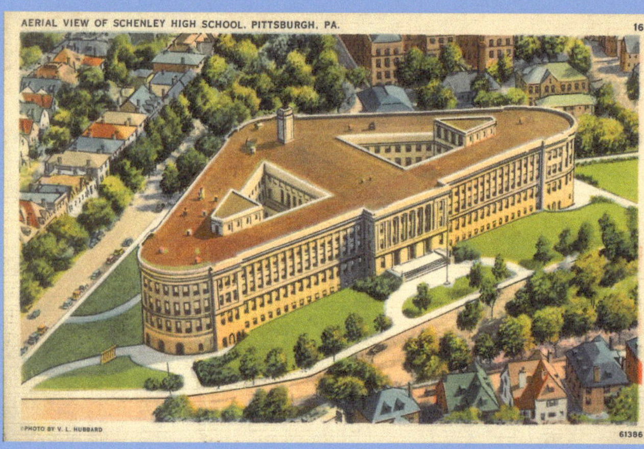

Postcard of Schenley High School, Pittsburgh News Company, ca. 1940; Carnegie Museum of Art

Spring Hill Elementary School (still in use as a school), and Prospect School (closed in 2006 and since converted to apartments).[12] During this period of school construction in Pittsburgh, the city's centralized School Board (1935–1954) maintained an in-house architectural team led by Marion M. Steen. As Staff Architect and later Superintendent of Buildings, Steen oversaw the construction of twenty-three new schools and major additions.[13]

The New Deal represented a form of federal architectural patronage that was unprecedented in its scale, as well as the explicit use of "building" for social welfare, translating into thousands of local public works projects and schools. It did not sponsor a single architectural style, but projects encompassed Beaux-Arts, classicism, Art Deco, and some innovative modernist experiments.

SCHOOL CLOSURES AND ALTERNATIVE FUTURES

After its controversial closure in 2008, Schenley High sat vacant until it was sold in 2013 and transformed into 180 luxury apartments by PMC Property Group. Alumni, preservationists, and several school board members argued that an architecturally significant school the district once insured for tens of millions was being "given away" for a fraction of its worth. One board member asked why a building he believed could fetch "ninety million" was being sold for five.[14] Others resented handing a public asset to a luxury developer when charter school and community reuse proposals were on the table.[15] Finally, many parents never accepted the original rationale for closing Schenley—dangerous asbestos—insisting the hazard had been overstated to justify shuttering the school, only to see the same shell marketed for private profit. The final design adaptation marketed many of the building's original features—including oak doors, classroom chalkboards, large windows, and high ceilings—as desirable amenities for private condominiums.

Several other Pittsburgh public schools from the pre-New Deal Era, most of which are over a hundred years old, have come to the same end as Schenley High. The Romanesque-style Latimer School in Deutschtown (built 1898) became the 77-unit boutique residential complex School House Apartments in 1985. In Upper Lawrenceville, the red-brick McCleary School (built 1900–1902) was decommissioned in 2012 and, between 2015 and 2017, was reborn as 25 condominium units.[16] Its promotional website brags of the condos' public school lineage: "original chalkboards, built-ins and post turn [sic] of the 20th Century details have been left in place."[17] The Fifth Avenue School, built as Pennsylvania's first fireproof school (1894), was closed in 1976 and redeveloped in 2012 into the 65-unit Fifth Avenue School Lofts. The building's preserved Gothic Revival detailing—including plaster ceilings and arched hallways—attests to the craftsmanship that once defined public investment in education.[18] Other examples abound: the Larimer School (1896–1980) is now being transformed into 35 mixed-income apartments; the Bayard School (built 1874) was redeveloped in 2018 into Italianate-style residential lofts; the Prospect School (1931), a striking Art Deco structure, was adapted into apartments

12 The New Deal also contributed some federal funds to complete the iconic Cathedral of Learning, a Pittsburgh landmark. "Cathedral of Learning (Continuing Work) Pittsburgh PA," Living New Deal, https://livingnewdeal.org/sites/cathedral-of-learning-pittsburgh-pa; Katie Blackley. "How the Works Progress Administration helped build Pittsburgh," 90.5 *WESA Pittsburgh's NPR News Station*, January 8, 2024.

13 "Pittsburgh Public Schools National Register of Historic Places Inventory–Nomination Form," U.S. Department of the Interior, September 30, 1986.

14 "School Board Votes in Favor of Selling Old Schenley High School Building," *WPXI.com*, February 28, 2013.

15 Chris Young, "Class Dismissed," *Pittsburgh City Paper*, January 31, 2008.

16 Tracy Certo, "Rehab of McCleary School Condos in Lawrenceville Preserves History for 25 Units," *NEXTPittsburgh*, November 17, 2015; Richard Cook, "Pittsburgh Then and Now: Fifth Avenue School," *Pittsburgh Magazine*, May 6, 2019.

17 "McCleary School Condos," https://mcclearyschoolcondos.com.

18 Richard Cook, "Pittsburgh Then and Now: Fifth Avenue School," *Pittsburgh Magazine*, May 6, 2019.

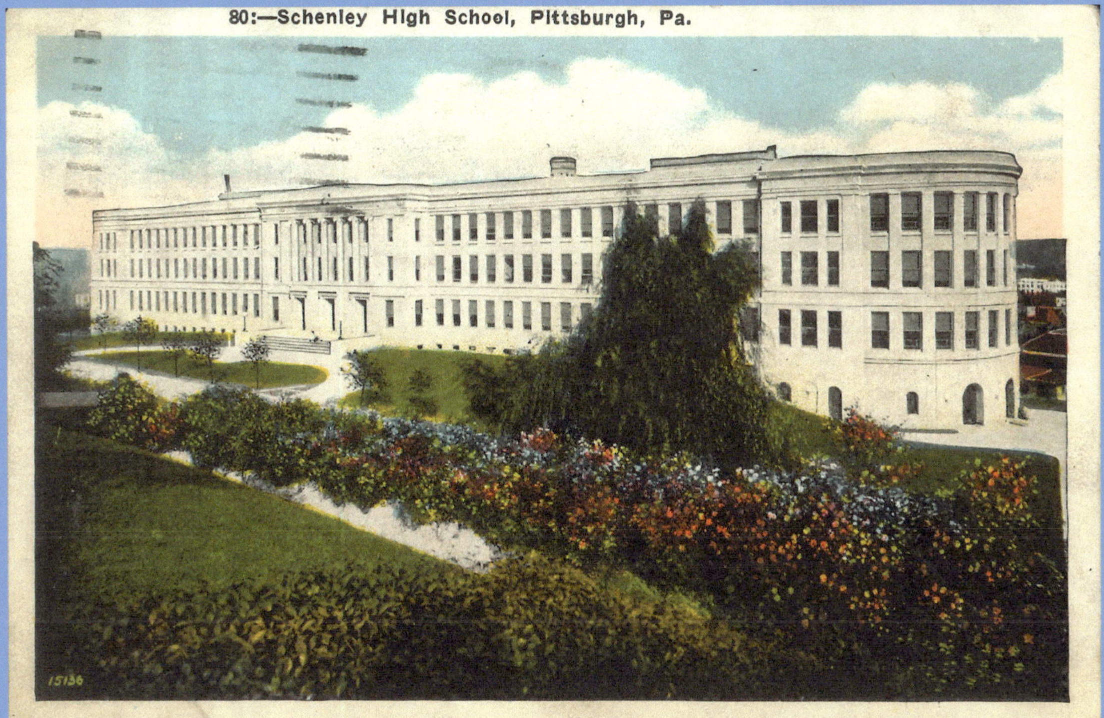

Postcard of Schenley High School, Minksy Brothers & Co., ca. 1920; Carnegie Museum of Art

post-2006; and the Deniston School in Swissvale (1902) began a $3 million conversion into 18 condominiums in 2017.[19] Impressively, most of these buildings, built through tax-payer public funds, are on the National Register of Historic Places.[20]

The hollowing out of public schools is the result of deliberate policies that prioritized markets over the commons. The rise of neoliberalism in the 1970s and 80s saw waves of disinvestment from public spending and public infrastructure, resulting in deep federal disinvestment, property tax-based funding models, and an education-for-profit model that favored private and charter schools. The ideal of public education as a shared civic project has eroded, disproportionately affecting poorer neighborhoods and communities of color.[21] A benchmark of inequality, by 2017 three American billionaires owned more wealth than 50% of the country, even as middle-class wages stagnated and worker productivity soared.[22] This is particularly relevant for public schools whose construction and upkeep depend on local property taxes. In Pittsburgh, large tax-exempt nonprofits and foundations make nominal contributions by way of taxes. This is why stagnant household incomes translate into chronically underfunded classrooms. Starved of resources, the district defers maintenance, public buildings deteriorate, and schools deeply cherished within their communities are sold off—an austerity spiral that steadily undermines both public assets and public trust.

The crisis facing public schools mirrors a broader pattern of infrastructural decline across the United States. Key infrastructure systems in the United States are rapidly aging and in need of care, repair, and replacement. A 2025 Infrastructure Report Card from The American Society of Civil Engineers graded core infrastructure systems, from transit to drinking water, in the "D" range.[23] Public Schools scored a D+, indicating poor, at-risk status. The over 98,000 public Pre-K through 12 schools serving nearly 50 million students are, on average, forty-nine years old. Despite this, "only 10% of total school spending in 2021–2022

19 Emily Stimmel, "A Historic, Rundown Swissvale Schoolhouse Will Soon House 28 New Condos, Some Affordable," *NEXTPittsburgh*, February 12, 2018.

20 Albert M. Tanler, "20 Pittsburgh Public Schools Designated as City of Pittsburgh Historic Structures," Pittsburgh History and Landmarks Foundation, March 2001.

21 For an insight into the racialized implications of neoliberalism in school policy, see: Lester Spence, *Knocking the Hustle: Against the Neoliberal Turn in Black Politics* (Punctum Books, 2015). Spence defines neoliberalism "as a loose set of ideas, [practices, and strategies], that market principles should govern how society should work."

22 Noah Kirsch, "The 3 Richest Americans Hold More Wealth Than Bottom 50% Of The Country, Study Finds," *Forbes Magazine*, January 25, 2018; Lawrence Mishel, Elise Gould, and Josh Bivens, "Wage Stagnation in Nine Charts," Economic Policy Institute, January 6, 2015, https://www.epi.org/publication/charting-wage-stagnation/.

23 American Society of Civil Engineers, *A Comprehensive Assessment of America's Infrastructure: 2025 Report Card*, 2025, https://infrastructurereportcard.org/wp-content/uploads/2025/03/Full-Report-2025-Natl-IRC-WEB.pdf.

was directed to facility expenses, a total that has been low for decades, and a majority of which is dedicated toward new construction versus maintenance of existing buildings."[24]

Pittsburgh Public Schools are a symptom of this larger national crisis of public education. Ninety percent of public schools face costly renovations. The Facilities Condition Index (FCI), a system used in building construction to determine the facility's physical condition, is a critical metric for determining school closures. The system considers the state of roofing, exterior and interior walls, windows, doors, as well as building systems like heating, air conditioning, plumbing fire and life safety, structural condition, technology, and accessibility. The FCI score is the ratio between the "cost to maintain and upgrade the facility to a good condition" versus the "cost to tear down and replace the facility, ranking buildings from 'good' to 'poor.'"[25] In Pittsburgh, PPS is moving forward with plans to close or "right-size" multiple public schools, largely based on recommendations derived from a FCI report prepared by a private consulting firm, though the exact modality of these closures continues to be debated.[26] Judging schools by their state of disrepair, after decades of deliberate defunding and neglect, reveals the circular logic of austerity. This is reflective of a deeper critique of the civilizational model of our contemporary time: a late-capitalist patriarchy where public policy is still shaped by paradigms that continue to favor austerity and disinvestment, while directly maximizing the growth and accumulation of private capital.

Yet, the district's impetus to close schools arises from some complex financial considerations. For instance, student enrollment in the school district has thinned for decades, symptomatic of national trends, falling from more than 40,000 in the late 1990s to around 18,380 today. Enrollment is expected to be under 14,000 by 2031.[27] As the population of schools shrinks, smaller cohorts leave half-empty buildings that are expensive to heat and staff. The average cost per student rises, as some city schools remain the lowest performing in the state. Administrators argue that combining two half-full buildings can lower costs per student and redirect scarce dollars to instruction; a slimmed-down footprint appears fiscally prudent. However, this translates immediately into school shutdowns and the permanent alienation of civic assets without involving neighborhood residents' considerations.

In 2013, Chicago shuttered fifty schools, the largest mass closure in U.S. history. Yet, ten years later, more than half of these structures remain unused, including ones that were sold to the private sector.[28] Rachel Weber, professor of urban planning and policy at the University of Illinois Chicago, makes the observation that in the rush to sell and privatize, communities living in close proximity to these schools were not involved in their futures. Others similarly argue that "there should have been some kind of priority given or weight to affordable housing developers and developers of senior housing… The city prioritized private, sort of market-led redevelopment instead."[29] In accordance with national trends, the current district policy and Pennsylvania School Code follow a common market-oriented neoliberal model where the district "will engage a real estate firm to assess the value of, market, and manage the sale of these properties."[30]

A school building, by way of its very presence in a community, creates forms of social infrastructure beyond the education of students. It provides a hub for parents and community members to meet, playgrounds to host sporting events, and large gathering spaces to host various functions—from job fairs to pop-up health clinics. When an

24 ASCE, *A Comprehensive Assessment of America's Infrastructure.*

25 For more on Pittsburgh Public Schools' Facilities Condition Index see, **Megan Tomasic,** "Pittsburgh Public Recommending 12 School Closures under Newly Revised Plan," *Pittsburgh Post-Gazette*, May 21, 2025; **Jillian Forstadt and Lajja Mistry,** "PPS Records Show 90% of Buildings Need Costly Renovations as District Weighs School Closures," 90.5 WESA, August 8, 2024.

26 At times the term "Facilities Utilization Plan" is used by the PPS, but the logic of austerity and "right-sizing" remains. For the most recent Future-Ready Facilities Plan, see: https://www.pghschools.org/about/superintendent-of-schools/future-ready.

27 **Lajja Mistry,** "While Pittsburgh's District Bleeds Students, a Few Schools Grow," *PUBLICSOURCE*, January 9, 2024.

28 **Lauren FitzPatrick, Nader Issa, Sarah Karp, and Alden Loury,** "Ten Years Later, More than Half of Chicago's Closed Schools Remain Unused," *Chicago Sun Times*, May 18, 2023.

29 **FitzPatrick, Issa, et al,** "Ten Years Later."

30 According to the PPS Closed Building Disposition Plan, "In accordance with Board Policy No. 814 and the Pennsylvania School Code any building disposition will follow established procedures. Upon the closure of the 10 additional facilities, the District will engage a real estate firm to assess the value of, market, and manage the sale of these properties." "Future Ready Facilities Plan," *Pittsburgh Public Schools*, last updated May 19, 2025, https://www.pghschools.org/about/superintendent-of-schools/facilities-utilization-plan-new.

underprivileged neighborhood loses a school, it loses a form of social infrastructure, a civic commons. A large, abandoned facility with boarded-up windows drives down local property values and deepens the sense of decline within the neighborhood. What if the cycle of viewing schools as "under-performing assets" were reversed? What if we considered schools as vital hubs of social infrastructure? Might community nonprofits and local businesses be invited to host a range of programs determined upon by the community for its needs—health centers, cooperative kitchens, makerspaces, after-hours libraries?

The city of Pittsburgh has a robust network of nonprofits, like the Pittsburgh Land Bank and the City of Bridges Community Land Trust (CBCLT), which demonstrate how property might be held in "banks" outside of real-estate speculation. These banks allow for the development of much needed long-term, affordable housing. Imagine, then, a "School Commons Trust" that folds surplus buildings into the same public interest portfolio that already shelters vacant lots for the City of Bridges Community Land Trust. The title would remain with the district or, perhaps, shift to local community organizations or nonprofits, who in turn might lease classrooms at symbolic rents in exchange for community engagement and care. Revenue would circle back into maintenance, creating fiscal sustainability. Because the structures already meet life safety codes, boasting generous daylight and wide corridors, their conversion costs are far lower than new construction. Likewise, their meaning is woven into local memory. Their reuse brings renewed life to streets and the neighborhood at large, where boarded-up windows once signaled abandonment.

Such alternative futures for public schools would endorse the value of these buildings as essential social infrastructures. Early twentieth century architects in Pittsburgh built schools so that working-class children might find a seat at democracy's table. These buildings were large, spacious public institutions that allowed for cross programming, heating, ventilation, and daylighting. They set the stage for education to become, in bell hooks' words, "a practice of freedom."[31] The New Deal established public patronage as a primary vehicle for public infrastructure and championed the building, extension, care, and repair of schools. Concurrently, it also produced mechanisms for the financing and building of social infrastructure at an unprecedented scale. At a time when architectural patronage has reduced almost entirely to the private sector, it is worth remembering that not so long ago, such patronage was tied to building public institutions of social resonance. To disregard these public assets—at a moment when the city is faced with several crises of social infrastructure, including an acute shortage of affordable housing—is to squander the public inheritance of the city and its communities. Even after the last school bell rings, can school buildings become what they have always aspired to be: spaces of shared learning and care that offer the courage to dream otherwise?

31 bell hooks, *Teaching to Transgress: Education as the Practice of Freedom* (Routledge, 1994), title page.

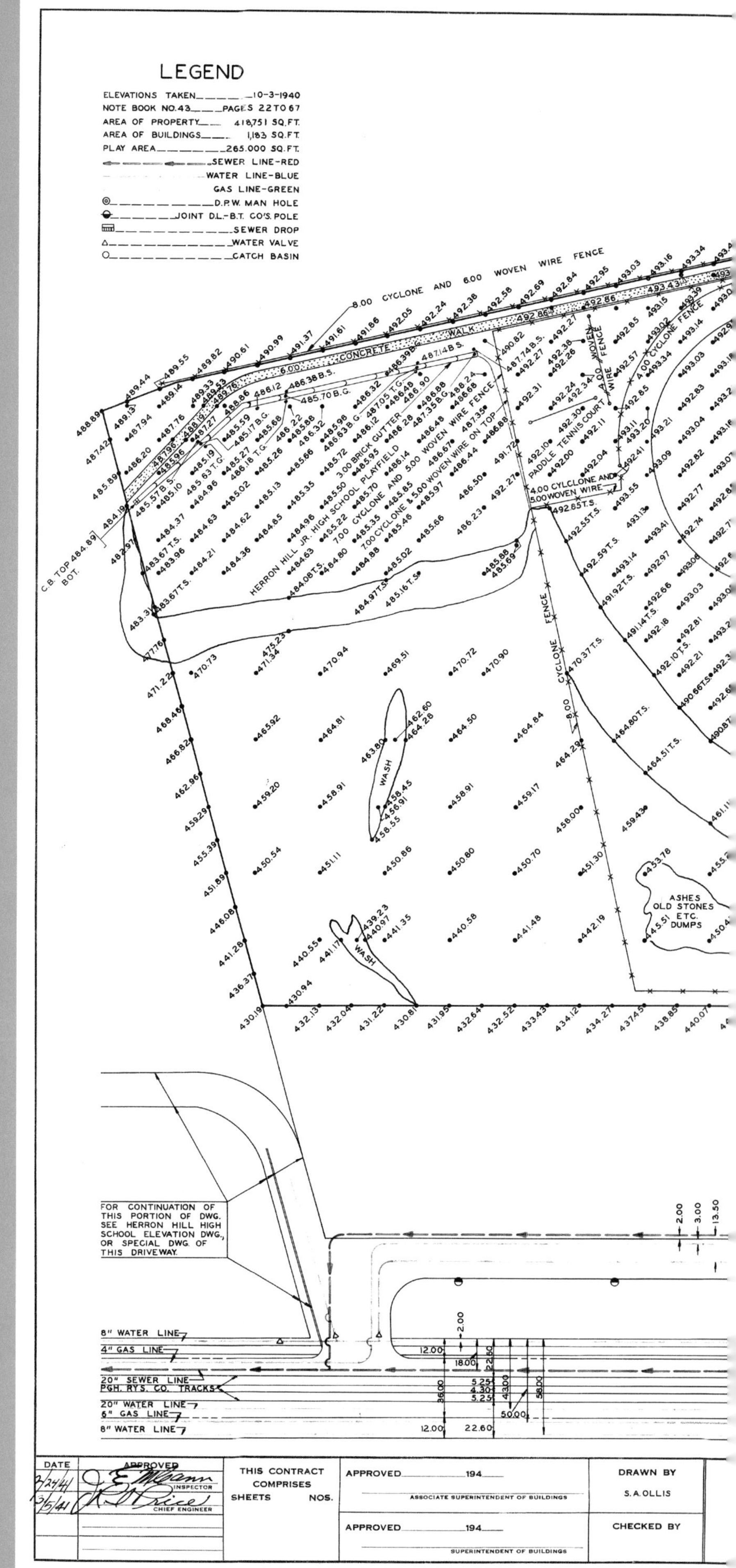
LEGEND
ELEVATIONS TAKEN___________10-3-1940
NOTE BOOK NO. 43_____PAGES 22 TO 67
AREA OF PROPERTY_____418,751 SQ. FT.
AREA OF BUILDINGS_____1,183 SQ. FT.
PLAY AREA_________265,000 SQ. FT.
SEWER LINE-RED
WATER LINE-BLUE
GAS LINE-GREEN
D.P.W. MAN HOLE
JOINT D.L.-B.T. CO'S. POLE
SEWER DROP
WATER VALVE
CATCH BASIN
8.00 CYCLONE AND 6.00 WOVEN WIRE FENCE
6.00 CONCRETE WALK
4.00 CYCLONE FENCE
PADDLE TENNIS COURT
4.00 CYCLONE AND 5.00 WOVEN WIRE
HERRON HILL JR. HIGH SCHOOL PLAYFIELD
3.00 BRICK GUTTER
7.00 CYCLONE 8.00 WOVEN WIRE FENCE
5.00 WOVEN WIRE ON TOP
CYCLONE FENCE
WASH
WASH
ASHES OLD STONES ETC. DUMPS
FOR CONTINUATION OF THIS PORTION OF DWG. SEE HERRON HILL HIGH SCHOOL ELEVATION DWG., OR SPECIAL DWG. OF THIS DRIVEWAY.
8" WATER LINE
4" GAS LINE
20" SEWER LINE
PGH. RYS. CO. TRACKS
20" WATER LINE
6" GAS LINE
8" WATER LINE
DATE
APPROVED
INSPECTOR
CHIEF ENGINEER
THIS CONTRACT COMPRISES SHEETS NOS.
APPROVED______194___
ASSOCIATE SUPERINTENDENT OF BUILDINGS
APPROVED______194___
SUPERINTENDENT OF BUILDINGS
DRAWN BY
S. A. OLLIS
CHECKED BY

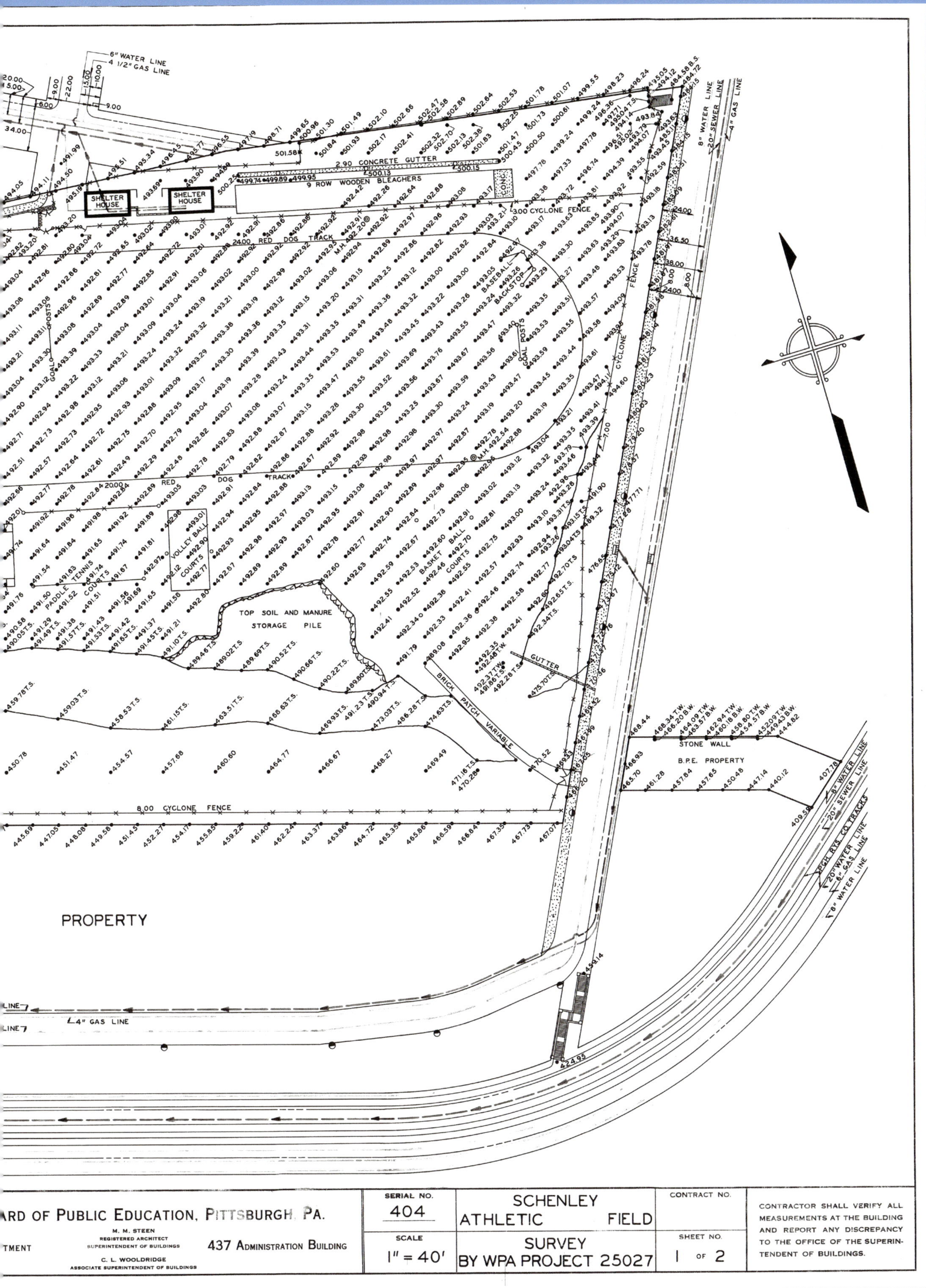
6" WATER LINE
4 1/2" GAS LINE
SHELTER HOUSE
SHELTER HOUSE
2.90 CONCRETE GUTTER
9 ROW WOODEN BLEACHERS
24.00 RED DOG TRACK
3.00 CYCLONE FENCE
BASEBALL BACKSTOP
GOAL POSTS
CYCLONE FENCE
8" WATER LINE
20" SEWER LINE
4" GAS LINE
RED DOG TRACK
20.00
VOLLEY BALL COURTS
TENNIS COURTS
PADDLE TENNIS COURTS
GOAL POSTS
BASKET BALL COURTS
TOP SOIL AND MANURE STORAGE PILE
BRICK PATCH VARIABLE
GUTTER
STONE WALL
B.P.E. PROPERTY
8.00 CYCLONE FENCE
PROPERTY
8" WATER LINE
20" SEWER LINE
P.R.R. CO. TRACKS
6" WATER LINE
6" GAS LINE
8" WATER LINE
4" GAS LINE
BOARD OF PUBLIC EDUCATION, PITTSBURGH, PA.
M. M. STEEN
REGISTERED ARCHITECT
SUPERINTENDENT OF BUILDINGS
437 ADMINISTRATION BUILDING
C. L. WOOLDRIDGE
ASSOCIATE SUPERINTENDENT OF BUILDINGS
SERIAL NO. 404
SCHENLEY ATHLETIC FIELD
SURVEY BY WPA PROJECT 25027
SCALE 1" = 40'
CONTRACT NO.
SHEET NO. 1 OF 2
CONTRACTOR SHALL VERIFY ALL MEASUREMENTS AT THE BUILDING AND REPORT ANY DISCREPANCY TO THE OFFICE OF THE SUPERINTENDENT OF BUILDINGS.

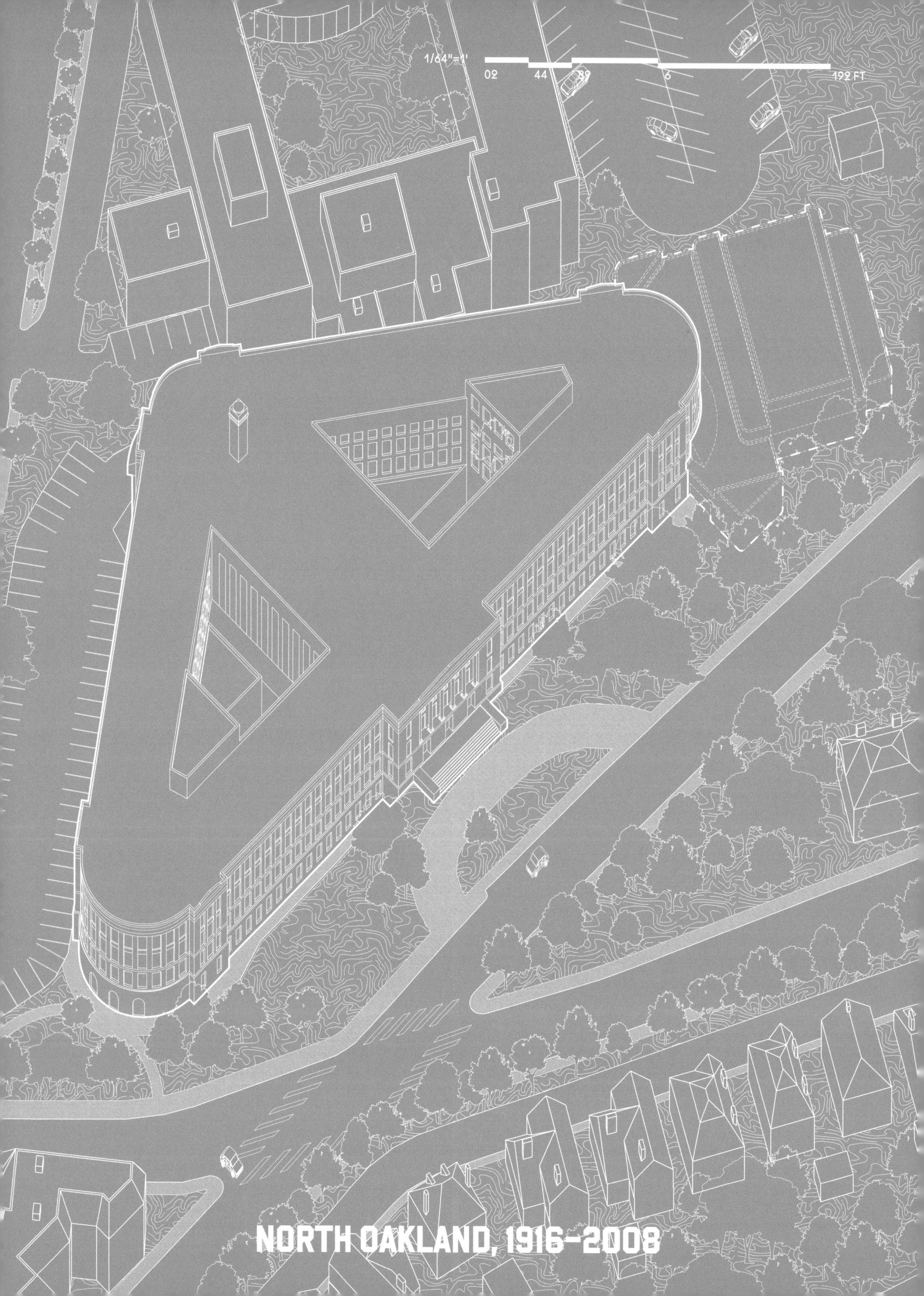

1/64"=1'
02   44   89   6   192 FT
NORTH OAKLAND, 1916-2008

Established as Pittsburgh Central in 1855, the city's first public high school was relocated to North Oakland and renamed Schenley in 1916. Architect Edward Stotz, Sr. designed the school's colossal, million-dollar building known as "the Triangle," which arranged classrooms, science labs, art and craft studios, and a swimming pool along three corridors, forming a sharp triangular loop around two central gymnasia and a tiered auditorium. For decades, the school served generations of working-class families and immigrants, particularly from the neighboring Hill District. Students received both academic instruction and hands-on vocational training, including trades and technical skills. In the 1980s, amid federal desegregation mandates, Schenley piloted specialized magnet programs and a teaching training lab that garnered national attention and boosted student enrollment. By the early 2000s, however, the district cited asbestos, deferred maintenance, and budget cuts to justify closing the school. Despite a determined community-led campaign to prevent its shutdown, the school closed in 2008. Today, it is a luxury apartment building; its civic purpose stripped away.

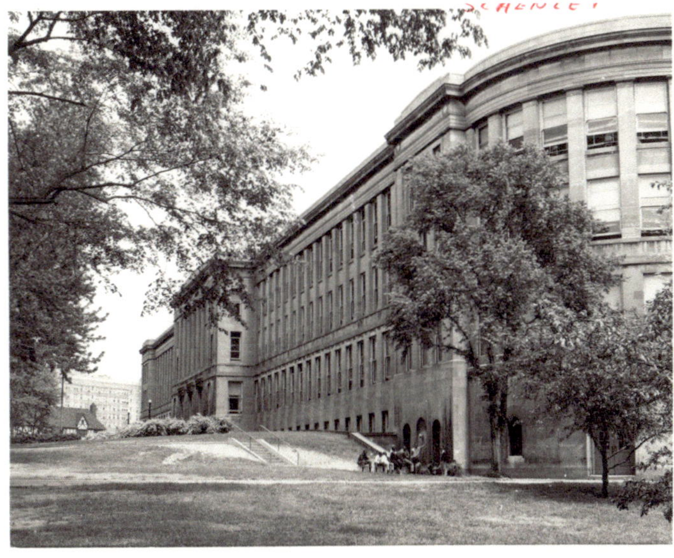

SCHENLEY HIGH SCHOOL

CAUGHT IN A TRIANGULAR LOOP James Hill

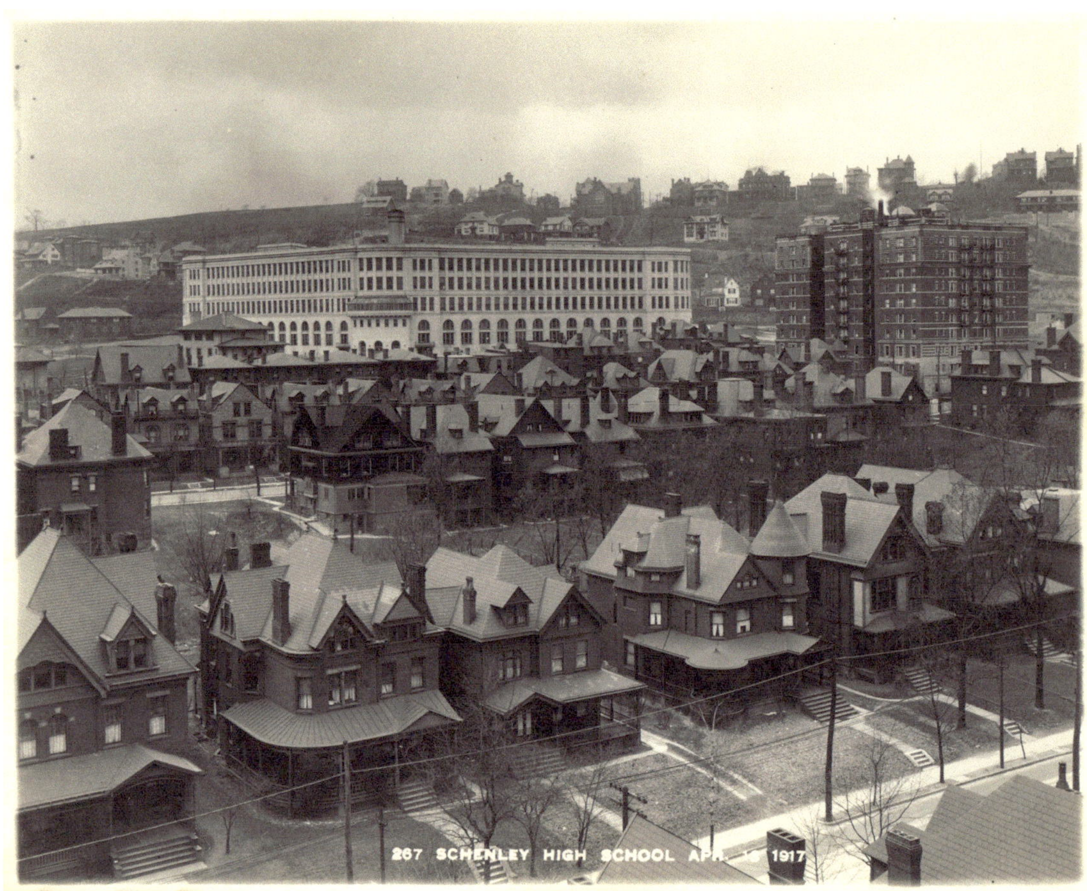

SCHENLEY high SCHOOL HAS always held an outsized space in My mind.

Previous page: Schenley High School, ca. 1950, photograph; Detre Library & Archives, HHC

Above: Schenley High School and surrounding neighborhood, April 13, 1917, photograph; Detre Library & Archives, HHC

As a child, Schenley was where my sister and cousins went to school, and where my uncle taught gym and coached track. The building was situated along the route my mother would take down Centre Avenue to my grandma's house in the Hill District. Otherwise hidden by foliage on the Hill or by the angles of other buildings in the East End, Schenley would suddenly explode into view each time we traveled the route. At age nine, it was the largest building I had ever seen. Today, I understand that, as America's first "million-dollar high school," it was meant to project the very ideals of public education: something bigger than yourself. Stable, important, and endless.

But, of course, everything does come to an end. Pittsburgh Public Schools experienced a wave of closures under its 2006 "Right Sizing Plan"—an initiative that primarily targeted elementary schools. At the time, my friends and I were in middle school, so these changes didn't really stick in my mind. We always thought that middle schools and high schools like Schenley were too eternal to ever be closed down.

My most vivid memories of Schenley come from the summer of 2007—just before my first day of freshman year. Pittsburgh Public Schools' 9th Grade Nation program had us spend a few days there, participating

in small classes that discussed summer reading while giving us a chance
to familiarize ourselves with the school. I had been to Schenley before,
of course, for various community programs, prom line-ups, and parent-
teacher conferences. However, as a prospective student, at just thirteen
years old, I approached the school on my own for the first time. For those
few days at Schenley, it was just the freshman class. There were no other
students in the halls, just various teachers preparing their classrooms. I initially remember thinking it was so quiet, but over time, as my friends and
I learned more about the school and its traditions, we slowly felt more
comfortable in the space.

At the time, Schenley just seemed, well, endless. Its unique triangular shape meant the halls lacked any clear beginning or end—a seamless
triangular loop. As I approached the massive oak front doors on my
first day of school in 2007, I thought for the first time that they were the
largest doors I had ever seen. Passing through them into the grand lobby,
the twenty-foot ceilings forced my eyes upwards so quickly that it was
almost easy to miss the nine-foot tall, larger-than-life statue of Augustus
Caesar placed along other friezes safeguarding the lobby. The auditorium where we had our first assembly was equally impressive, with its
massive proscenium arch framed by a pipe organ proclaiming the school's
motto: "Enter to Learn, Go Forth to Serve." It all felt so serious—an
undeniable jump from my previous smaller elementary and unremarkable
middle school buildings.

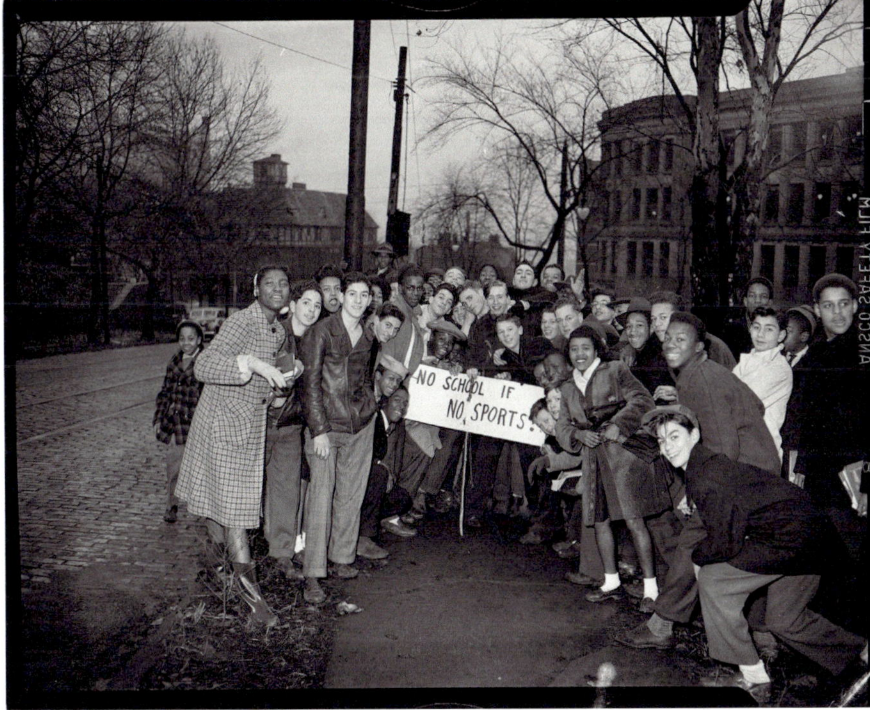

Charles "Teenie" Harris, Outside Schenley
High School, Pittsburgh, PA, November 1945,
photograph; Carnegie Museum of Art, HFF

By the end of 9th Grade Nation, our teacher suggested we finish
our summer reading on the front steps of the school. We filed out of those
grand doors, spread out into groups, and sat down outside on a beautiful
day. With my back to the limestone walls, I sat cross-legged on the right-
hand side of the steps with my copy of *The Last Chance Texaco* in hand as
a gust of wind blew by. I glanced upward to witness two magnolia trees
shed a few of their limited remaining leaves and the school towering over
us. I read the words "Schenley High School" carved in stone and, in that
moment, it just clicked—this was my school now, too.

During a busy freshman year, I learned that quiet was *not* the normal state of Schenley. School traditions, from pep rallies and musicals to the school chant, were loud and echoed through the halls. Schenley was just as much its triangular walls as it was the magnetic energy from an eclectic and diverse mix of students and staff, who made it special amongst the district's high schools. I loved it. I learned that the quiet moments were meant to give way to the loud energy that made the school hum.

After the school year ended, I returned to drop off a few books and found myself, once again, in a rather empty and quiet Schenley High School. At the beginning of the year, this quiet and contemplative experience felt cool, but after a full year there, it no longer felt right. At that moment, I was completely unaware that I would never return as a student to Schenley and all of its noise again. The following school year, the other freshman and I were relocated to Reizenstein Middle School in East Liberty, where we, Schenley's last graduating class, would continue to carry the Schenley Spartans banner while the school was being "phased out." There had been such a vicious public battle to save the school. Many of my friends and I participated in various rallies. I always thought Schenley's closure would be a temporary change, never its end.

Despite having only attended the school for one academic year, my class and I felt more and more protective of Schenley, its name, and its traditions as we said a long goodbye. Even after I graduated from Reizenstein with one of the last Schenley High School diplomas, the school continued to be a constant topic at Board of Public Education meetings. Questions lingered: What would happen to such a prominent place and location next? Should it reopen? Should it be sold to a charter school?

After being sold by Pittsburgh Public Schools in 2013, the Schenley High School building re-opened as apartments a few years later. I took a tour not long after renovations were finished, curious to see what had become of the building. I was surprised to see that, in many ways, it was recognizable, but it was quiet again, which didn't feel right. I haven't been back since, and I no longer drive down that part of Centre Avenue. Some great public buildings are better left existing as loud memories.

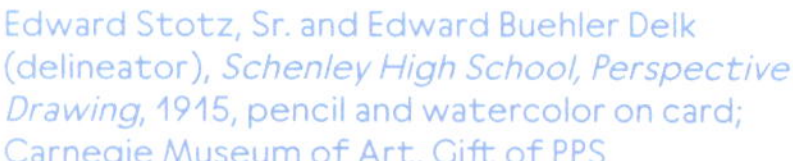

Edward Stotz, Sr. and Edward Buehler Delk (delineator), *Schenley High School, Perspective Drawing*, 1915, pencil and watercolor on card; Carnegie Museum of Art, Gift of PPS

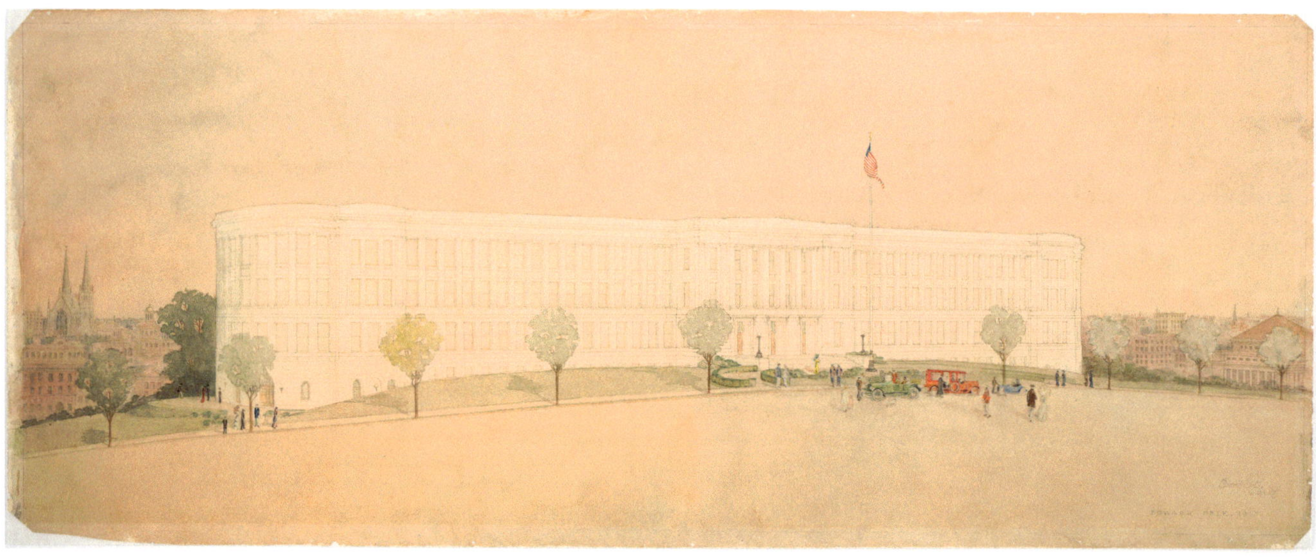

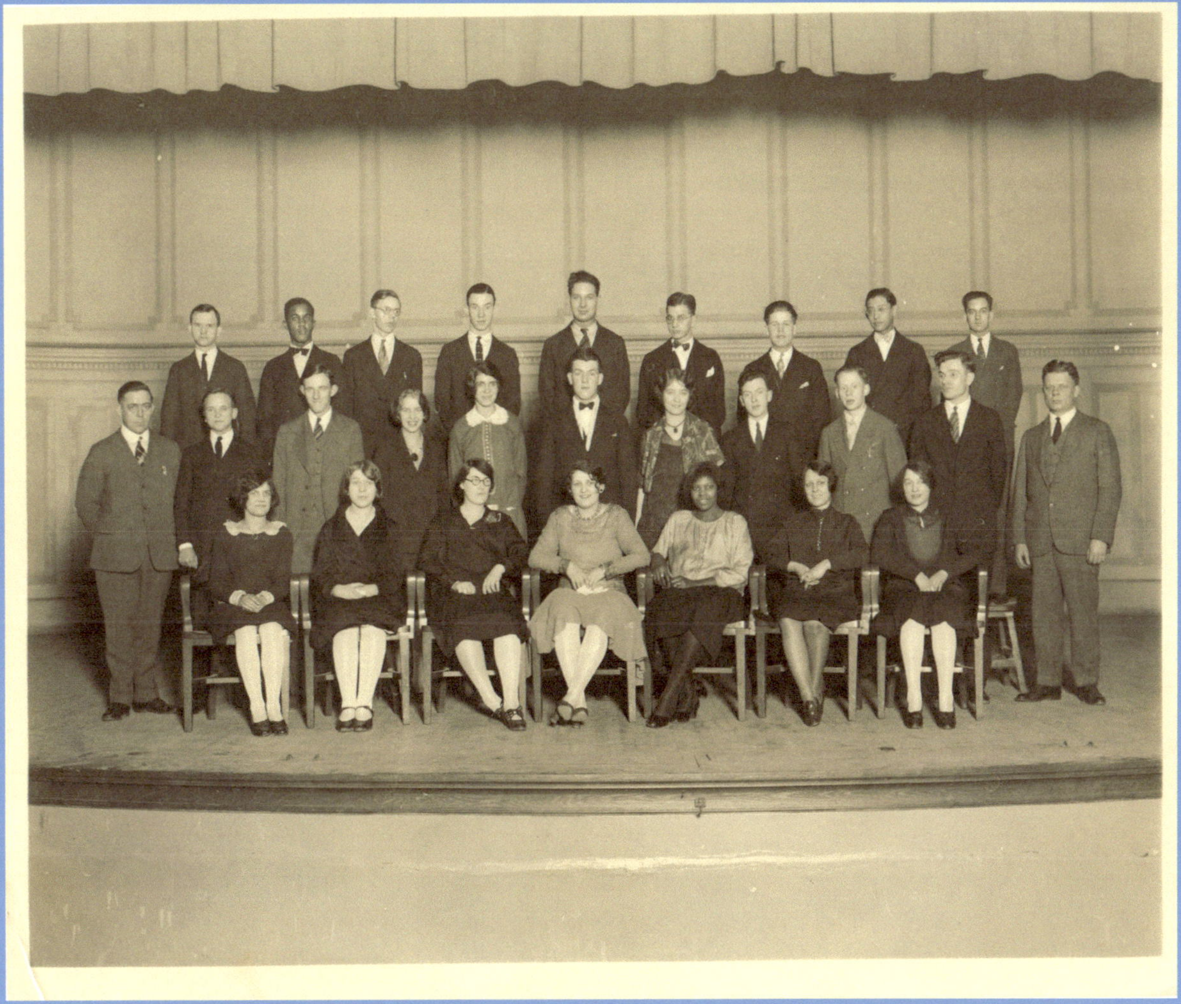

Group picture of Schenley Standard Evening High, 1926, photograph; Pittsburgh Board of Education Archives, CLP

James J. Bonner, senior English teacher at Oliver High School, Nancy Lewonas, Robert Dunscomb, Sally Stephen, Vivian Brooks, and two unidentified County Health Department employees, 1969, photograph; Detre Library & Archives, HHC

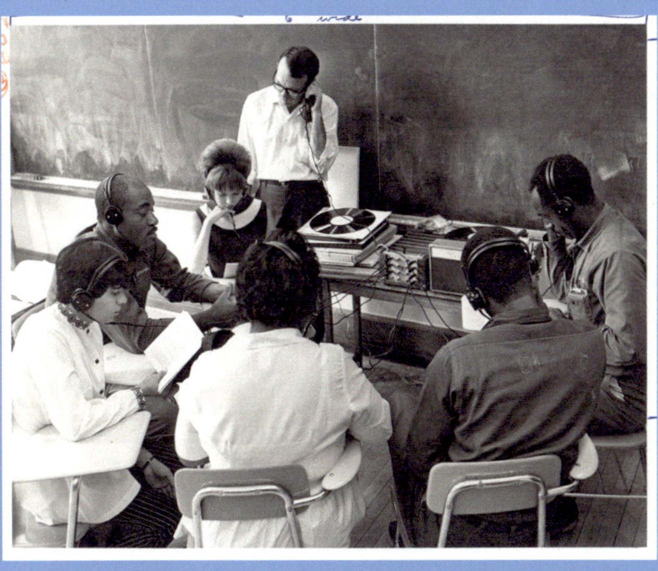

JAMES HILL   Schenley High School

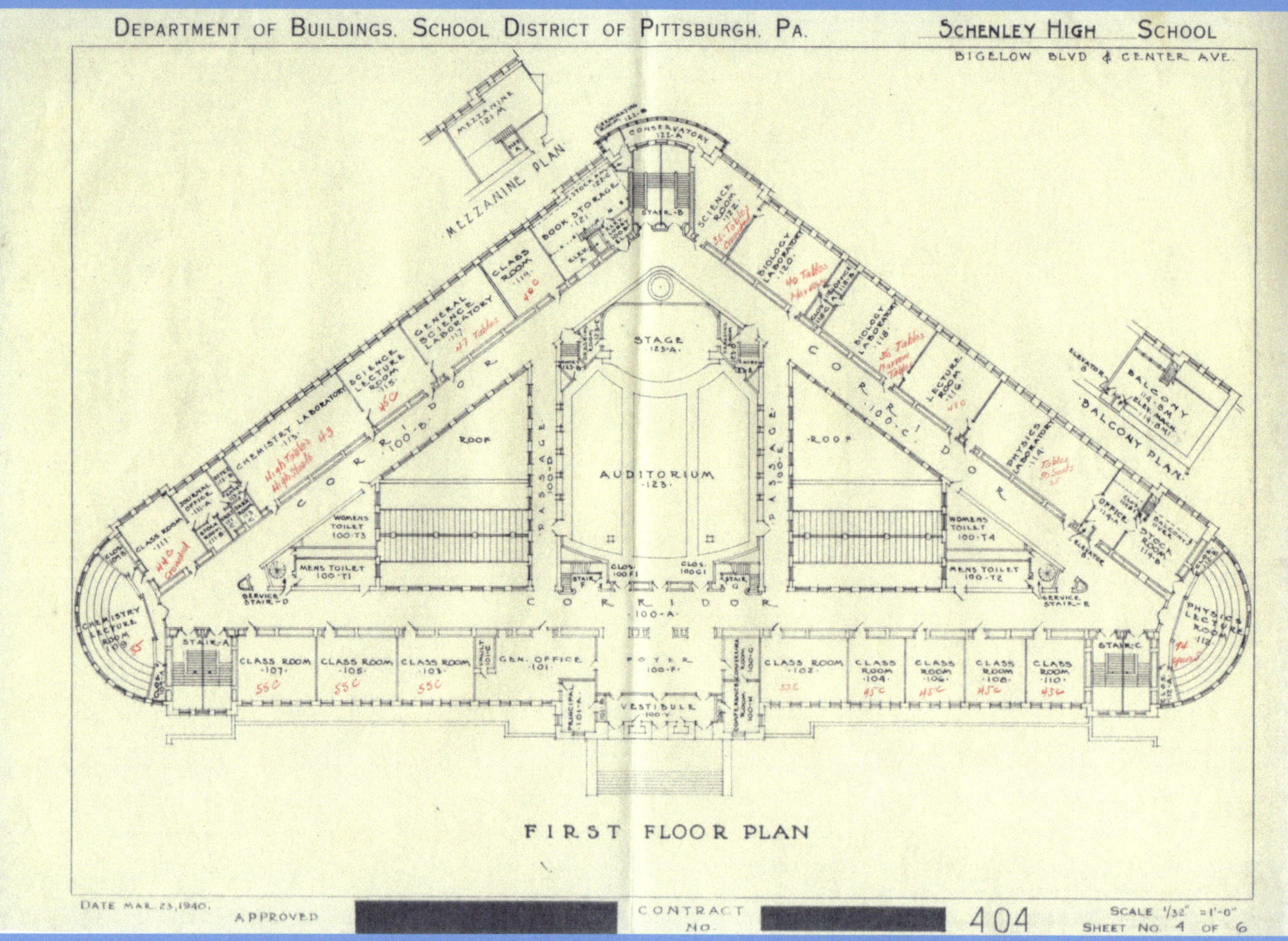

Edward Stotz, Sr., Schenley High School, First Floor Plan, 1916, architectural drawing; PPBF

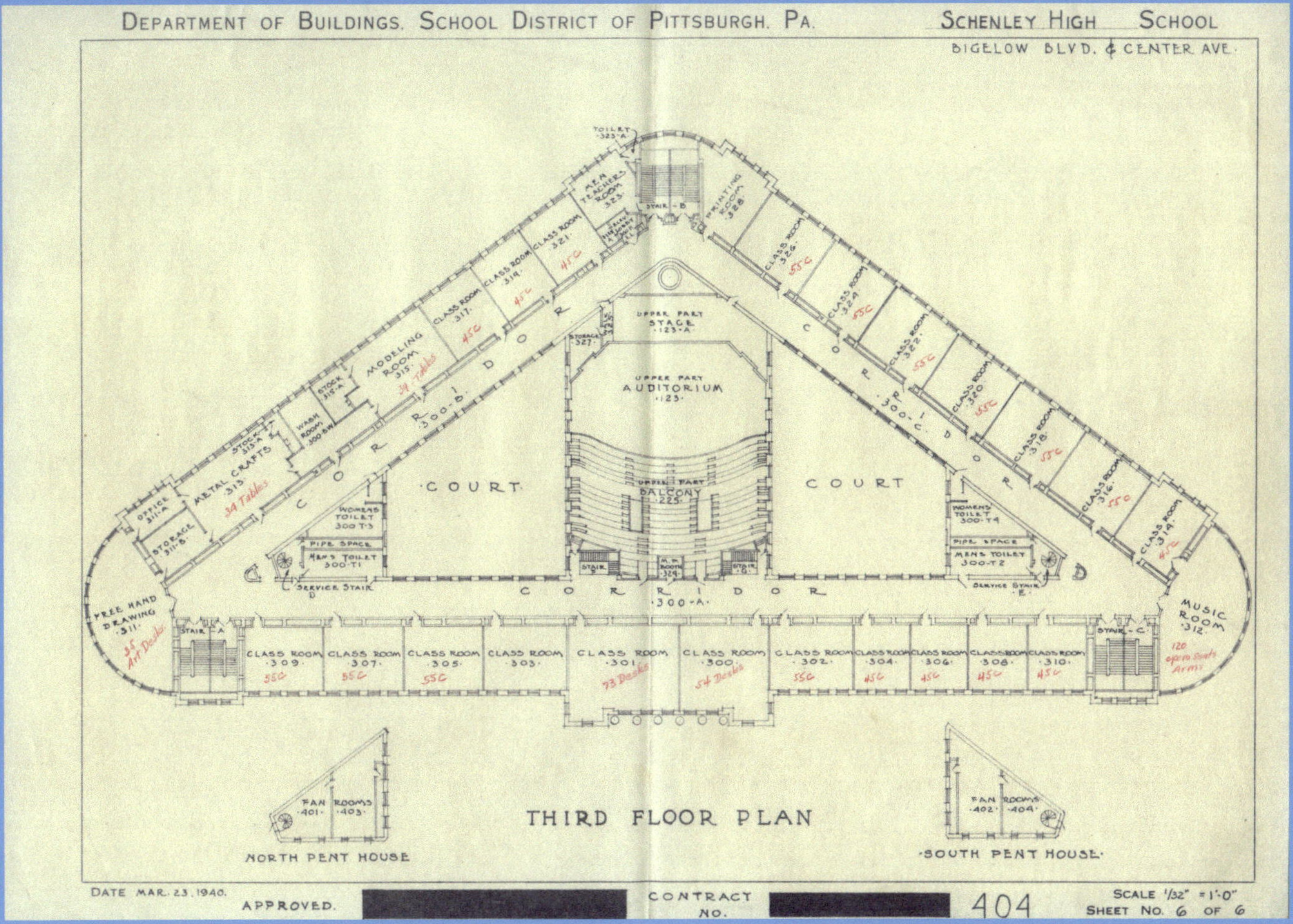

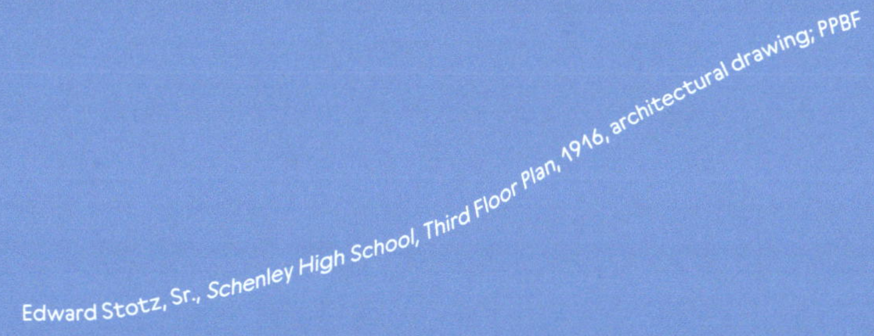

DEPARTMENT OF BUILDINGS. SCHOOL DISTRICT OF PITTSBURGH, PA.
SCHENLEY HIGH SCHOOL
BIGELOW BLVD. & CENTER AVE.
THIRD FLOOR PLAN
COURT
COURT
CORRIDOR
UPPER PART STAGE 123-A
UPPER PART AUDITORIUM 125
UPPER PART BALCONY 225
MODELING ROOM 315
METAL CRAFTS 313
FREE HAND DRAWING 311
OFFICE 313-A
STORAGE 315-B
WOMENS TOILET 300-T3
PIPE SPACE
MEN'S TOILET 300-T1
SERVICE STAIR
STAIR A
STAIR B
STAIR C
WOMENS TOILET 300-T4
PIPE SPACE
MENS TOILET 300-T2
SERVICE STAIR
MUSIC ROOM 312
CLASS ROOM 309
CLASS ROOM 307
CLASS ROOM 305
CLASS ROOM 303
CLASS ROOM 301
CLASS ROOM 300
CLASS ROOM 302
CLASS ROOM 304
CLASS ROOM 306
CLASS ROOM 308
CLASS ROOM 310
CLASS ROOM 317
CLASS ROOM 319
CLASS ROOM 321
CLASS ROOM 323
CLASS ROOM 325
CLASS ROOM 327
CLASS ROOM 320
CLASS ROOM 318
CLASS ROOM 314
TOILET 323-A
FAN ROOMS 401 403
FAN ROOMS 402 404
NORTH PENT HOUSE
SOUTH PENT HOUSE
DATE MAR. 23, 1940.
APPROVED.
CONTRACT NO.
404
SCALE 1/32" = 1'-0"
SHEET NO. 6 OF 6

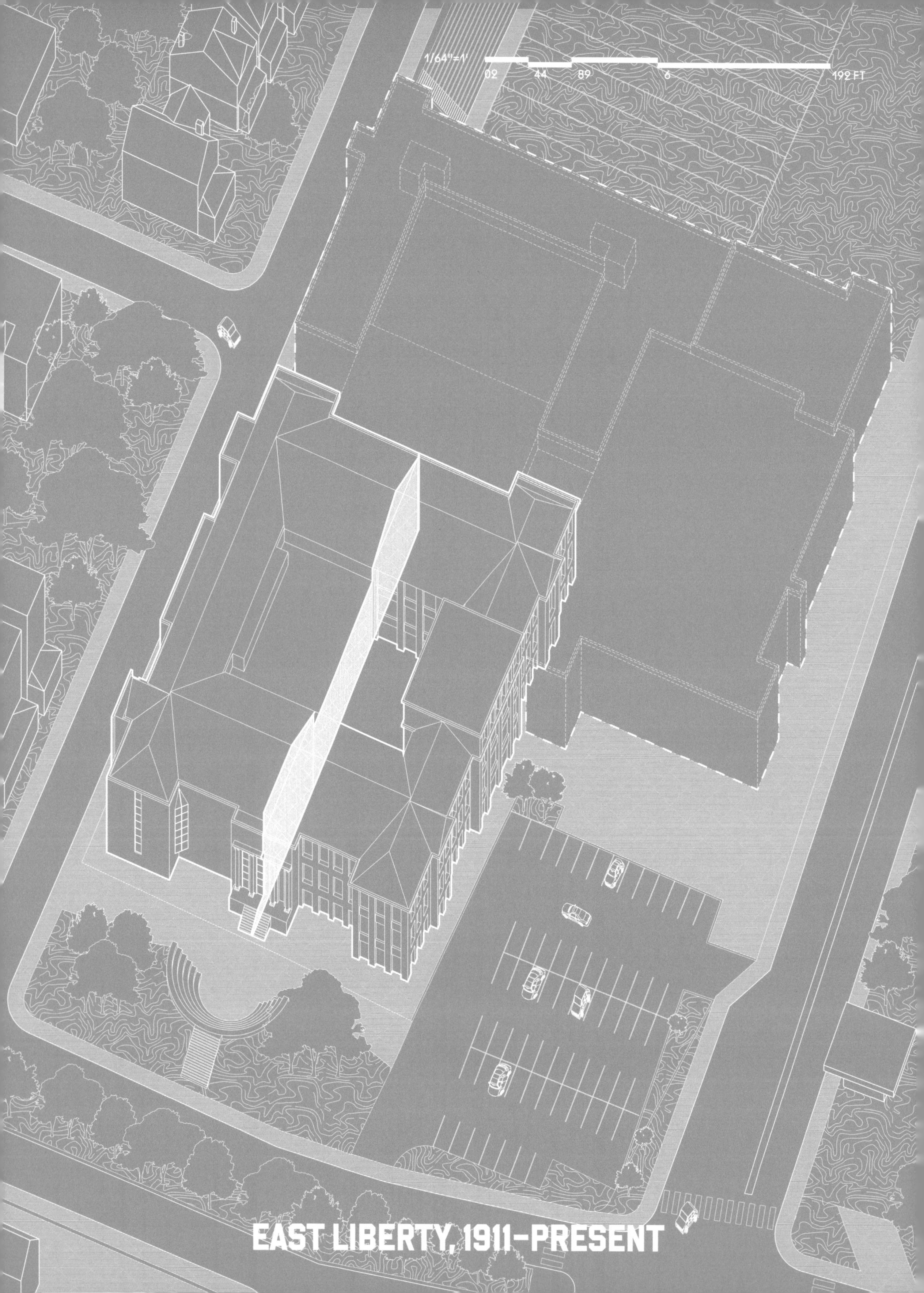

1/64"=1'
02
44
89
6
192 FT
EAST LIBERTY, 1911–PRESENT

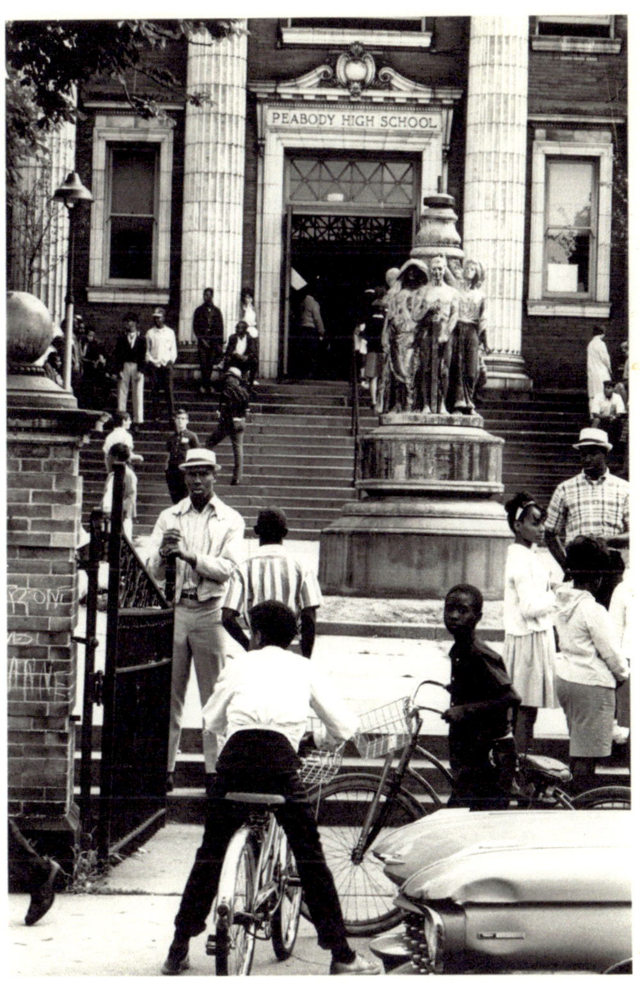

Located in East Liberty, Peabody High School's lifespan has mirrored the changes in its surrounding neighborhood, including disinvestment, urban renewal, and structural erasure. The site's first school opened in 1870; it was replaced in 1901 by a Neoclassical building designed by Charles Bartberger, then renamed Peabody High in 1911. In 1925, architect Edward B. Lee expanded the building with a new auditorium, gym, swimming pool, and choir room. Its final major renovation, in the late 1970s, was more subtractive. Architects encased its original columns and fenestrated facade behind a flat expanse of red brick, obscuring the building's exterior ornamentation and removing natural light from most classrooms. After nearly a century of operation, Peabody closed in 2011. The next year, it reopened as the Barack Obama Academy of International Studies 6–12—a magnet school with an International Baccalaureate curriculum. The building remains a layered archive of educational change—where each addition or concealment reflects both the city and nation's shifting priorities in public schooling.

PEABODY HIGH SCHOOL/OBAMA ACADEMY

A MIRROR OF STAINLESS STEEL

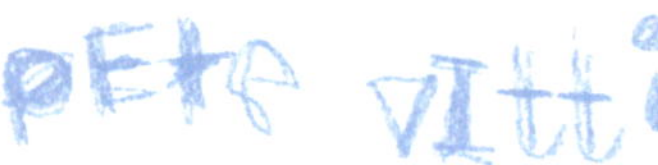

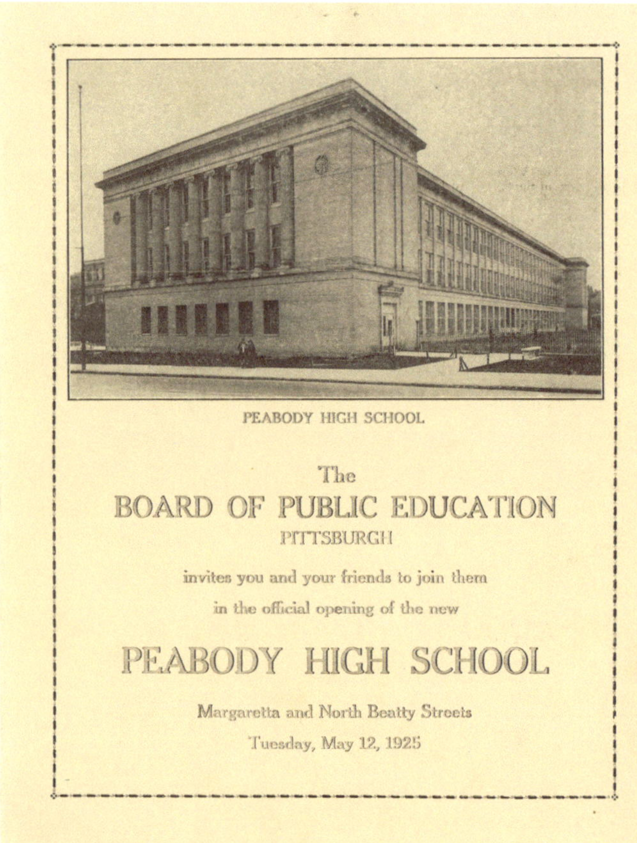

Above: Opening invitation to Peabody
High School, May 12, 1925, pamphlet; Pittsburgh
Board of Education Archives, CLP

Previous page: Front entrance to Peabody
High School, 1969, photograph; Detre Library &
Archives, HHC

In 2010, after teaching at Schenley High School for seventeen years, I made the transition to the Barack Obama Academy of International Studies, which took on the International Baccalaureate portions of the former North Oakland school. Two years later, when the Obama Academy moved locations from Reizenstein, in the city's East Liberty neighborhood, to the Peabody building, it was a bit of a surreal experience to return to the same school I had previously attended and graduated from in the early 1980s. Back then, Peabody was a comprehensive school that was buzzing with a plethora of clubs, sports, art programs, and other activities. In 1983, my graduating class consisted of 350 students—a remarkably large cohort equal to the high school's entire student enrollment (grades 9-12) in the years leading up to its closure.

Upon my return to the Peabody building as a teacher in 2012, I noticed almost immediately that not much had changed. The school's interior walls remained covered in the same drab, white tiles, and the long corridors and hallways were lined by the same six-inch red and black lockers I used to store my own backpack and school supplies as a student. Even the bathrooms acted like a kind of time capsule, featuring the indestructible stainless steel sinks and mirrors (yes, stainless steel mirrors) from the 1980s. The old desks that I sat in thirty years prior were still in use. I would point this out to my students: "I once sat in the same desks that you are sitting in now …No, really…I sat in those exact desks!" It seemed that the school hadn't changed since it was renovated in the late 1970s—a renovation that encased the beautiful former Neoclassical structure in a sarcophagus of brick-and-mortar without windows. At the time, I remember reading in the newspapers that the architects' decision to remove all windows from classrooms was motivated by the belief that limiting views of the outdoors would redirect and enhance student focus.

As I reflect on my collective experiences at Peabody—as a student at the former comprehensive school and, more recently, as a teacher at the Obama Academy magnet school—I do believe that things have been both lost and gained over the years. For instance, I recall when a classmate and good friend of mine, David Bendet, participated in what was known as the "scholars program" at Peabody. We had "tracking" back when I was a student, so students were either placed on a college or vocational pathway. The benefit of attending a comprehensive high school, such as Peabody, was that students were occasionally presented with the opportunity to take elective courses outside of their track. One semester, David, who was enrolled in the college pathway, decided to take a mechanical drawing class—a course intended for predominately vocational-technical or "vo-tech" students. But as it turned out, the class inspired him to pursue an architecture degree in college, which developed into a life-long passion and career. In recent years, I have witnessed how this ability for students to experiment and gain new perspectives has been limited by the emergence of specialized schools in the 1990s as well as the No Child Left Behind (NCLB) Act of the early 2000s. As a teacher during these decades, I witnessed a pedagogical shift that prioritized standardized science, math, and English tests over arts and elective programs. Today, students are encouraged to choose a specialization before starting high school, and sometimes even before entering sixth grade. This new reality of our educational system makes me wonder: How is it possible for a twelve year old student to know what they want to do as a career? Are we doing students a disservice by withholding access to a broad spectrum of experimentation that can only be accessed through a comprehensive education?

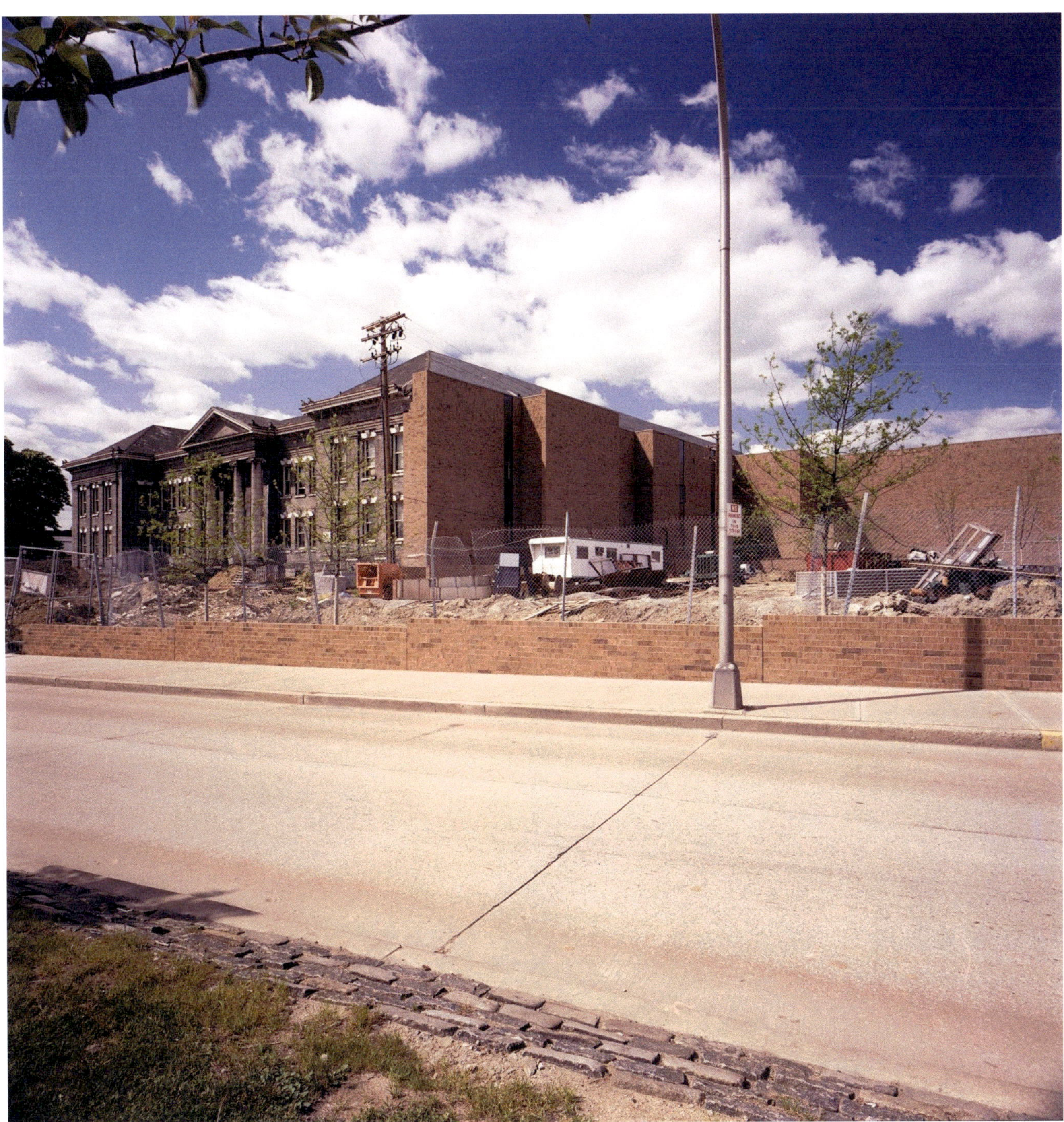

Renovation in progress at Peabody High School, 1975–1978, photograph; Preservation Pittsburgh & Doug Conzolo

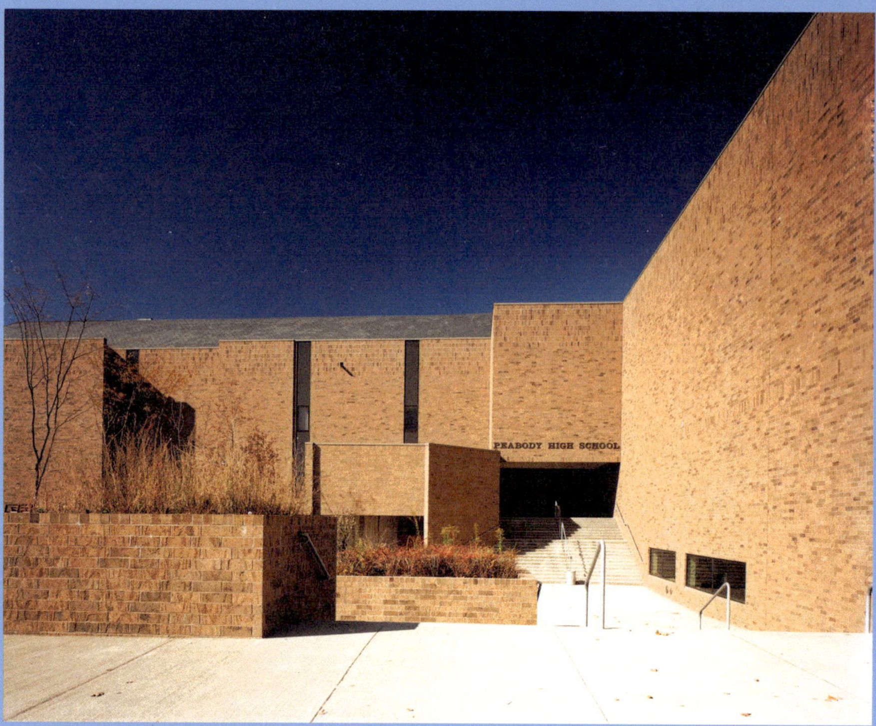

Main entrance of Peabody High School, 1978, photograph; Preservation Pittsburgh & Doug Conzolo

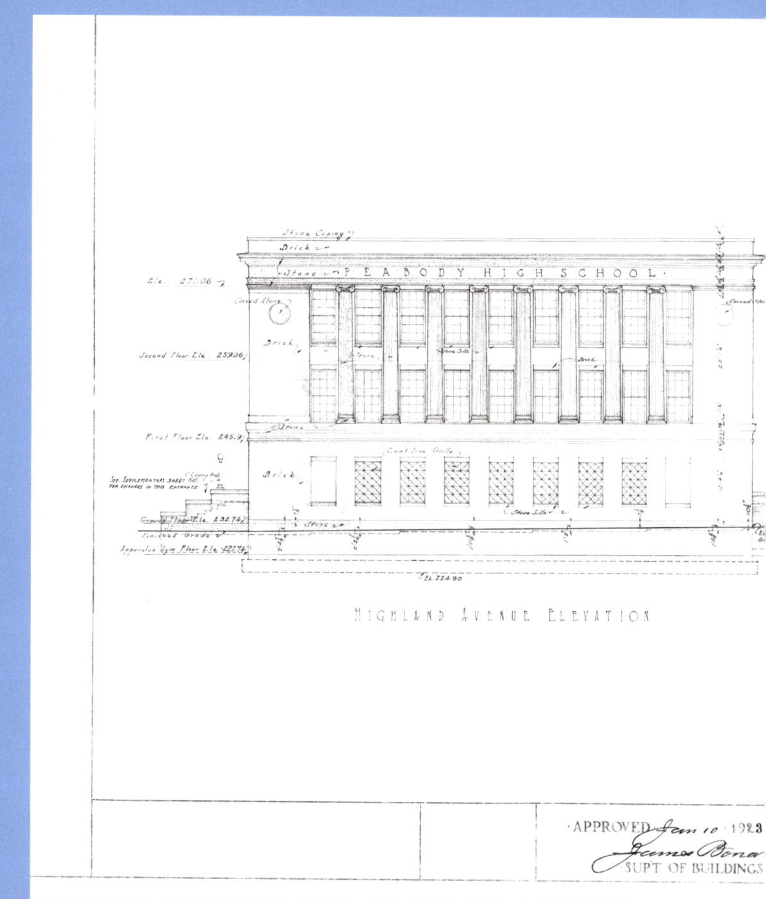

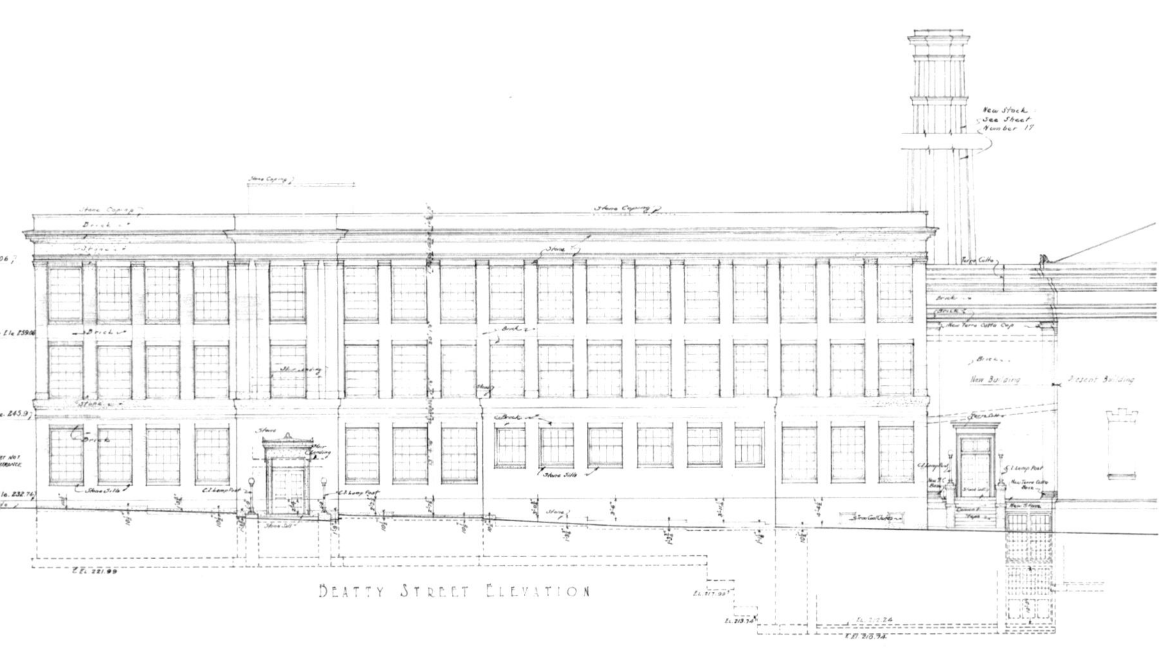
BEATTY STREET ELEVATION

FINAL WORKING DRAWINGS

PEABODY HIGH SCHOOL ADDITION
Margaretta Beatty Streets & Highland Ave Pittsburgh Penna.
BOARD OF PUBLIC EDUCATION · SCHOOL DISTRICT OF PITTSBURGH PENNA

EDWARD · B · LEE · ARCHITECT
REGISTERED IN PENNA
CHAMBER OF COMMERCE BUILDING
PITTSBURGH PENNA

CONTRACT Nº 1016

·ELEVATIONS·
·SCALE·ONE·EIGHTH·INCH·EQUALS·ONE·FOOT·

9

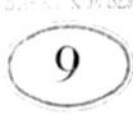

UPPER HILL DISTRICT, 1928–PRESENT

Perched on a hillside in the Upper Hill District, Herron Hill Junior High opened in 1928 as a monumental red brick building. Designed by James T. Steen & Sons, the school with its strict symmetry and massive scale expressed the imperatives of public education in the early twentieth century: institutional and foreboding. In 1974, the building was closed for an expansion by architects Damianos and Pedone, who added a rotated cubic volume at the complex's entrance. This addition broke the building's formal symmetry and reconfigured the interior to introduce open classrooms, a cafeteria, and other communal spaces. Two years later, it reopened as Margaret Milliones Middle School, renamed for the Pittsburgh educator and civil rights leader. Known as an "integration crusader," Milliones worked alongside Dr. Martin Luther King Jr. and fought for desegregation, gifted programs, and Black student retention. A professor of Black studies at the University of Pittsburgh, she was elected to the school board in 1976 and served until her death in 1980. Milliones 6–12, University Preparatory remains in operation as a secondary magnet school.

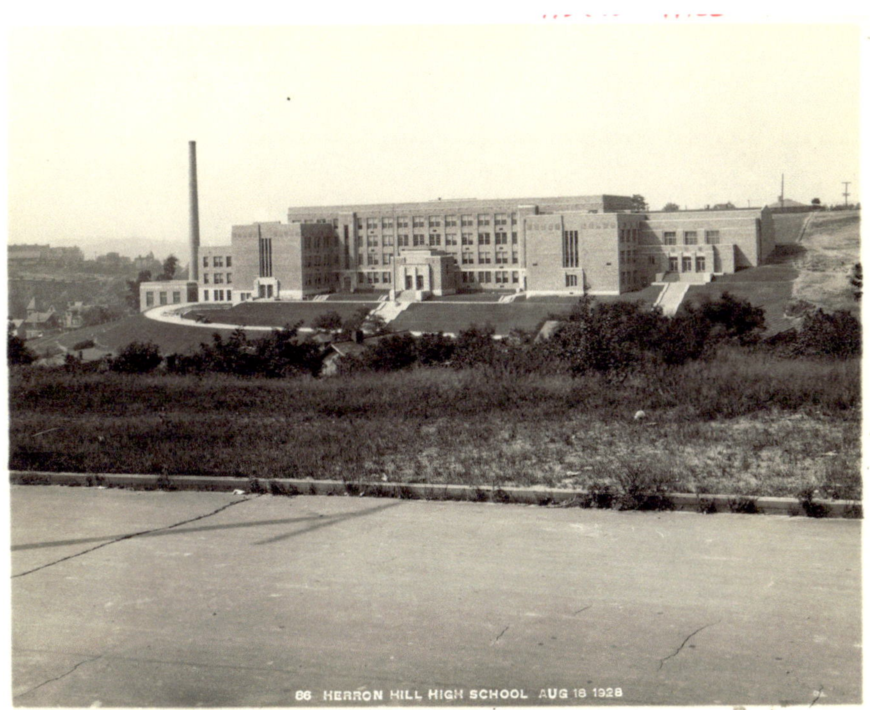

HERRON HILL / MILLIONES UNIVERSITY PREP

AN UPHILL BATTLE *Jillian Forstadt*

When University Preparatory School opened at Margaret Milliones Middle School in 2008, district leaders presented it as an innovative partnership between Pittsburgh Public Schools and the University of Pittsburgh—with promises of laptops, tutoring, and college readiness. The initiative was meant to serve as a launchpad for college-bound students and a model for university-district collaboration. But in the years since, the university has backed away from its initial commitments at UPrep Milliones. Some community members viewed this decision as a promise broken, while university officials faulted a rocky relationship with the school.[1] In November 2024, only a quarter of UPrep Milliones students were on track to earn the Pittsburgh Promise college scholarship—the second-lowest eligibility rate of all the district's high schools. PPS board member Sala Udin (see Dr. Sala Udin & Dana Bishop-Root, p.66), a longtime Hill District resident and activist, has observed the Milliones building over multiple experiments promised to improve student outcomes. "I think the bottom line is that it was easier to conceptualize and implement physical changes than it was to create academic improvement," Udin says. "And that's true today."

The building, initially Herron Hill Junior High School, was renamed in the late 1970s for PPS board member Margaret Milliones, who represented the board district in which the school is located until her death in 1978. Milliones was a fervent proponent for integration in the Hill District, the heart of Pittsburgh's historic Black community.[2] After multiple desegregation orders in 1960s and 70s, PPS spent more than six million dollars renovating the building—adding eighteen thousand square feet and transforming its learning spaces into an open-space environment with modular walls. The district attempted to recruit four hundred white students to Herron Hill before reopening the school in 1976.[3] Few enrolled, triggering another desegregation order the following year.[4]

Udin remains skeptical of architectural fixes without structural change: "I waited to see whether or not [an open concept] would produce better academic achievement. It didn't," Udin says. "We have waited to see the concept of University Preparatory take shape. It didn't." PPS is again considering how to address segregation, achievement gaps, and a staggering budget deficit. A sweeping facilities utilization plan would close nine buildings and renovate more than a dozen others to house modified programs. UPrep Milliones would be replaced by a STEM-focused middle school program—an extension of the popular PPS SciTech magnet high school in the city's Oakland neighborhood. The district plans to spend $375,000 to upgrade the Milliones building, adding a new art room and converting one of the school's computer labs into a high-tech workshop. On a tour of the school this summer, former UPrep principal Eric Graf said, aside from those changes, it would be a turnkey project. "I do think obviously it's an amazing and historic building that's served the public for a hundred years now. And I hope that whatever comes next, it's continued to be seen by the school community as a place where people can send their children to get a quality education and live their life

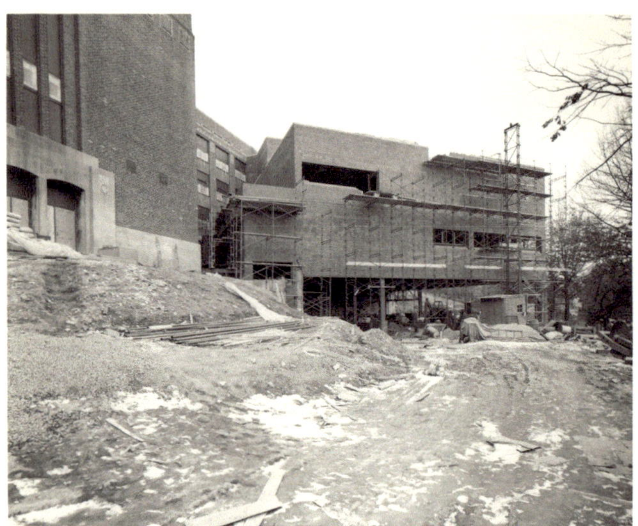

Above: Herron Hill/Milliones under construction for extension, January 1976, photograph; Detre Library & Archives, HHC

Previous page: Herron Hill High School, August 18, 1928, photograph; Detre Library & Archives, HHC

1 Alexandra Ross, "UPrep's Resets: A School Meant to Bring Pitt's Resources to Hill Students Goes Back to the Drawing Board," *Public Source*, February 28, 2023, https://www.publicsource.org/pittsburgh-public-pps-uprep-milliones-university-preparatory-hill-district-pitt/.

2 *Pittsburgh Post-Gazette*, July 15, 1976.

3 As shared by former principal Robert Nicklos, who helmed Herron Hill Junior High from 1969 to 1974, in *Three Principals Reflect on Herron Hill*, 1977, Carnegie Library of Pittsburgh.

4 *Pittsburgh Post-Gazette*, February 26, 1977.

boldly." But Graf, who served as the school's principal until 2025, noted the process to close schools is a political one. The Milliones building was closed in 2006, along with seventeen other schools. Board of Public Education members voted the following year to reopen it as an arts-focused middle school companion to the Creative and Performing Arts Magnet School in Downtown Pittsburgh, but that plan was quickly abandoned. UPrep Milliones instead opened to house students displaced by the recent closure of Schenley High School in nearby Oakland. "I think for a while, [the school has] kind of faced a little bit of an uphill battle in terms of acceptance, in that regard," Graf says.

If turned into a SciTech middle school, educators at Milliones will likely be tasked with public persuasion. It's something they've done time and again as the district tried to rebalance its racial composition through reconfigurations and bussing. "I would basically say to all the SciTech parents and teachers in that school community too, [that] if the transition happens, look at this move as an opportunity to create something new," Graf adds. For Udin, real transformation begins with historical reckoning: "I think you cannot chart a way forward unless you examine the history and use that examination to help you plan a path forward. And of course, there is the danger of somebody being blamed. Tough. We need to take a hard, tough look at what happened."

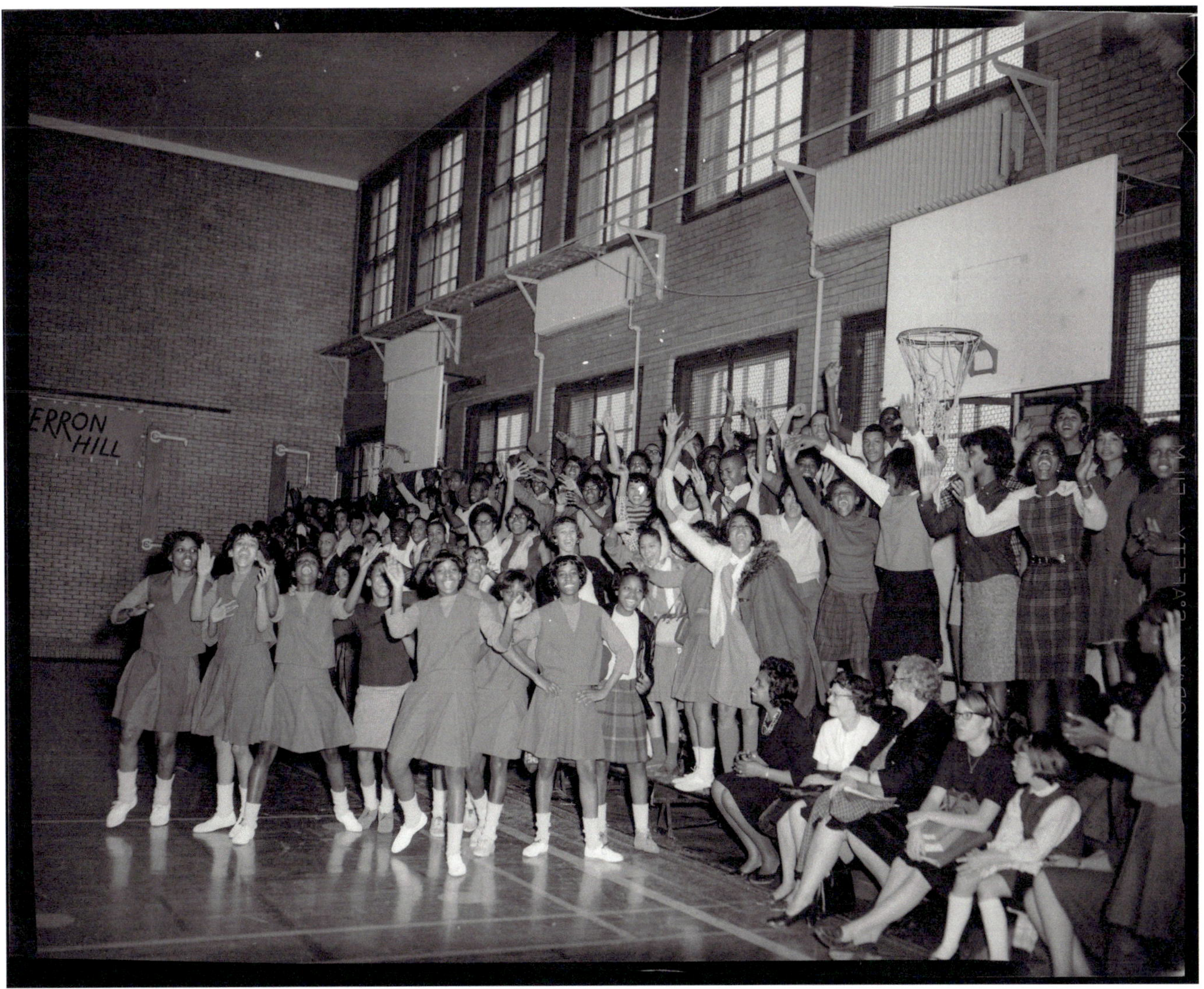

Charles "Teenie" Harris, *Crowd scene with cheerleaders in Herron Hill gym*, c. 1950–1965, photograph; Carnegie Museum of Art, HFF

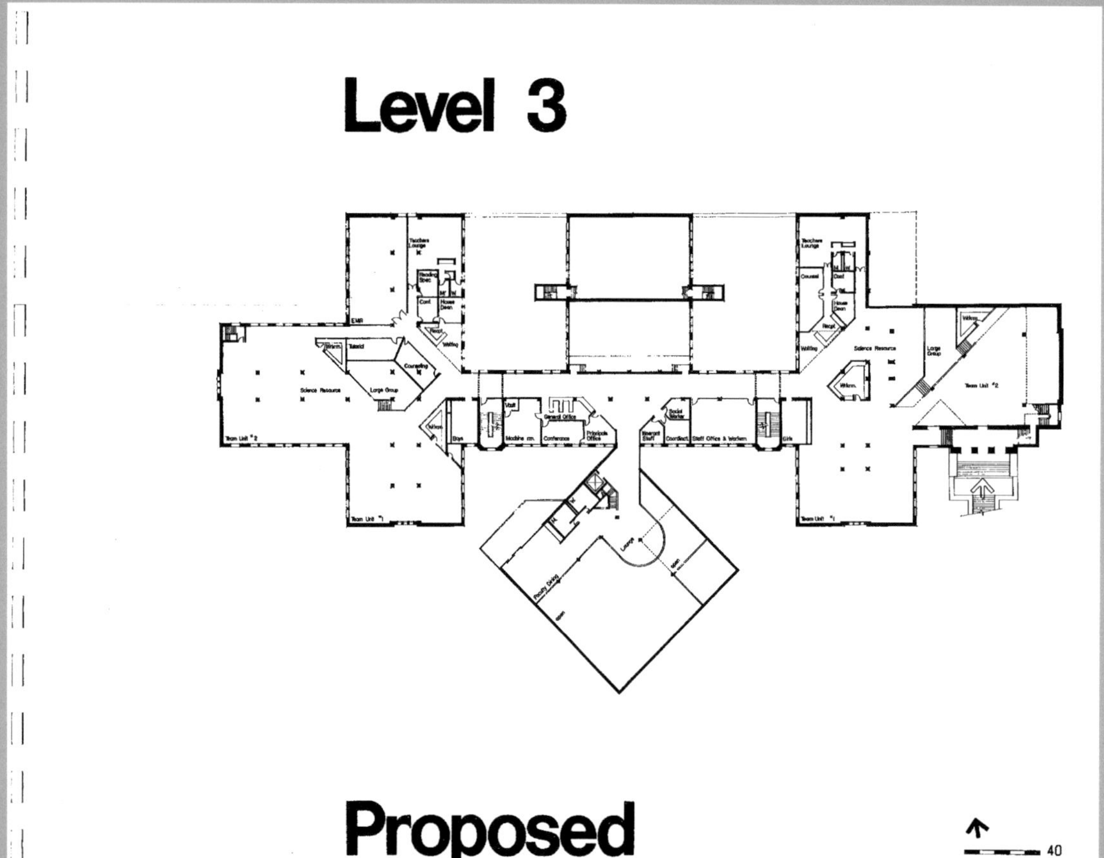

Level 3
Proposed
40

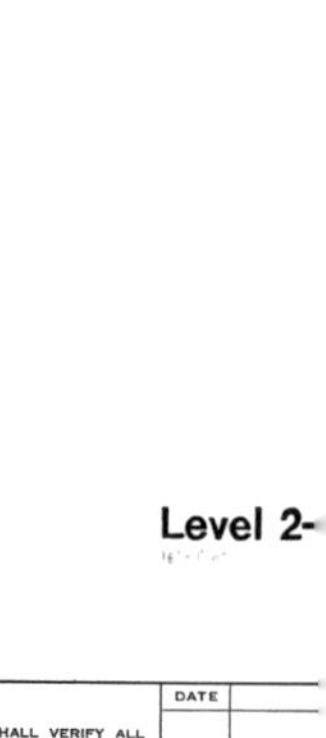

Level 2-
CONTRACTOR SHALL VERIFY ALL
MEASUREMENTS AT BUILDING AND
REPORT ANY DISCREPANCY TO THE
OFFICE OF THE FACILITIES DIVI-
SION.
DATE

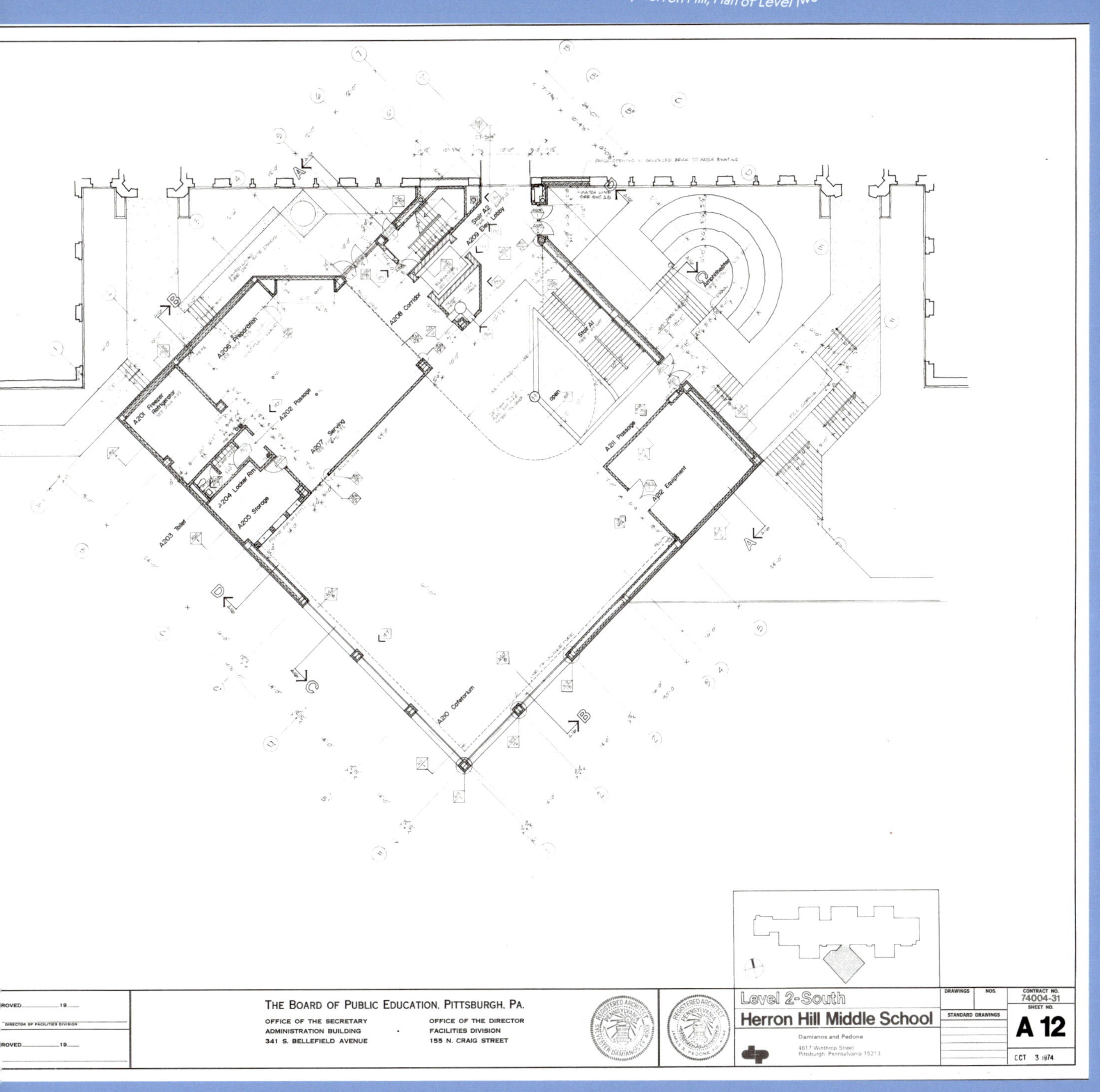
Level 2-South
Herron Hill Middle School
Damianos and Pedone
4617 Winthrop Street
Pittsburgh, Pennsylvania 15213
THE BOARD OF PUBLIC EDUCATION, PITTSBURGH, PA.
OFFICE OF THE SECRETARY
ADMINISTRATION BUILDING
341 S. BELLEFIELD AVENUE
OFFICE OF THE DIRECTOR
FACILITIES DIVISION
155 N. CRAIG STREET
CONTRACT NO.
74004-31
SHEET NO.
A 12
DRAWINGS NOS.
STANDARD DRAWINGS
OCT 3 1974
APPROVED 19
DIRECTOR OF FACILITIES DIVISION
APPROVED 19

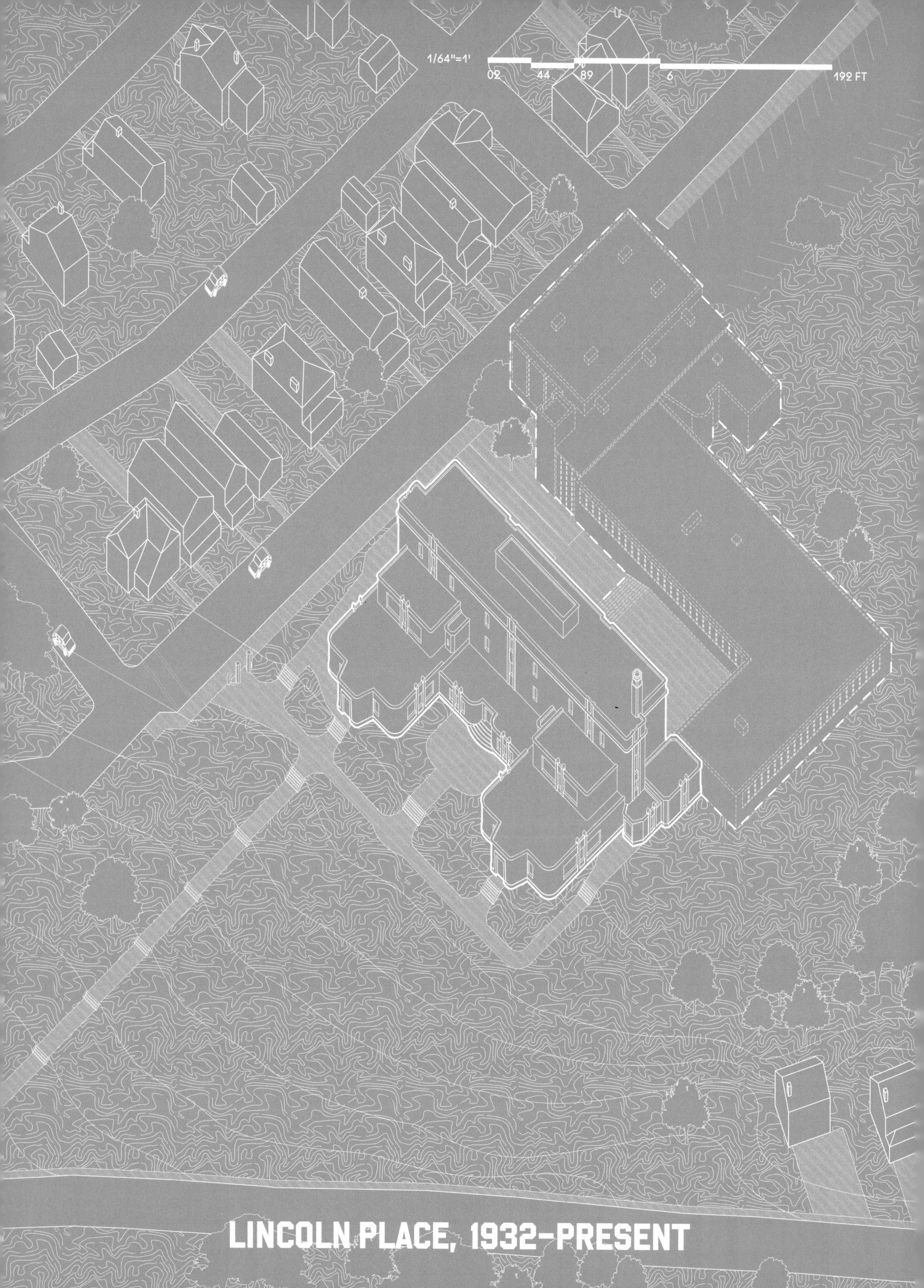

1/64"=1'
02 44 89 6 192 FT
LINCOLN PLACE, 1932-PRESENT

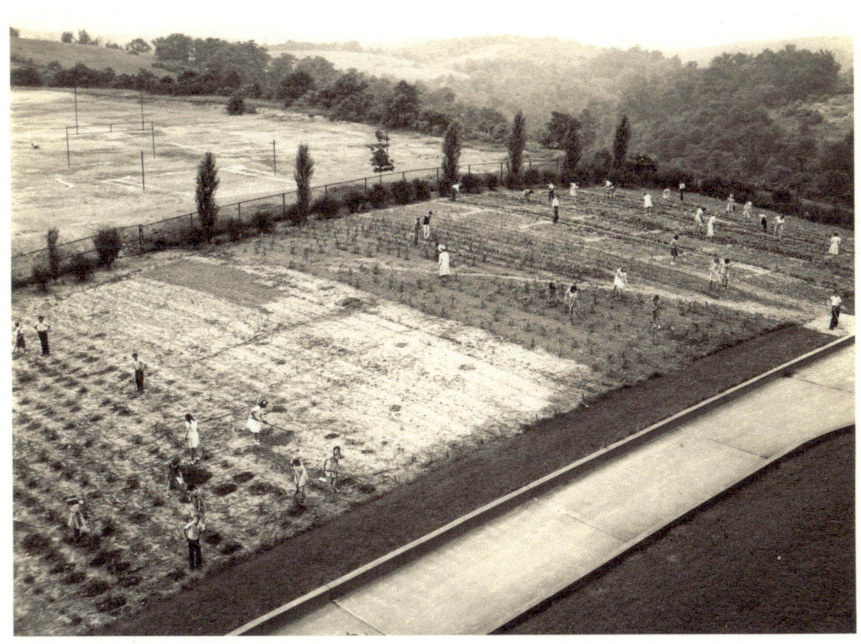

MIFFLIN ELEMENTARY & JUNIOR HIGH

Previous page: Gardening at Mifflin Elementary School, ca. 1950, photograph; Detre Library & Archives, HHC

The following drawings come from a *Mifflin Creative Writing* project in 1978, compiled by staff and edited by Mrs. Dolores K Sebastian.[1] In the forward to the booklet, Jean McKenney, Principal of Mifflin School, explains that "one of the goals we had for this year [1978] was to have each child express [their] thoughts and feelings through writing so that people would understand [them] better."

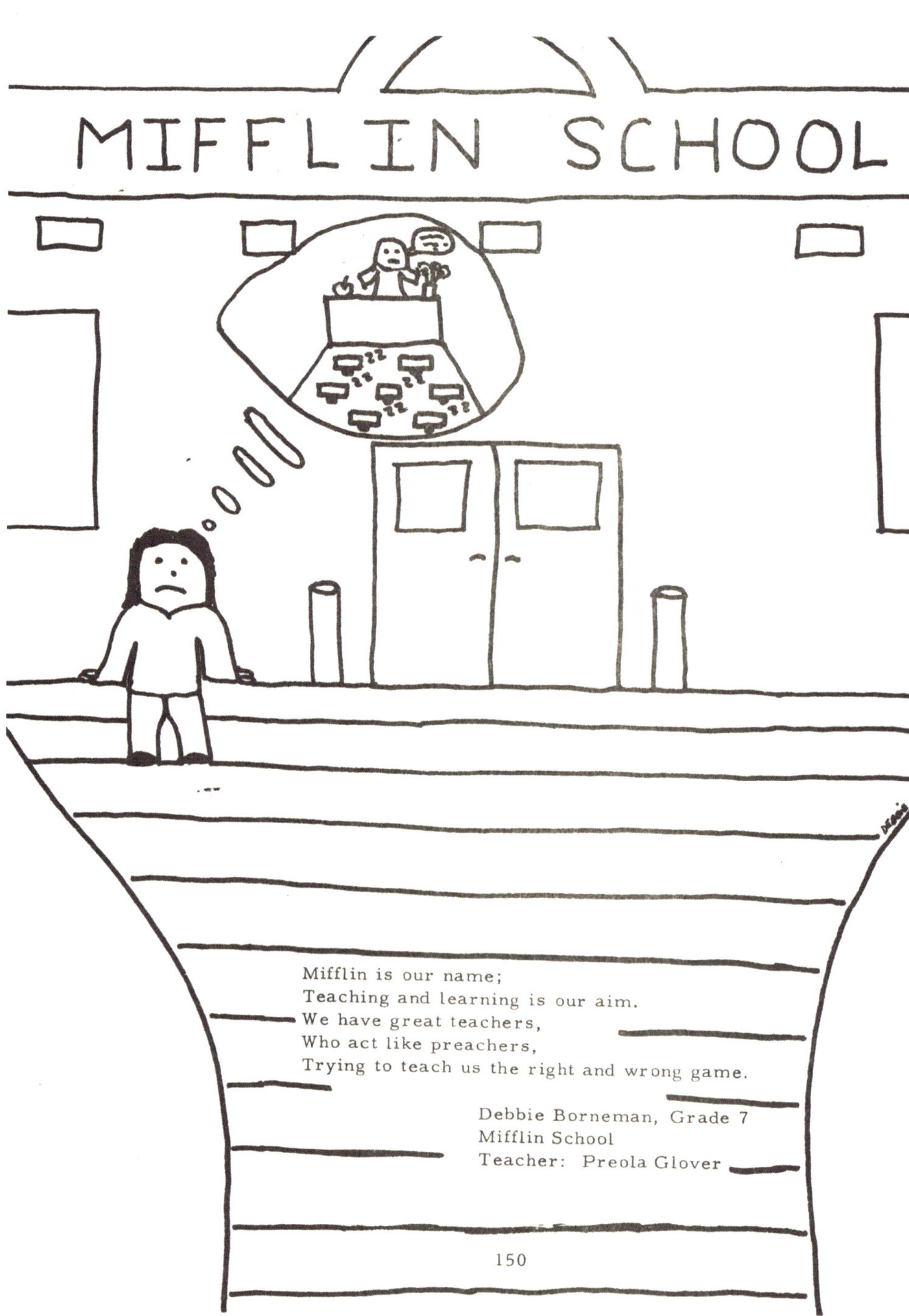

1 Staff included Preola Glover, Dolores Sebastian, Jerome Baxter, Iris Smith, Judith Werner, Gladys Kelly, Ruth Davis, Jean Donley, Eileen Barry, Assunta Tyskiewicz, Della Navaroli, Rosalie Sachs, Ida Stavor, Maryanne Philbrick, Patricia Hanobik, Karen Mamajek, Judith Morgan, and Lois Kotler.

McKenney describes the creative process: "from the kindergarten circle to the eighth grade English class, from the foundations to the chimney peaks, Mifflin students plied their way through couplets and rhymes, imagery and personification, cinquains and limericks, synonyms, allegories, and iambic pentameter. Exchanges of ideas, independent research, refinement and polishing, flowed spontaneously … illustrations were avidly provided by proud authors, poets, composers, and artists."

Drawing from their immediate surroundings, Mifflin students depicted buses, classrooms, and teachers. The figures on steps or balancing on bouncy balls are a small sampling of Mifflin students' view of their school.

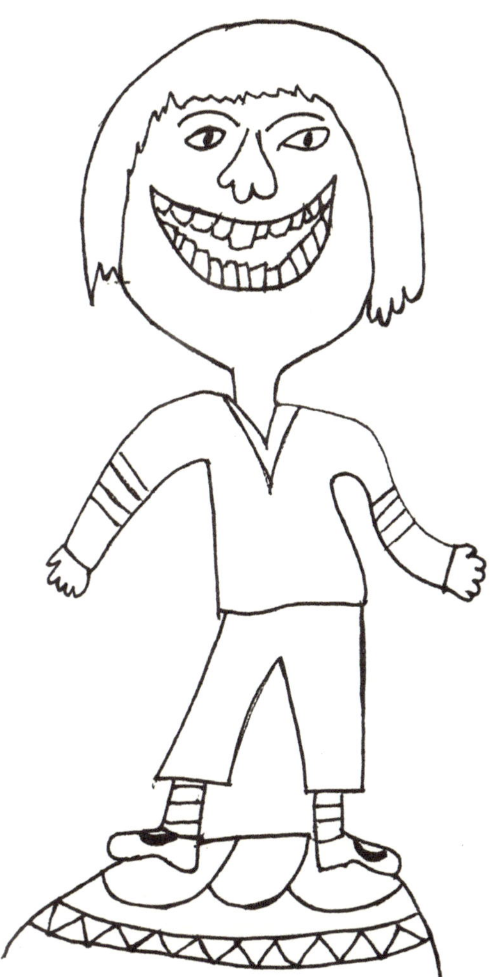

Robby Capozzolo
Grade 3
Miss Hanobik

54

Left: Sherry Williams, "My Wish," *Mifflin Creative Writing*, 1978, bound notebook, p. 10; Detre Library & Archives, HHC

Right: Kevin Todd, "My Wish," *Mifflin Creative Writing*, 1978, bound notebook, p. 13; Detre Library & Archives, HHC

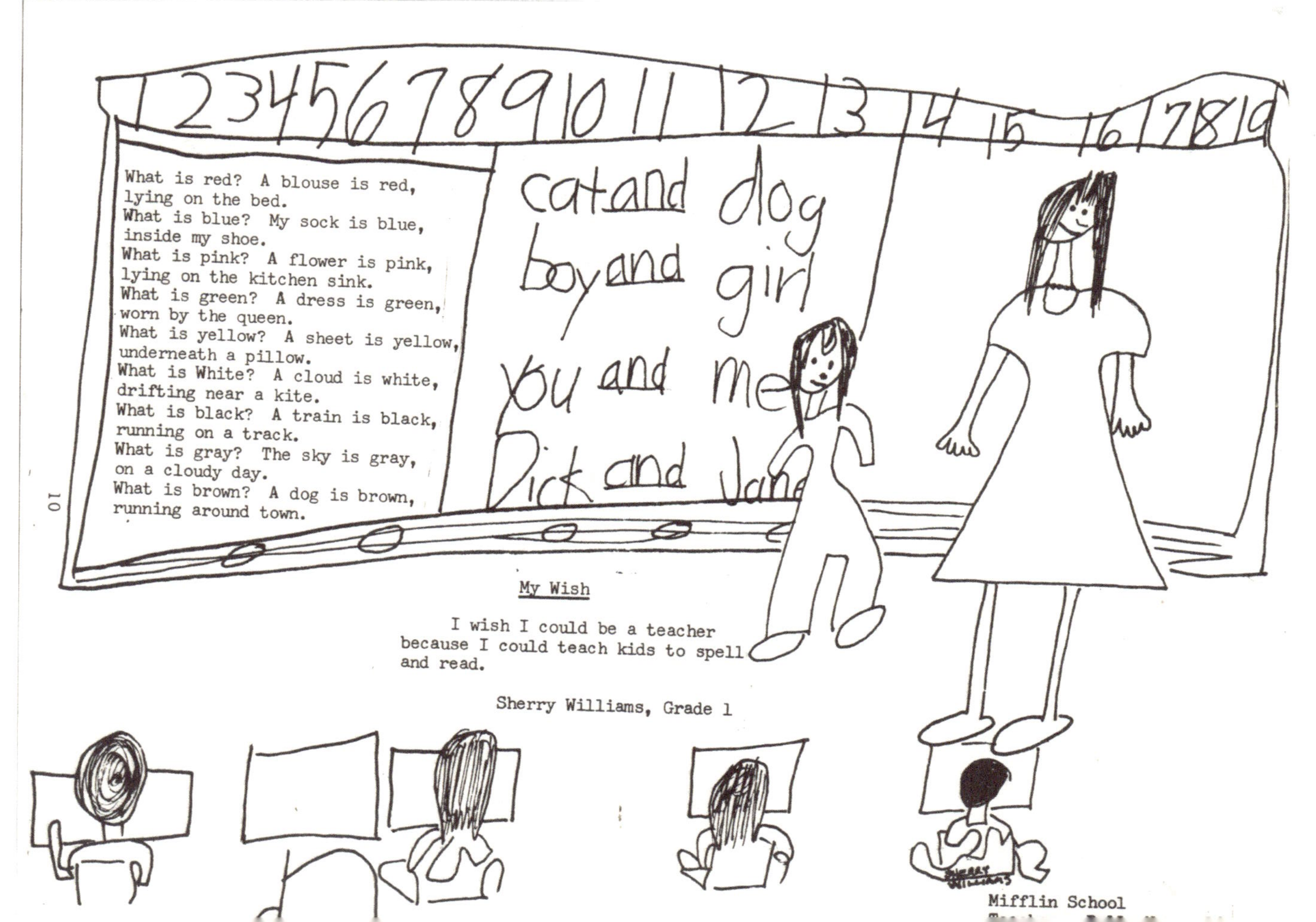

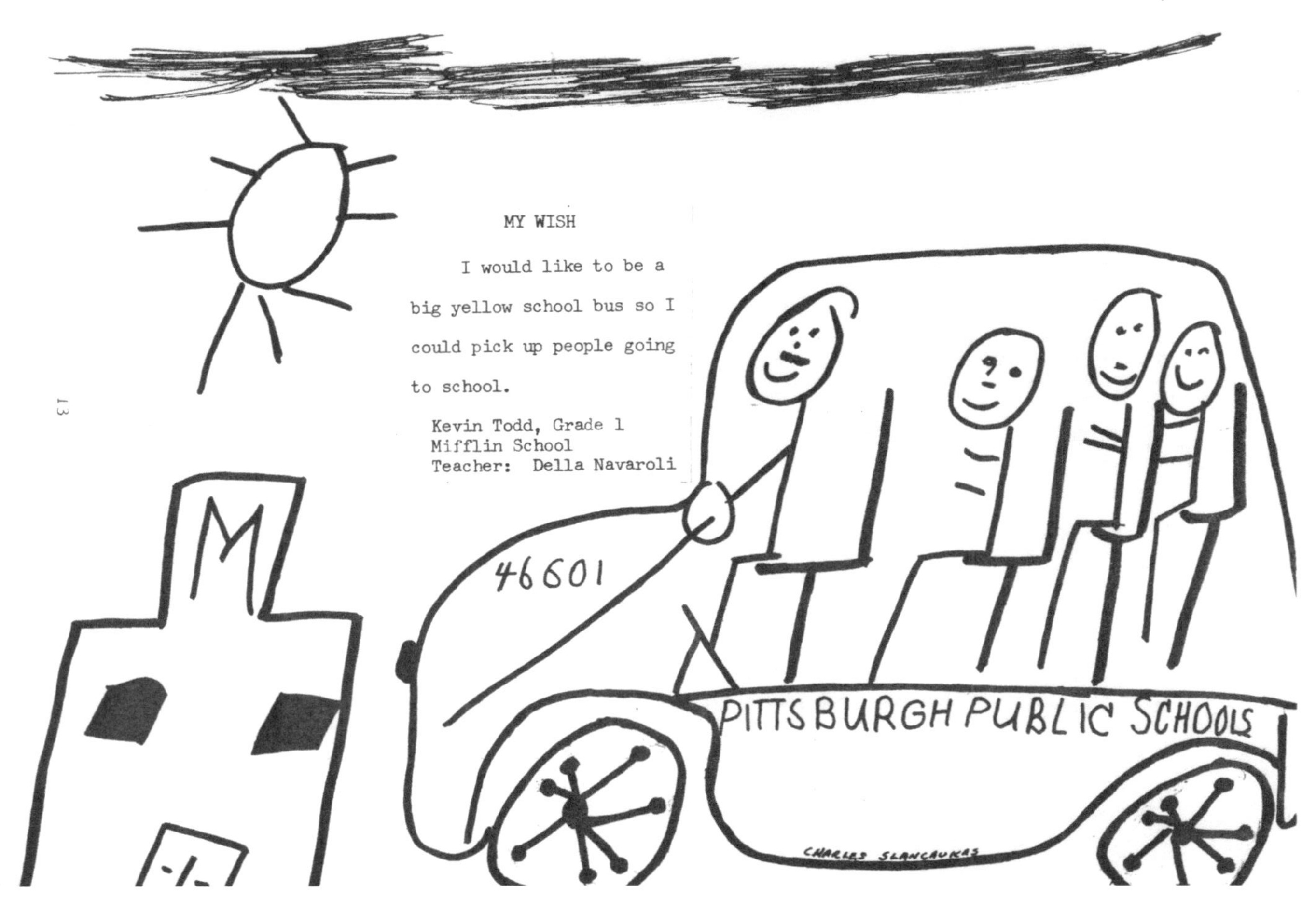

MY WISH

I would like to be a big yellow school bus so I could pick up people going to school.

Kevin Todd, Grade 1
Mifflin School
Teacher: Della Navaroli

13

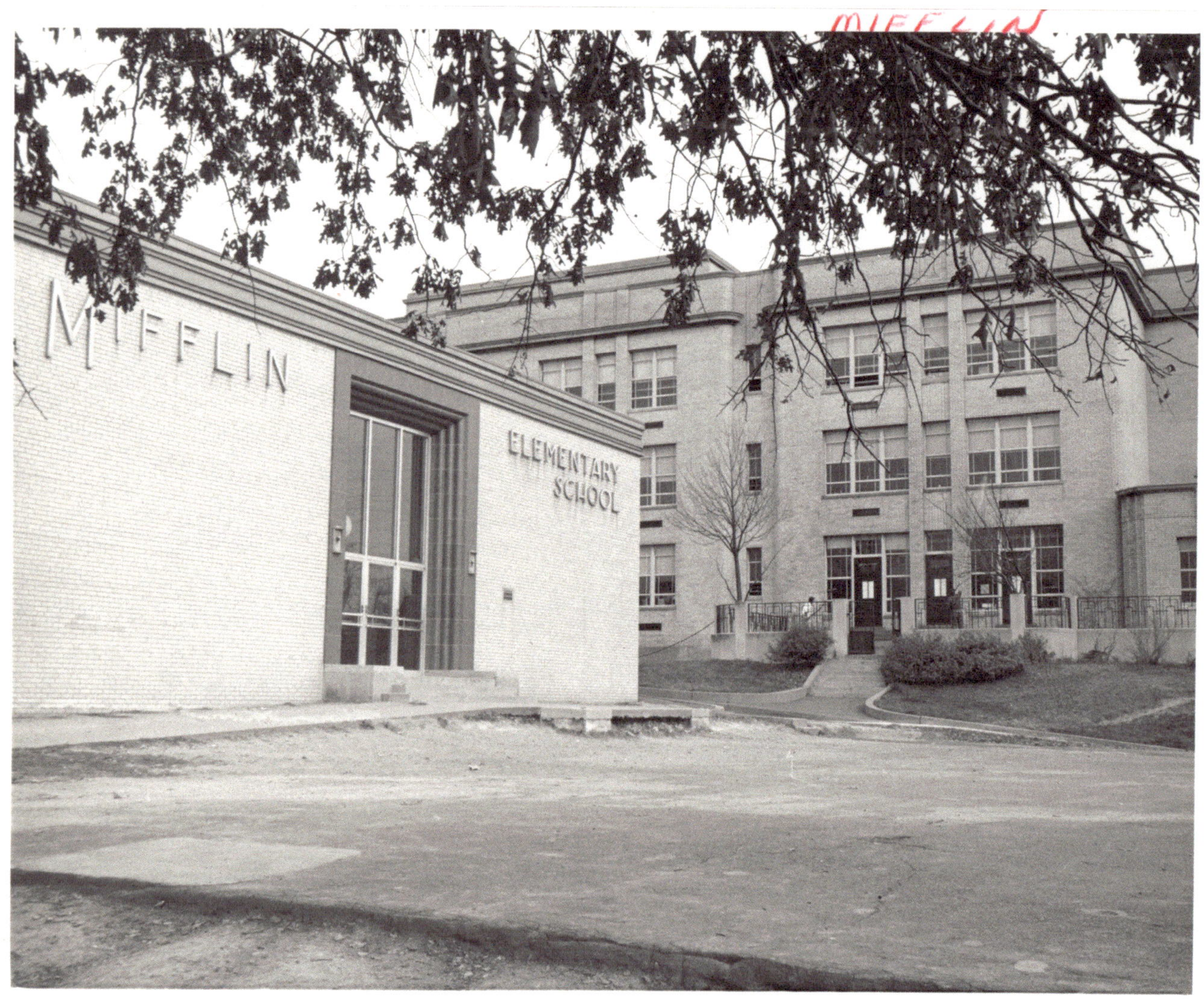

Above: Entrance of Mifflin Elementary School, ca. 1950, photograph; Detre Library & Archives, HHC

Below: Student gardening radishes, ca. 1950, photograph; Detre Library & Archives, HHC

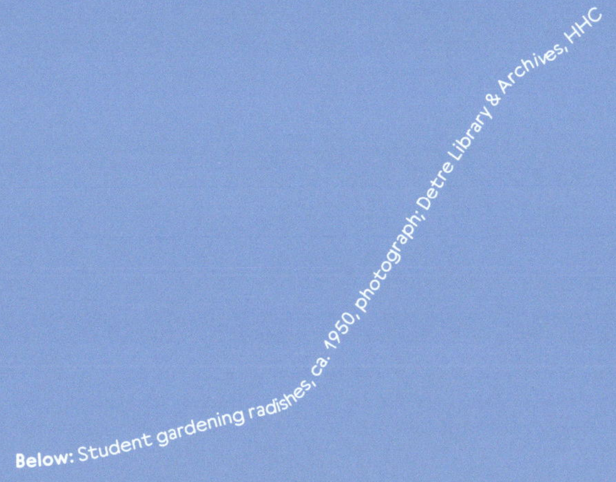

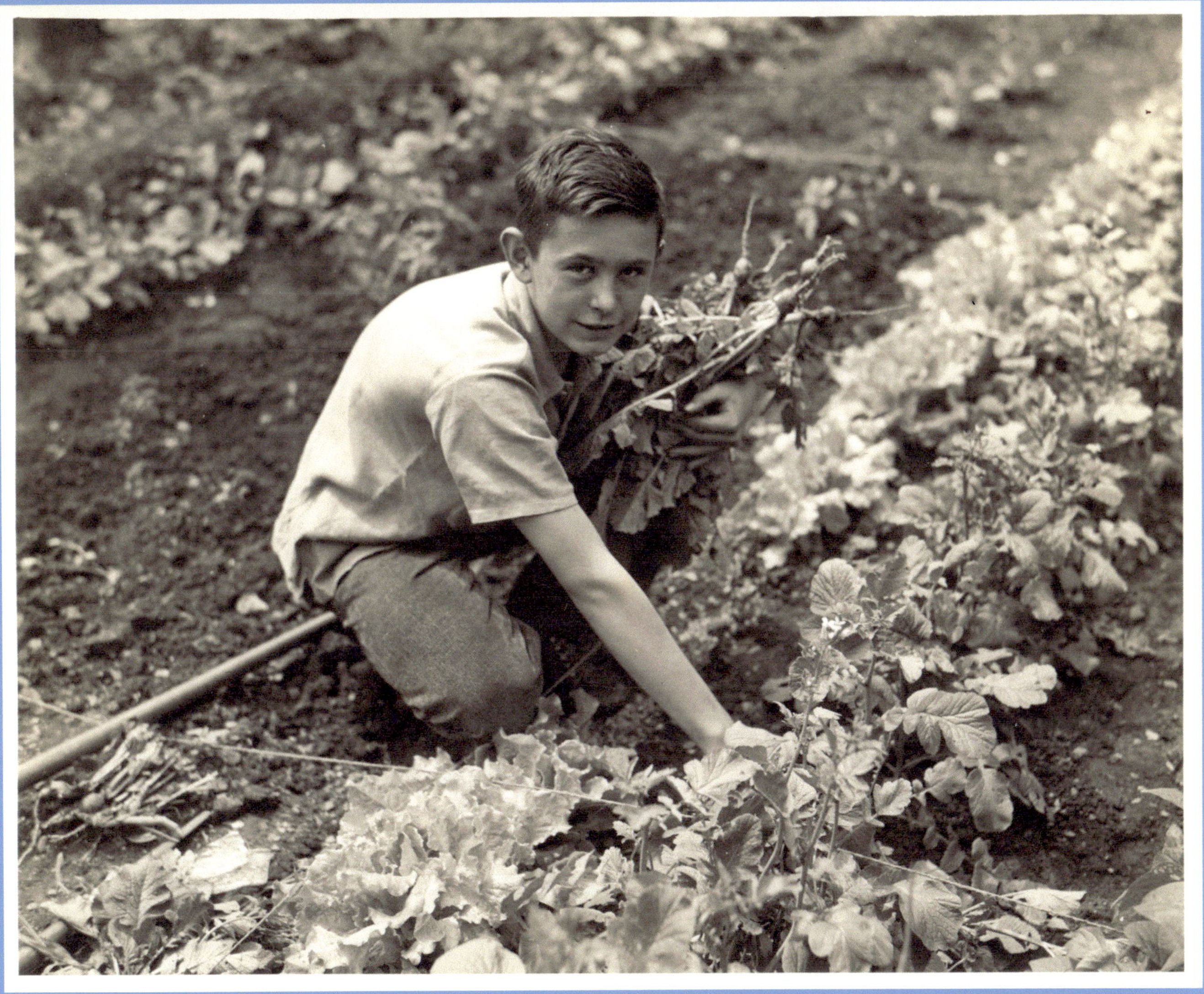

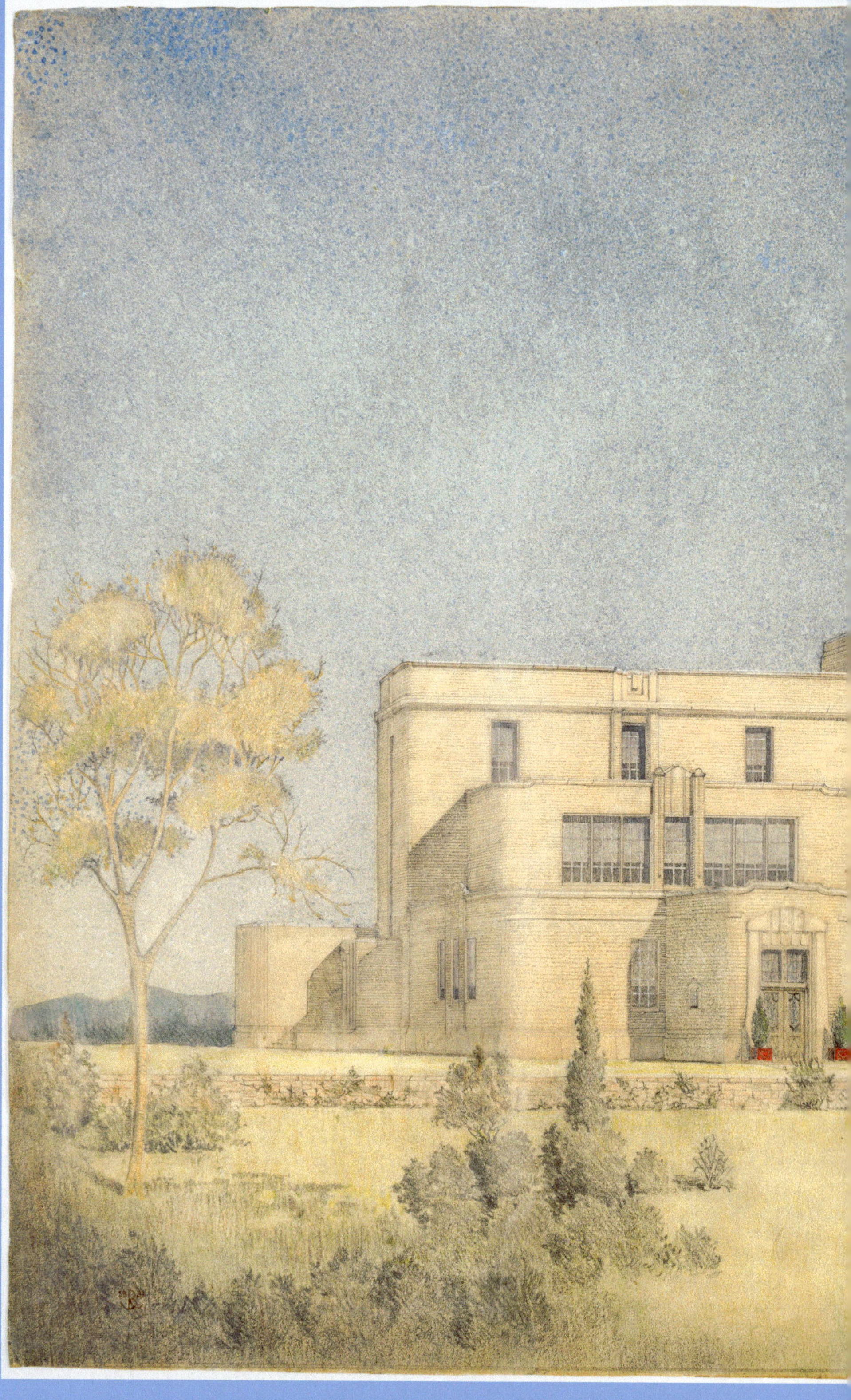

Link Weber &Bowers and Otto R. Eggers (delineator), *Mifflin Elementary School, Perspective Drawing,* 1931, pencil and watercolor on card; Carnegie Museum of Art, Gift of PPS

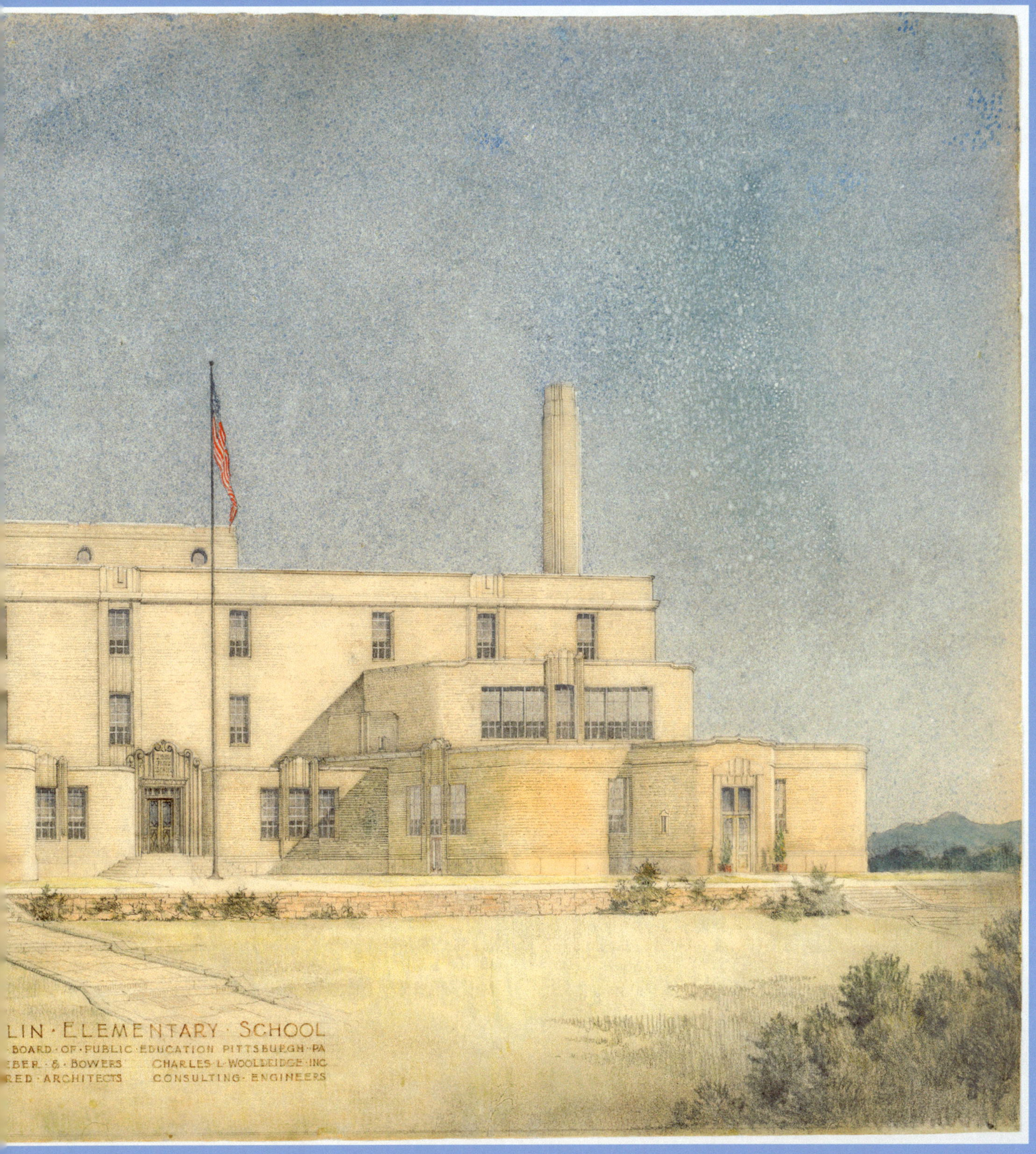
LIN·ELEMENTARY·SCHOOL
BOARD·OF·PUBLIC·EDUCATION PITTSBURGH·PA
EBER·&·BOWERS   CHARLES·L·WOOLDRIDGE·INC
RED·ARCHITECTS   CONSULTING·ENGINEERS

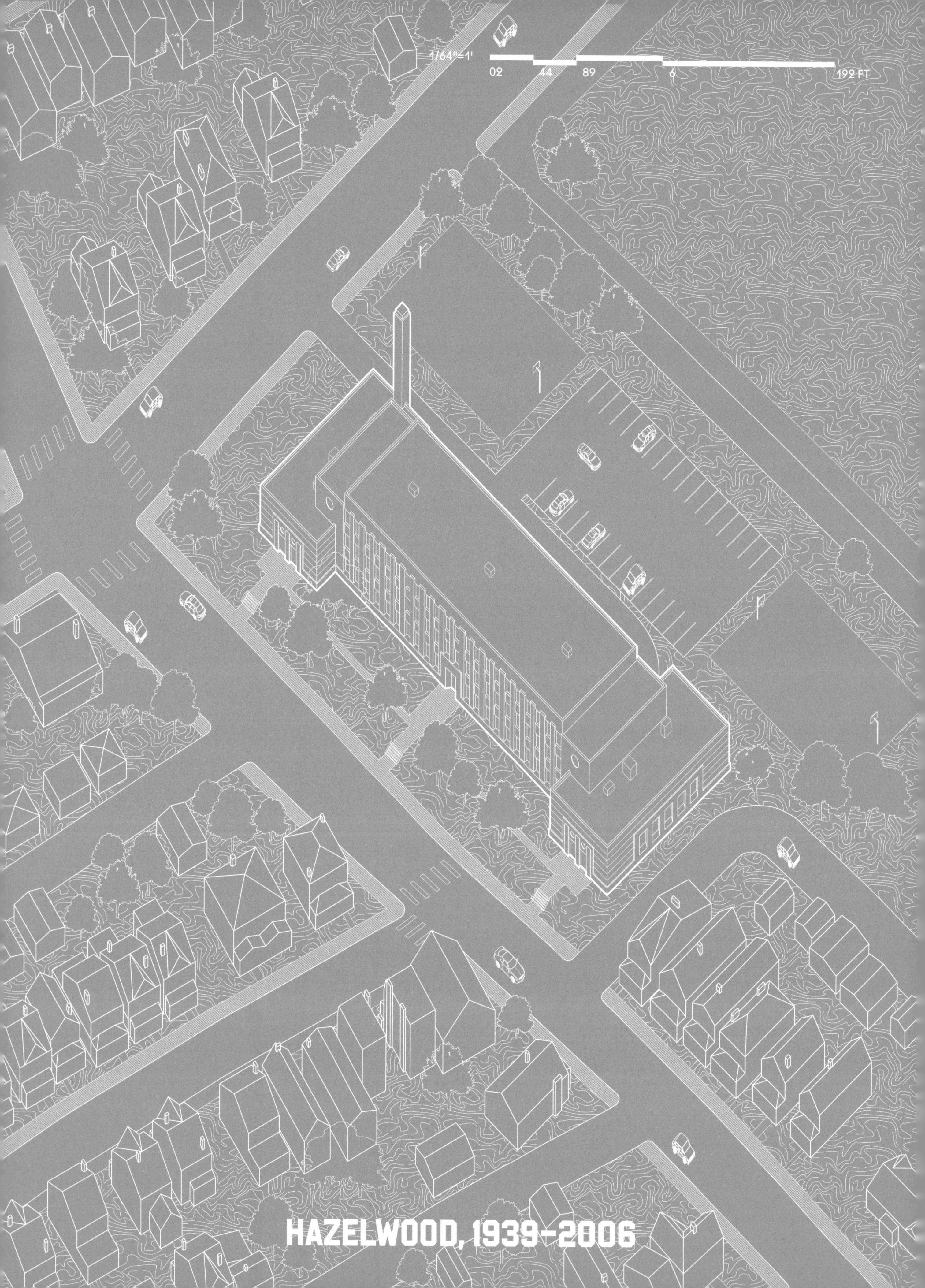

1/64"=1'
02 44 89 6 192 FT
HAZELWOOD, 1939–2006

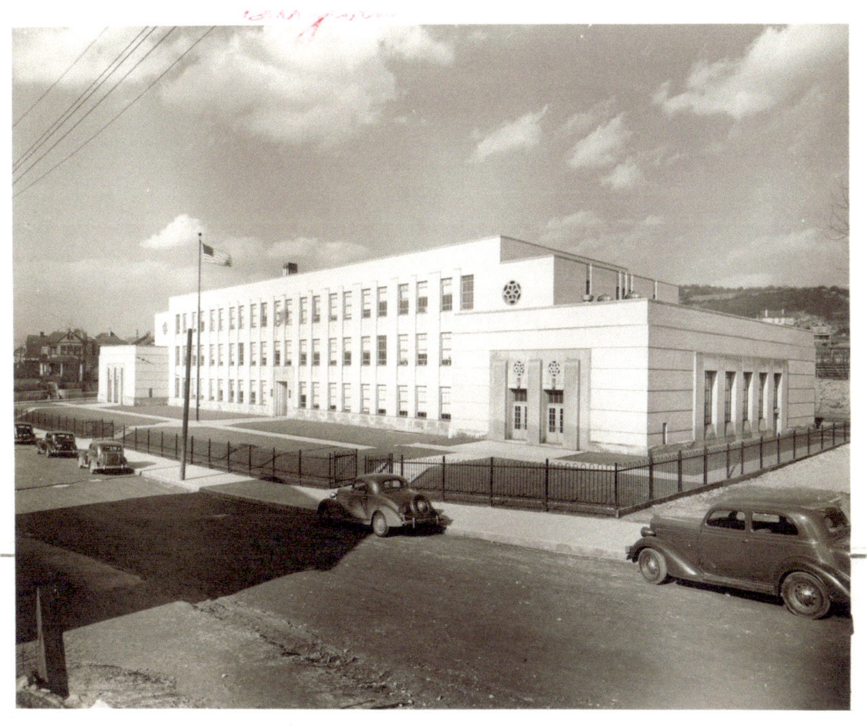

BURGWIN ELEMENTARY

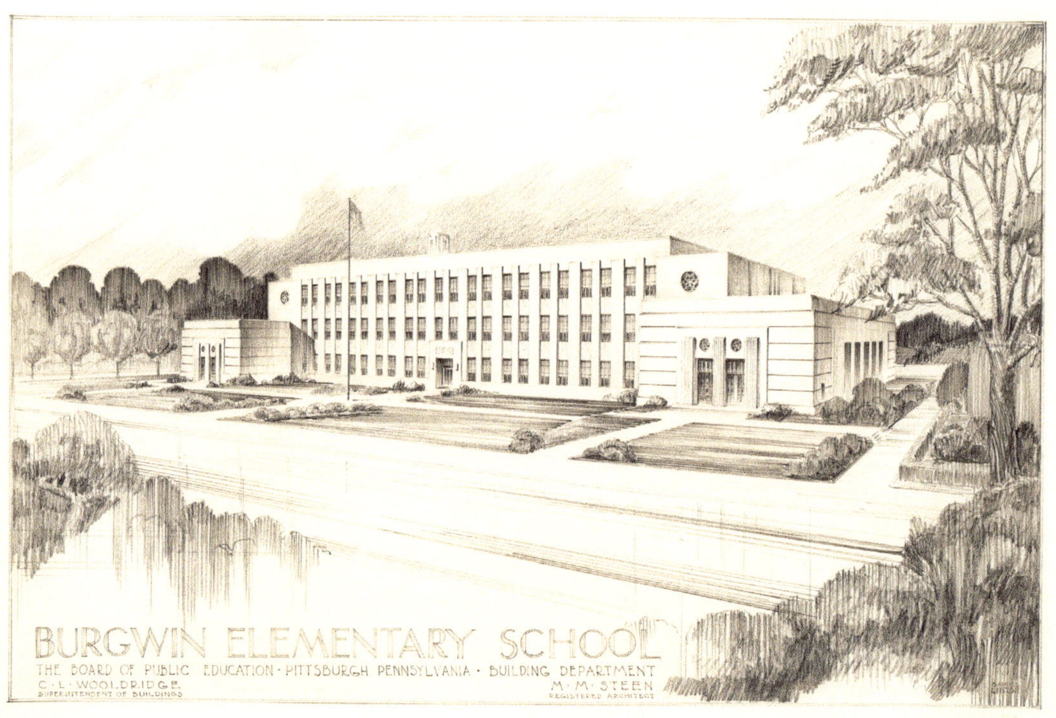

Above: Marion M. Steen and Samuel Linton (delineator), *Burgwin Elementary School, Perspective Drawing,* 1936, pencil and crayon on card; Carnegie Museum of Art, Gift of PPS

Previous page: Burgwin Elementary School, ca. 1940, photograph; Detre Library & Archives, HHC

In 2006, the Pittsburgh Board of Public Education decided to close Burgwin Elementary School on the grounds that the school wasn't meeting the state's academic standards, and that attendance was too low to merit keeping the school open. The closure caused an uproar throughout the Greater Hazelwood area, particularly after community-led research revealed that, among the elementary schools slated to be closed due to poor academic performance, Burgwin was performing at or above the state's standards with student attendance at capacity. A true neighborhood school, Burgwin provided after-school programs and worked with community-based and non-community-based programs to supplement gaps in educational services.

The Board of Public Education conducted a series of public meetings where Greater Hazelwood community members gave comments for three minutes each to persuade the Board to reverse their recommendations regarding the closure of the school. In advance of each meeting, Hazelwood-based organizations brought in several busloads of people and packed the meeting room. Despite the overwhelming display of support and public outcry, and despite data demonstrating that the school was performing up to state standards with a full complement of students in attendance, the Board still voted to close Burgwin Elementary in 2006.

This decision was made as part of a district-wide "realignment" proposal, marking the third time within a five-year span that our community had to endure one of our schools closing. We watched as our children suffered the consequences of having to relocate and be bussed to different schools spread across eight different communities. With the closure of Gladstone Middle School in 2001, our Catholic school in 2003, and Burgwin Elementary in 2006, the families of Greater Hazelwood faced the reality of their children having no local access to a formal public education. But this time, leaders from the Greater Hazelwood community were proactive in addressing PPS representatives and found ways to work with the district to produce logistics that wouldn't include moving Hazelwood students.

After Burgwin's closing, we came together as a community to discuss the method that the Board of Public Education was using to shut down schools and the logistical outcomes. We discovered that the schools in economically advantaged neighborhoods were not being touched. We also discovered that some of these schools needed more students in the building to justify keeping them open and, therefore, sought the enrollment of children from low-income communities.

Today, the top priority for the parents of Hazelwood is to reestablish and guarantee community access to formal public education once again. Children need to be in an environment where they have a sense of belonging, significance, and security. They also deserve to feel that they are free to be who they are and to learn how they learn. In the last fifteen years, the number of students graduating from high school and choosing not to attend a four-year university has grown tremendously.

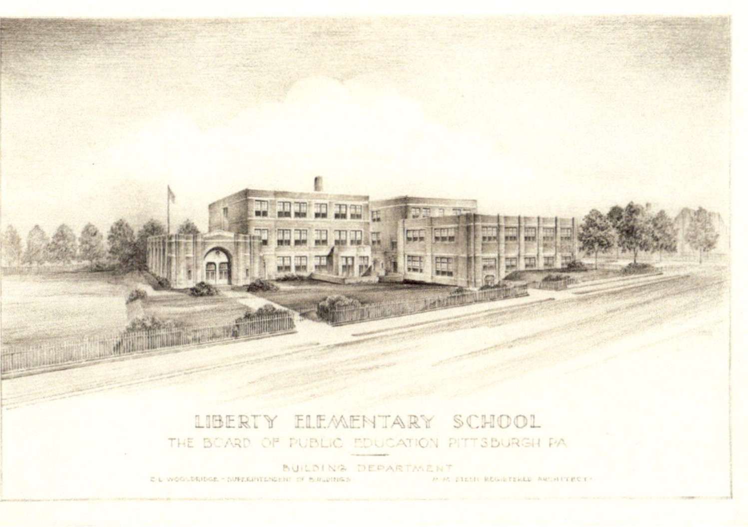

Marion M. Steen and Samuel Linton (delineator), *Liberty Elementary School, Perspective Drawing,* 1936, pencil and crayon on card; Carnegie Museum of Art, Gift of PPS

But I believe that education is everywhere, and where there is education, there is opportunity. This was part of the driving force behind the creation of the Center of Life: I wanted to do my part to make a better community, to make a safer community that has access to the best resources and education. I wanted to have a part in that. From the beginning—when the Center was operated by just my wife, myself, and a handful of volunteers—we built our non-profit practice on the basis of four community pillars: access to early learning, access to jobs and resources, access to mental and physical healthcare, and access to the arts and sciences. Any community structured around those four pillars is not a community that can easily be underserved. They're going to be full of people who actually know how to do things and know what it means to manage wealth and control their own economy. The Center of Life is not about offering a safety net; it's about taking the initiative and doing the hard work to make sure that there's a secure, stable place for our children and our children's children.

Now, the Center of Life employs close to forty people and offers a variety of educational opportunities: from family strengthening sessions and healthcare resources to music, athletic, and entrepreneurial programs. We have partnerships with hospitals and universities, including the Community College of Allegheny County as well as the Robotics Institute at Carnegie Mellon University. Our goal is to offer a spectrum of services to our community. We saw that there were a lot of services that could have been offered through the schools, and that were offered through schools that were now out of our community, to support families, children, and youth. So, we stepped in to fill that gap.

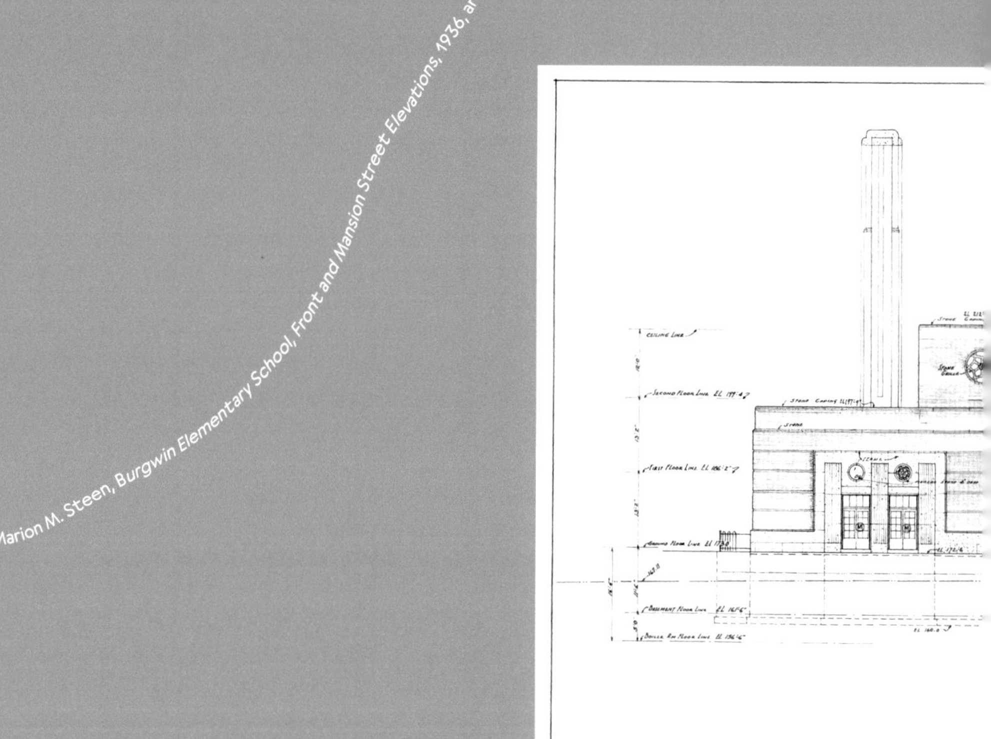

Marion M. Steen, Burgwin Elementary School, Front and Mansion Street Elevations, 1936, architectural drawing; PPBF

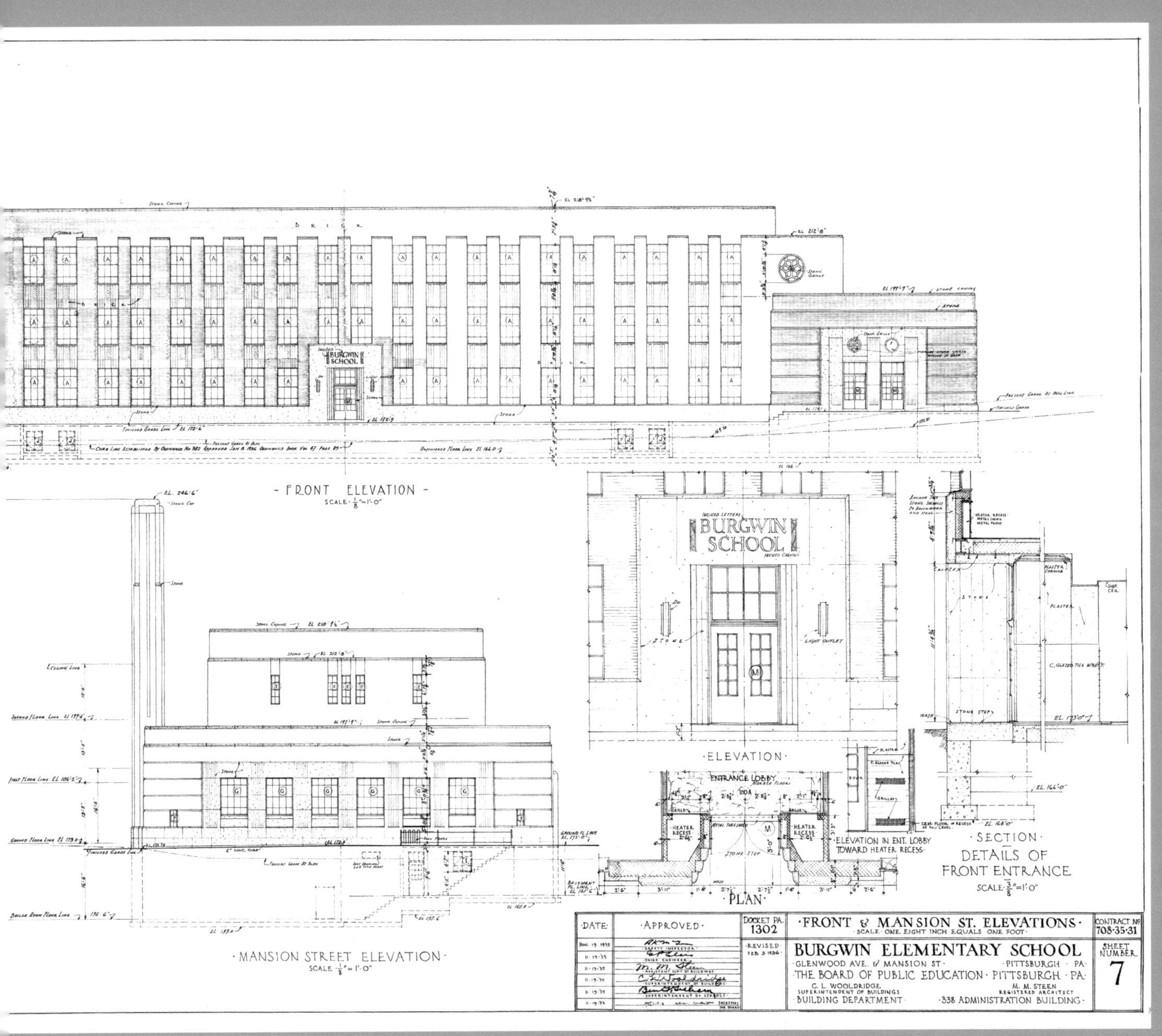
BURGWIN SCHOOL
- FRONT ELEVATION -
SCALE 1/8" = 1'-0"
- MANSION STREET ELEVATION -
SCALE 1/8" = 1'-0"
BURGWIN SCHOOL
ELEVATION
ENTRANCE LOBBY
HEATER RECESS
HEATER RECESS
PLAN
ELEVATION IN ENT. LOBBY TOWARD HEATER RECESS
SECTION
DETAILS OF FRONT ENTRANCE
SCALE 3/8" = 1'-0"
DATE:
APPROVED
DOCKET PA.
1302
REVISED
FEB 3 1936
CONTRACT No
708-35-31
FRONT & MANSION ST. ELEVATIONS
SCALE ONE EIGHTH INCH EQUALS ONE FOOT
BURGWIN ELEMENTARY SCHOOL
GLENWOOD AVE. & MANSION ST.   PITTSBURGH · PA·
THE BOARD OF PUBLIC EDUCATION · PITTSBURGH · PA·
C. L. WOOLDRIDGE   M. M. STEEN
SUPERINTENDENT OF BUILDINGS   REGISTERED ARCHITECT
BUILDING DEPARTMENT   ·338 ADMINISTRATION BUILDING·
SHEET NUMBER
7

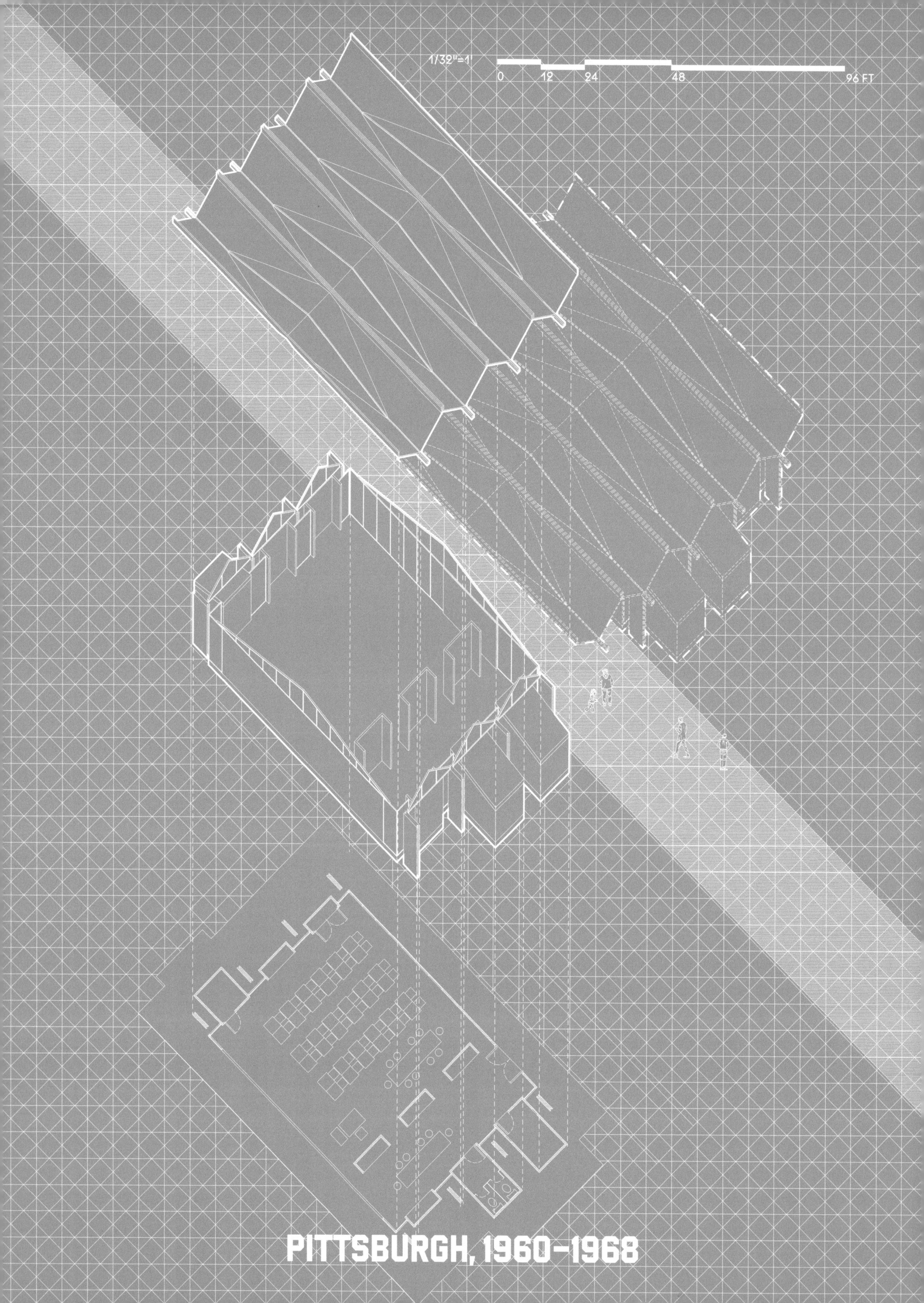

1/32"=1'
0 12 24 48 96 FT
PITTSBURGH, 1960-1968

In the early 1960s, a special committee formed in Pittsburgh to explore the idea of demountable schools as a spatial response to overcrowding and shifting urban populations. Led by architects John Pekruhn, Dahlen Ritchey (Deeter & Ritchey), and Lawrence Wolfe (Wolfe & Wolfe), the committee proposed several designs for self-contained classrooms, capable of expanding or contracting based on need and equipped with lighting, ventilation, and heating. Designed to be modular and prefabricated, these temporary structures were framed as low-cost, flexible, and quickly deployable units for neighborhoods lacking adequate school infrastructure. The architects' studies and preparatory drawings for the proposed schools shed light on the committee's material and structural experimentations with industrial materials. Supported by regional manufactures, the demountable schools project concluded with the construction of two prototyped systems: the first developed six steel units near Philip Murray Elementary, and the second yielded four concrete units organized into two classrooms near Homewood Elementary.

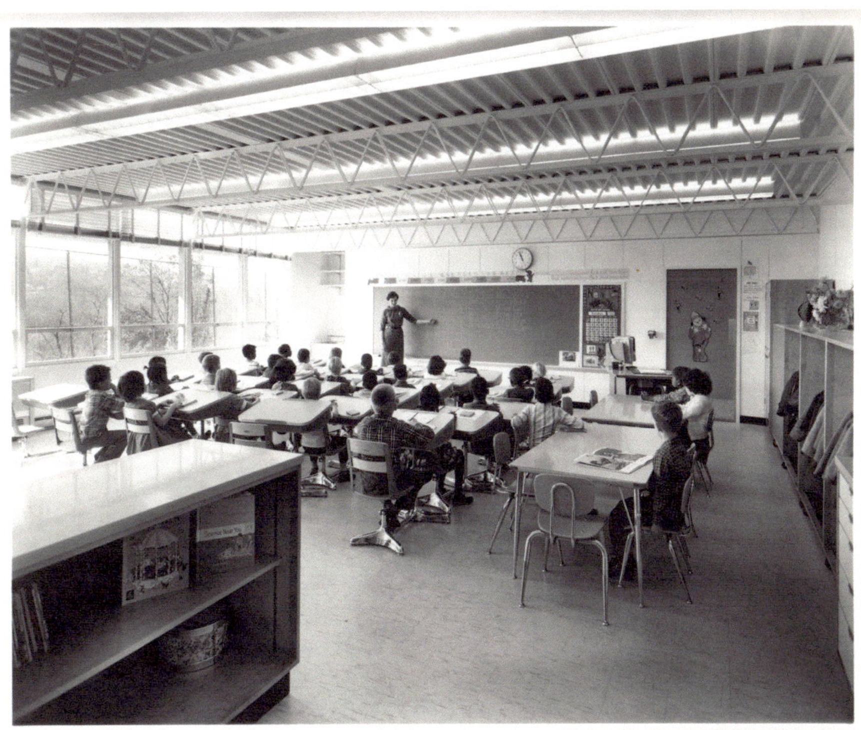

DEMOUNTABLE SCHOOLS

PATIENTLY WAITING: COMMUNITY, CONNECTION, AND CURIOSITY Lynn Kawaratani

"Demountable" is not a word I expected to encounter when I began working in an architecture archive. Administrations change. Old materials get buried or lost. Drawings curl at the edges. Slides fade. Reports gather dust. With limited space and resources, most institutions discard what feels outdated or of minor significance. But sometimes, a collection survives—preserved, patient, and waiting for someone to notice. That is the story of the Demountable Schools in Pittsburgh.

I stepped into the role of manager at the Carnegie Mellon University Architecture Archives (CMUAA) in August 2022. The archive has been growing since 1984, now encompassing thousands of drawings and records from hundreds of architects. As I continue to explore its holdings, I have found that understanding these materials often means reaching beyond the archive itself—building community to rebuild context. Brittany Reilly, the chair of the Modern Committee of Preservation Pittsburgh, introduced me to the Demountable Schools proposal while she was researching the work of architects Lawrence and Anthony Wolfe in local elementary schools. Reilly, a longtime user of the archive and now a key collaborator, is committed to amplifying Pittsburgh's often-overlooked modern architectural legacy. Her inquiry led me to a remarkable set of documents—sketches on tracing paper, meticulous presentation drawings, and a final report with photographs and usage metrics—traces of a project that has all but disappeared from the city's built environment.

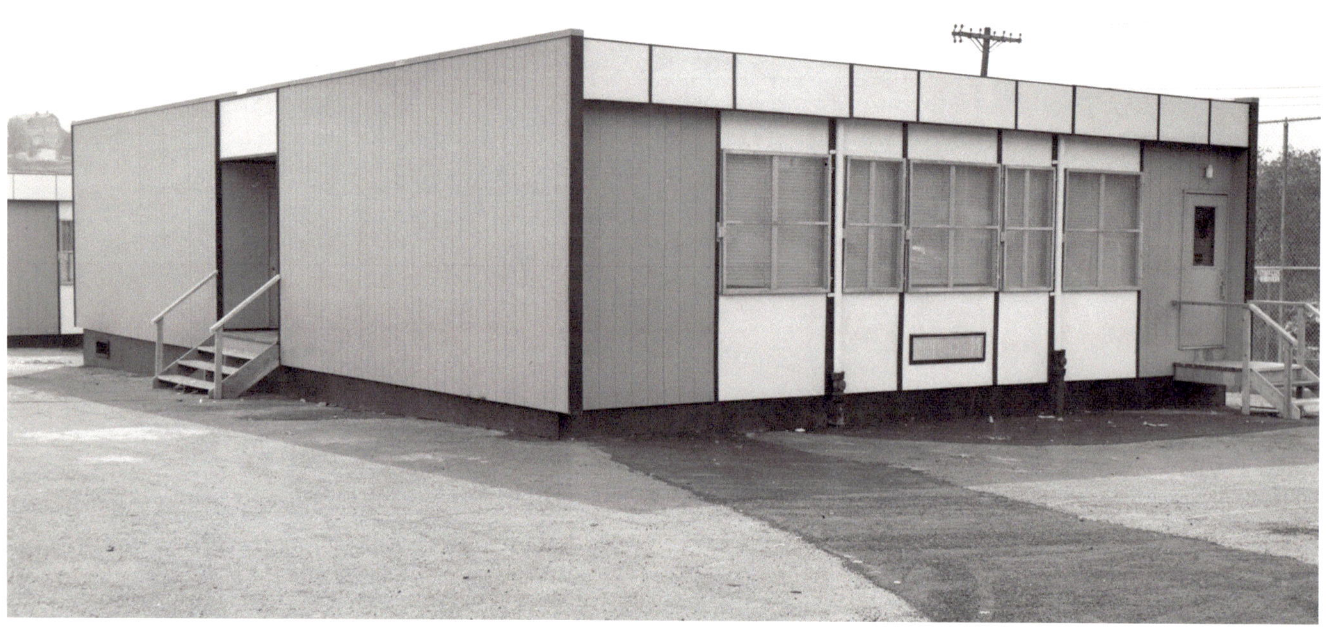

Although undated, the Demountable Schools project was likely developed in the early 1960s, when many large cities in the United States were grappling with the challenges of shifting populations and uneven growth. The drawings are unsigned, but the report begins with a preface by Richard L. Barrick, the Educational Facilities Coordinator of the Pittsburgh Board of Public Education. It lists Superintendent of Schools Calvin E. Gross—who served between 1958 and 1962—as a key participant. Led by a special committee of architects, including Pittsburgh-based John Pekruhn, the project explored the feasibility of a modular building system that could respond quickly to changing demographics and neighborhood needs.

The report outlines specific conditions for such flexibility: the use of steel and concrete from local industries; strategies for navigating Pittsburgh's steep and winding topography; climate-responsive spatial layouts; and most crucially, the ability for units to function independently, even on sites lacking infrastructure. Four modular bays could be joined to form a classroom, then disassembled and moved by truck to a new location. It was an experimental logic of mobility and adaptation—an architecture that might anticipate where children would need to learn next.

Only a handful of these prototypes were ever built. One was demolished; the other remains standing in deteriorated condition, having neither moved nor aged particularly well. The innovation behind their portability is no longer visible; the buildings themselves no longer speak. The prototypes do little to communicate the experimental ideas behind their original design. Instead, it is the archive that allows their story to be told through initial concept sketches and multiple design iterations, each carrying the markings of an idea in formation and the impulse of architects responding to a pressing contemporary question. The hand-drawn renderings evoke more than construction technique; they reflect the era's aspirational ideas of classroom learning, filtered through the language of midcentury modernism.

Without archives, the critical context preserved in these records would be lost. When the curators of *after school* visited the archives with a list of school buildings they were researching, I shared the Demountable Schools materials with them. It was a moment to expand the circle. In our current time of educational upheaval and uncertainty both in the Pittsburgh Public Schools and in the nation as a whole, we are confronted once again with the need to rethink the future of schools and, perhaps more critically, the architecture of education. The materials nestled within the CMUAA speak from the past, offering insight into what was explored before and what might spark the next transformation.

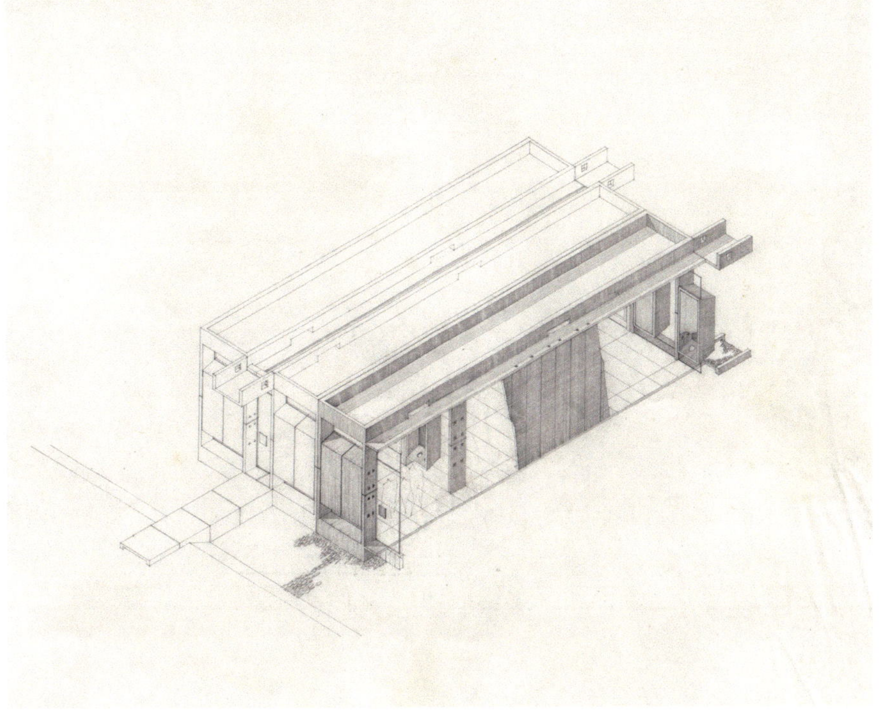

John Pekruhn, et al, *Demountable School, Concrete Study, Axonometric Drawing*, 1961–1962, pencil on tracing paper; CMUAA

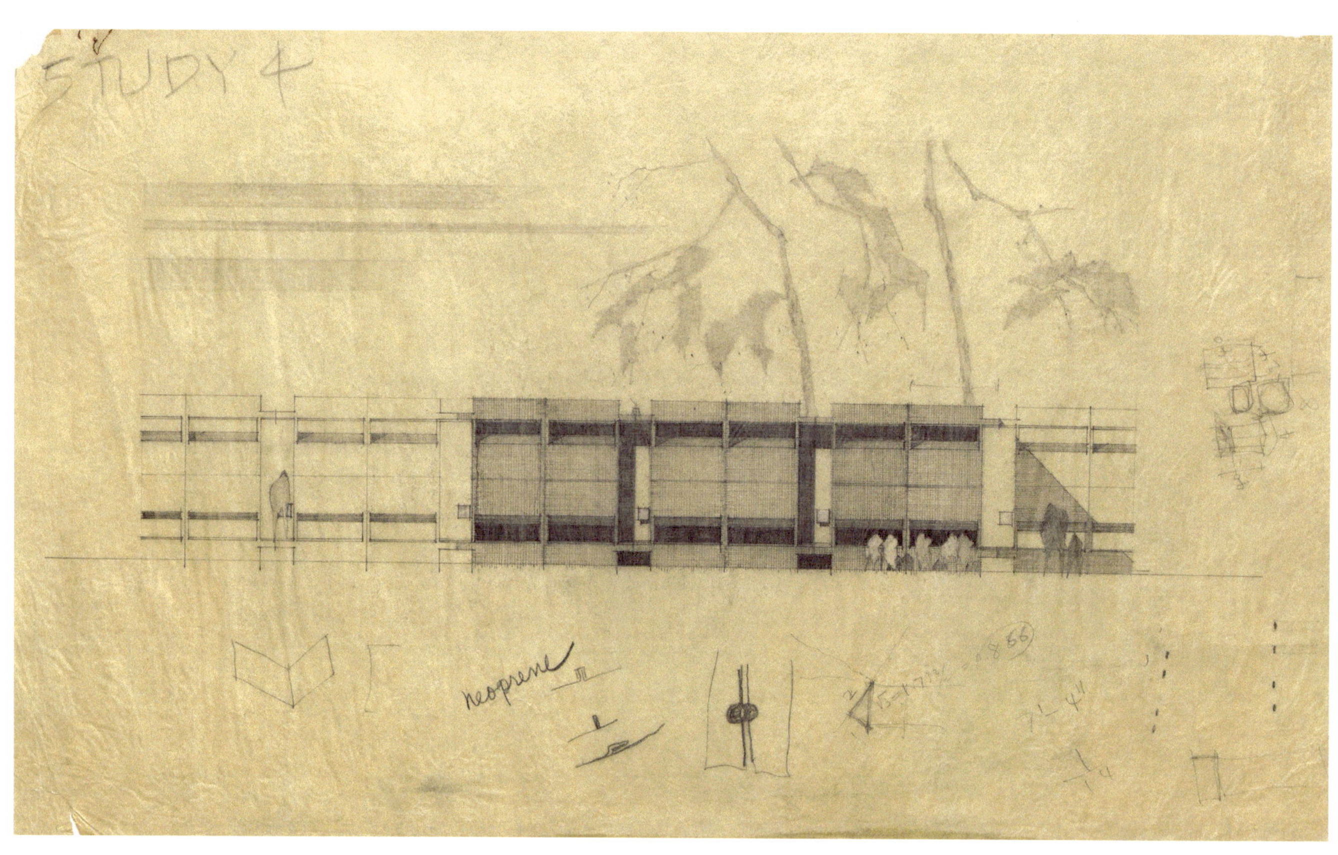

John Pekruhn, Lawrence Wolfe, Anthony Lee Wolfe, Russell Orrin Deeter, and Dahlen K. Ritchey, *Demountable School, Concrete Study, Elevation*, 1961–1962, pencil on tracing paper; CMUAA

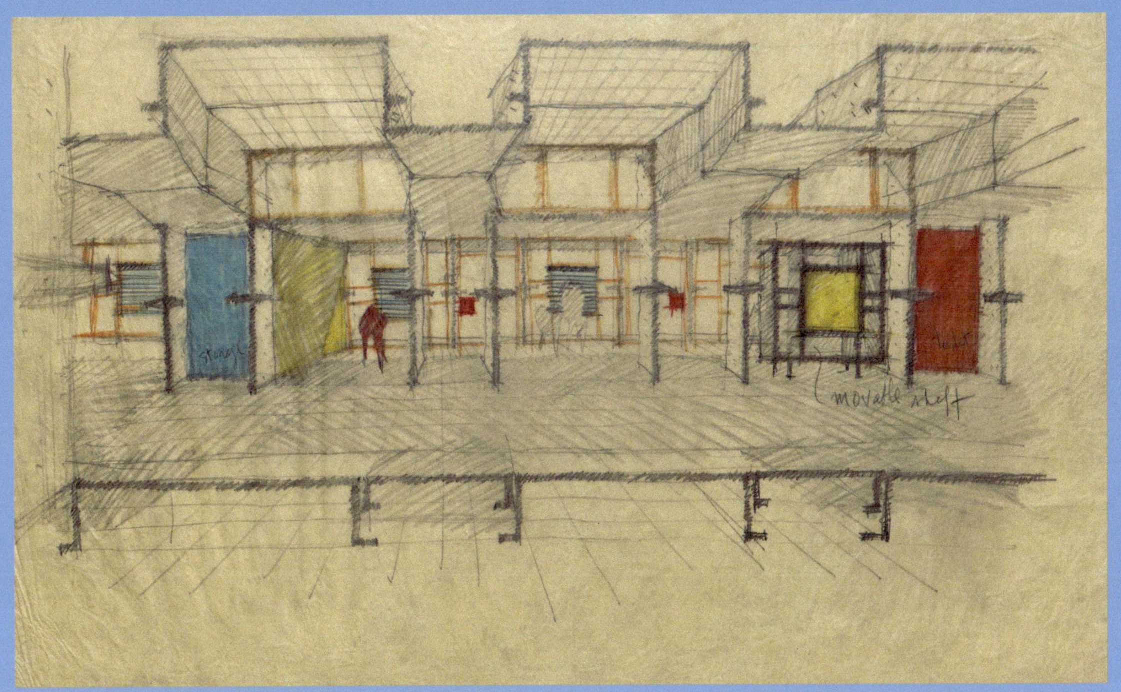

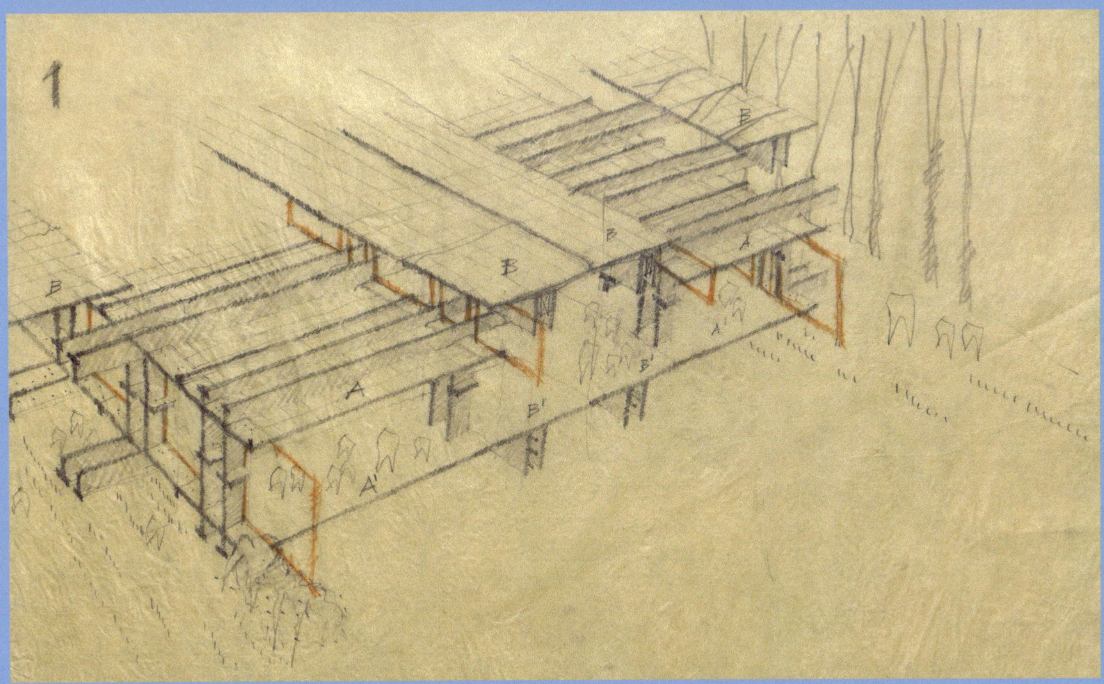

Top: John Pekruhn, et al, *Demountable School, Aluminum Study, Perspectival Section Sketch,* 1961–1962, pencil and crayon on tracing paper; CMUAA

Bottom: John Pekruhn, et al, *Demountable School, Steel Study, Axonometric Sketch,* 1961–1962, pencil and crayon on tracing paper, CMUAA

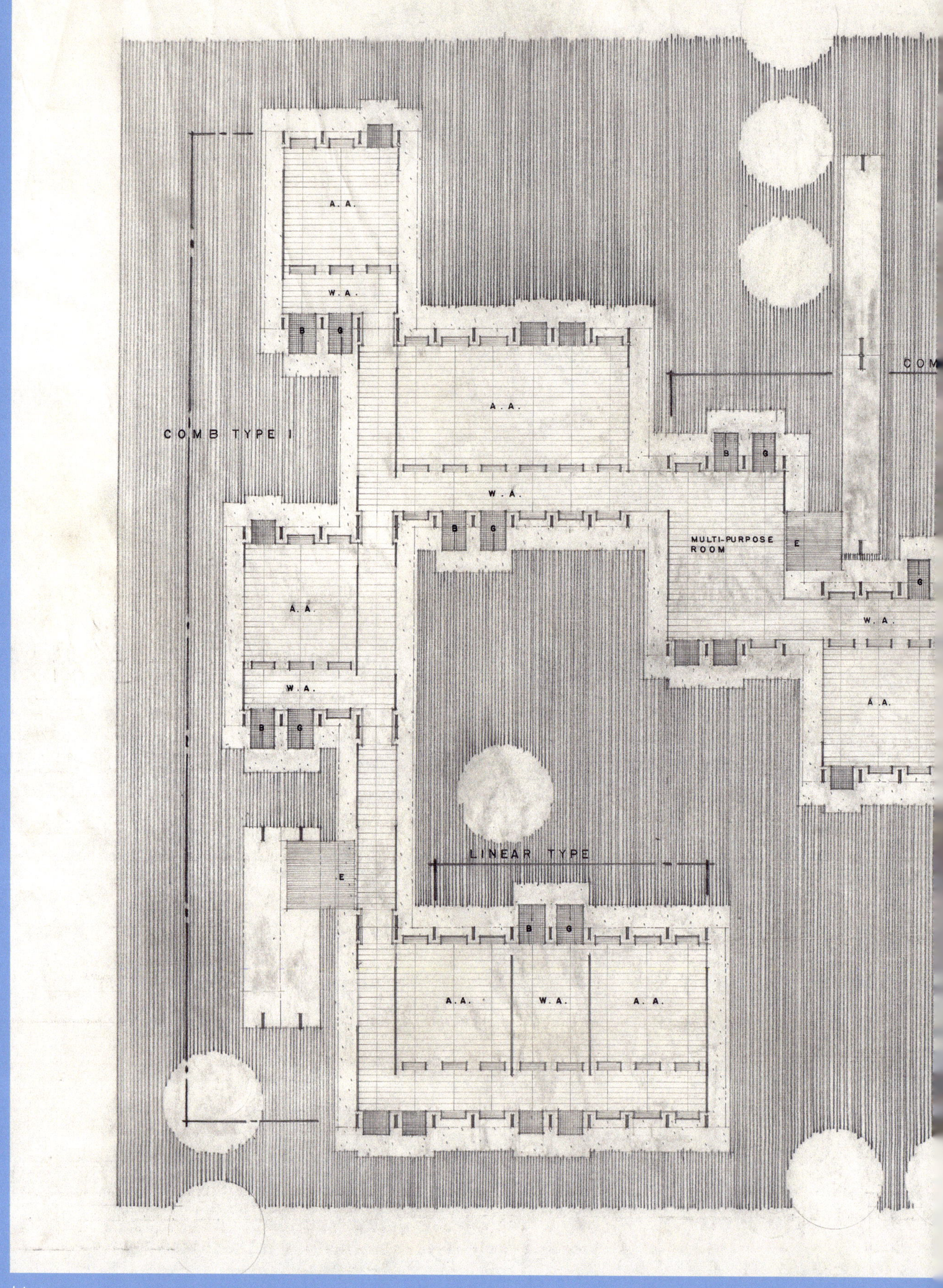

John Pekruhn, et al, *Demountable School, Aluminum Study, Plan, 1961–1962*, pencil on tracing paper; CMUAA

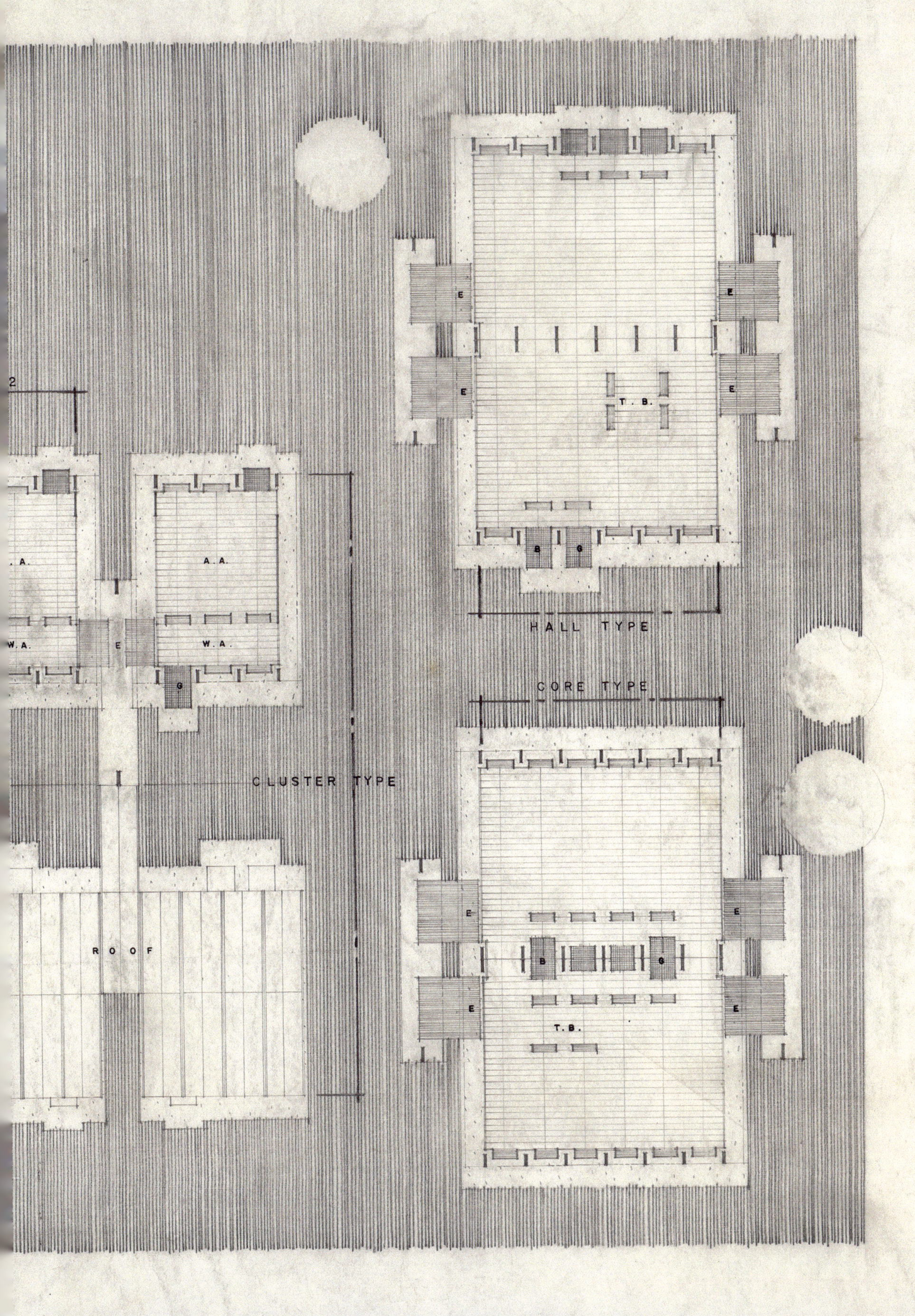

LYNN KAWARATANI   Demountable Schools

BROOKLINE, 1960-PRESENT

The Pioneer School opened in 1960 as a
tuition-free public school for students
with disabilities. Predating the 1975
passage of the Individuals with Disabilities
Education Act (IDEA), which mandated
free and accessible public education for all
students with disabilities, the school
integrated classroom instruction with
on-site physical, occupational, and
speech therapies, ensuring students
received simultaneous access to
instruction and care. At the time of
its construction, Pioneer, like many
special education programs established
midcentury, was pushed to the city's
periphery in the South Hills neighborhood
of Brookline. Afforded by the school's
suburban location, architect Burton
Kenneth Johnstone, then chair of
University of Pennsylvania's Department
of Architecture, was able to design a
spacious and sprawling one-story building
with wide corridors and doorways for
wheelchair access, adaptive classroom
spaces, and brightly lit common areas.
Special attention was also paid to the
design of outdoor spaces, which included
a covered play area and sensory gardens.
The Pioneer Education Center, renamed
in 1978, continues to serve students
ages five to twenty-one, sharing its campus with South Brook Middle School.

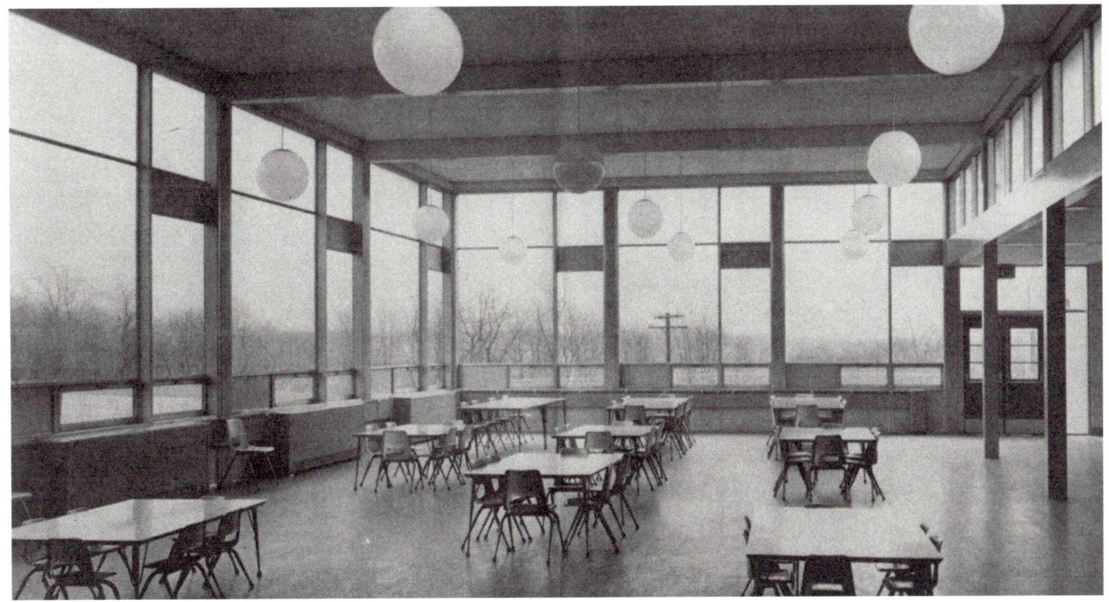

PIONEER EDUCATION CENTER

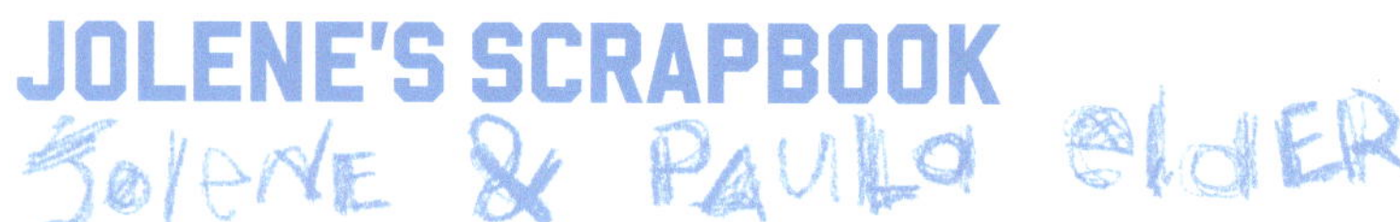

JOLENE'S SCRAPBOOK

Jolene & Paula Elder

The following pages offer a glimpse into a mother-daughter narrative within the broader context of disability advocacy, inclusive education, and community building. Born in 1981, Jolene Elder began her educational journey in the infant program at Easterseals Western and Central Pennsylvania and continued at the Pioneer Education Center from the age of four until her graduation in 2002. During her time on the Brookline campus, Jolene produced a range of creative work, documenting aspects of her everyday life as a student at Pioneer and her engagement with

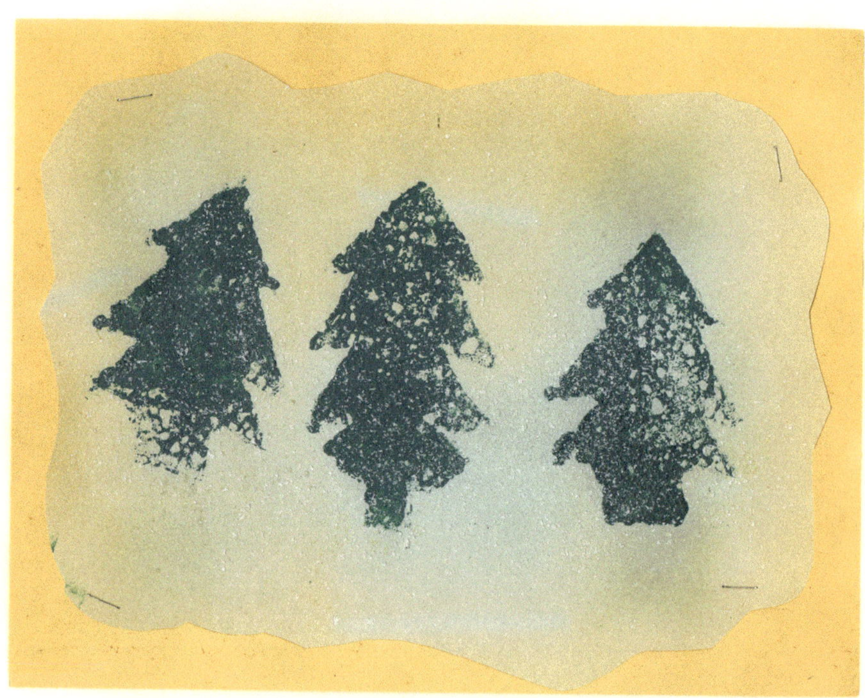

Some evergreen trees stand tall in the snowstorm!

10

the natural world. Across each page of Jolene's scrapbook, her collages capture seasonal details and textures of the suburban landscape around her—clusters of evergreens weathering a winter storm and found materials like leaves, twigs, pressed flowers, and a bottle cap, carefully arranged and preserved.

From the beginning, Jolene's mother, Paula Elder, was actively involved in her daughter's educational experience at Pioneer, eventually becoming a substitute teacher and later employed as a paraprofessional at the school. In 1997, when Pioneer was faced with the potential of closure, Paula wrote a powerful letter, part of which was featured in a story published by the local newspaper. In her statement, Paula advocated for the school to remain open in order to continue to serve and support Jolene and other local students with disabilities.

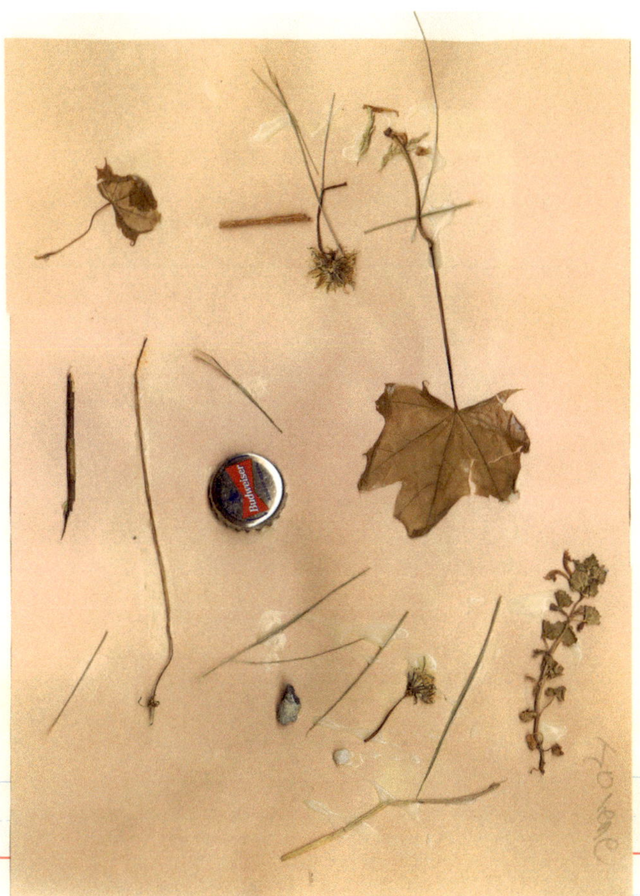

On a scavenger hunt with her buddy Jolene found these items. Can you name all of them?

Left: Jolene Elder, *Evergreens in the Snowstorm*, 1995, painted paper collage; Detre Library & Archives, HHC

Right: Jolene Elder, *Scavenger Hunt*, 1995, multimedia collage; Detre Library & Archives, HHC

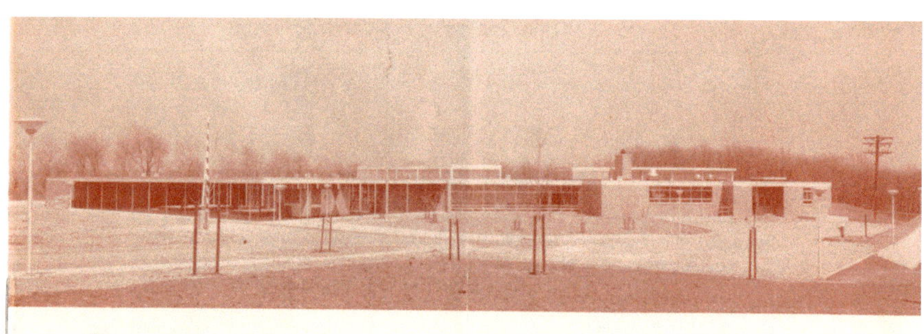

Program

for
the

Dedication

of
the

Pioneer
School

Tuesday
May Seventeenth
1960
Pittsburgh - Pennsylvania

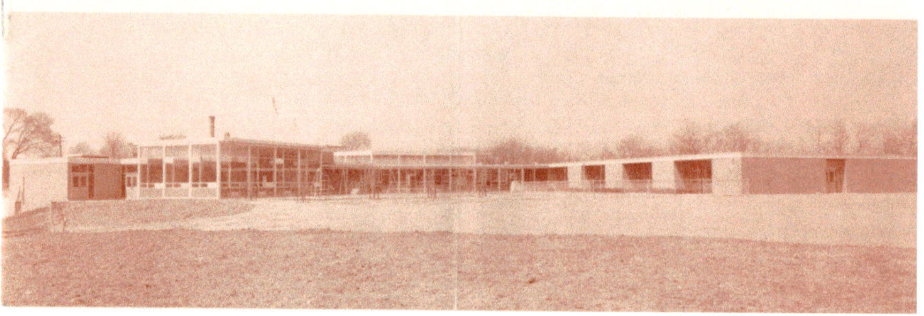

Paula Elder, Letter, 1997, transcribed archival document with original annotations; Detre Library & Archives, HHC

Hello, I am Paula Elder, a parent of a multiply handicapped 16 year old, Jolene. And I am here on behalf of her. I want to thank you in advance for opening your minds and listening to different alternatives to closing Pioneer.

Jolene has attended Pioneer since she was 4 1/2 years old. I'm sure you all know how hard it is to send a child off to kindergarten. But imagine how hard it was to send a child so completely dependent on someone for all her needs. How relieved I was to find that Pioneer School, its program, staff and safe and nurturing environment were completely suitable to her. Pioneer was indeed built with her in mind.

Pioneer has grown since 1985. The parents raised money for a Handicapped-Accessible Playground. For most of our children, this was the first time that they were on swings or a merry-go-round. They have a safe place to walk or ride a bike. Air-conditioning was put in all the rooms to be regulated to fit the needs of the children.

Today, 12 years later, Jolene has accomplished many things I never thought possible. Although, Jolene will always be dependent on others for most of her needs, she has almost mastered feeding herself. She can use a walker through the halls, and bike around the track. She has learned to trust the routine and is secure ~~here~~ at Pioneer. And I am secure that she is safe. Jolene only has 4 more years before she graduates, but I feel I must also fight for the other children to have the same right to ~~chose~~ choose Pioneer.

When some of you visited our school last month, I'm sure you were able to see students that were happy, safe and thriving. And I am sure you also noticed that many of the students were without the use of their legs, many were without their voices, and some without their eyesight or hearing. Please do not take another thing from them. Hear their voice. Leave the Pioneer Program in the building for which it was built.

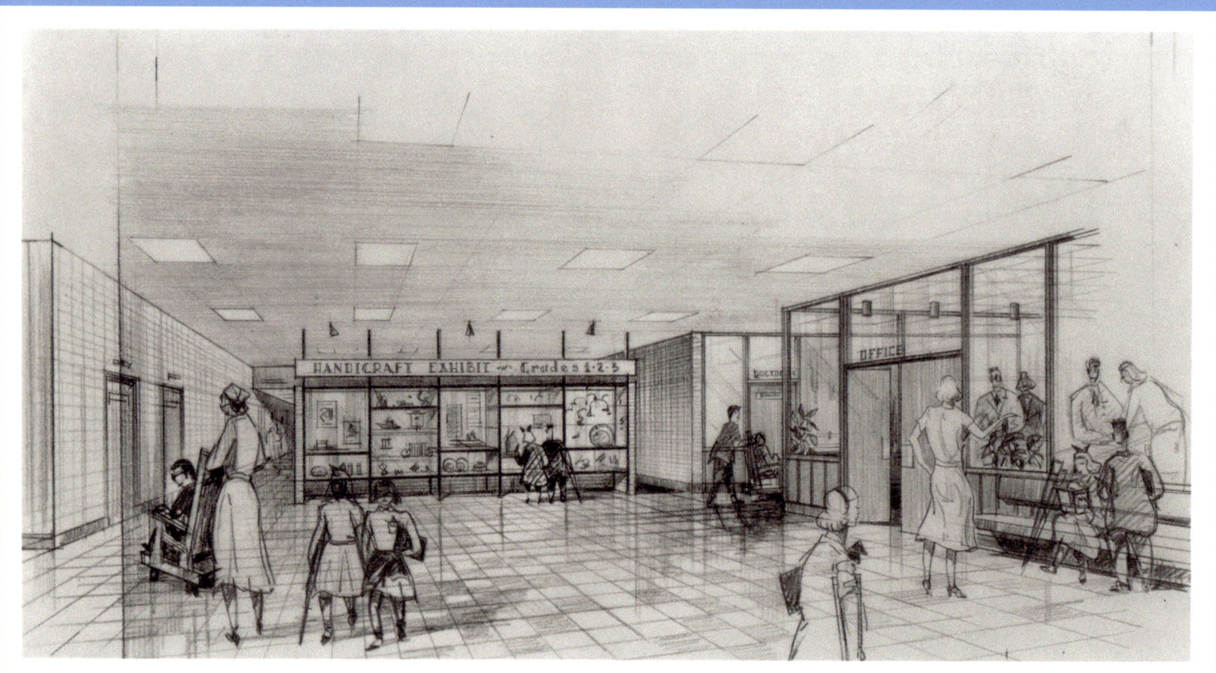
HANDICRAFT EXHIBIT — Grades 1-2-3
OFFICE

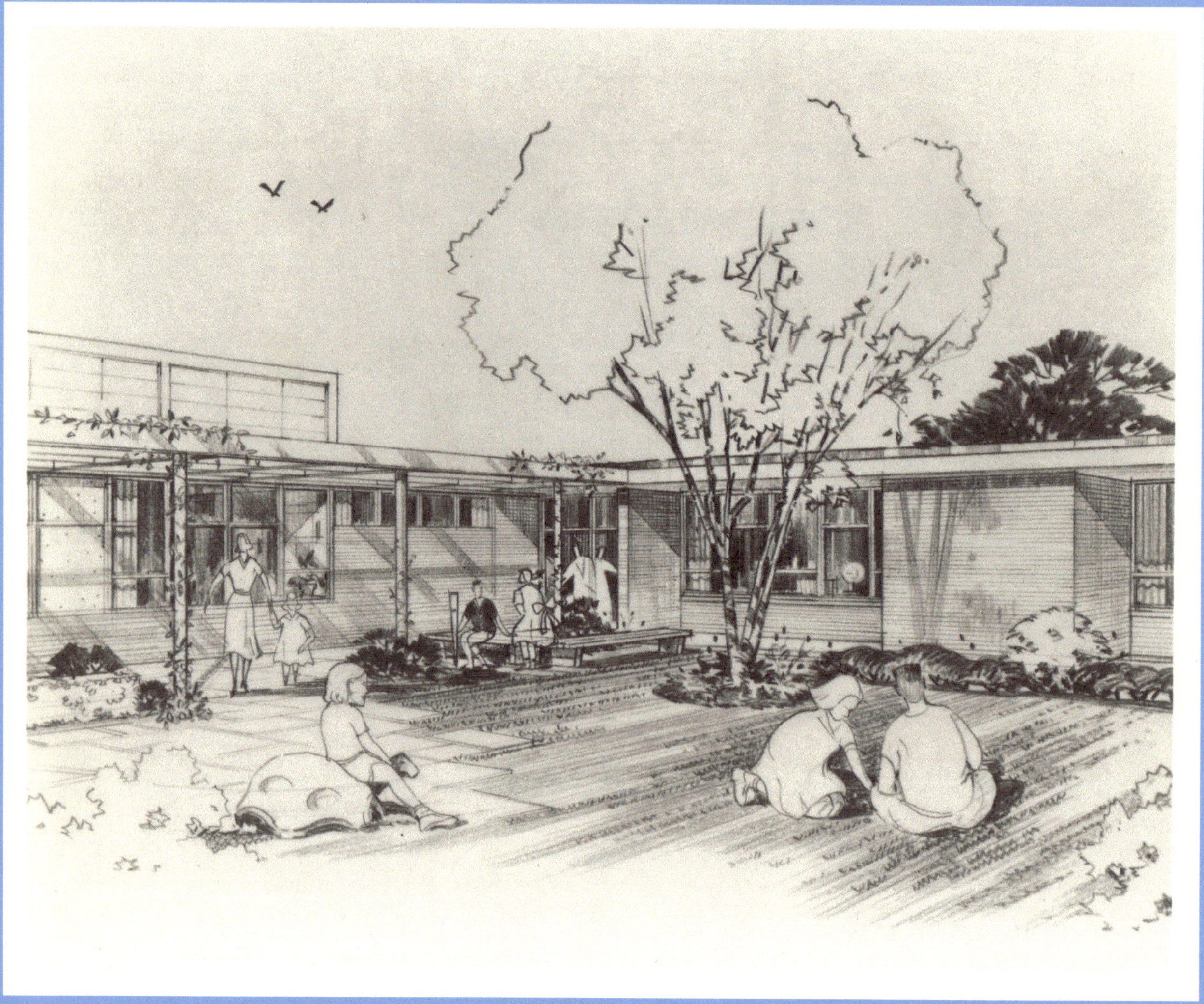

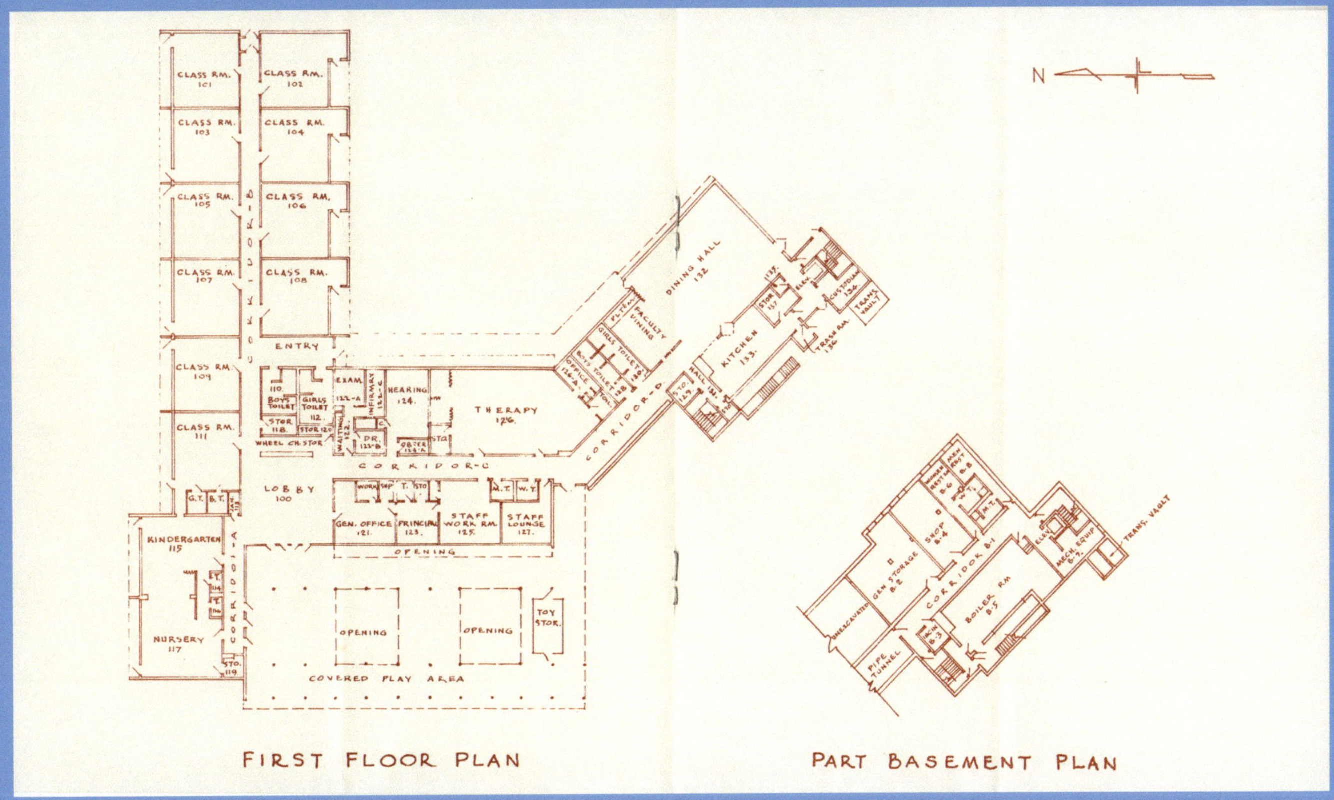

Architectural plan in the Program for the Dedication of the Pioneer School, May 17, 1960, pamphlet; Pittsburgh Board of Education archives, CLP

Left top: Burton Kenneth Johnstone, *Pioneer School, Architectural Rendering of Handicraft Exhibit,* ca. 1957, pencil on paper; Detre Library & Archives, HHC

Left bottom: Burton Kenneth Johnstone, *Pioneer School, Architectural Rendering of Outside Play Area*, ca. 1957, pencil on paper; Detre Library & Archives, HHC

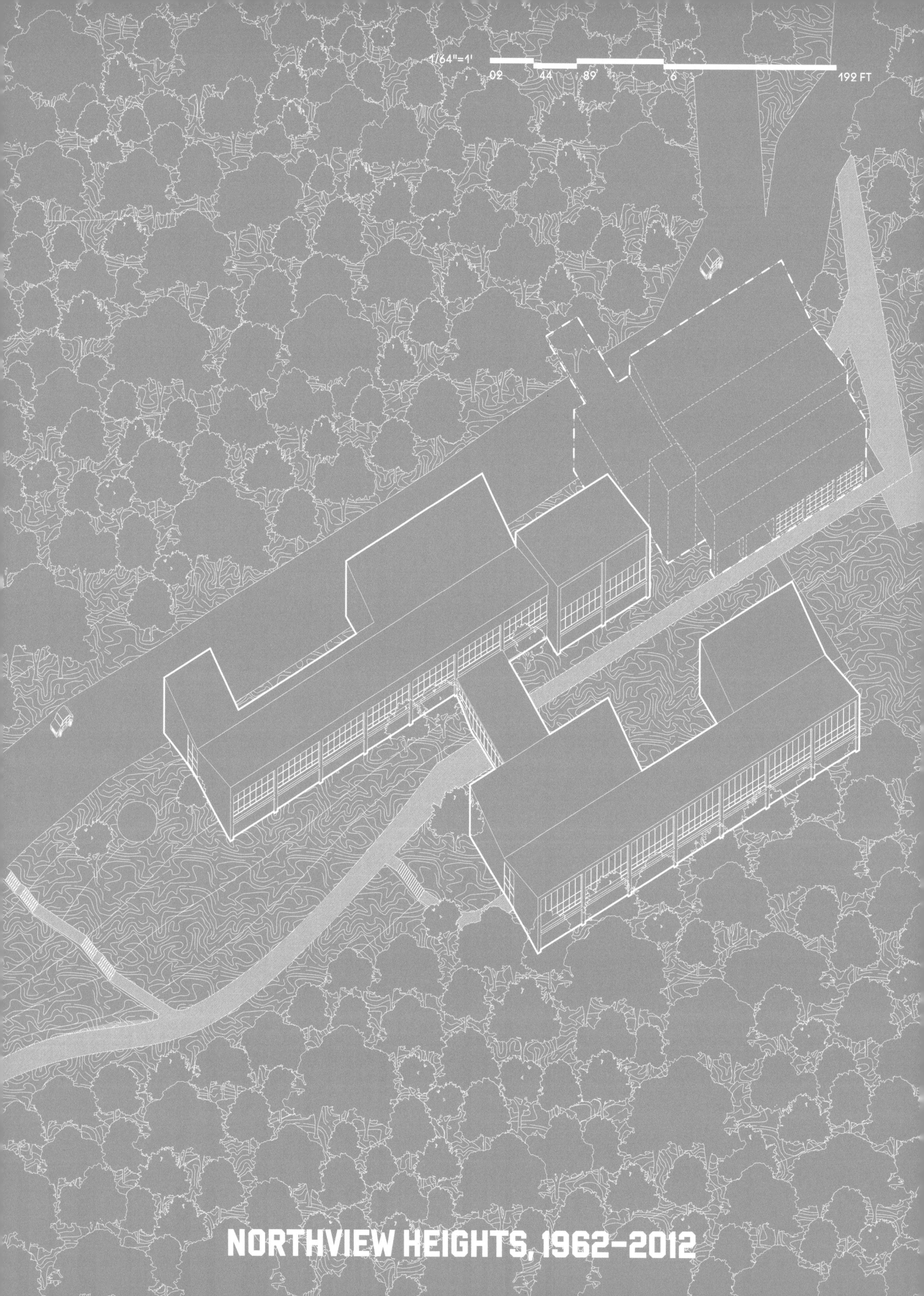

1/64"=1'
02   44   89'   6   192 FT
NORTHVIEW HEIGHTS, 1962-2012

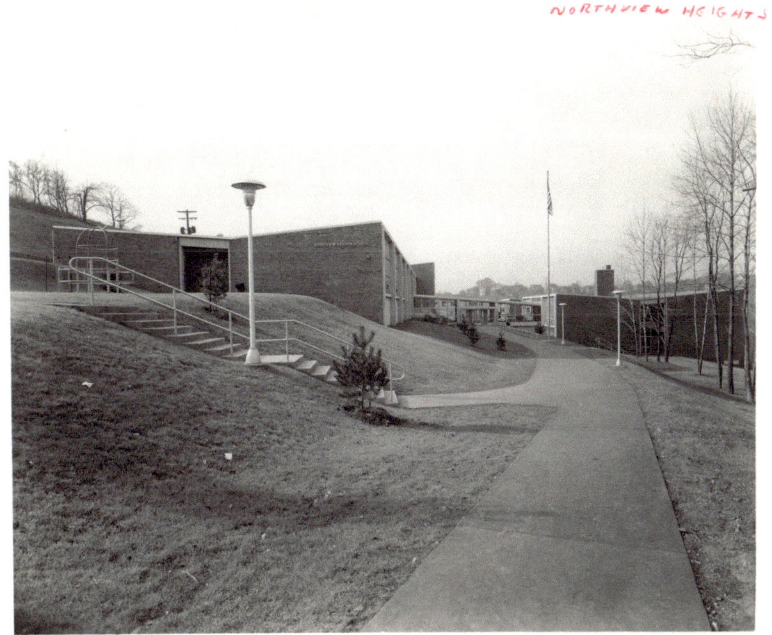

NORTHVIEW HEIGHTS ELEMENTARY

FROM DISPLACEMENT TO REOPENING: NORTHVIEW HEIGHTS AND THE LONG ARC OF REFORM LAJJa MiStRy

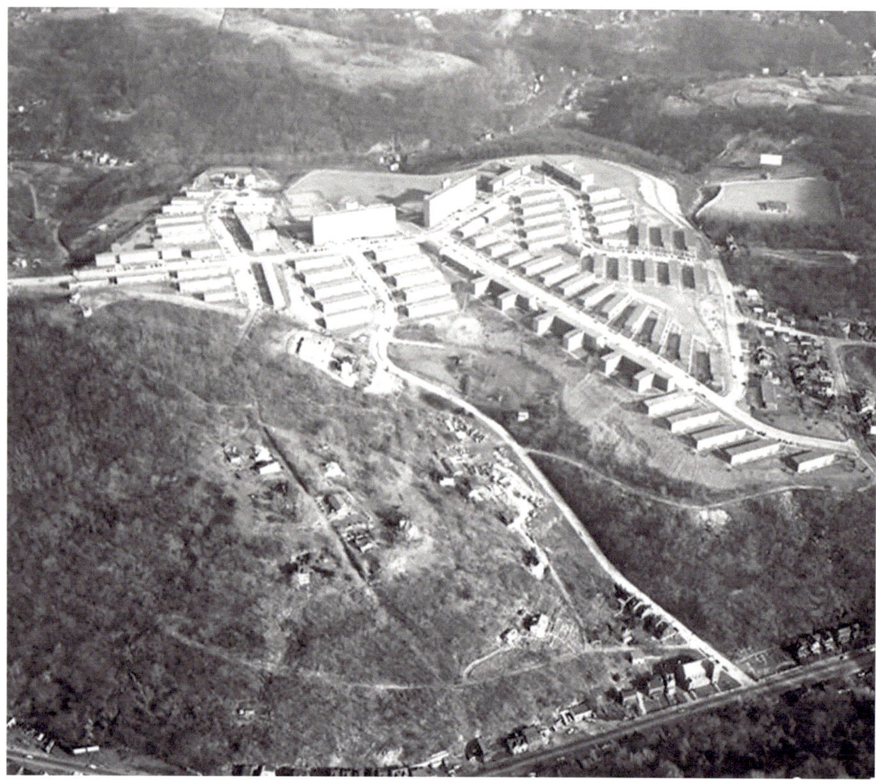

Above: Rick Barie, Aerial view of the Northview Heights public housing project, ca. 1964, photograph; Allegheny City Historic Gallery

Previous page: Northview Heights Elementary, November 15, 1962, photograph; Detre Library & Archives, HHC

Tucked away behind the lush canopy of Mt. Pleasant Road, the sprawling Northview Heights PreK-8 building is easy to overlook. The building has sat vacant since Pittsburgh Public Schools closed it in 2012, citing low enrollment. Now, under a new proposal that includes shuttering twelve schools in the district, the Northview Heights school building could once again open its doors. The plan to reconfigure the district, nearly two years in the making, would reopen the building as an elementary school and an English Language Development site in the fall of 2028, after undergoing major renovations.

The Northview Heights neighborhood was born out of displacement. Built in 1962, as part of Pittsburgh's urban renewal efforts, it became home to many Black families displaced from the Hill District by federally funded clearance campaigns. Designed with a single point of entry, physically isolated from surrounding neighborhoods, and burdened with a legacy of surveillance and underinvestment, Northview Heights exemplifies how state-led redevelopment has reshaped Black life in Pittsburgh. The Northview Heights elementary school opened in 1962, the same year that Pittsburgh's Housing Authority opened Northview Heights Mid-Rise. Many residents enrolled their children in the school, which served Northview Heights, Spring Hill, and Perry Hilltop. The potential reopening of the Northview Heights school building has elicited layered responses from Northview Heights residents—not simply hopes or concerns, but conditional strategies shaped by years of disinvestment, segregation, and displacement.

Today, Northview Heights is also home to African immigrant and refugee communities, including a significant Somali Bantu population. Many of their children attend King PreK-8 in the Allegheny Commons North Park, while those in the English Language Development program cross the bridge to attend Arsenal PreK-5 in Lawrenceville, a neighborhood from which many Somali families were displaced by rising rents in the early 2000s.

Fatima Muhina, president of the United Somali Bantu of Greater Pittsburgh, has reservations about the Northview Heights elementary school re-opening. While most of her kids attend charter schools, one son is currently enrolled at the Northview Heights Early Childhood

Center housed in the vacant Northview Heights school building. Muhina says the proposed plan does not foster inclusion, and reopening the school would lead to further segregation. All of the kids at her son's preschool are Somali Bantu or from other Black communities. "I would like my kid to go somewhere like, you know, when he transitions out of kindergarten, he's gonna meet other types of people, which he's not seeing right now." Muhina also worries that concentrating low-income students in one building would reinforce harmful perceptions. "It might not be true but based on your ZIP code and the school you attended, you're already profiled," she says. For the plan to work, Muhina says the district should make efforts to diversify schools and bring students from other neighborhoods to Northview Heights. Under the proposed plan, students from Northview Heights, Spring Garden, Spring Hill City View, Summer Hill, and Troy Hill would attend the new elementary school.

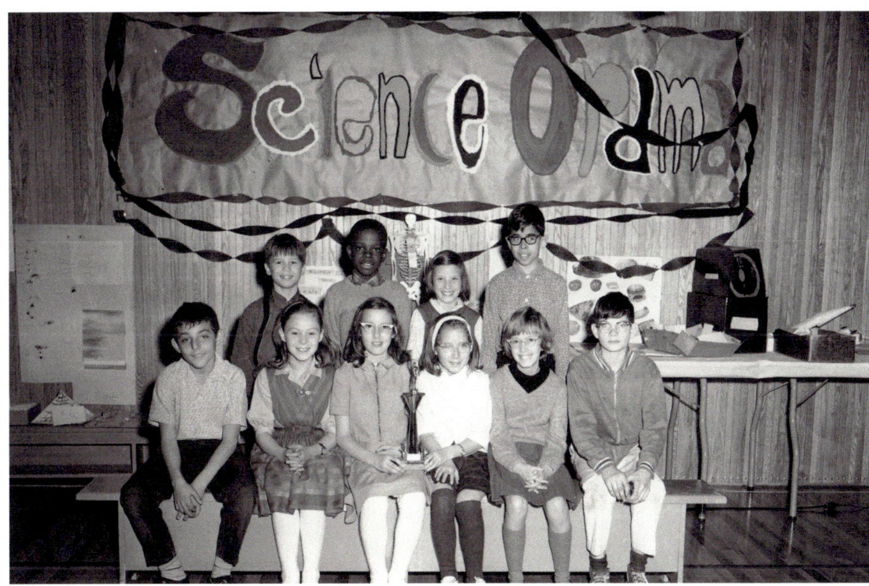

Charles "Teenie" Harris, Science O'Rama Competition, Northview Heights Elementary School, Pittsburgh, PA, 1966, photograph; Carnegie Museum of Art, HFF

Many members of the immigrant community also feel reopening the school is a "double-edged sword"—a logistical relief with social and educational risks. Aweys Mwaliya, president of the Somali Bantu Community Association of Pittsburgh, says having a school within walking distance would relieve many families of the long daily bus rides to King or Manchester PreK-8. Still, he echoes Muhina's concerns about isolation and equity: "It's just been forced by policies implemented all these years. This is all created chaos and also a challenge for the students and their families." Mwaliya fears that reopening Northview Heights will further disrupt education for students who would have to move from King, Manchester, or Spring Hill schools.

For longtime residents like Renita Freeman, the school's return represents more than convenience. It offers the possibility of revitalizing the community. A Northview Heights resident since 1970, Freeman attended the school along with all her siblings, children, and grandchildren. She says bringing the school back could connect an isolated Northview Heights community to school activities, which is a challenge when those kids are bussed to King or Manchester. "As long as we're ambassadors of positive change, I think it can go that way. We need to get people that want to see the change, that are encouraging new families and old families that can go back to go back," Freeman said. Rochelle Preston, another longtime resident, echoes the desire to see the school reopened: "It's just going to waste. It would be good to bring some life back to it." At the same time, Preston emphasizes that any reopening must account for students returning from multiple schools and the disruptions they've already experienced.

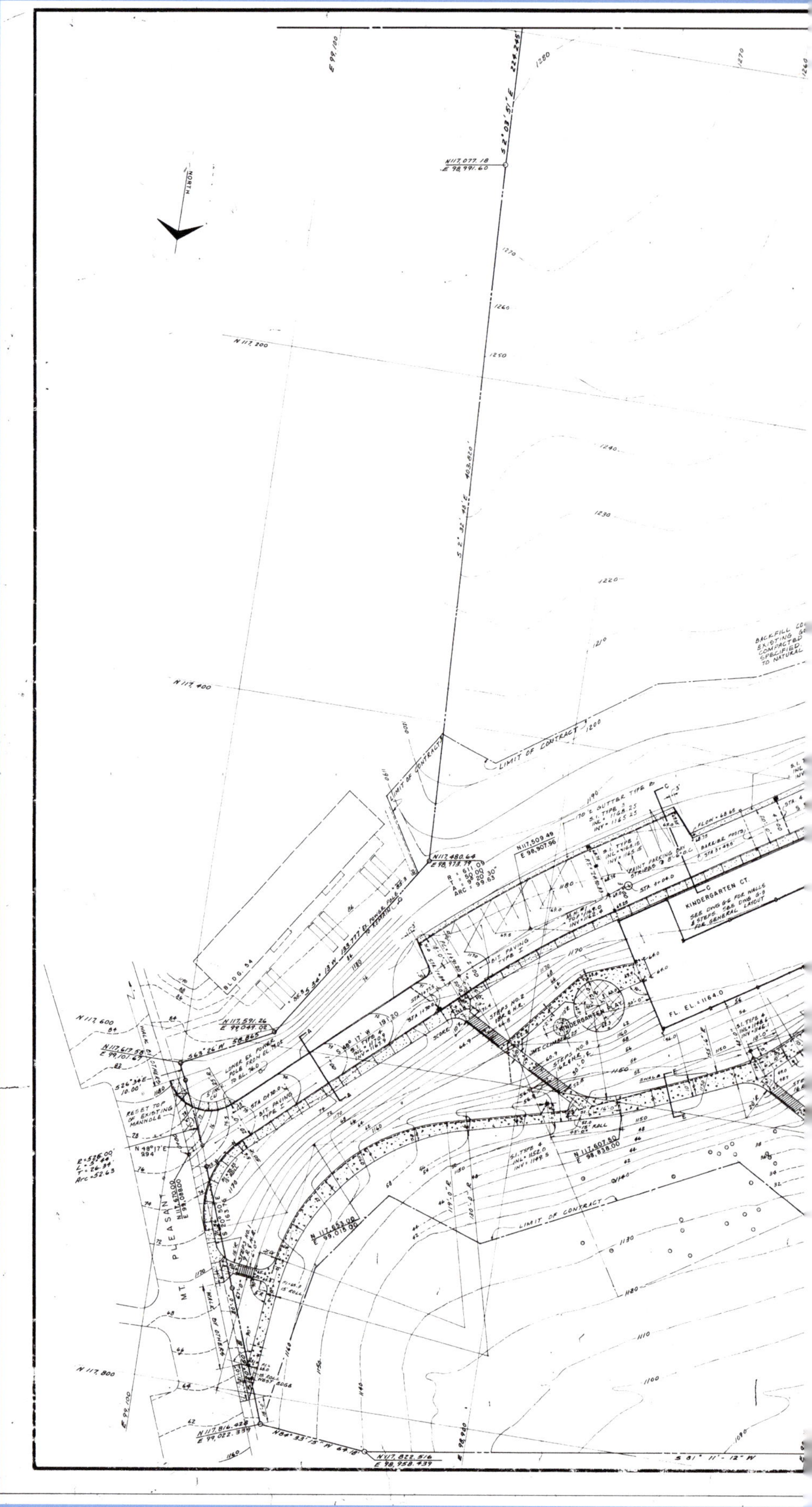

Deeter and Ritchey, *Northview Heights Elementary, Site Plan*, 1961, architectural drawings; PPBF

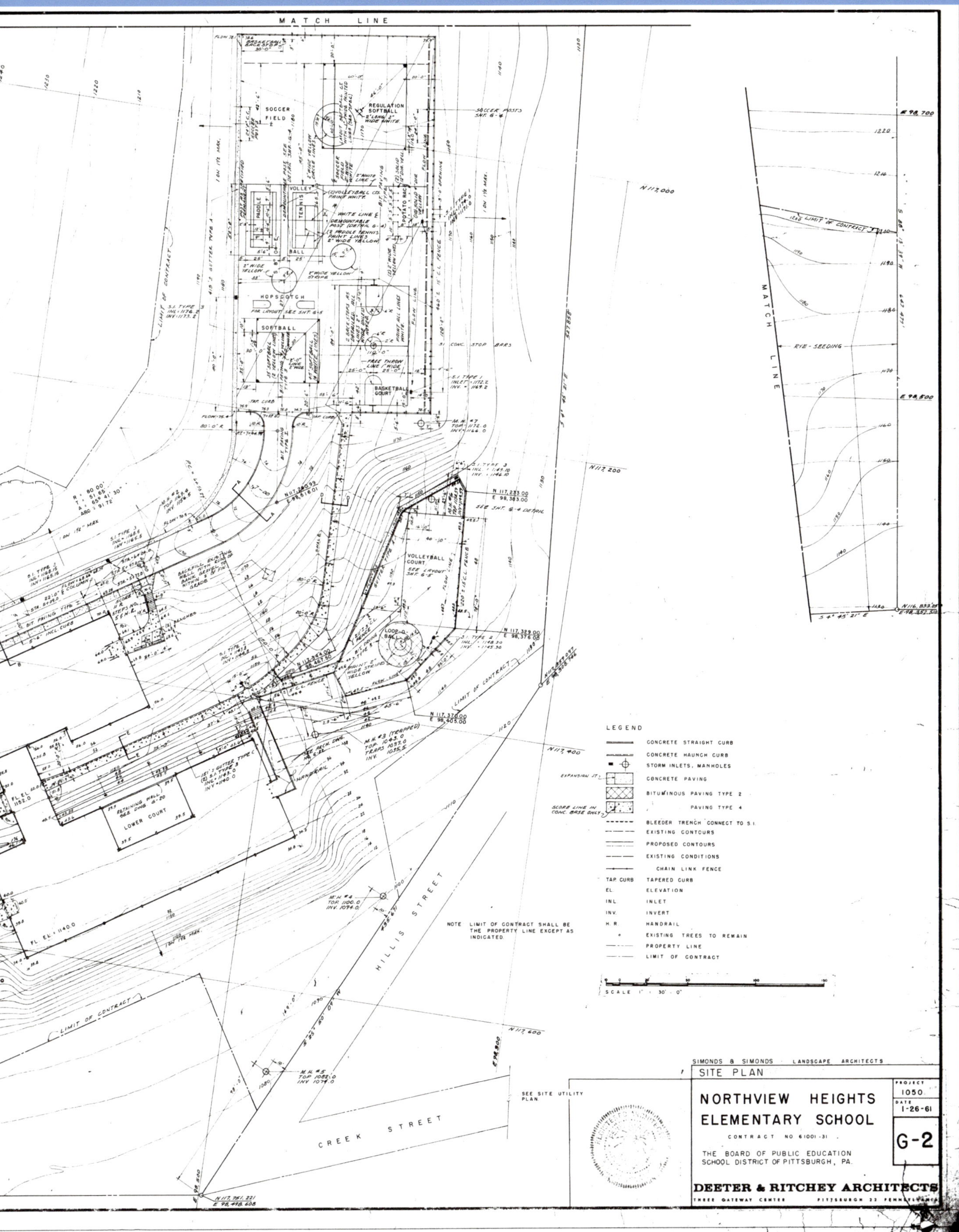

MATCH LINE
SOCCER FIELD
REGULATION SOFTBALL
VOLLEY TENNIS
PADDLE BALL
HOPSCOTCH
SOFTBALL
BASKETBALL COURT
VOLLEYBALL COURT
SEE LAYOUT SHT. 6-4
LOWER COURT
RETAINING WALL SEE DWG 6-20
RYE - SEEDING
SEE SITE UTILITY PLAN
NOTE LIMIT OF CONTRACT SHALL BE THE PROPERTY LINE EXCEPT AS INDICATED

HILLIS STREET
CREEK STREET

LEGEND
CONCRETE STRAIGHT CURB
CONCRETE HAUNCH CURB
STORM INLETS, MANHOLES
CONCRETE PAVING
BITUMINOUS PAVING TYPE 2
PAVING TYPE 4
BLEEDER TRENCH CONNECT TO S.I.
EXISTING CONTOURS
PROPOSED CONTOURS
EXISTING CONDITIONS
CHAIN LINK FENCE
TAP. CURB   TAPERED CURB
EL   ELEVATION
INL   INLET
INV.   INVERT
H.R.   HANDRAIL
EXISTING TREES TO REMAIN
PROPERTY LINE
LIMIT OF CONTRACT
EXPANSION JT.
SCORE LINE IN CONC. BASE ONLY

SCALE 1" - 30' - 0"

SIMONDS & SIMONDS · LANDSCAPE ARCHITECTS
SITE PLAN
NORTHVIEW HEIGHTS ELEMENTARY SCHOOL
CONTRACT NO 61001-31
THE BOARD OF PUBLIC EDUCATION
SCHOOL DISTRICT OF PITTSBURGH, PA.
DEETER & RITCHEY ARCHITECTS
THREE GATEWAY CENTER   PITTSBURGH 22 PENNSYLVANIA
PROJECT 1050
DATE 1-26-61
G-2

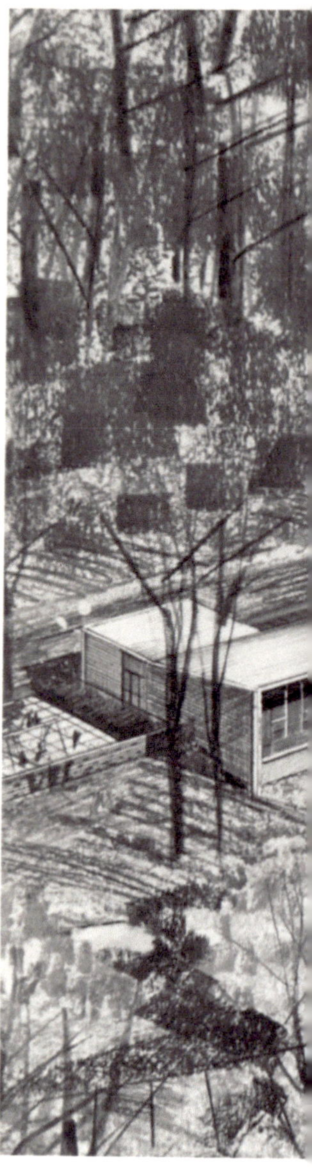

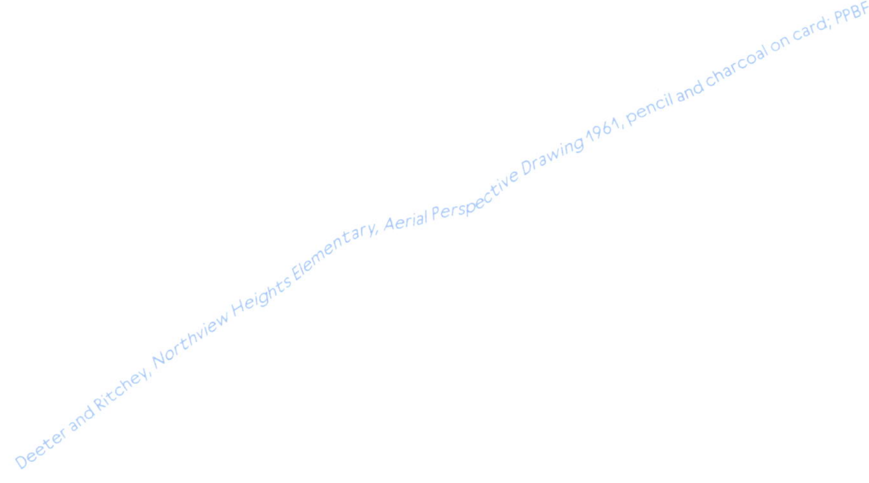

Deeter and Ritchey, Northview Heights Elementary, Aerial Perspective Drawing 1961, pencil and charcoal on card; PPBF

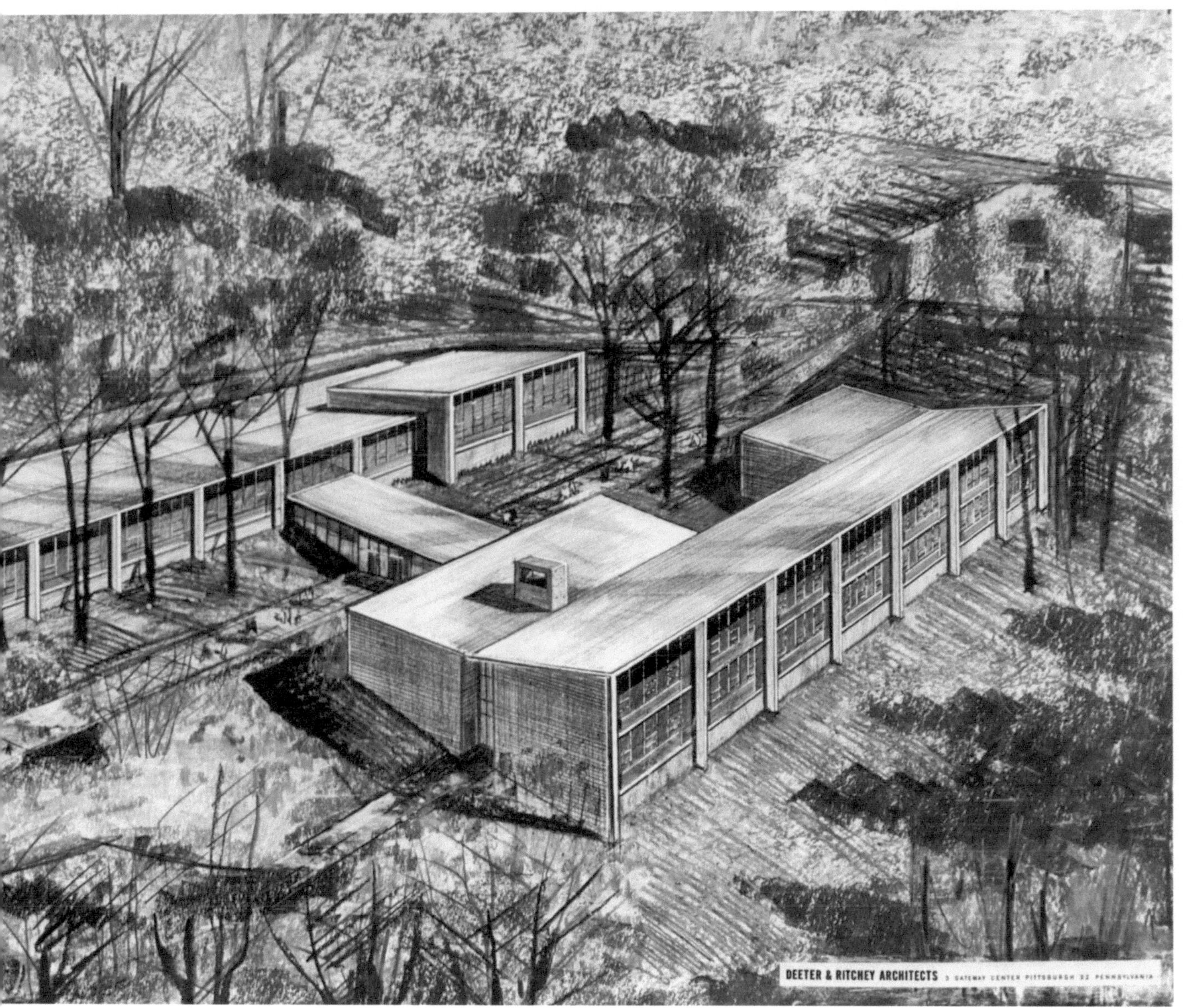

Northview Heights Elementary

1/32"=1'
0   12   24   48   96 FT
MANCHESTER, 1970

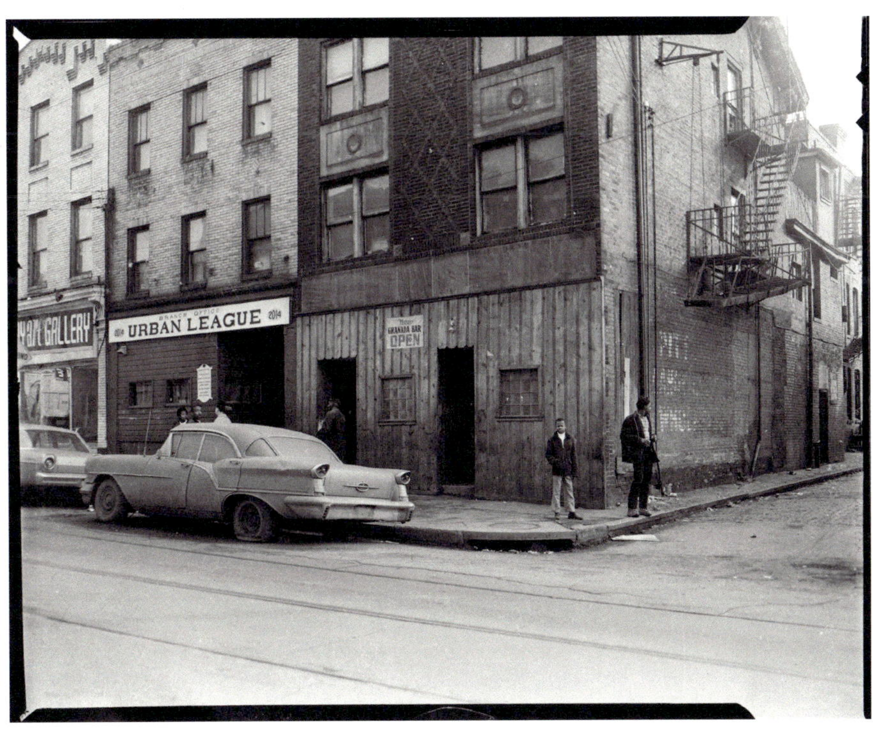

STREET ACADEMY

OH SINNERMAN, WHERE WE GOING TO RUN TO ALL ON THAT DAY?

Justin Laing

Histories of Black nationalist, socialist, and Pan Afrikanist tendencies and the efforts to win national liberation from the U.S. white settler colony have been introduced to Black children in the context of their families since the womb, and earlier, for centuries. However, the struggle to develop teaching and learning that centers these kinds of praxes outside the home has been a challenge for just as long. This essay will rely largely on my experience helping to begin and teach in the Omega Doctor Carter G. Woodson Academy, a Saturday Academy started by the Iota Phi Chapter of Omega Psi Phi Fraternity. For more than a decade, the Academy has taught children and youth ages six through sixteen for periods of six to ten weeks. The teaching is put in dialogue with work in a formation that has a mission to increase socialist praxis among Black people in Allegheny County, the Black Socialist Formation.

The mission of the Academy is rooted in historian and author Dr. Carter G. Woodson's notion of "the miseducation of the negro." Dr. Woodson explained this miseducation as a process perpetuated both by the U.S. educational system and the Black professional classes.[1] This Academy could be classified as an example of a fugitive pedagogy in the sense employed in Jarvis Givens' *Fugitive Pedagogy: Carter G. Woodson and the Art of Black Teaching*, as well as a "street academy" in the context of this collection.[2] Through the Academy, we engage such topics as Malcolm X and the Black Power movement, histories of how whiteness and Blackness were constructed, and revolutionary Pan Afrikanism. Our intent is to water the seed of interest in Black radicalism that students' families have planted, in hopes it might further blossom. Students have engaged enthusiastically with these topics, particularly when there is physical movement, games, and fun included. Many enjoy being challenged with unfamiliar concepts like Pan Afrikanism or learning about countries like Burkina Faso and its current leader, Ibrahim Traore.

But our efforts have raised questions and gentle criticisms. It is not students' interest or teachers' ability to design Black radical lesson plans that has drawn questions but the development of a Pan Afrikanist or national liberatory education at a greater scale. We simply do not have the institutions to deliver this type of education at the desired level that would really challenge the miseducation program of the state. This is a particular problem at this time when the state is being used by revanchist tendencies within the capital class to win back the small gains that Black people have won in state-sponsored education. We see this in the work to ban books and frame Black history as "reverse racism."

The challenge of a plethora of local efforts, small models, fractals, those that we are naming as "street academies," or fugitive pedagogies, if you will, feel rooted in certain political tendencies that resist the ideas of seeking state power, which has been objective of nationalist, Pan Afrikanist, and socialist projects. In this way, do frameworks of fugitive pedagogy or marronage act as a counter ethos to the nationalist liberational schools, which emerged during the 1960s as part of a larger body of work by an organization like the Black Panthers? In terms of fugitivity, where do we imagine our children can escape to when, for example, we are faced with eleven U.S. military command centers that both encompass the planet and reach into space with a mission of full spectrum

[1] For more in-depth reading on this process of cultural indoctrination, not teaching, defined and described by Dr. Carter G. Woodson as "the miseducation of the negro," please reference: **Dr. Carter G. Woodson,** *The Mis-Education of the Negro* (The Associated Publishers, 1933).

[2] Jarvis Givens is an American scholar and professor of education who examines and identifies Woodson's counter-canon approach to Black Education as a decolonizing practice of "fugitive pedagogy." **Jarvis Givens,** *Fugitive Pedagogy: Carter G. Woodson and the Art of Black Teaching* (Harvard University Press, 2023).

dominance? My concern is that our praxis of fugitive pedagogies seems to fit well within the neoliberal era best summarized by Margaret Thatcher's claim that, with the defeat of the Soviet Union, *there is no alternative.* In the way they leave state power relatively unchallenged and rather seek to let a thousand flowers bloom, might "fugitivity" or "street academies" be more of an expression of this quickly receding neoliberal era than one that combats its core logics like actual maroonage did? Have these logics of resisting both the benefit and possibility of challenging state power contributed to a weakening of nationalist, Pan Afrikanist, and socialist movements because we are not teaching its core assumptions?

There is an opportunity for those of us who have cut our teeth in the street academy and fugitive pedagogy space to bring our educational visions to the context of larger organizations committed to movements that challenge the ruling class and its use of the state. Because as U.S. imperialism gets even more overt and aggressive, the slightly modified words of the Negro spiritual come to mind, "Where we gonna run to all on that day?"

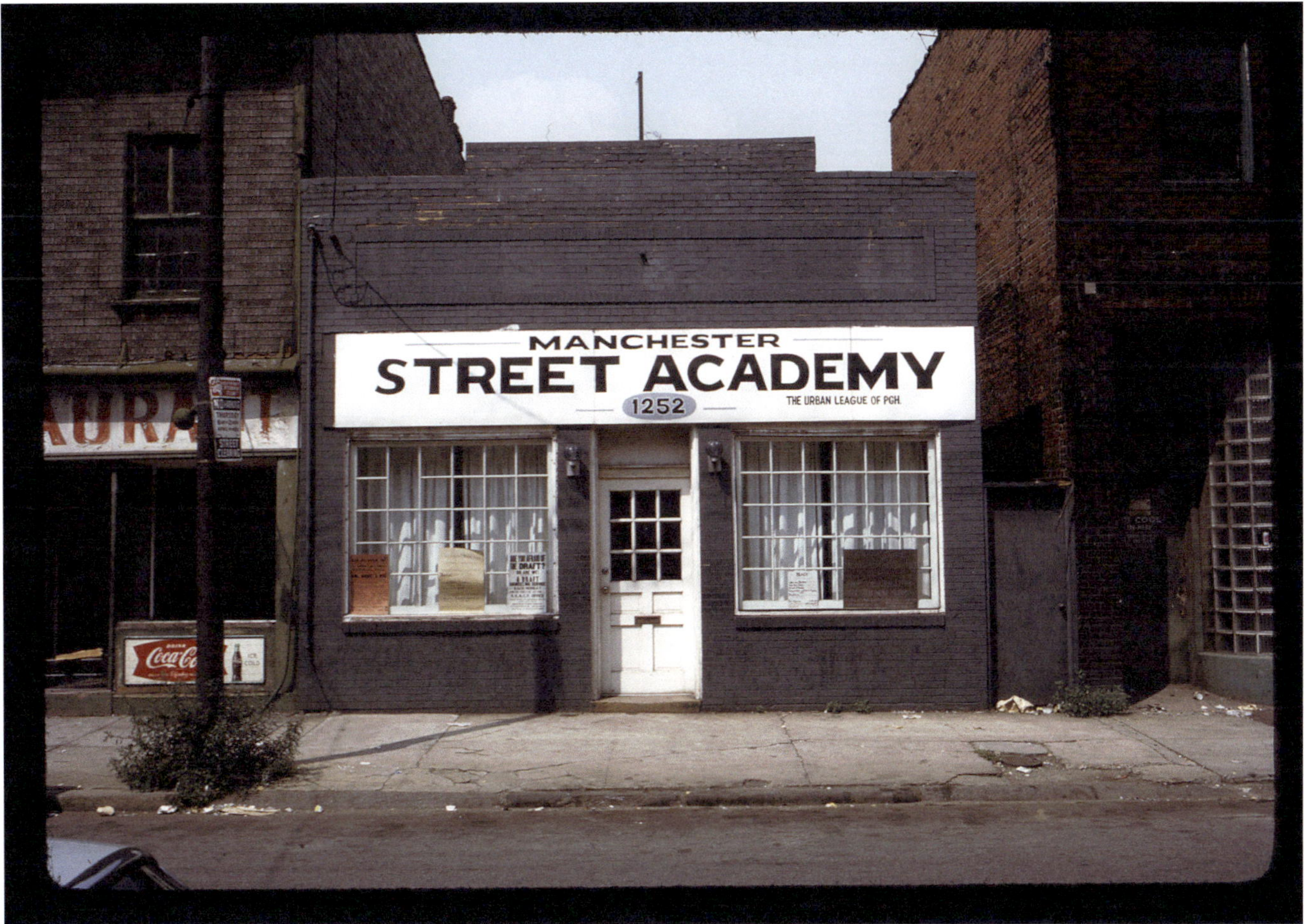

Below: Manchester Street Academy, 1970, photograph; Pittsburgh City Archives

STREET ACADEMY

<u>September 1969 to June 1970</u>

101 Students enrolled in Street Academy

42 Regular Attendees

9 graduated - 3 with diplomas and 4 with certificates
5 were admitted to college

25 students attended summer school in 1970 - all the students were high school grads and had been accepted in college

<u>September 1970 to June 1971</u>

167 Students enrolled

15 students graduated - 9 with diplomas and 6 with certificates
11 are attending college, one is working
1 business school
19 summer school enrollment

<u>September 1971 to June 1972</u>

58 students enrolled - 25 of which were old students (have not graduated from SAP as of yet)

11 students graduated - 1 attended college
13 summer enrollment

<u>STUDENT/TEACHER RATIOS</u> (Of those enrolled and those who attended)

1969 - 70 - 6 teachers and 101 enrollees but only 42 students actually attend class
student: teacher ratio is 17:1 and 7:1

1970 - 71 - 6 teachers and 167 enrollees
student: teacher ratio is 17:1

1971 - 72 - 6 teachers and 57 enrollees
student: teacher ratio is 9:1

<u>TOTALS</u>

245 students enrolled (including 25 who attended summer school in 1970)

29 graduated - 18 received diplomas and 11 received certificates

20 attending college
2 working
7 no word

9/18/72

STREET ACADEMY PROGRAM

PROGRESS REPORT

March 13, 1972

<u>Curriculum and Schedule Changes</u>

The curriculum of the Street Academy Program includes the following courses:

1. English 1
2. English 11
3. English 111
4. English 1V
5. Shakespeare
6. Afro-American Literature
7. General Science
8. Biology
9. Chemistry
10. Physics
11. American History
12. World Culture
13. Economics
14. Afro-American History
15. Algebra 1 and Geometry
16. Algebra 11
17. Basic Mathematics
18. Remedial Mathematics
19. Intermediate Mathematics 1
20. Intermediate Mathematics 11
21. Calculus
22. Trigonometry
23. Reading

Afro-American Literature, Shakespeare, Advanced Science, Calculus, and Trigonometry have been added to the cirriculum as electives.

<u>Curriculum and Schedule Changes</u>

The schedule that is currently in use is more flexible than the one used previously. Students are now being placed in the levels on which they are functioning in all subject areas. Prior to this time, placement tests were given in reading and English only; and students were assigned to the Transition 1, Transition 11, Prep 1 or Prep 11 levels according to the scores received on these two exams.

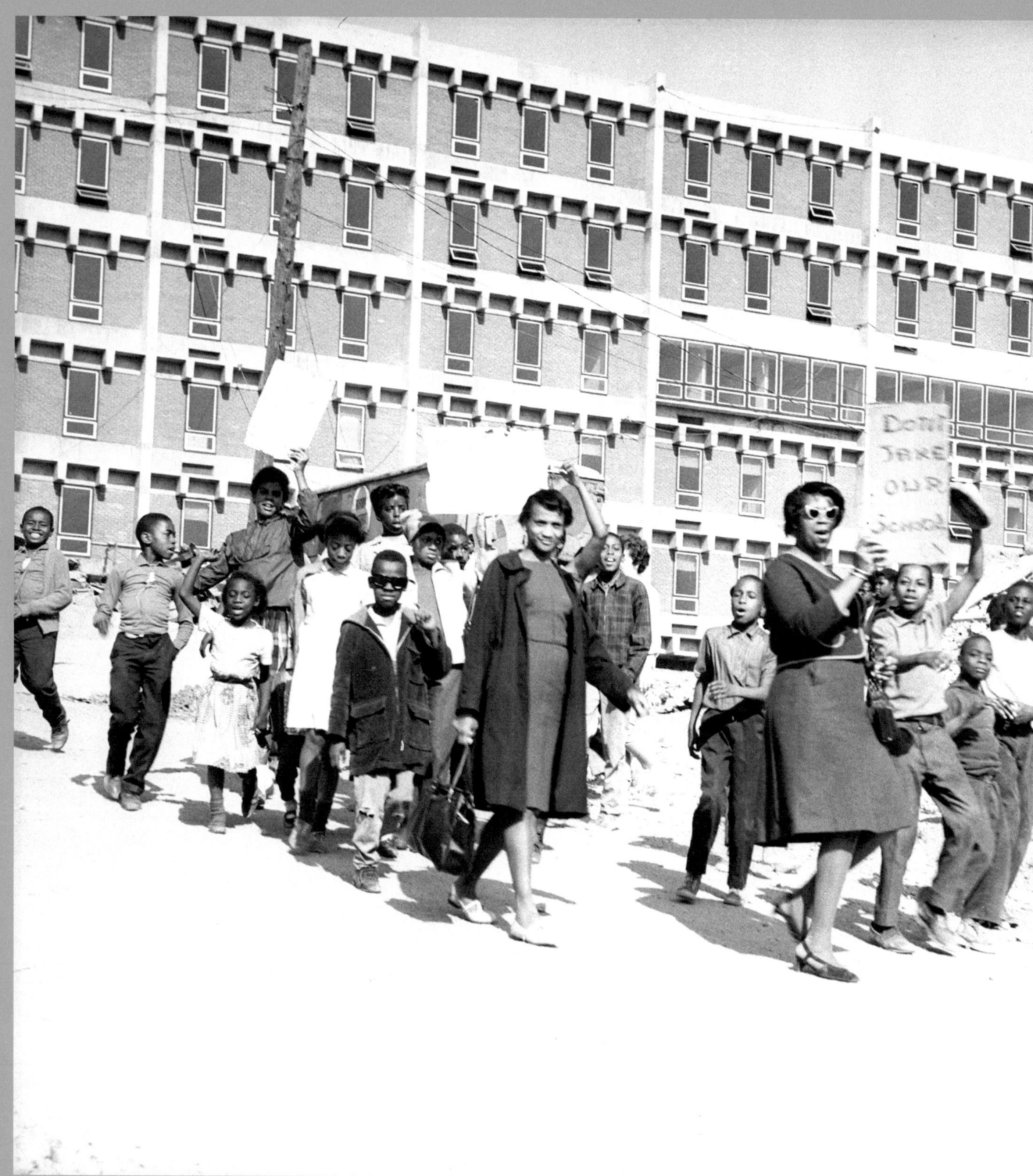

DON'T
TAKE
OUR
School

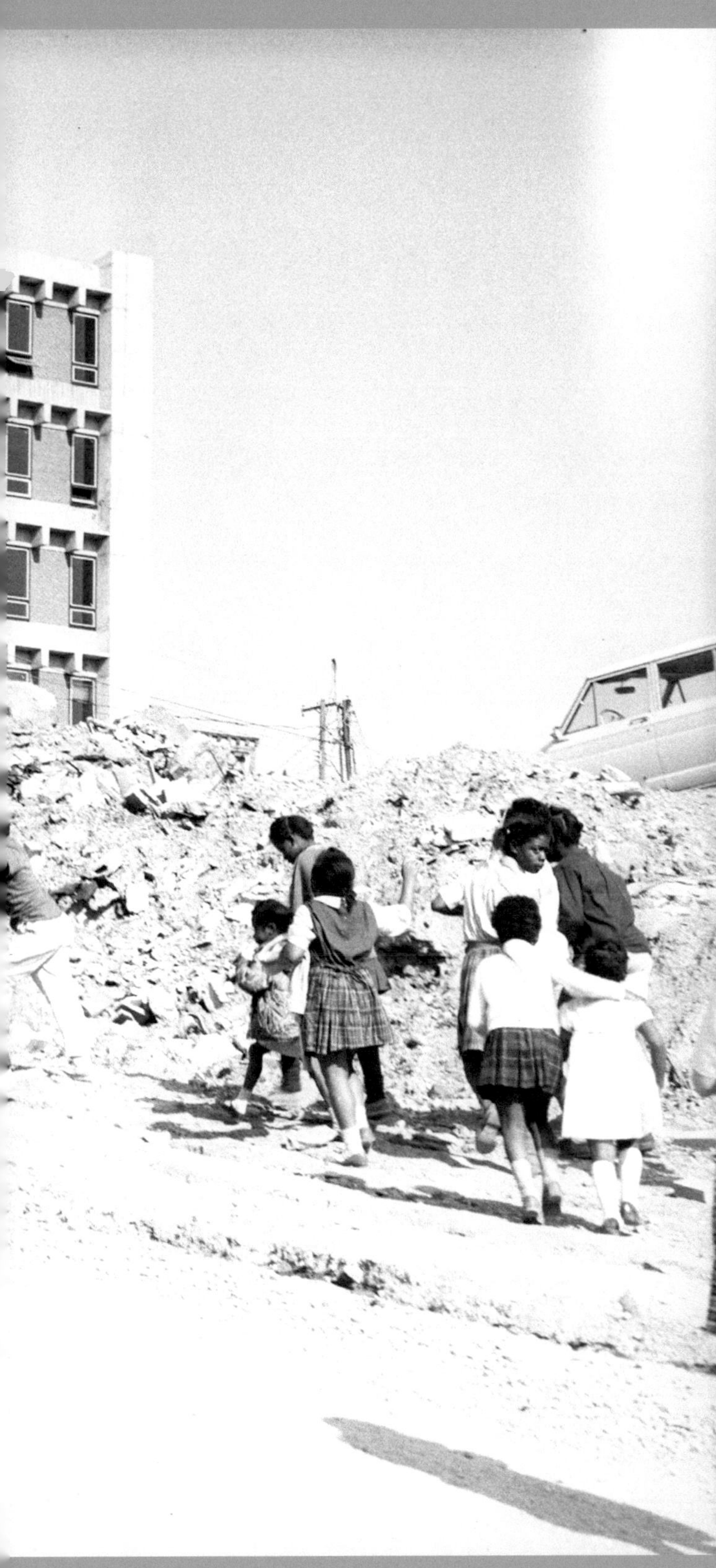

Charles "Teenie" Harris, Outside Columbus Elementary School, North Side, Pittsburgh, PA, 1967, Photograph, Carnegie Museum of Art, HFF

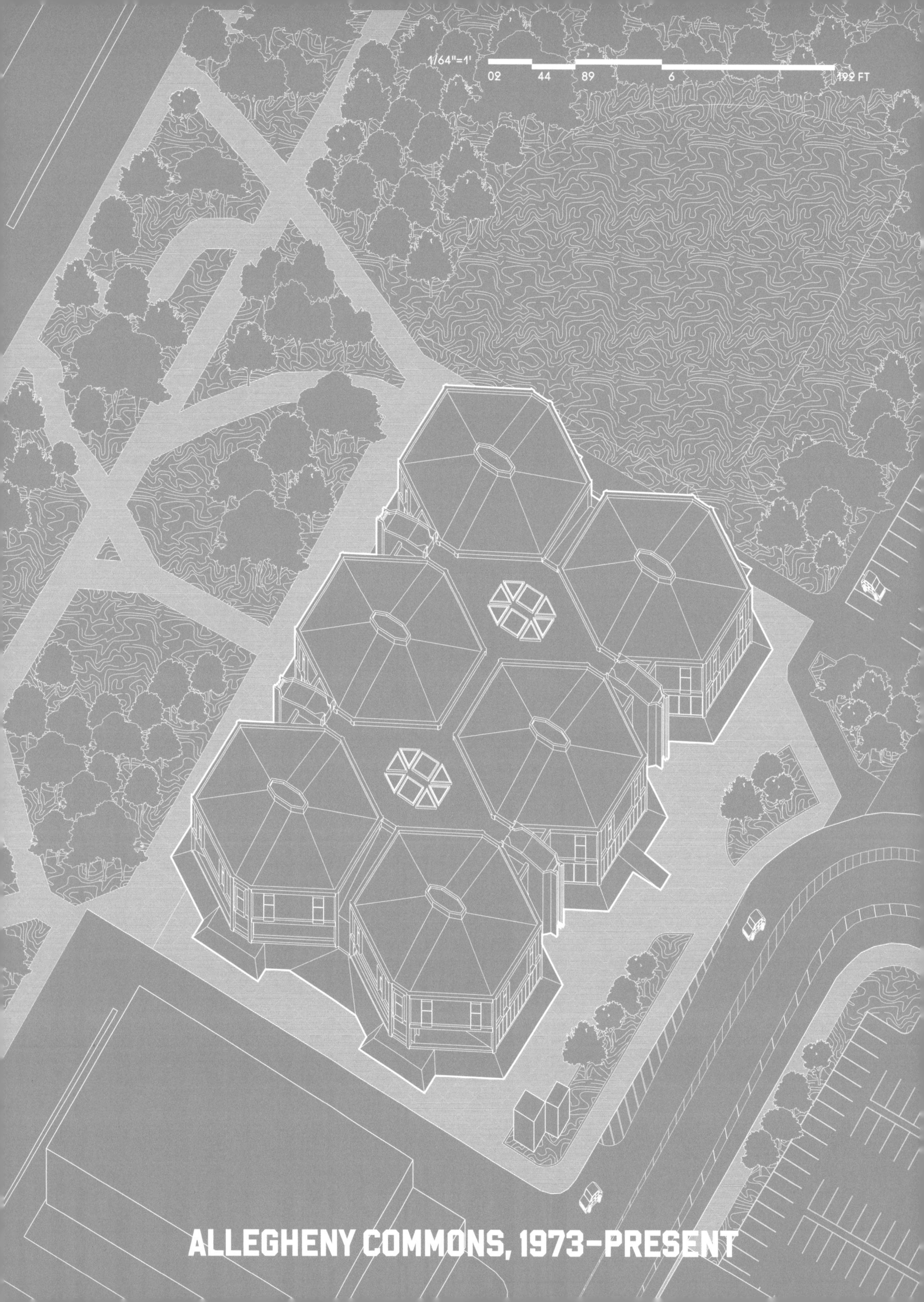

1/64"=1'
02
44
89
6
192 FT
ALLEGHENY COMMONS, 1973-PRESENT

Opened in 1973 alongside Allegheny
Commons Park, Martin Luther King Jr.
Elementary was part of a brief but radical
experiment in school design. Architects
Liff Justh & Chetlin designed a building
composed of repeating clusters of interlocking hexagonal units. Departing from
the corridor-and-classroom model, the
school instead embraced six open
"pods" with movable wall dividers that
supported group work, lectures, and
self-guided learning. The plan also integrated advanced systems for lighting
and air circulation, visible in the reflected
ceiling plan. This open classroom model—
popularized nationally in the 1960s and
70s—soon faced challenges: noise, lack of
structure, and administrative resistance.
By the 1980s, the layout had largely fallen
out of favor. Today the building stands
as a rare spatial artifact of pedagogical
experimentation—one that prefigured
current debates about flexible classrooms and collective learning.

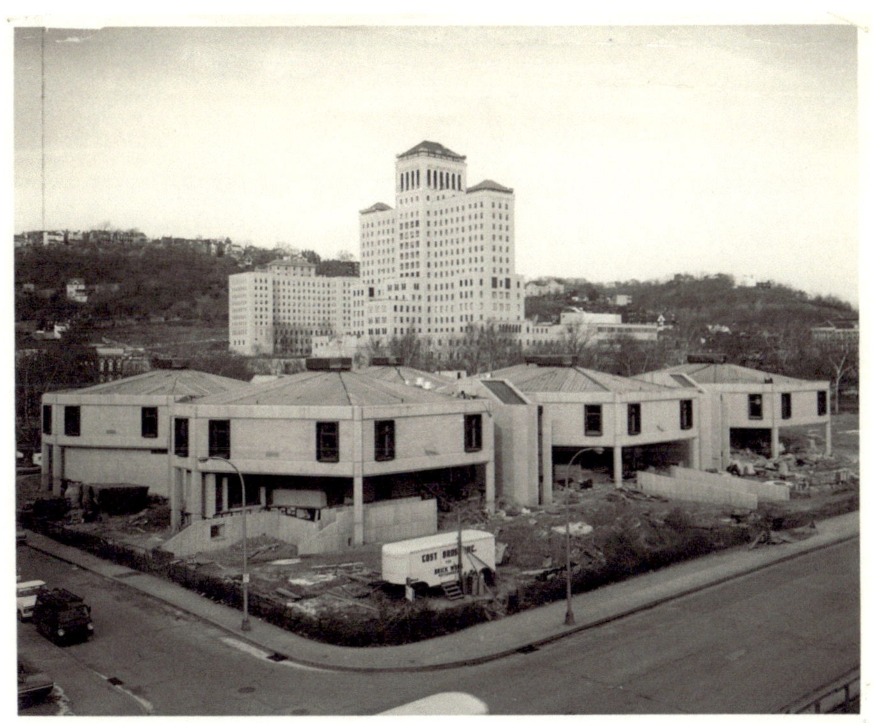

MARTIN LUTHER KING JR. ELEMENTARY

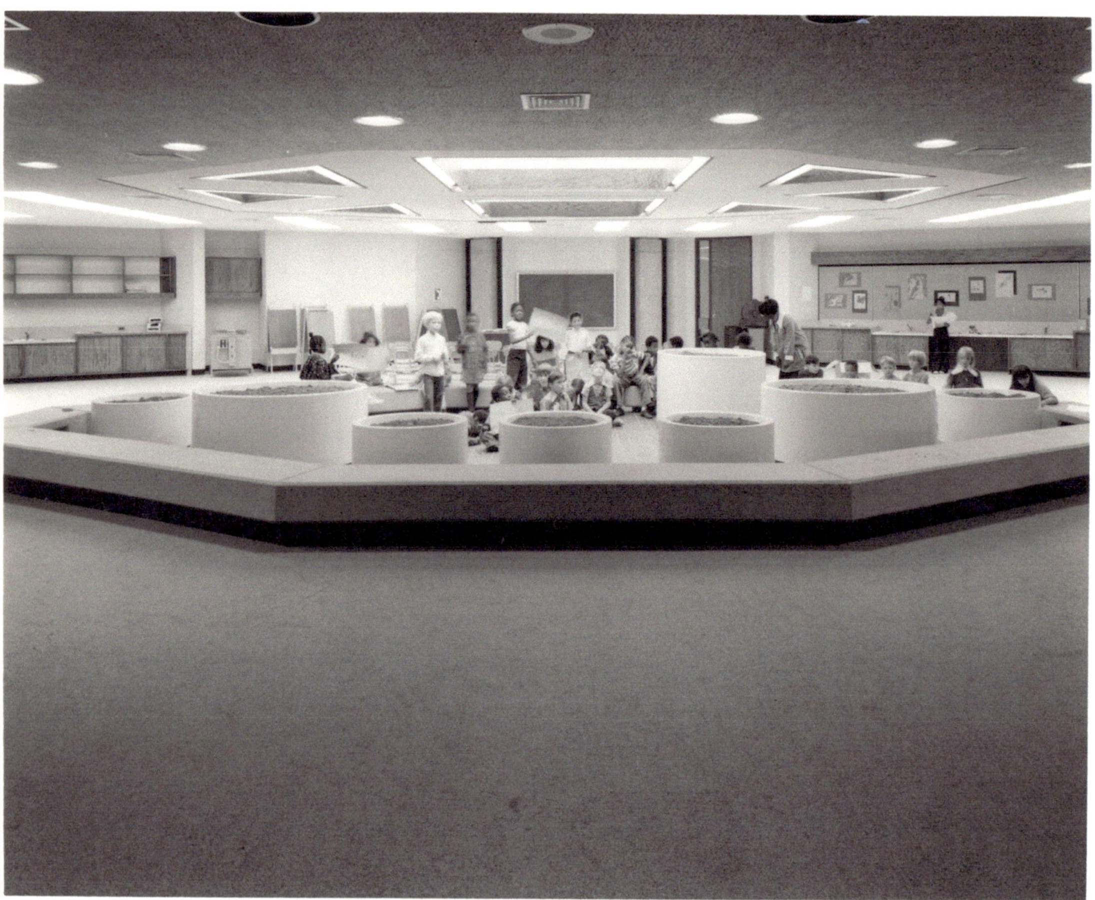

INTRODUCTION
BY NOAH FRITSCH

Previous page: Martin Luther King Jr. Elementary School, ca. 1973, photograph; Detre Library & Archives, HHC

The first time I really talked with my great-uncle about buildings, I was a high school student and had just finished an apprenticeship at the Pittsburgh Landmarks Association. There, I learned to draft from seasoned architects who loved line weights and teaching kids how to use a scale. I remember one day bringing my drawing plates to Martin's house in Mount Lebanon; they barely fit through the front door. We cleared the dining room table, and I nervously laid them out. After my over-labored description of a small grocery with housing in Homestead, Martin said: "The word you're looking for is contextual. You designed a contextual building. That's all you need to say."

From then on, our relationship was defined by my periodic visits— the most consequential of which were during my semester breaks while I was studying architecture at Syracuse University. The following text reflects many of our conversations over the past eight years.

NOAH FRITSCH
Can we begin by discussing how the Martin Luther King Jr. School project came across your desk?

MARTIN CHETLIN Well, in 1969, myself and my partners were awarded the project to design the North Side Elementary School, later renamed the Martin Luther King Jr. School. The building opened in 1973.

NF Remind me who your partners were. What was their background?

MC I had two experienced partners a generation older than me. Bernie Liff, an architect, and Milton Justh, a civil engineer. They both graduated from Carnegie Tech in 1935 and formed their practice shortly thereafter. I didn't join their firm until around 1959. Working for them was a learning experience that gave me confidence.

NF With two established partners behind you, two Carnegie Libraries recently completed (one in East Liberty and one in Squirrel Hill), and a number of years teaching architecture at Carnegie Tech, you were presented with the fresh responsibility of this elementary school. Am I correct in saying that you led the school's design?

MC Yes. I designed the school, and all my experiences up until that point prepared me for the job. I don't remember if I campaigned for it, but I do know that the door opened so that I could be a reasonable candidate for the MLK Jr. school. The President of the Board of Public Education was Mrs. Reizenstein, and at the time, the Board wanted something new. To think about education differently. They were contemplating the idea of open classrooms.

NF Before we discuss the actual design of the Martin Luther King Jr. School, can you briefly tell me about your own educational background?

MC Well, when I started my studies at Carnegie Tech in 1945, I was only seventeen years old. My professors had a big influence on me—namely, my professor who led the first two years of design studio. He was an artist, a muralist, named Kindred McLeary. A wonderful instructor, capable of communicating the basics of form and space to you—pure design. And as a graduate student, I was a teaching assistant for Hans Vetter, an Austrian architect. The way he taught encouraged you to use your imagination to interpret what a design program required.

NF An understanding of abstract composition from McLeary and a critical position on program from Vetter—I see their influence on you and your design of MLK Jr. Did you receive any assistance in the process of developing the project?

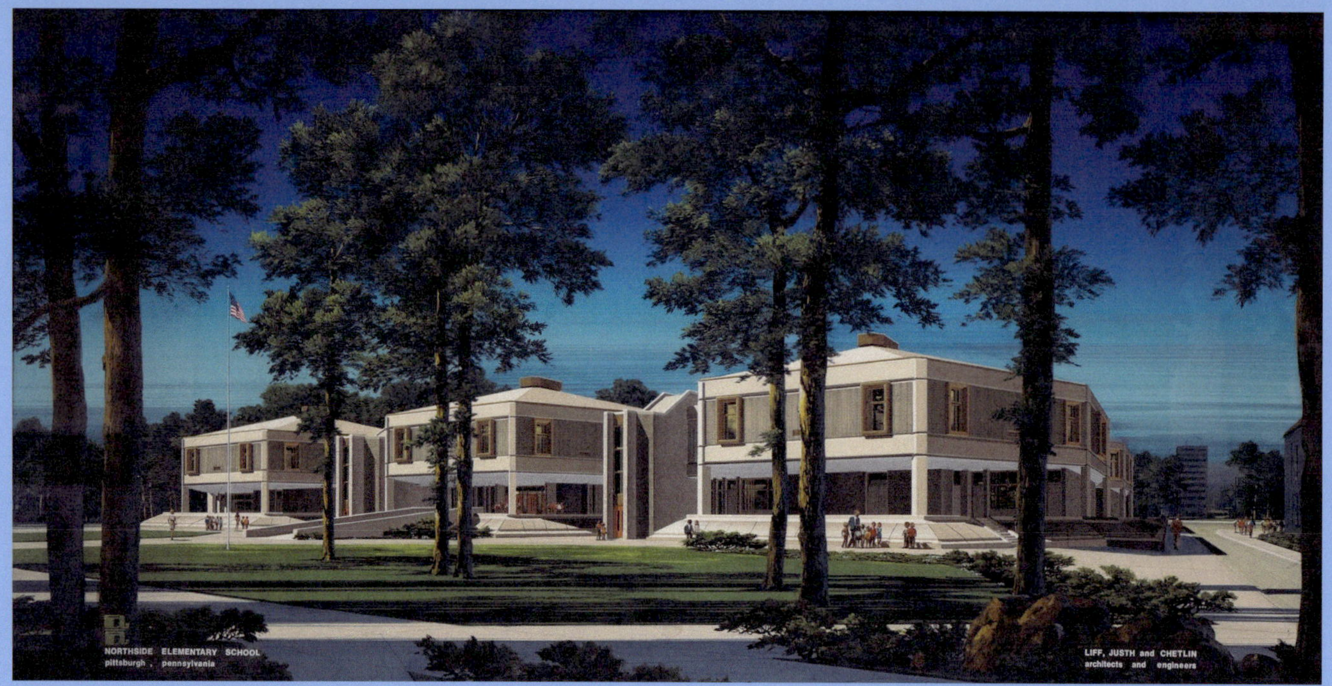

Liff Justh and Chetlin, *Martin Luther King Jr. Elementary School, Perspective Rendering*, 1973, tempera on card; PPBF

MC   The people on the Board who ran facilities were either one class or two classes behind me at Carnegie Tech, so we were all familiar with one another. A lot of the work we did together was conversational. I knew they wanted a certain amount of open planning for the school, but you couldn't do that on the ground floor. It didn't make sense because you couldn't differentiate the outdoor play areas from indoor teaching areas with open planning. So, I raised the open classrooms to the second floor with columns.

NF That was the diagram, the main idea.

MC   Yes, that was the diagram: a terrace and pilotis. The system I proposed was a series of six hexagons raised on columns that were split by a ten-foot corridor. It was half a hexagon, ten feet in between, and another half hexagon. The classrooms were situated on either side of the corridor, and that became the basis for the design. The terraces below eventually provided flexibility for expansion, but the Board of Public Education later enclosed these platforms.

NF Very interesting! Did anyone else contribute to the design of the school?

MC   Betty Jean Radvak, the principal of the school and a very sharp person, was involved in the project from early on. She gave her input, which was that we needed classrooms with an outside play area or terrace. This was the most efficient way to keep the size of the building from taking up more of the Allegheny Commons Park.

NF So, was there a kind of alchemy between you and the educators?

MC   There was input from the rest of the administration, yes. The idea was to have classrooms to test varying levels of openness. We did one set with three classrooms that all opened up into one space, and they could be separated back into three spaces. It was a demonstration.

NF Did they believe that the design of a building could support a new way of learning?

MC   See, the MLK Jr. school was separate from other projects the Board had previously undertaken, which didn't form an opinion.

NF An opinion on education?

MC   Yes. The MLK Jr. school was a huge statement about education. At the time, open classrooms were becoming popular.

NF   And you agreed with that idea?

MC   In the late 1960s, it was uncertain how to teach in open classrooms. Each teacher got to decide how "open" they wanted their classroom. I didn't believe in designing classrooms with open space willy-nilly. If the teachers wanted to take the partitions out, they could open up one whole half of the second floor. It had to be flexible so that the design could suit the way they wanted to teach.

NF   Were the open classrooms also on the ground level?

MC   No. The ground level was the kindergarten, which was designed differently. It could exist in a pod of four classrooms on its own. We were able to put a terrace outside of each classroom and an entrance on each side, whereas the pods on the second floor could be opened or divided with partitions.

NF   I find the overall figure of the plan to be quite striking.

MC   The real wonder of the project was that, during my meeting with the community on the North Side, some residents told me they didn't believe it would ever happen.

NF   Why didn't they believe it would happen?

MC   Because they'd been fooled so many times before and told me so when I met with them. They were promised everything and nothing ever came of it.

NF   Were they welcoming to you as an outsider proposing this school in the park?

MC   I don't think people ever complained about its intrusion into the park. The intention was always to build a school that fit into the park as much as possible. I was always conscious of this.

NF   Conversely, the building always struck me as autonomous and object-like. The system of half hexagons is small enough for the parts to read as a whole.

MC   No, it is not autonomous; it is contextual. The building was always imagined as part of the park: connected via the terraces, angled corners, second-floor overhang, and the way it faces the street on one side allowing the other half to be firmly situated within the park. I relied on the system of interlocking hexagons to create a setting for the building that acted like a transitional space. If the building was made of rectilinear boxes, it would have had too strong a presence in the park. Like a box that's blocking the view of everything. You wouldn't be able to see around the corners.

NF Now I finally understand the hexagon form. It's a square with the edges cut off. The potency of the school comes from choosing the right problems—the view in a park and the need for a softer edge to control monumentality. Speaking of transitional spaces, not only is the building raised on pilotis, but it is elevated on a platform with edges that taper downward into a sloped hip. What were you thinking about when you drafted this design?

MC   It was important to go up visually and create a space for the building to transition out of the park. Practically, the school also needed privacy for the terrace play areas and separation from traffic on the one side.

NF Did you know that people throughout Pittsburgh now go there to skateboard? Your design of the tapered hip has evolved.

MC *(Laughs)* Do they go up those slopes?

NF Yeah, they go up the slopes and then back down. It is one of the city's main skateboarding spots.

MC I did not realize!

NF The lives of buildings are strange!

Adaptability:

The structure shows a concern for the future with adaptability to a whole range of educational goals: movable partitions that can transform space from open to enclosed; and floors designed so that every area can support the same maximum loading.

Involvement:

In addition to their responsibilities for architectural design and for construction supervision, Liff, Justh and Chetlin were instrumental, along with the Board of Education, in the school's successful acceptance by the community. From the earliest planning stages, they attended meetings with community leaders and neighborhood representatives to discuss the proposed plans and to explain how the design concept related to the educational philosophy and to the needs of the community. At the same time, teachers were going into the homes of incoming students to give parents a preview of education as it would be practiced at Martin Luther King.

Success:

As a result, the school's first year of operation was an unqualified success. Educational progress is ahead of schedule. There is peak utilization of the facilities for educational and for community functions.

From all points of view—educational, architectural, and sociological—Martin Luther King has more than reached its initial goals. The foresight and cooperation of all those involved has made it a full partner in the educational process and in the life of the community.

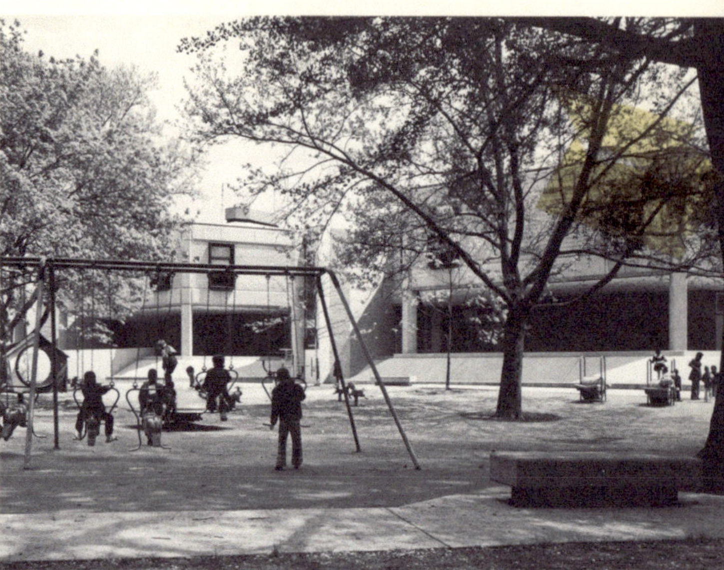

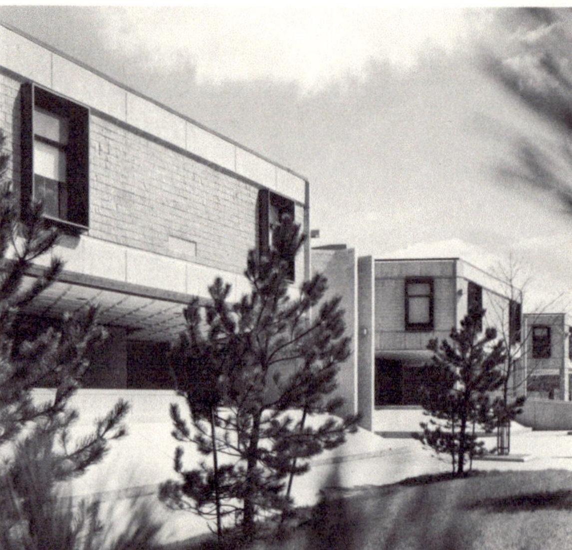

Profile on Martin Luther King Jr. Elementary School, 1973, pamphlet; Detre Library & Archives, HHC

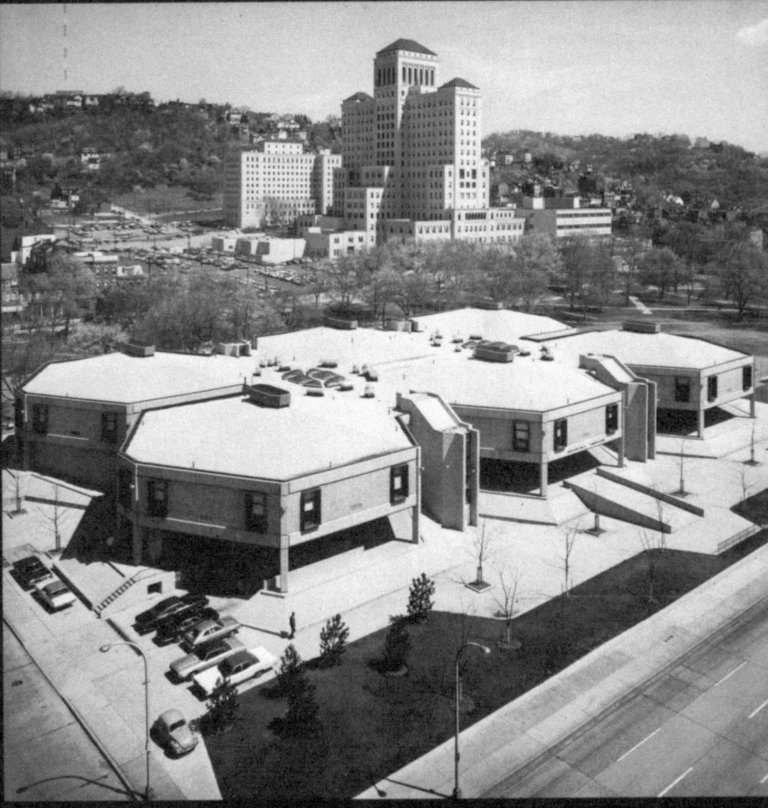

NOAH FRITSCH & MARTIN CHETLIN   Martin Luther King Jr. Elementary

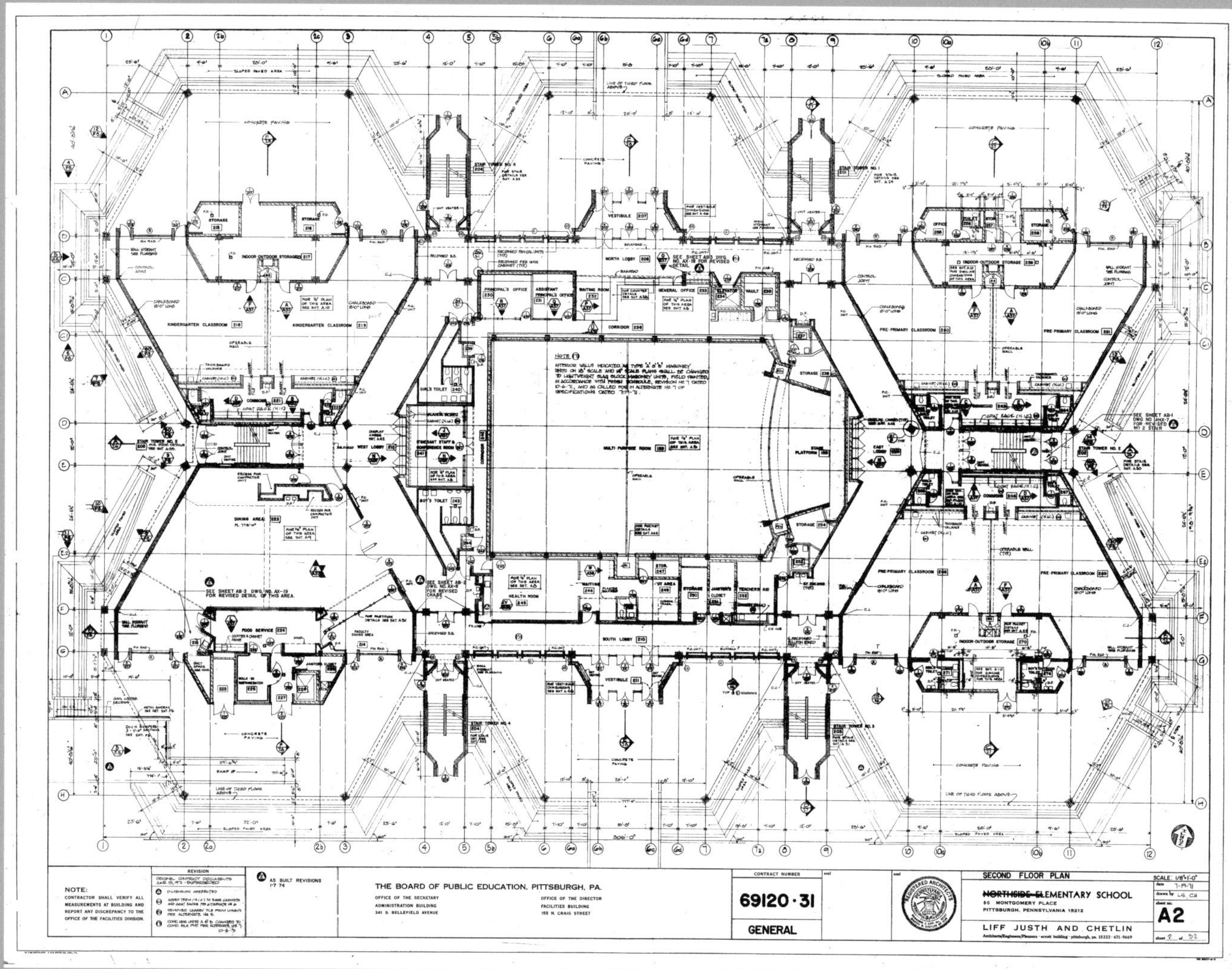

Liff Justh and Chetlin, Martin Luther King Jr. Elementary School, Second Floor Plan, 1971, architectural drawing; PPBF

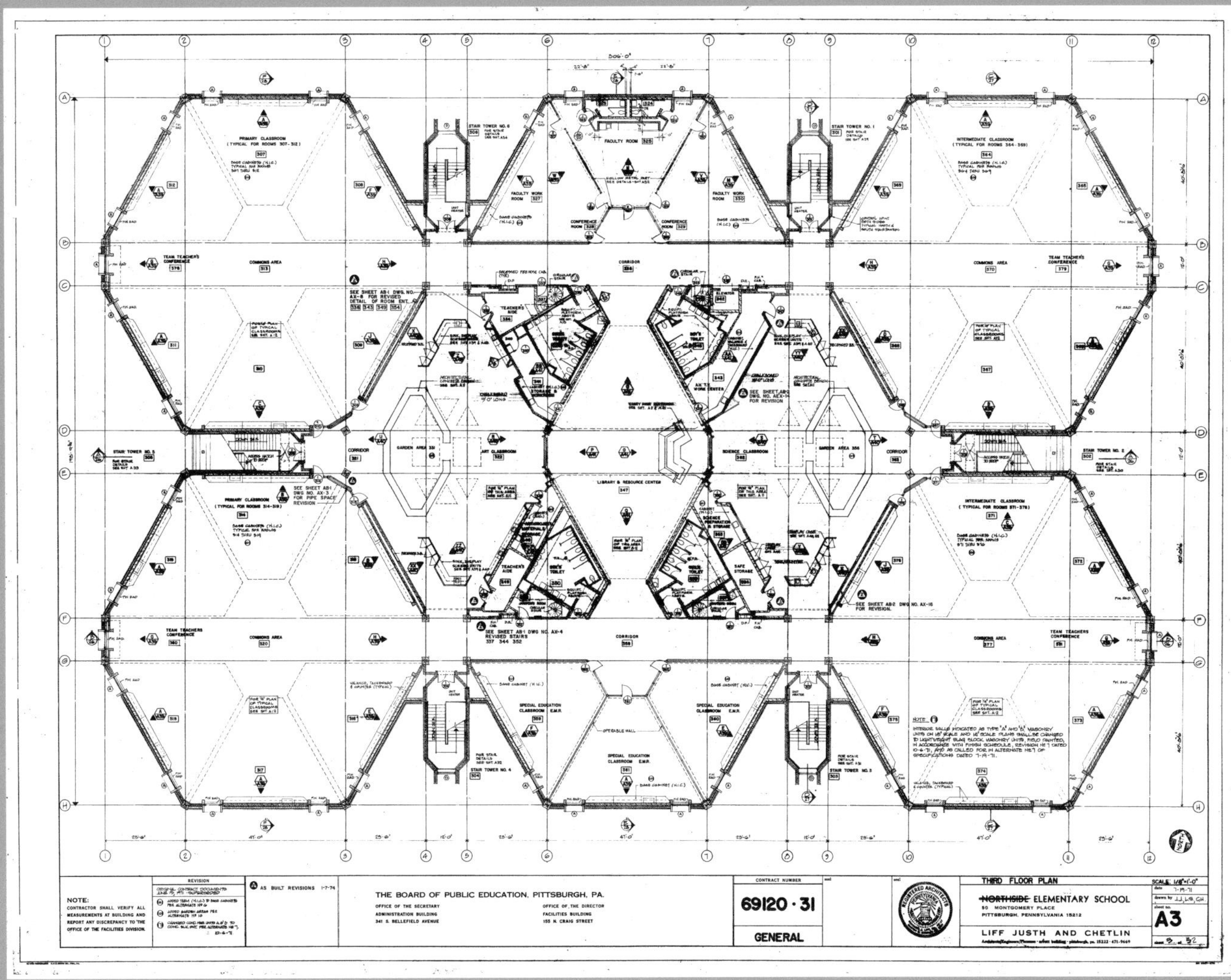

Liff Justh and Chetlin, Martin Luther King Jr. Elementary School, Third Floor Plan, 1971, architectural drawing; PPBF

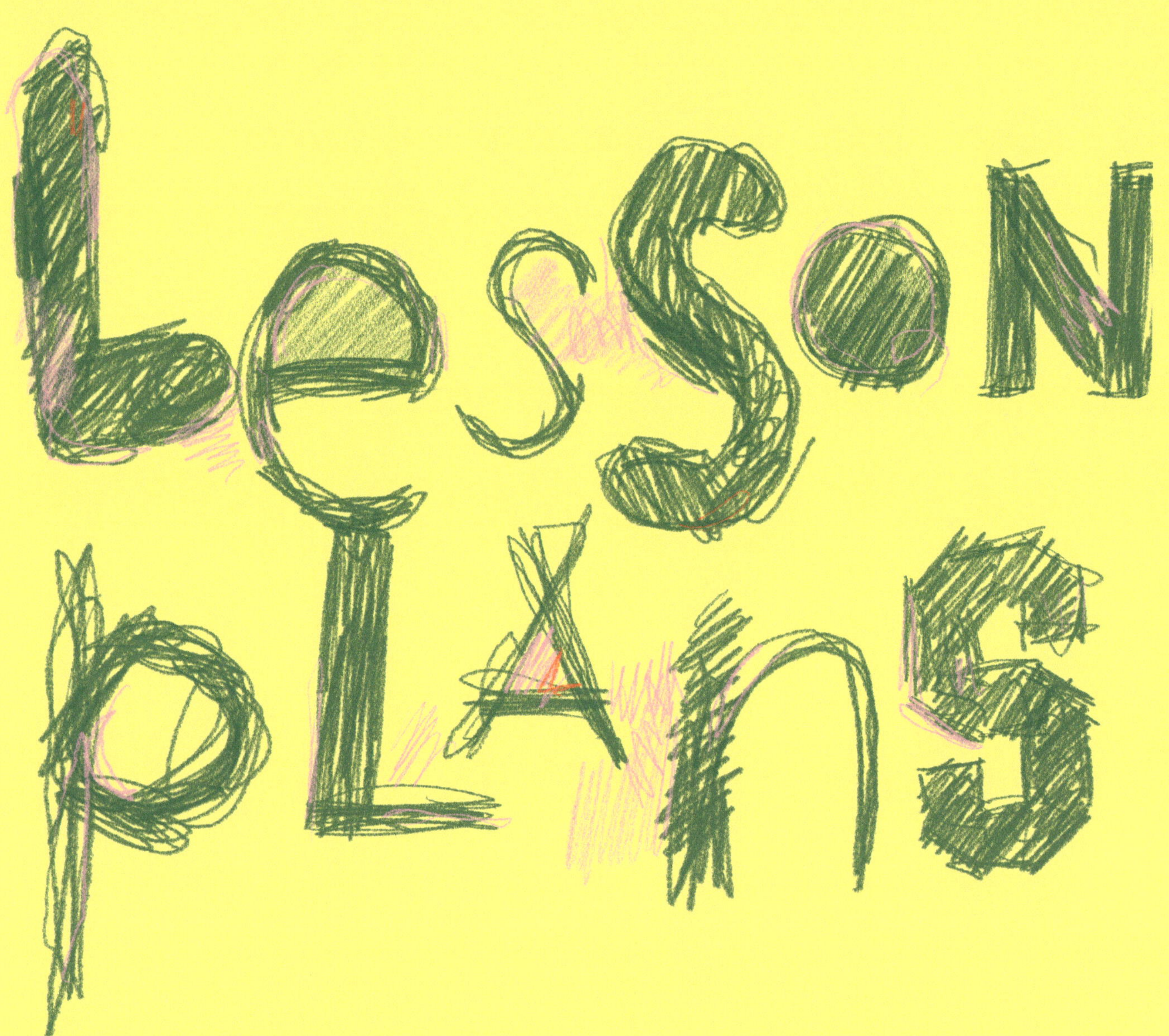

Lesson
plans

Lesson plans—the blueprints of instruction—structure the rhythms of classrooms lined with desks, tiled floors, and fluorescent lights. Yet no two students learn alike, and the generic lesson plan rarely accounts for the lived experiences of those engaged or silenced by daily instruction, particularly when curricula restrict inquiry around race, gender, or sexuality. The following section gathers contributions from contemporary architects, artists, and educators who reimagine lesson plans as sites of uncertainty, improvisation, and productive error. Their work foregrounds knowledge-making as embodied, intergenerational, and transnational: linking the Black Panther Party's Free Breakfast Program to contemporary food sovereignty; staging site-responsive exercises that center craft and creativity; weaving community-based knowledge into the building of schools and artist residencies; and inviting young learners to imagine and resist everyday mechanisms of control. Across national and international contexts, gardens, museums, and community centers emerge as classrooms where play becomes pedagogical, movement central, and the distinction between instructor and student begins to blur.

LIFE LESSONS: INFORMAL, STRUCTURED, AND SUBVERSIVE

RACHEL DELPHIA

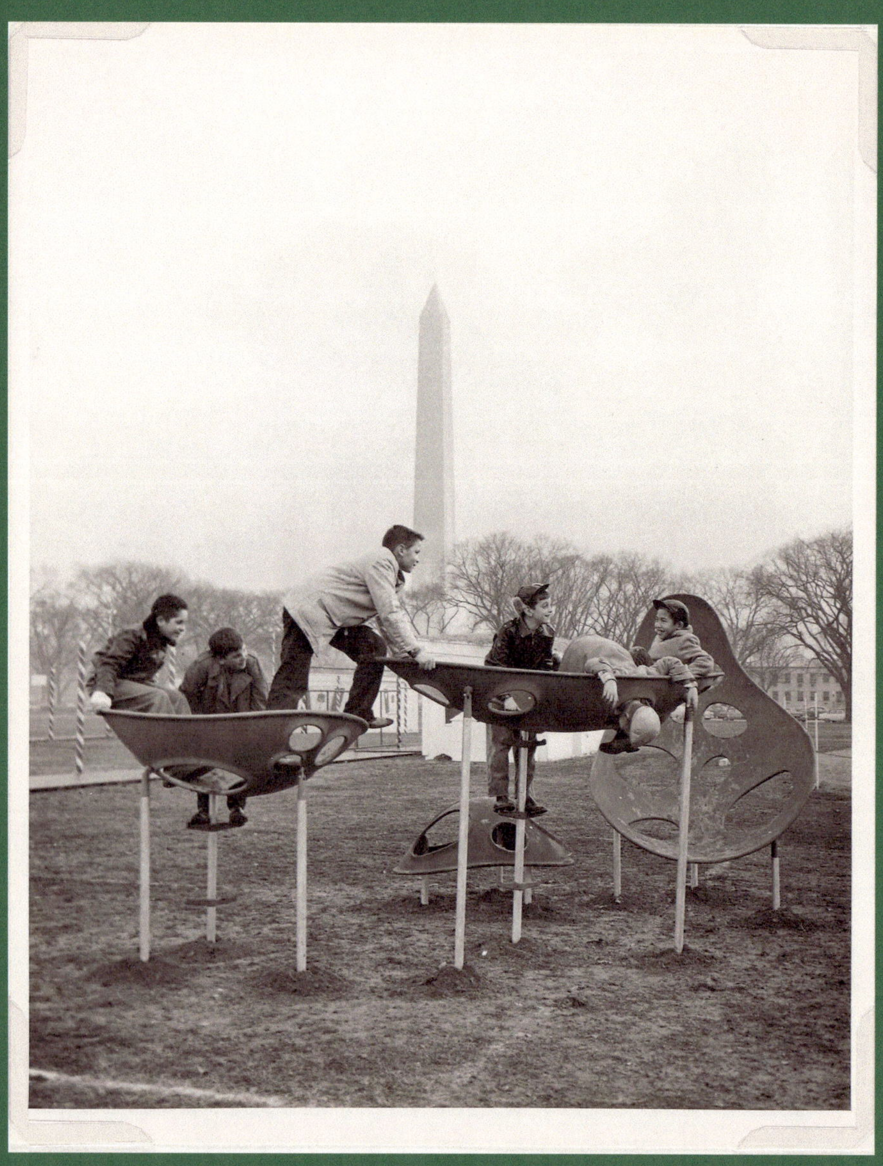

INFORMAL LESSONS

Lifelong learning begins in the first embrace of interaction between infants and caregivers. I found the first year of each of my children's lives to be nothing short of magic—if also a sleep-deprived, anxiety-ridden marathon.[1] Parenthood is, undeniably, a miraculous immersion in the innate human ability and drive to learn. Months before a neurotypical child meets milestones like articulating words, eating solid food, or even grasping an object on purpose, its *sentience* and *will* are remarkably evident. Sense by sense, babies intuitively seek input. Through constant observations, tests, and feedback loops, their synapses fire and make millions of new connections. Without specialized training or facilities, loving adult caregivers expertly provide infants' first life lessons. This is nature's design.[2]

To make sense of these remarkable early learning experiences, some cognitive psychologists have drawn metaphors from the language of computing, imagining the newborn brain as a system which learns through trial, error, and constant revision. In other words, babies are not passively waiting for formal instruction. They come equipped with "powerful learning mechanisms that allow them to spontaneously revise, reshape, and restructure their knowledge. … Children think, observe, and reason. They consider evidence, draft conclusions, do experiments, and search for the truth," even as infants.[3]

The earliest bits of evidence arrive to the infant mind via the senses—touch, sight, sound, taste, and smell. Obstetricians and doulas lay a newborn on their mother's chest within minutes of being born, letting bare skin touch bare skin. Birth wrests a tiny creature from the only environment it has ever known: the warm, dark embrace of the uterus. In the bright, cold, airy world, skin-to-skin contact offers reassurance through touch. *I am here. You are here. We are in this together.* Over the coming hours, days, and weeks, caregivers hug, pat, tap, poke, tickle, kiss, wipe, bounce, bathe, and swaddle their infant—inadvertently teaching them about the sensory abilities of their skin. Babies learn that touch can be pleasant, surprising, or painful. They also realize that touch can be all-encompassing (a wet bath) or localized (a kiss on the head). In time, they begin to initiate contact—reaching for a hand, pressing a cheek—and to test their own impact through scratches, swats, and kicks.

Newborn babies do not see like adults do, yet their burgeoning sight is perfectly adapted for early cognitive growth. While distance vision is fuzzy, the baby can see quite well at a focal length of about a foot, perfect for taking in the faces of caregivers. Babies are primed to closely observe human faces and will begin imitating facial expressions at only one month old.[4] They learn to differentiate the countenances of multiple loved ones and to correlate expressions with both positive and negative conditions. When an older infant encounters something unexpected, they will look to a parent's face for cues. If mom is calm, they stay calm. If mom is scared, they deduce that there must be cause for alarm.

Doctors presume that babies can hear indistinct sounds from inside the womb, especially their mother's voice as it resonates in the adjacent diaphragm. Infants may have a head start on recognizing this voice above all others, but they quickly assimilate knowledge of the voices they hear day to day. Cooing and vocalizing their own sounds, they experiment with rhythm, pitch, and inflection. Baby talk between adults and infants establishes spoken language as a reciprocal, communicative activity. Infants also soon recognize that sound emanates *from* something or someone.

---

[1] Basic shelter, sustenance, and safety are lacking for many American infants, and their parents may not have access to a living wage, nutritious food, paid parental leave, or affordable childcare. These challenges persist from birth to graduation. Human interaction might be the first educational infrastructure; yet systemic disparities affect families and young children persist.

[2] Throughout this essay, I draw on my own, subjective experiences as a mother of two daughters. As both parent and scholar here, I rely on the work of cognitive psychologist Alison Gopnik and her co-authors. See: **Alison Gopnik, Andrew N. Meltzoff, and Patricia K. Kuhl,** *The Scientist in the Crib: Minds, Brains, and How Children Learn* (William Morrow and Company, Inc., 1999).

[3] **Gopnik, et al.,** *The Scientist in the Crib,* 7, 13.

[4] **Gopnik, et al.,** *The Scientist in the Crib,* 12–13, for the authors' take on the history of epistemology and philosophy as it relates to child development. See also the writings of Plato, John Locke, Jean-Jacques Rousseau, and John Dewey.

Smell is another powerful tool for infants, who can identify their primary caregivers by scent as well as sight and sound. Growing babies meet new people and experience new places and substances, each with associated smells. They both respond innately and look to their caregivers to confirm whether they find smells to be pleasant, just acceptable, or repugnant. These are social signals that prepare children to live not just in *the* world, but in *their* world.

Taste offers infants a similar opportunity to deduce clues about their immediate context while also expressing their individual preferences. They may spit out a new food dozens of times even as an adult affirms that it is edible and nutritious. Older siblings may delight in introducing a range of strong flavors just to see how the baby will react. A pinch of salt, sugar, spice, or a drop of lemon juice may comprise baby taste lesson 101.

Of course, babies also combine their sensory inputs. One afternoon, in early 2017, I found my five-year-old on the couch with her father and four-and-a-half-month-old sister, listening to Soul Coughing's *Lazybones*. My husband cradled the baby in a sitting position while he and big sister tapped their thighs to the driving beat. The baby started tapping along: not half-heartedly but fully committed and on tempo. Flabbergasted by her participation, they stopped, but she looked perplexed. She made eye contact with her dad and started tapping again. It was a non-verbal comment, question, and cue combined. "Hey, we were doing a thing. Why did you stop? Let's do it again!" That day she discovered that her family could engage in a group activity involving visible and tactile movement in response to sound and that this shared experience could bring connection and joy. *We are all here. We are in this together.*

What is the point of all of this, beyond the reflections of a parent? The point is that children's education begins immediately, almost imperceptibly, in a world of wonder accessed through the senses. Through direct interaction and modeling behavior, we teach babies to process sensory information and to recognize a sense of self. They learn material properties, spatial relationships, gravity, and cause and effect. They acquire a basic facility with language, both receptive and productive. In short, they learn to live in a world of things, spaces, and other living beings. Simply by caring for their basic needs, interacting with them directly, and giving them access to observe our daily lives, we provide a primer for living.

STRUCTURED LESSONS

At some point, depending on the provisions of national, state, and local governments, parents entrust their preschoolers, kindergarteners, or older children to the teachers, administrators, and school boards who make up their local educational institutions. The informality of early childhood learning gives way to a newfound structure, both conceptually and physically. There are weighty new questions: What will be taught? How? In what facilities? And, to what end?

From Plato to John Locke, Western philosophers have long pondered the nature of knowledge, the capacity to learn, and the relationship to qualities like truth and virtue. Do children arrive in this world inherently good or bad? Can they tap into the *anamnesis* of pre-existing knowledge, or must the instructions be inscribed onto the *tabula rasa* of their nascent minds? Are children inherently unruly, as Freud argues, driven by the unchecked impulses of the primal *id*? Or, in the model of Romantics

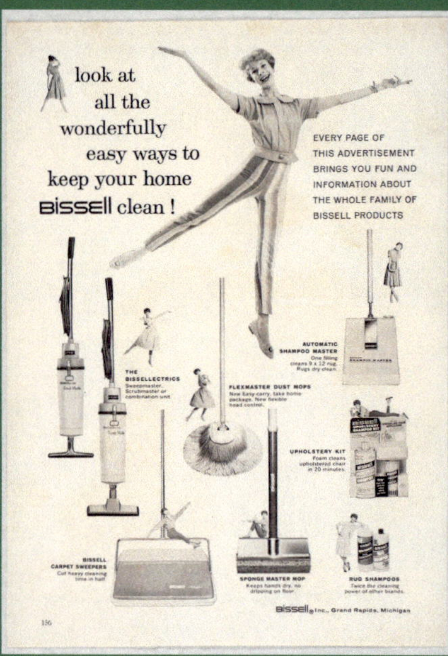

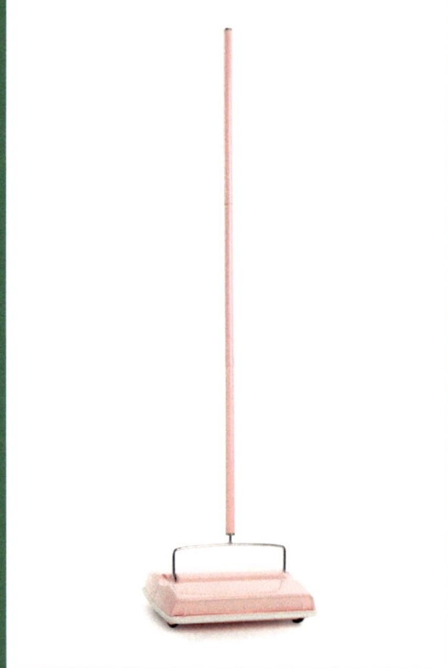

Top: Bissell products advertisement from *Good Housekeeping*, October 1960, magazine excerpt; Carnegie Museum of Art, Gift of Jewel Stern

Bottom: Peter Muller-Munk Associates, *Bissell Inc. Little Queen Carpet Sweeper*, ca. 1960, enameled steel, vinyl, rubber, chromium-plated steel, and natural bristles; Carnegie Museum of Art, Gift of Jewel Stern

like Jean-Jacques Rousseau, are impulse and imagination admirable merits of youth, stamped out, regrettably, by formal education? Is the goal of education transmitting knowledge or developing character? Should schooling mold children in the model of socially constructed "ideal" adults or support them to become whomever they want to be? Who reaps the ultimate rewards of education: the pupil or society?

Answers to these questions drive educational approaches, from curriculum to pedagogy to the design of classrooms and their contents. Such questions are not only philosophical, but highly personal and political as well. Students in Pennsylvania have a right to public education, as governed by The Pennsylvania Public School Code of 1949 (also known as Title 24).[5] Yet the commitment to equitably serving every child is not easily fulfilled. To invoke a popular image from Diversity, Equity, Accessibility, and Inclusion workshops of the early 2020s, individuals of different heights will need different amounts of lift to see over the same fence. In practice, educational "fences" may be physical (the absence of an elevator in an aging school building) or psychological (a lesson that perpetuates an outdated social hierarchy). The flip side of public education being guaranteed is that it is also *compulsory* for students aged six to eighteen, requiring schools to constantly find the appropriate amount of "lift" for each pupil. Balancing standards with individualization at scale is an estimable, herculean, and never-ending task.

In a polarized political climate public, debate often swirls around curriculum—the "standards-based sequence of planned experiences where students practice and achieve proficiency in content and applied learning skills."[6] Pennsylvania's State Academic Standards are approved and published by the State Board of Education and include more than dozen subject areas, from English Language and Mathematics, to Civics and History, to Sciences, Arts and Humanities, Geography, and Economics. The guidelines for each subject area begin with the same lofty promise.

> Pennsylvania's public schools shall teach, challenge and support every student to realize his or her maximum potential and to acquire the knowledge and skills needed to… [e.g.]… Recognize critical processes used in the examination of works in the arts and humanities, … Explain geographic tools and their uses, [or] … Explore and develop an understanding of fractions as numbers.[7]

Chart after chart provides a panoply of desired outcomes by subject and age, which correlate to standardized exams for tested subjects. On the one hand, academic standards provide a practical baseline for accountability and establish goals for shared knowledge across the population. On the other hand, no curriculum is neutral, and standards do not necessarily serve all pupils equally.

The pitfalls of establishing curricular standards are also borne out in textbooks, which are tactically revised and approved by the states. Dana Goldstein's 2020 article in the *New York Times* exposed the effects of partisan politics on what children read in the classroom, which differs between red states and blue states. Goldstein writes, "in a country that cannot come to a consensus on fundamental questions—how restricted

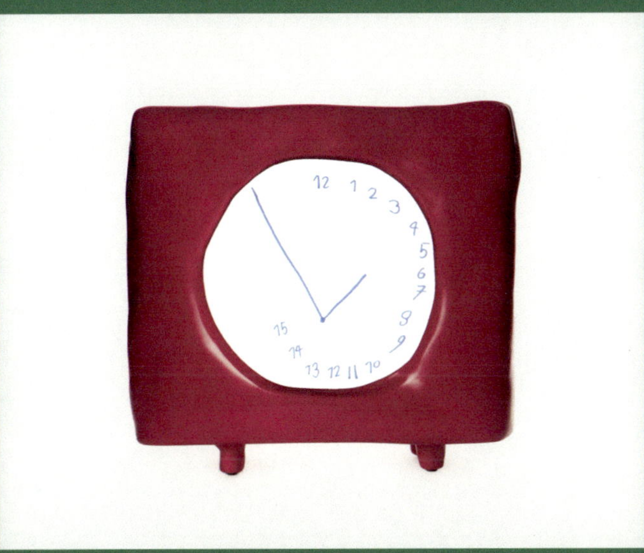

Maarten Baas, *Children's Clock*, 2022, stainless steel, clay, digital equipment; Carnegie Museum of Art, Women's Committee Acquisition Fund

5 Pennsylvania Public School Code of 1949, March 10, 1949, P.L. 30, No. 14, Cl. 24.

6 "Curriculum Definition," State of Rhode Island Department of Education https://ride.ri.gov/instruction-assessment/curriculum/curriculum-definition.

7 Pennsylvania State Academic Standards, 9.3.3.A, 7.1.9.A, and CC.2.1.3.C.1. https://www.pa.gov/agencies/stateboard/resources/regulations--policy/state-academic-standards.

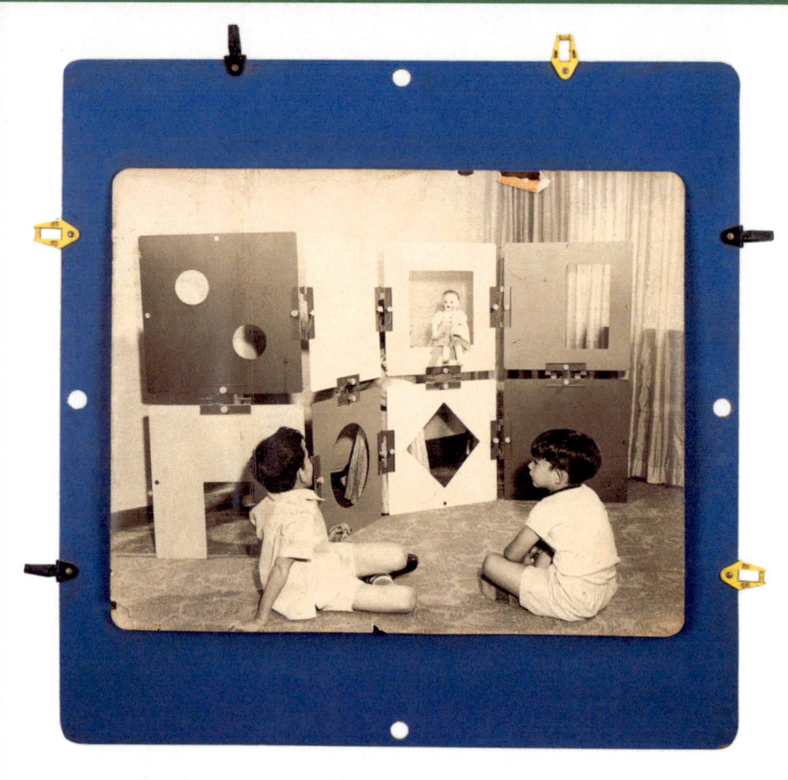

Orin Raphael, *Playspaces,* ca. 1955, pressed wood, plastic, and steel; Carnegie Museum of Art, Gift of the family of Orin M. Raphael

capitalism should be, whether immigrants are a burden or a boon, to what extent the legacy of slavery continues to shape American life—textbook publishers are caught in the middle."[8] Students in Texas and California both learn about the Harlem Renaissance, but a Texas history book is more circumspect in describing the quality and relative importance of the intellectual and artistic output of this early twentieth century movement.

Indeed, teachers toe the line where structures meet individual learners. Core standards and textbooks become scaffolding and tools, with teachers as the expert mediators who utilize the best pedagogical approaches and specific lessons for their students. Ideal scenarios assume teachers have the resources they need, financially and beyond *e.g.,* professional development, support services, and the time to invest in lesson planning. Teachers and students also need safe, comfortable spaces that are conducive to learning, outfitted with appropriate equipment, and flexible enough to accommodate the needs of each body and mind. Yet systems intended to support order and discipline—hallmarks of many traditional school settings—can place undue constraints on individuals. Carpets with colorful dots maintain distance between seated students, but they fail to accommodate all bodies. A preponderance of right-handed desks or scissors signals to lefties that they are outliers. Spaces designated "boys" and "girls" assert normative, binary expressions of gender.

Designed objects, both inside and outside the classroom, reflect attitudes and expectations about childrearing and its results. Carnegie Museum of Art's collection preserves several toys from earlier eras that prescribe traditional gender roles for young women. The Ideal Toy Corporation in Hollis, New York produced miniature plastic dishes in imitation of the *American Modern Casual China* designed by Russel Wright for the Steubenville Pottery Company, Ohio in 1937. The organic shapes and playful colors of Wright's designs for adults encouraged more casual dining and entertaining in the American home. The cardboard carton for the toy dishes features dancing images of pink, yellow, and powder blue teacups and saucers above an illustration of a pigtailed girl pouring tea. "It's FUN to serve your friends in real Russel Wright dishes. … just like mother's," reads the caption. While both father *and mother* have their feet up on the cover of Mary and Russel Wright's *Guide to Easier Living,* 1950, the toy promotes a world in which girls play at hosting tea parties, a structured lesson along a well-constructed path to housewifery, thinly-veiled as play.[9] The Grand Rapids, Michigan-based company Bissell, which cornered the adult housekeeping market in the 1950s and 60s with their boxy mechanical carpet sweepers, offers another. Their *Little Queen Carpet Sweeper* (ca. 1960) designed by the Pittsburgh firm Peter Muller-Munk Associates, is a fully functional miniature model that provided the perfect prop to mimic household chores. Unsurprisingly, it is also pink.

8 **Dana Goldstein,** "Two States. Eight Textbooks. Two American Stories," *The New York Times,* January 12, 2020.

9 **Mary and Russel Wright,** *Mary and Russel Wright's Guide to Easier Living,* 1st ed. (Gibbs Smith, 1950).

SUBVERSIVE LESSONS

Designed objects and spaces can codify and reinforce societal structures, like the ubiquitous classroom wall clock minding beginnings, lessons, lunch breaks, and dismissals, *ad nauseum*. But designs can also push back: subverting prevailing ideas and making room to unlearn.

A prime example is the *Children's Clock* (2022) by Dutch designer Maarten Baas. Baas' clocks pose playful and provocative questions about marking time. At the Salone del Mobile, Milano, in 2009, he launched a series called *Real Time*, comprising twelve-hour film performances as timekeeping devices. The *Children's Clock* is the latest iteration. The cartoonish, polymer clay housing sports a round digital screen in lieu of a clockface, which Baas animates by combining 720 distinct one-minute videos to complete one twelve-hour cycle. Baas recorded each video from a fixed camera pointed down at the table where 720 children each drew their assigned time *e.g.* 10:01 or 3:55. The completed clock has a curious effect on viewers: although they can technically read the time at any given moment, they are inclined to linger and *watch* the moving images. More than numerals or hand positions, the clock portrays humanity. Its hands are big and small, dark, light, and in between, uncertain and decisive. Some children draw the numbers first. Others jump right into the hour and minute hands. They use pencil, marker, crayon, or paint, and their styles range from minimalist to ebullient. Ironically, the durational video clock reminds audiences that time is, in fact, fleeting. Each featured child is growing up. Perhaps the viewer, transfixed, shakes off the enchantment of time thus recorded and recalls that life's ultimate resource is ticking away, minute by minute.

As Alexandra Lange has written, architect- and designer-made toys in the mid-twentieth century gave children open-ended tools to engage creatively with objects and space. One of the most famous is the Tyng Toy (1949) designed by Anne Tyng (an architect who later designed an elementary school in Bucks County, Pennsylvania). The eleven-piece toy set included plywood cutouts of various abstract shapes and circles, complete with holes and notches to fit together, as well as dowels that could serve as axels.[10] The *New York Times* remarked that children might find parallels to their parents' efforts trying to assemble the era's new knock-down furniture. But whereas putting together furniture might have stressed the era's adults, for the children there were no right or wrong answers, just unbridled play.[11]

Another toy designed for open-ended construction was Orin Raphael's *Playspaces* (ca. 1955), a set of colorful panels that could connect to form walls, boxes, and environments, inspired by the cardboard boxes that Raphael's children used imaginatively. Raphael studied design at the New Bauhaus in Chicago and later married Elizabeth Rockwell Raphael, founder of Pittsburgh's avant garde art gallery *Outlines* and the Society for Contemporary Craft. Orin Raphael's interest in non-traditional pedagogy extended to his personal life. A father of three daughters, he was the vice president of the Play School in Pittsburgh's Squirrel Hill neighborhood, "a non-profit, state registered nursery school of pre-kindergarten children … dedicated to progressive child education" where children were free to play in the manner of their choosing.[12]

In the built environment, designer David Aaron created playgrounds full of possibility. His play structures came under the auspices of the Aluminum Company of America's (ALCOA) Forecast program, a multi-pronged design and advertising effort to promote playful and

10 **Alexandra Lange,** "Toys as Furniture / Furniture as Toys," *iSimultaneous Randomness and Order: the Fibonacci-Divine Proportion as a Universal Forming Principle,* (PhD diss., University of Pennsylvania, 1975).

11 **Lange,** "Toys as Furniture."

12 "Sq. Hill Play School Elects New Officers for Guides," *The American Jewish Outlook,* December 23, 1949, 59.

innovative uses for aluminum in the late 1950s. Aaron's imaginative playground consisted of amoeboid, cast aluminum shells in various colors and propped off the ground in assorted orientations. Pierced with holes of different sizes, the parabolic planes resembled Swiss cheese, albeit with hand and foot holds and curious portals big enough for kids to pass through. According to Aaron, children's play was serious business. His structure could "be used for hiding and seeking, climbing and sliding, and letting imagination run wild."[13]

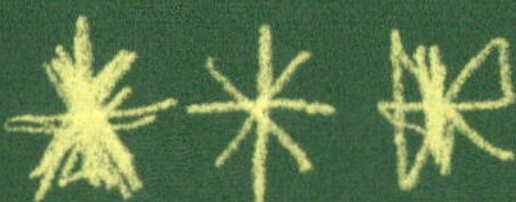

An infectiously open and joyful spirit infuses the projects above. How delightfully perverse of Baas to render a clock face with children's delineations in real time, some of which are so scribbly as to be illegible. To see this clock is to unlearn, to conjure a time when you didn't know how to read, let alone draw, an analog clock, to ponder the simple act of mark-making and schematic representation. Raphael and Aaron similarly invite users to rethink the body's relationship to the built environment. While typical floors, walls, or chairs, exude familiar affordances for normative postures like standing, leaning, or sitting, these play structures unleash the potential to shape and inhabit space differently. Hills, valleys, partitions, boxes, tunnels, and peep holes constitute landscapes of possibility for being bored, rambunctious, pensive, theatrical, or mischievous. With various colors, shapes, and materials, the play structures stimulate the senses of sight and touch. Little bodies, smelling sweet and sweaty, activate these objects, adding incidental thuds and clonks, as well as intentional sounds from knocking hands, tapping sticks, and experimenting with vocal echoes and projection. Keep an eye on the toddlers; someone will venture a lick or taste a mouthful of dirt. Set free by design, the playful inhabitants return to their earliest sensory lessons.

Tucked away in the archives of Pittsburgh Public Schools, a series of folders from 1972 provide a glimpse of experimental curriculum for "perceptual development"—everything that unfolds so naturally for infants— extended to a classroom of young learners. Lesson plans for developing tactile senses ask children to assume a position of their choice while describing what parts of their body are touching the floor, reaching into a bag of objects and identify them by touch, or matching physical samples (a sponge, feather, or marble) to images of things with a similar feel. Other pages outline lessons for developing "olfactory" or "gustatory" senses, such as tasting related or contrasting foods: raw carrot/cooked carrot, olive/pickle, Swiss cheese/Velveeta, or sugar/salt.[14]

Amid the very real challenges of administrating public education, *after school* asks us to consider how communities might reclaim this sense of wonder and self-determination. How might school be re-imagined? Can it channel the freedom of erector sets and climbing structures? Can learning be unbound, like the neuroplastic infant brain? What third places might be built to support not only learning, but *unlearning* as well, and to teach topics of great value that have never been codified into the core curriculum?

13 **Darrin Alfred,** "Serious Business: the Wonderful Imaginative Spirit of ALCOA's Forecast Program," in *Serious Play*, edited by Monica Obniski and Darrin Alfred, (Yale University Press, 2019); 208–210.

14 Folder 2: Guidelines, 1972, Series II: Curriculum and Instruction, Subseries 2: Courses of Study, Pittsburgh Public Schools Papers (1848–1999), MSS#117, Thomas & Katherine Detre Library & Archives at the Senator John Heinz History Center, Pittsburgh, Pennsylvania.

OBJECTIVE: The pupil will savor and discriminate among various tastes.

CONCEPTS AND/OR TYPES OF ACTIVITIES	*ACTIVITIES*	*RESOURCES AND MATERIALS*

One learns in many ways. Tasting is one of these ways.

Prepare a "taste tray" containing paired samples of food with distinctive tastes and texture.

Tray
Food samples

Examples
raw potato-mashed potato
raw carrot-cooked carrot
olive-pickle
sugar-salt
apple-pineapple
orange-lemon
swiss cheese-velveeta
sucker-gumdrop
cracker-cookie

Explain to the child that some things will taste pleasant and that others might be bitter or sour or hard. Constantly reassure him/her that nothing on the tray will hurt him. Offer a sweet taste after a bitter one.* (See the following page.)

Encourage discussion of food likes and dislikes, favorite meals, birthday meals, and picnics.

Ask questions to heighten the child's perception of the differences in the tastes and texture of foods and his/her memory of good things tasted in the past.

Examples
"Which do you like better, a hamburger or a hot dog? Why?"
"Would you rather eat watermelon or a grape? They both have seeds that get in your mouth."
"Does your mother make you eat things you don't like? What are they?"
"Surprise your mother. Eat a little bit the next time without complaining."

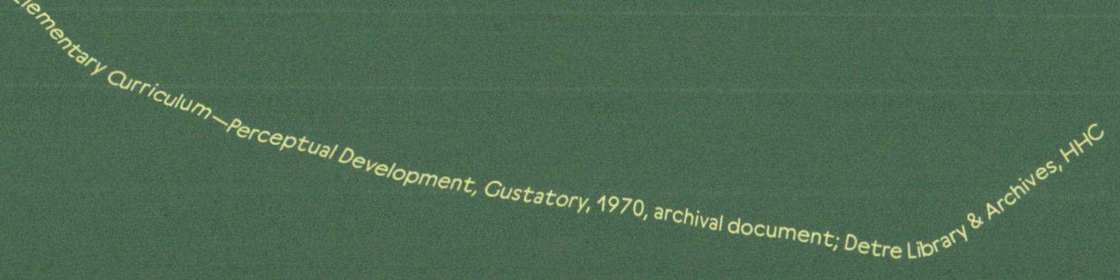

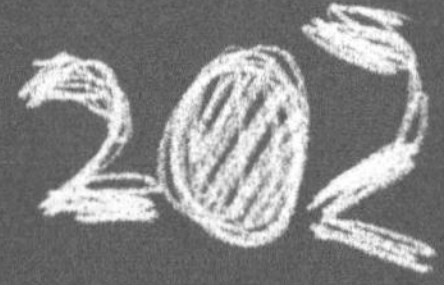

A CHILD
FLOATING IN SPACE

DANIELLE DEAN

THE AMERICAN DREAM OF EDUCATION

PREREQUISITES: None

COURSE DESCRIPTION

I have long been interested in the industrialization of the imagination, individual and collective. I have thought about this in a multitude of ways: from the language we use to articulate our worlds to how our imaginations have been taken over by sociopolitical ideas that prioritize the accumulation of capital above all else.

For example, when I was in art school, I looked through archival collections of magazines—from a time when magazines were more important than the Internet—and analyzed the language of adverts found in them. The texts often grappled with ideas of individualism, consumption, and competition. I had just moved to the United States for school, and as I was exposed to these ideas and affects in the archive, I, too, began to feel them percolate into my everyday conversations and personal relationships. This experience made me realize how ideologies influence our perception of the world intimately—how we come to see it, feel it, and know it.

What does it mean to look out at the wonders of the world spread out across a vast landscape that surrounds you and realize you cannot see it but through a set of predetermined ideas which prioritize extraction? How did we learn to see the world in this peculiar way?

To consider the ecology of education today, I spoke with Wayee Chu, partner at Reach Capital, a venture fund focused on companies in education and technology. She contributes to the future of educational access through online teaching technology and tools, including AI tutors. In conversation, she explains that, "Futurists in education generally believe that the traditional model of schooling—standardized, time-bound, and credentials-first—is outdated. They envision a system that is flexible, learner-driven, and continuously evolving with technology and societal needs." The benefits of online school appear to parallel those originally proposed by the Pittsburgh Board of Public Education's Great High Schools: a series of mega-schools, prominent in a movement of architects, designers, and technology-advocates reimagining education during the 1960s Civil Rights era. However, whereas the Great High Schools plan proposed five high school education parks with massive forty-acre campuses for student bodies of five thousand to six thousand each, futurists in education imagine a system that can reach many students simultaneously but with much less physical infrastructure.

I saw, perhaps naively, this movement from Zoom meetings to AI agents in the classroom as modeling a post-Fordist future for the classroom: a future where students are plugged into an assembly line of education that privileges economical mass-learning through data-driven customization. This parallels the Pittsburgh Board of Public Education's investment into strategies where student activity, time, and movement are governed by maximum utilization of space and resources, as seen in their 1973 *Feasibility Study* prepared by architects Damianos and Pedone.

The contradiction between a post-Fordist dream of individualization and free choice becomes evident in the face of increasingly oligarchical and centralized power structures in technology, which now reach into education through the inclusion of corporate AI products within online learning tools.

However, even in the 1960s and 70s, the Pittsburgh Urban League critiqued and addressed issues and inadequacies they found within the Board of Public Education's mass schooling models and desegregation plans. Within their community, they created pedagogical strategies and initiatives that aimed at uplifting Black youth through their Community School Model and the Street Academy program. Their counter-educational projects offer instructive parallels and guiding questions for our class.

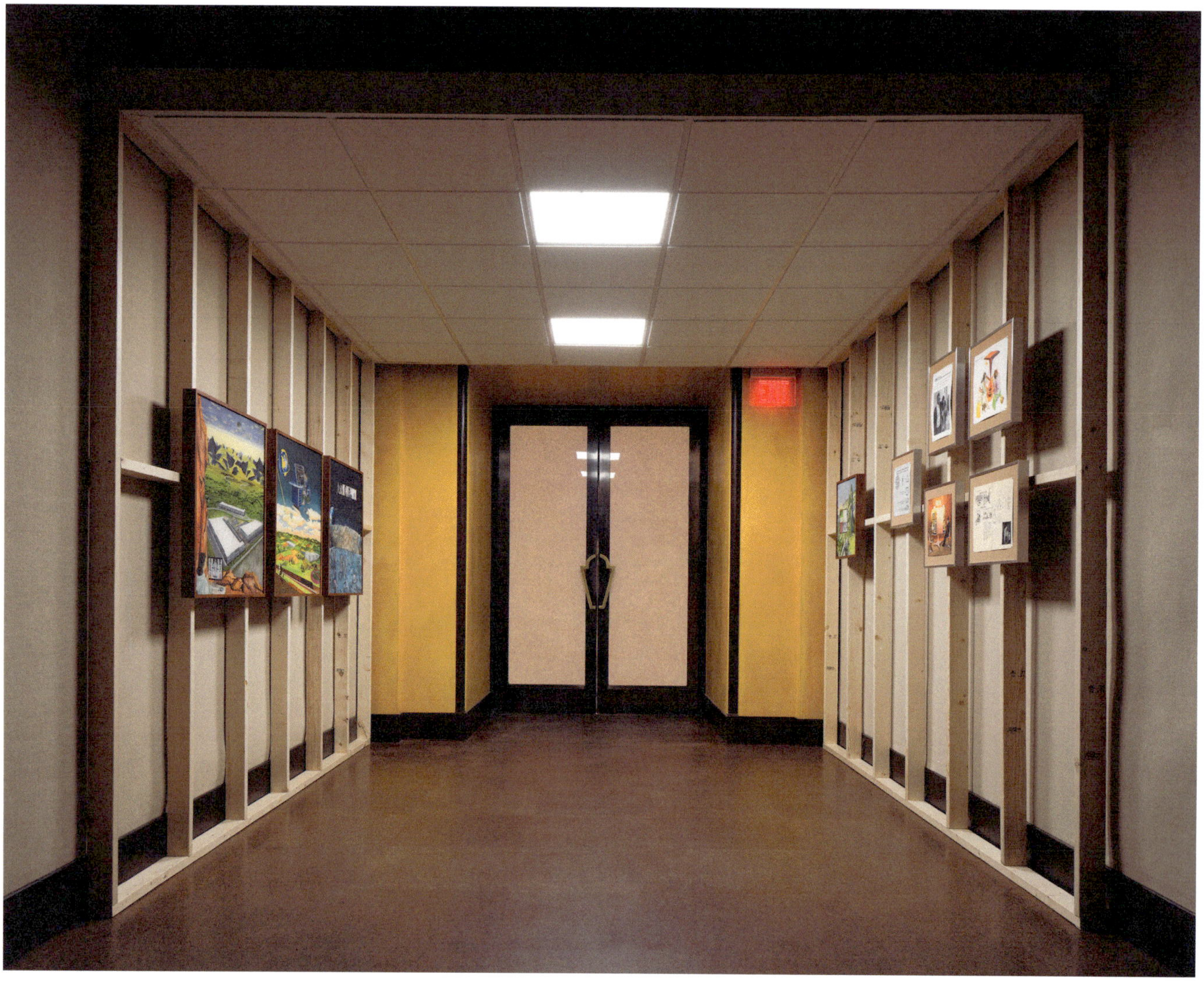

Danielle Dean, *A Child Floating in Space: The American Dream of Education*, 2025, watercolors on silk and paper, embroidery, installation view of *after school*, Carnegie Museum of Art, 2025; photo: Zachary Riggleman

COURSE
QUESTIONS

01 In our increasingly techno-feudalist and disconnected digital landscape, how can we re-imagine resistance strategies for the future of education?

02 How can we reconsider education to make space for free thought and the construction of more just futures today?

03 What does it mean when our imaginative processes become centralized by massive corporate monopolies?

04 How might we create alternatives in this capitalist, post-Fordist, post-AI landscape for online education and optimization?

05 Can you write a list of three things that would activate answers for the above questions in concrete terms? For example, might this include the abolishment of private schools? The unionization of all students and teachers? Implementing a curriculum that centers on the study of cooperative models of education and economic organization?

Danielle Dean, *The Homework Machine (1981)*, 2025, watercolor on paper, embroidery; Courtesy of the artist

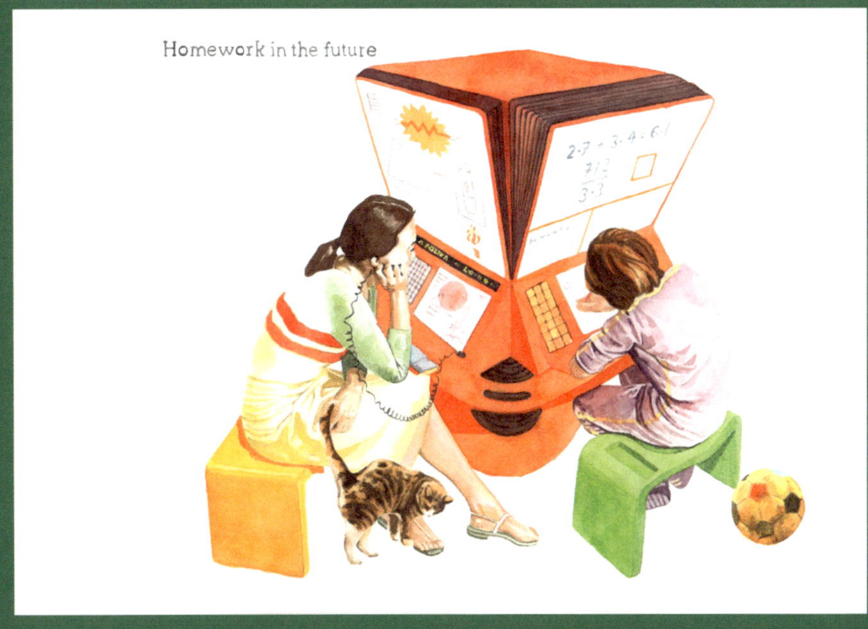

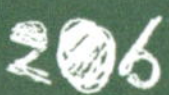

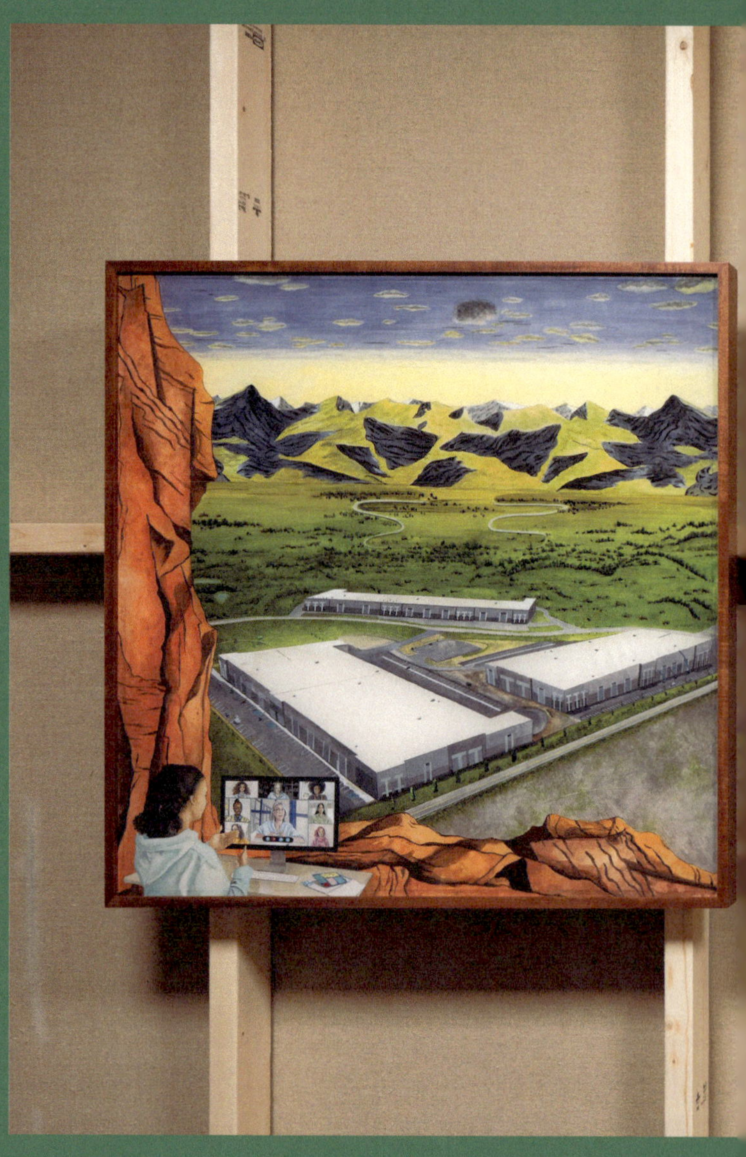

Danielle Dean, installation view of *Mega School (Ford; Amazon)*, *Child Floating in Space (United States Steel Corporation; Pennsylvania Railroad)*, and *Astra Nova (Ford)* 2025, watercolors on silk, embroidery (works listed left to right) in *after school*, Carnegie Museum of Art, 2025; photo: Zachary Riggleman

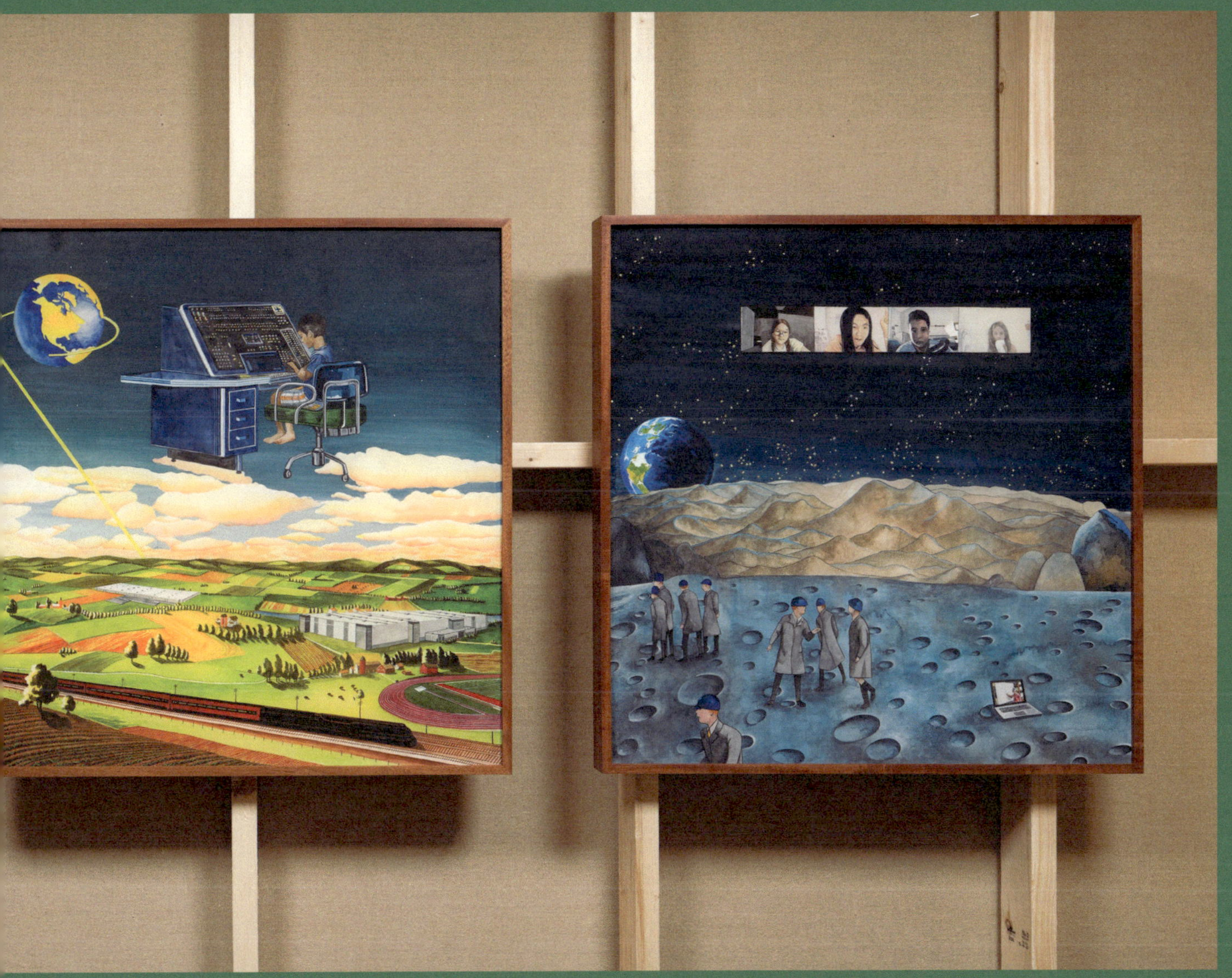

A Child Floating in Space

208

AMERICAN GAZE

CREATING PLACE

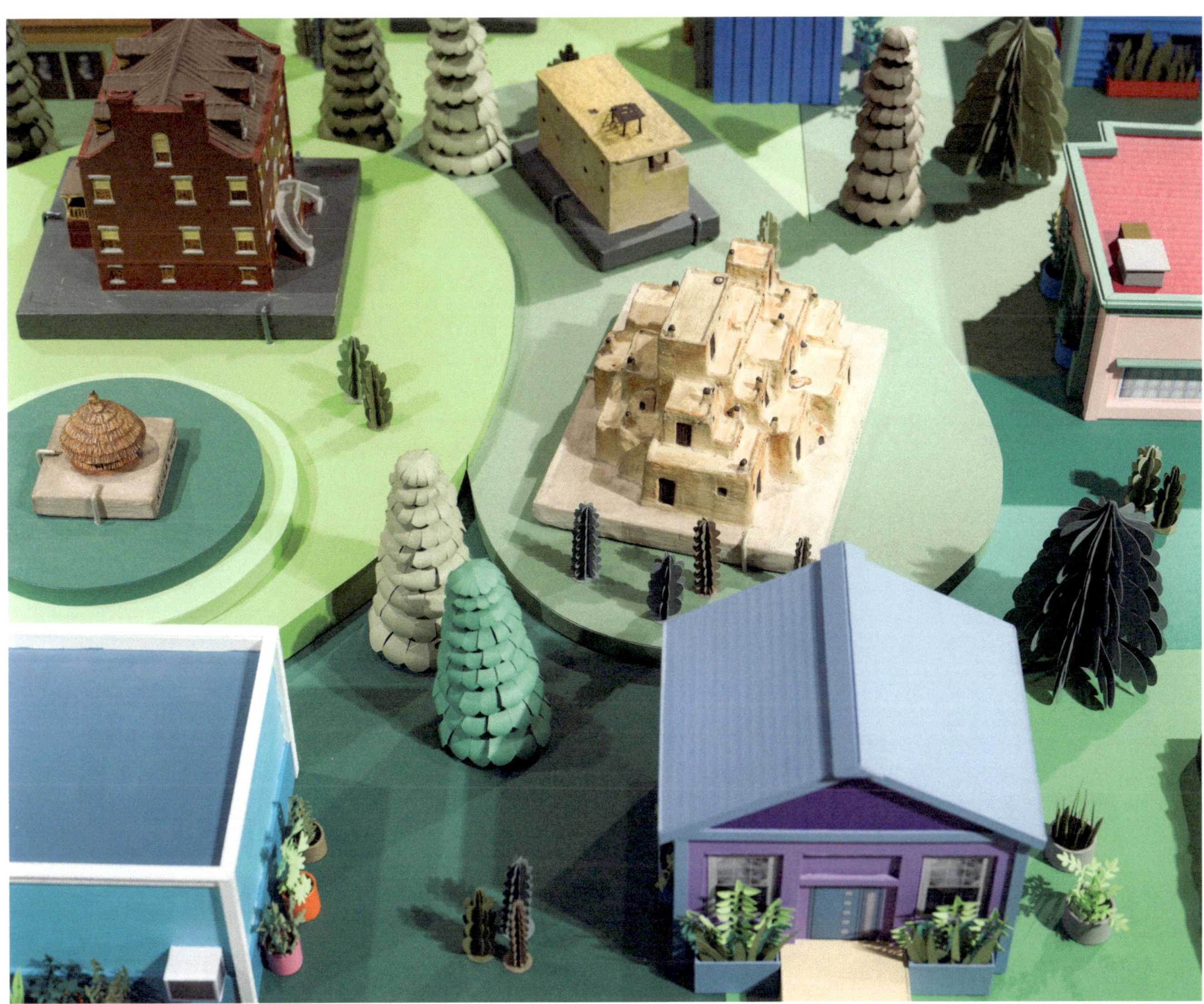

COURSE DESCRIPTION

Hand-painted signage, vibrant colors, satellite dishes, and iron gates are not anomalies within urban landscapes but authentic expressions of cultural identity and agency. They are also the architectural details often erased by gentrification. In my work, I am reasserting their presence within the built environment of working-class neighborhoods, particularly those imprinted on by Latinx cultures, with intention and pride. How can architecture shape identities and how can we, in turn, reshape architecture?

Above: Ana Serrano, Detail of *American Gaze*, 2025, paper models and plaster cast Works Progress Administration, Pennsylvania Museum Extension Project (1935–1943), installation view of *after school*, Carnegie Museum of Art, 2025; photo: Zachary Riggleman

MATERIALS

Start with cardboard. Cardboard's accessibility as an everyday material makes it a powerful tool. It's readily available; you will most likely already have it in your home. By choosing cardboard, we are also subverting the traditional material hierarchies of fine art. We are taking a material that is seen as disposable and elevating it. Cardboard is also easy to manipulate; all you will need are scissors or a blade.

While you're gathering your cardboard, think about the connections between you, your community, and cardboard. Do you or your community see cardboard as disposable? Is it repurposed, and if so, what does it become? Are community members collecting it for money? Have you seen it used in creative ways?

⁰¹ PLACE AS SELF

Now reflect on a place in your neighborhood that has shaped your identity, perhaps your own home or the corner store. If you don't have a place in mind, take a walk in your neighborhood. Observing the details of the built environment you inhabit is a great way to start analyzing your surroundings. Which architectural elements are unique to that space? Which details do you connect with? I often look for things that tell me more about the people who inhabit the space.

I look for what is planted in their garden or how they've adorned their personal spaces. Everything is telling a story and everything has a history. Now think of gentrification. It is not an abstract force; it manifests physically in the built environment. Pay attention to color; one of the first things to disappear during processes of gentrification is color, everything turns neutral. What other changes do you observe?

⁰² CONSTRUCT

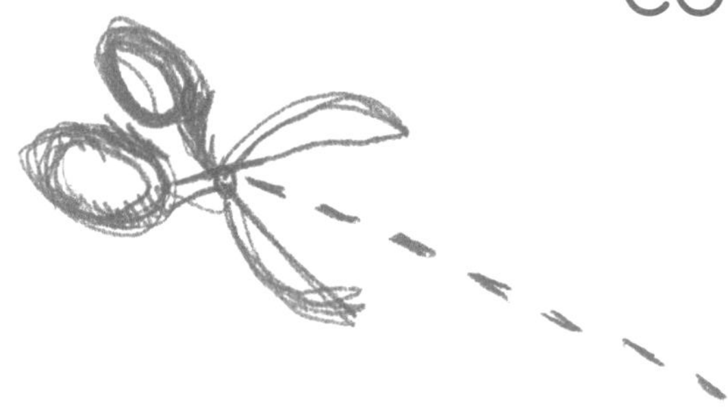

Using your cardboard, begin modeling a miniature version of that space. Add the architectural details that make it unique to you. In doing this, you're not just recreating architecture; you're adding your identity onto it. This place doesn't have to be an exact replica of an existing building; you can also imagine a place that is an amalgamation of all the architectural details you connect with.

⁰³ INTERVENTION

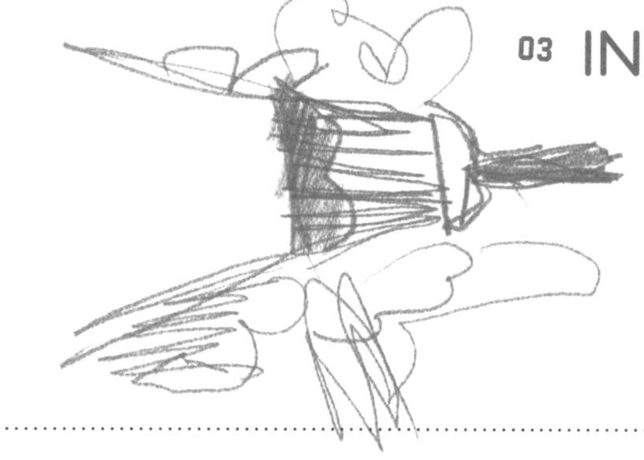

Now, take your model and introduce a change: What would this place look like after gentrification? Maybe a small mom and pop shop becomes a corporate store. Maybe the mural on the wall is painted over. How does this transformation feel? What disappears? What survives?

⁰⁴ RESIST

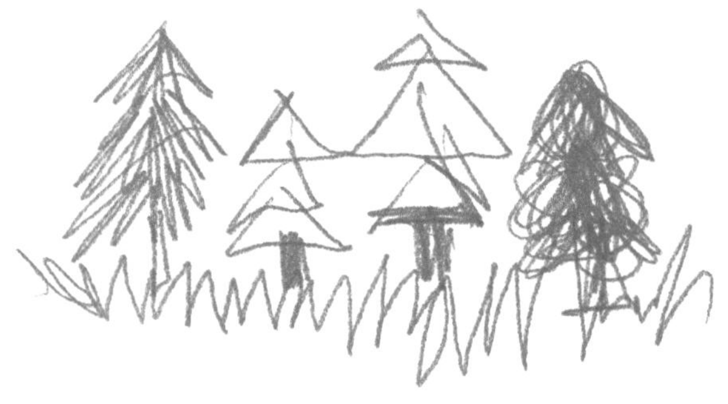

Then, as an act of resistance, rebuild. Add elements that restore your presence. Make something louder, more colorful, more permanent. Through this process, we learn how architecture is not neutral. It can reflect values, histories, and systems of power. But by taking it into our own hands, we reclaim agency. Now, with your model, can you begin to envision a future where communities remain rooted and your identity is preserved?

Ana Serrano, Template for a house, 2025; Courtesy of the artist

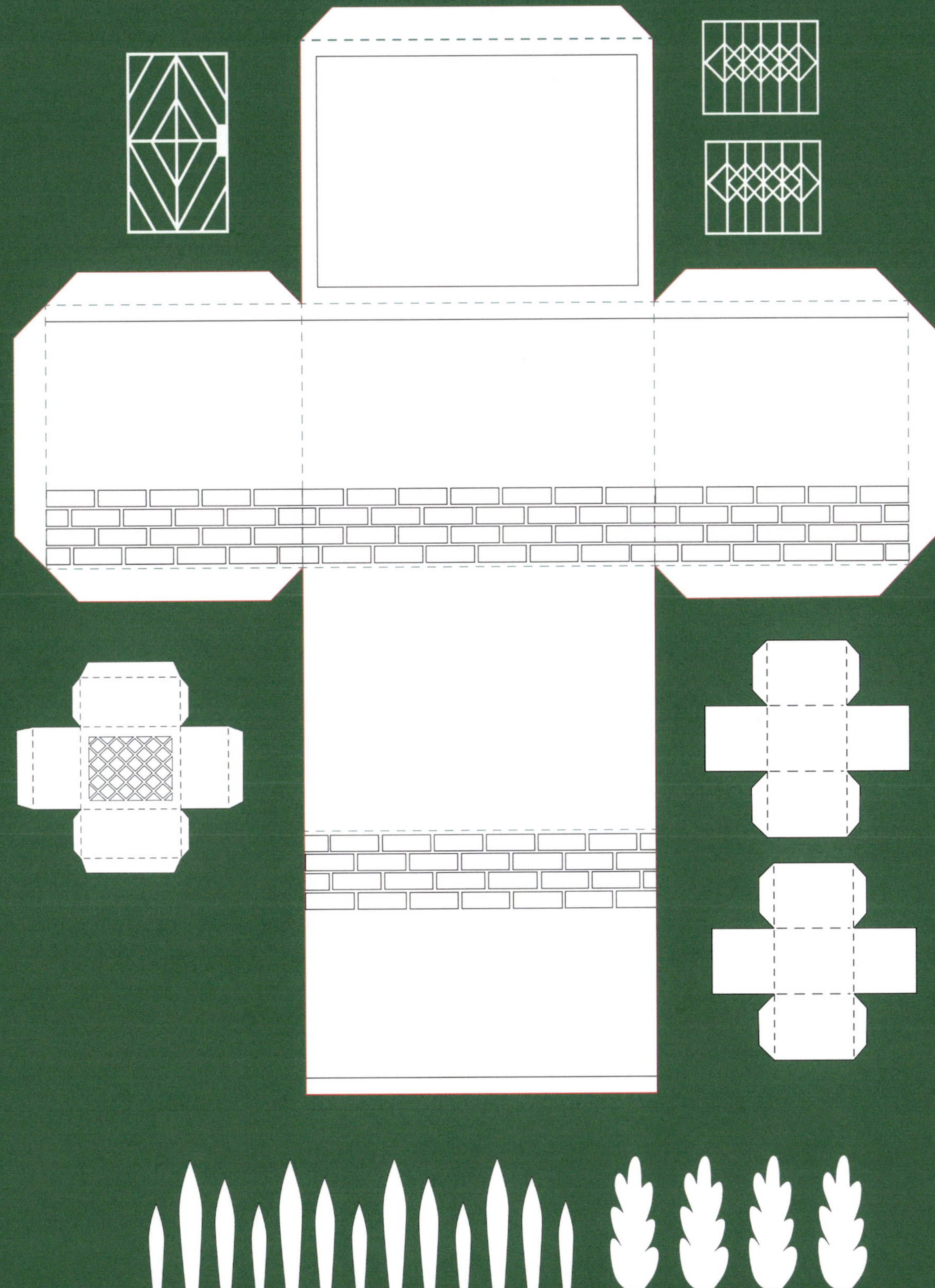

ANA SERRANO
American Gaze

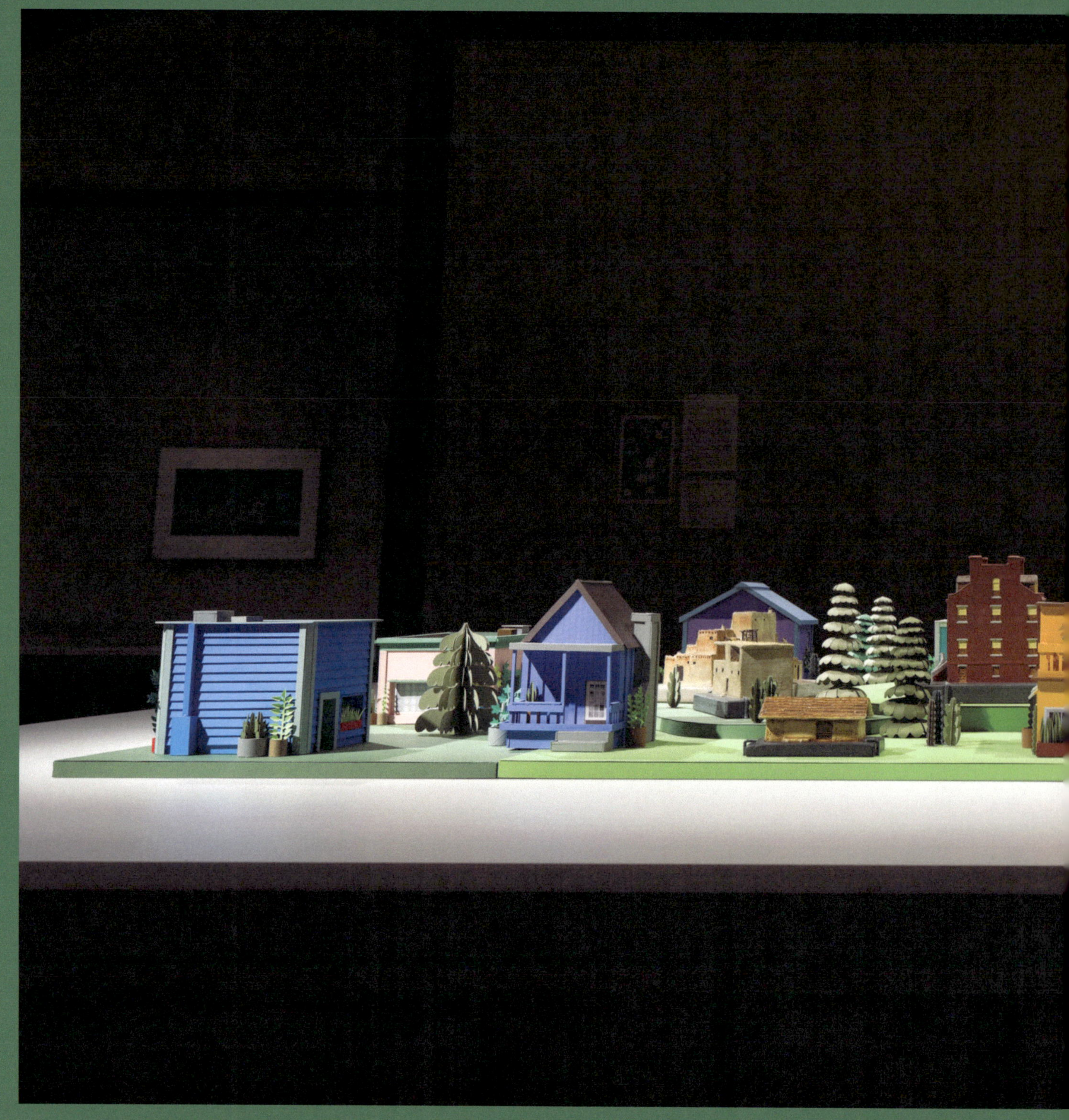

Ana Serrano, *American Caze*, installation view of *after school*, Carnegie Museum of Art, 2025; photo: Zachary Riggleman

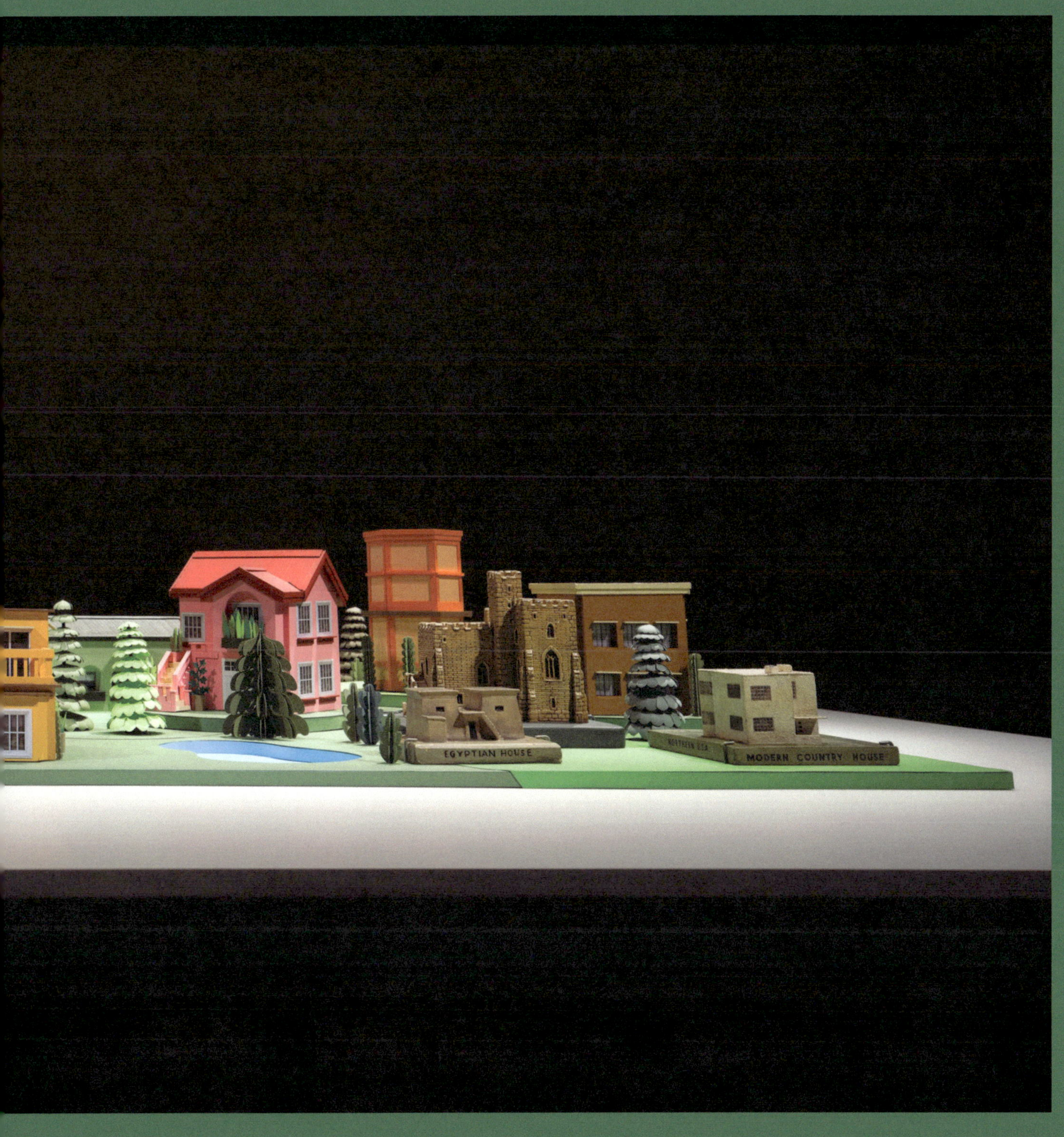

ANA SERRANO   American Gaze

214

Formal Abstraction
Profit
Assimilation
Discipline
Individualization

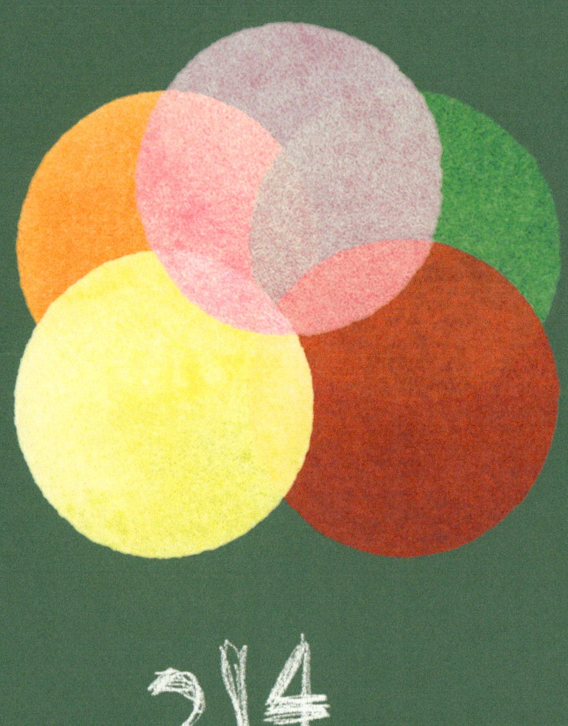

LOTS OF DOTS

THE STUDENT BODY

The installation *Lots of Dots* takes as its point of departure the classroom carpet of the same name, made by the U.S. company "Joy of Carpets" and designed for schools specializing in disciplinarian pedagogy. The installation points to the ways in which the formal abstraction of educational spaces is often a manifestation of individualist and universalist ideologies.

Below is a lesson plan meant to be realized with seven- to nine-year-olds—the age group the carpet is designed for. The template is one used by art teachers-in-training at Massachusetts College of Art and Design, where I teach. Using this template forced me to navigate the constraints of the public education system in the United States, while aiming to explode those same constraints. Increasingly, being an educator invested in solidarity and liberation involves finding ways to check institutional boxes while simultaneously pointing to the obsolescence of those boxes.

GRADE LEVEL: ☒ 3rd–5th Grade ☐ 6th–8th Grade ☐ 9th–12th Grade
LENGTH OF LESSON: A single eighty-minute session or two forty-minute class periods
NUMBER OF STUDENTS: 6–10

LESSON SUMMARY
Summarize this lesson in two to three sentences. What is your elevator pitch?

Using the *Lots of Dots* carpet, students will be facilitated in considering how architecture and design impact them physically and emotionally. Through movement exercises and conceptual prompts, the students will also be facilitated in disrupting the traditional use of the classroom carpet, with the goal of equipping them with tools for thinking critically about architecture and design, particularly in spaces that they are forced to inhabit.

ESSENTIAL QUESTIONS

What are one to three conceptual questions that your lesson explores? You might look to the National Standards and State Frameworks for help.

How does the built environment impact people psychologically and emotionally?

What is the connection between classroom design and how students move in the space?

How do young people find ways to push back against the demands made on them by classroom design?

How can adults facilitate young people's agency in designing and navigating regimented spaces such as classrooms?

NATIONAL & STATE STANDARDS

These standards are the content and skills students need to know by the end of a course. Identify the standards that this lesson helps your students master.

NATIONAL STANDARDS
4th VA:Cr1.1.4a: Brainstorm multiple approaches to a creative art or design problem.

5th VA:Cr1.1.4a: Identify and demonstrate diverse methods of artistic investigation to choose an approach for beginning a work of art.

MASSACHUSETTS ARTS CURRICULUM FRAMEWORK
3-4.V.Cr.03: Refine and complete artistic work. Respond to an artistic challenge and draft possible resolutions.

1-2.V.Co.10: Synthesize and relate knowledge and personal experiences to make art.

Left: Gabo Camnitzer, Color chart in *The Student Body*, 2021, excerpt; Courtesy of the artist

LEARNING OUTCOMES

**These are what a student will be able to do at the end of the lesson.
Include three to four student learning outcomes for this specific lesson.**

01   Students will be able to think critically about the design of the spaces they inhabit.

02   Students will be able to consider the ways the built environment affects how they think, feel, and move.

03   Students will be able to experiment with using their bodies in novel ways, in relation to the built environment.

04   Students will be able to design a classroom carpet.

HOW ARE YOUR GOALS SMARTIE?

**Describe how one to three of the following course SMARTIE goals are directly tied to this lesson:
Specific, Measurable, Action-Oriented, Realistic, Time-based, Inclusive, Equitable**

01   **Specific and Strategic:** Students will demonstrate their ability to think critically about classroom design.

02   **Measurable:** N/A

03   **Actionable:** Students will understand how they can use their bodies in experimental ways.

04   **Rigorous, Realistic, Results-Focused:** Students will create their own classroom carpet designs.

05   **Timed:** Students will have 80 minutes to work.

06   **Inclusive:** Students will be encouraged to incorporate their lived experiences into the work being done.

07   **Equitable:** Students will be encouraged to participate in the ways that feel comfortable and constructive to them based on their specific capacities. Students can abstain from any activity at any time. Water and snacks will be available.

PERSONAL RELEVANCE TO STUDENTS

How might you provide an opportunity for students to make connections between this lesson and their lives, interests, or identity?

This lesson will facilitate students in thinking critically about the relationship between the spaces they inhabit and how those spaces make them act and feel. They will be asked to build on their experiences of schools to express their agency in classroom settings.

CLASSROOM SETUP

Describe the physical setup of your room and explain how you will leverage this set up to enhance learning.

The "classroom" consists of a dark open museum gallery, 30 feet by 17 feet 11 inches with high ceilings. A 10 foot 9 inch by 13 foot 2 inch carpet will be in the center. The carpet is illuminated by a lighting rig that is suspended directly above the carpet. The lighting rig slowly cycles through the color spectrum, concealing and revealing colors in the carpet.

INSTRUCTIONAL COMPONENTS AND AGENDA

Agenda: *Outline how your lesson will unfold.* Use this as a way to organize and plan the different instructional components into logical and manageable segments. *Indicate times (and how long will you spend on each instructional component of the lesson).*

	INSTRUCTIONAL COMPONENT	WHAT WILL YOU DO?	WHAT WILL YOUR STUDENTS DO?
8:00AM–8:10AM	**Preliminary Activity:** Icebreaker. Hook / Introduction	Ask the students to sit in a circle on the carpet and name an emotion the installation is making them feel. Have students stand around the carpet. Ask them what they see, what they think it is, and how it makes them feel.	The students hear their voices in the space and make a connection between their feelings and the built environment. Discuss the carpet and its effects on their bodies and minds.
8:10AM–8:15AM	**Review / Prior Knowledge:** Considering classroom design and its relationship to the bodies of students	Ask the students about their favorite classrooms. Ask them why those classrooms were the best. Then ask about their least favorite classrooms. Ask the students: Who designs classrooms? Why do you think they make them look the way they do?	Students articulate their lived experiences of classrooms and tie them to the topics being discussed today.
8:15AM–8:20AM	Providing Context for the Carpet	Ask the students if they have ever encountered a carpet like this. If so, how were they asked to sit on it? Describe the use of the carpet and how students are made to sit on the dots with their backs straight and hands folded.	Students reflect on disciplinarian pedagogy and how it makes them feel.
8:20AM–8:30AM	**Teaching / Instruction:** How can we use movement to experiment with new uses for existing classroom designs?	Lead the students in a series of movement exercises on the carpet.	The students are asked to choose dots on the carpet to sit on and respond to the following prompts: 1. Make yourself as small as possible within your square. 2. Make yourself as big as possible within your square. 3. Reach out as far as possible without letting your feet leave your square. Touch the hand of the student furthest away that is still within reach. 4. Within your square, strike a pose that you think wouldn't be allowed within a strict classroom. 5. Within your square, strike a pose that you think your teacher at school would like. 6. Jump around the carpet trying to stay only on circles whose color is visible, as the light causes them to appear and disappear.

	INSTRUCTION	WHAT YOU DO	WHAT STUDENTS DO
8:30AM-8:35AM	**Student Participation:** Inverted power dynamic	Ask the students to return the parameter. Tell them they will now become the "teachers." Ask them to tell me a specific dot to sit on, and to direct me to do different poses and movements on the carpet.	The students direct me, in the process experiencing what it is like to be a teacher directing students.
8:35AM-8:40AM	Collective Reflection, Metacognition, Formative Assessment	Ask the students to share the thought processes behind their instructions for posing my body.	The students describe the reasoning for the different directions they gave me and reflect on the experience of being the teacher.
8:40AM-8:45AM	Collective Movement Exercise	Ask the students to cover as much of the carpet with their bodies as possible.	The students lay out on the carpet, taking as much space as possible.
8:45AM-8:50AM	Cartographic Choreography	Students are given fluorescent markers and a handout with an outline of the carpet. The students are asked to trace a path for someone to follow across the carpet.	1. Students mark their paths. 2. Students exchange papers with one another and follow the paths made for them by their peers.
8:50AM-9:00AM	**Assignment:** Classroom carpet design	Give the students a blank piece of paper and ask them to draw their ideal carpet, using fluorescent markers.	The students design their ideal classroom carpet.
9:00AM-9:05AM	Formative Assessment / Group Critique	Have the students share their designs with each other.	Students share their designs explaining the decision they made.
9:05AM-9:15AM	Summative assessment	Facilitate a conversation about the day's activities with questions such as: What did you find interesting today? What was fun? What was hard? What do you think is the relationship between the design of a room and how you feel in your body within the room?	The students reflect on the day's activities by responding to and expanding on questions and comments from me and their peers.
9:15AM-∞	Wrap Up / Closing / Soft ending	Facilitate closing activity related to time and productivity in school, with questions such as: Have you ever been in school and felt frustrated at how long something took, or how little time you had to do something? Do you feel like you have enough time to play in school? Who makes the decisions about time in school? What happens when we lose track of time in school? What would happen if you created our own definition of time? What would school look like without clocks? What if we all did what we wanted for as long as we wanted? Ask the students to do whatever they want in the space, for however long they want. When they are done, they can leave.	The students can stay and play in the installation for as long as they like. The museum has to remain open for as long as they choose to stay.

Gabo Camnitzer, *Lots of Dots*, 2021, carpet and light fixture, installation views of *after school*, Carnegie Museum of Art, 2025; photo: Zachary Riggleman

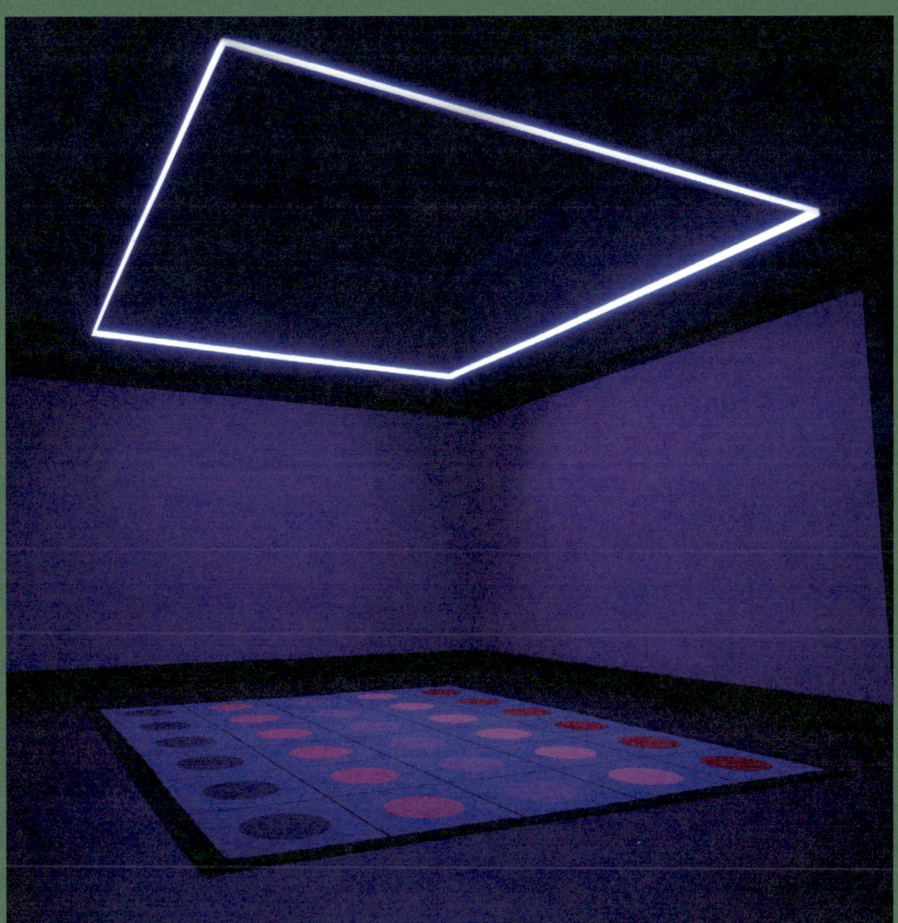

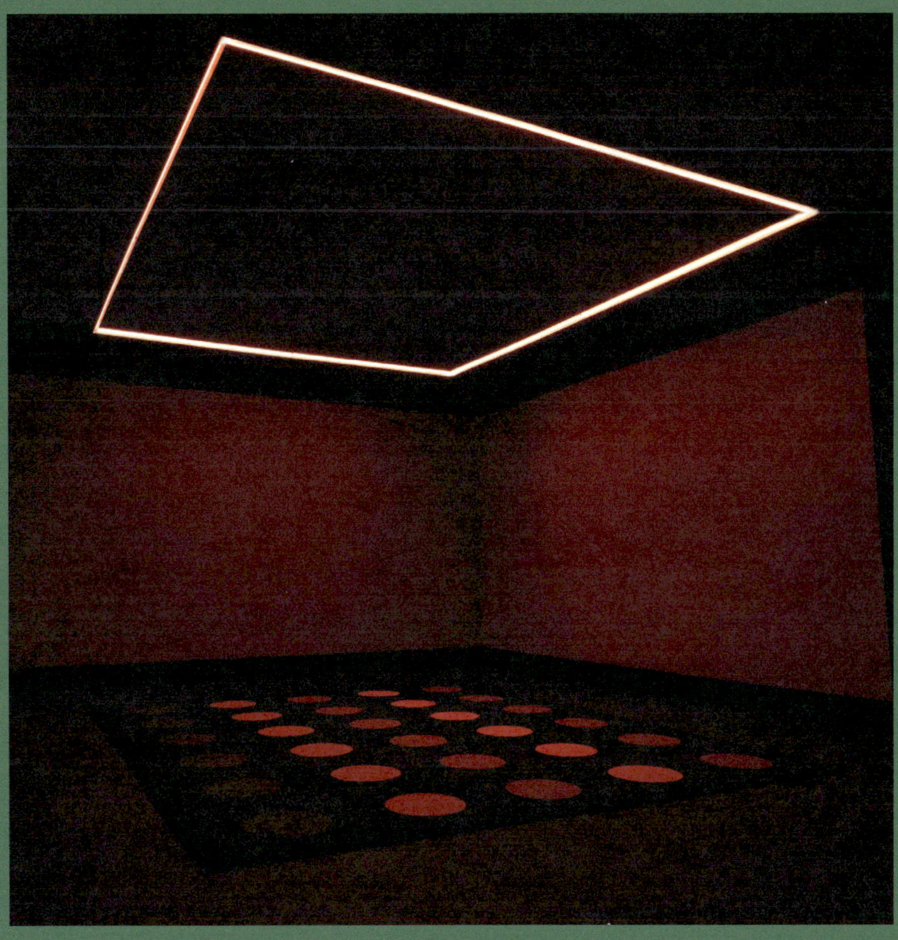

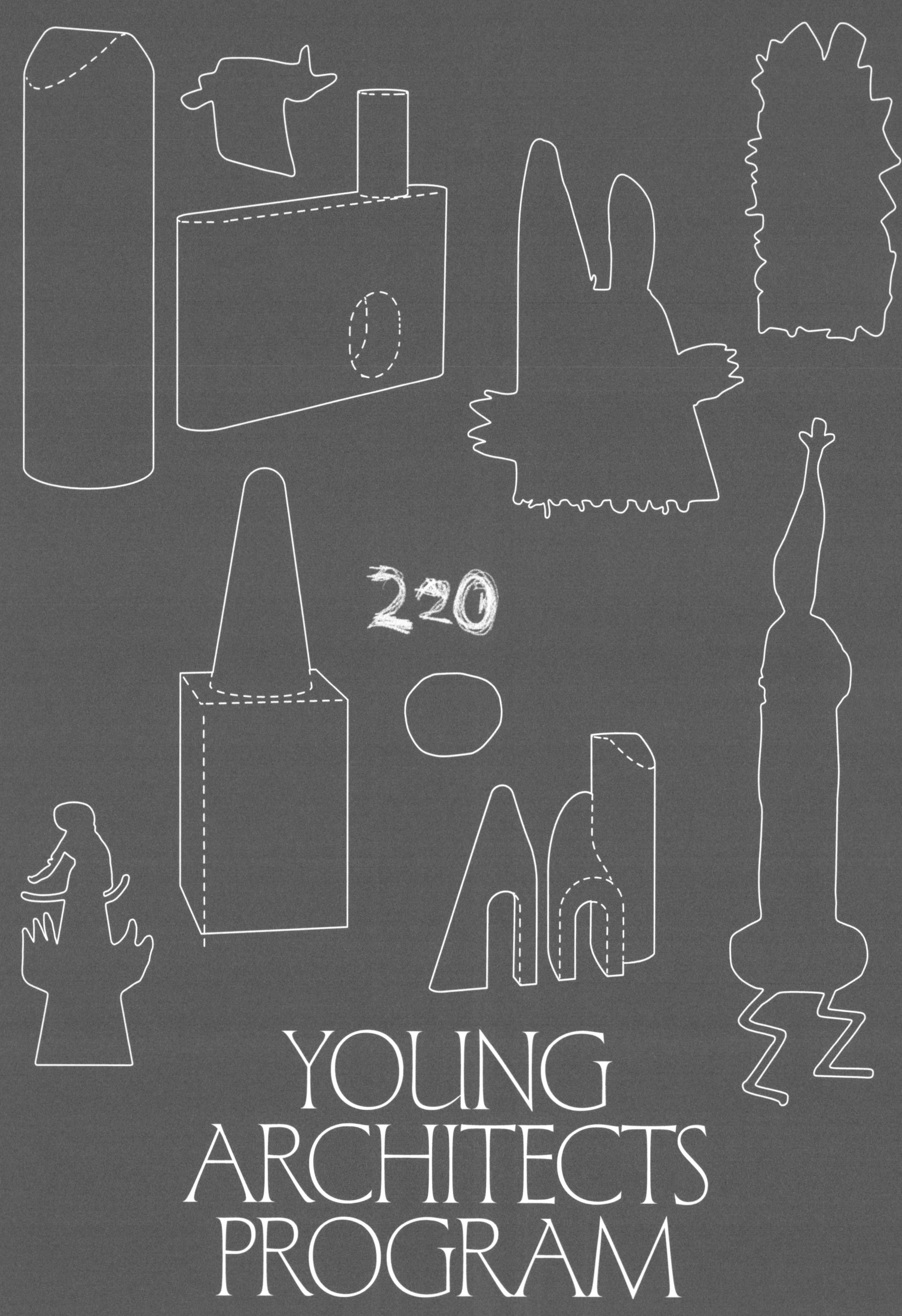

2 2 0
YOUNG
ARCHITECTS
PROGRAM

LEAH WULFMAN & JIN MEISENBERG
TAKE A WALK

LEAH WULFMAN

As a column becomes a chimney with balloons, becomes a tower, becomes a mountain, doors and windows open up new spaces and stories, promoting an iterative retelling of architectural forms and elements. This lesson plan asks participants to leverage and activate different ways of viewing the built environment through a variety of perspectives and associations, major and minor histories and narratives, speeds and scales.

JIN MEISENBERG

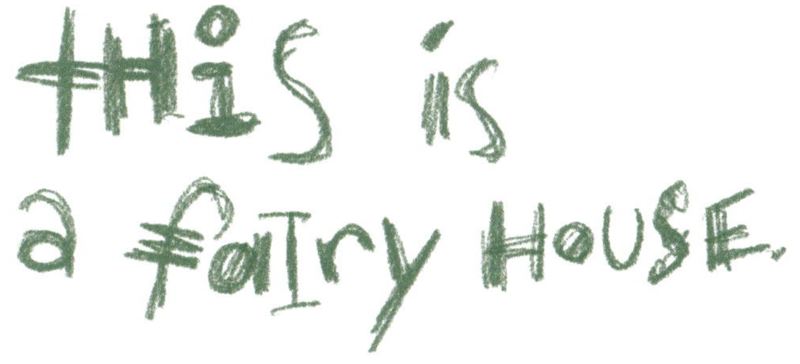

This is a funny dinosaur, a rhinoceros.

This is for me a rainbow angel. It's super special; it can make hoops and turns like a good, good flyer.

This is a sand-clock house, it can fly. It has three crowns on it; that's why it can fly.

This is an eye house; it has something special. The eyes can move, close, and fly.

This is the littlest, thinnest house. It can transform into a tree or a big, big eyeball.

The biggest, biggest, biggest house of all is something even more special. It is a rainbow dot. They are super special; they can fly and jump away. But the most special is the spiral on top of the house; it has pink dots. They are super special as they can swim inside of the spiral. And because I love uzumaki! Uzumaki means spiral, and it is a story. It is a little bit scary because everyone loves uzumaki!

Hmm... I think it's a little clock for me inside of a rainbow, rainbow house. People make rainbows inside; they make them with stardust and water and rainbow colors, glitter, and of course, stars—nothing else.

A flying home. A chicken home. It says, "Bok bok bok." No, it says, "Kukeldifooooo." It walks like a chicken, and it has a chicken tail.

It's a water home, where water comes out. They make water just out of water! They squirt it out of the home to make everyone wet! They just have fun.

Left: Leah Wulfman, Stencil template for *Young Architects Program*, 2025; Courtesy of the artist

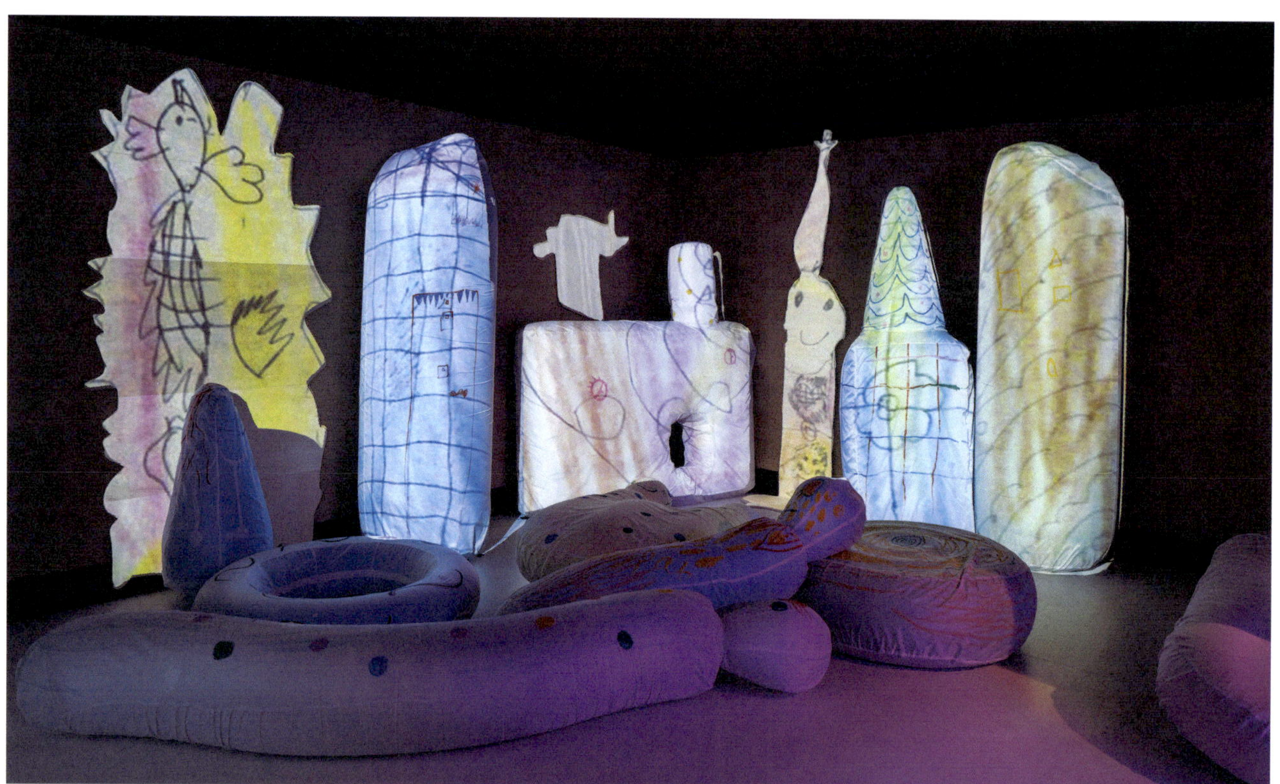

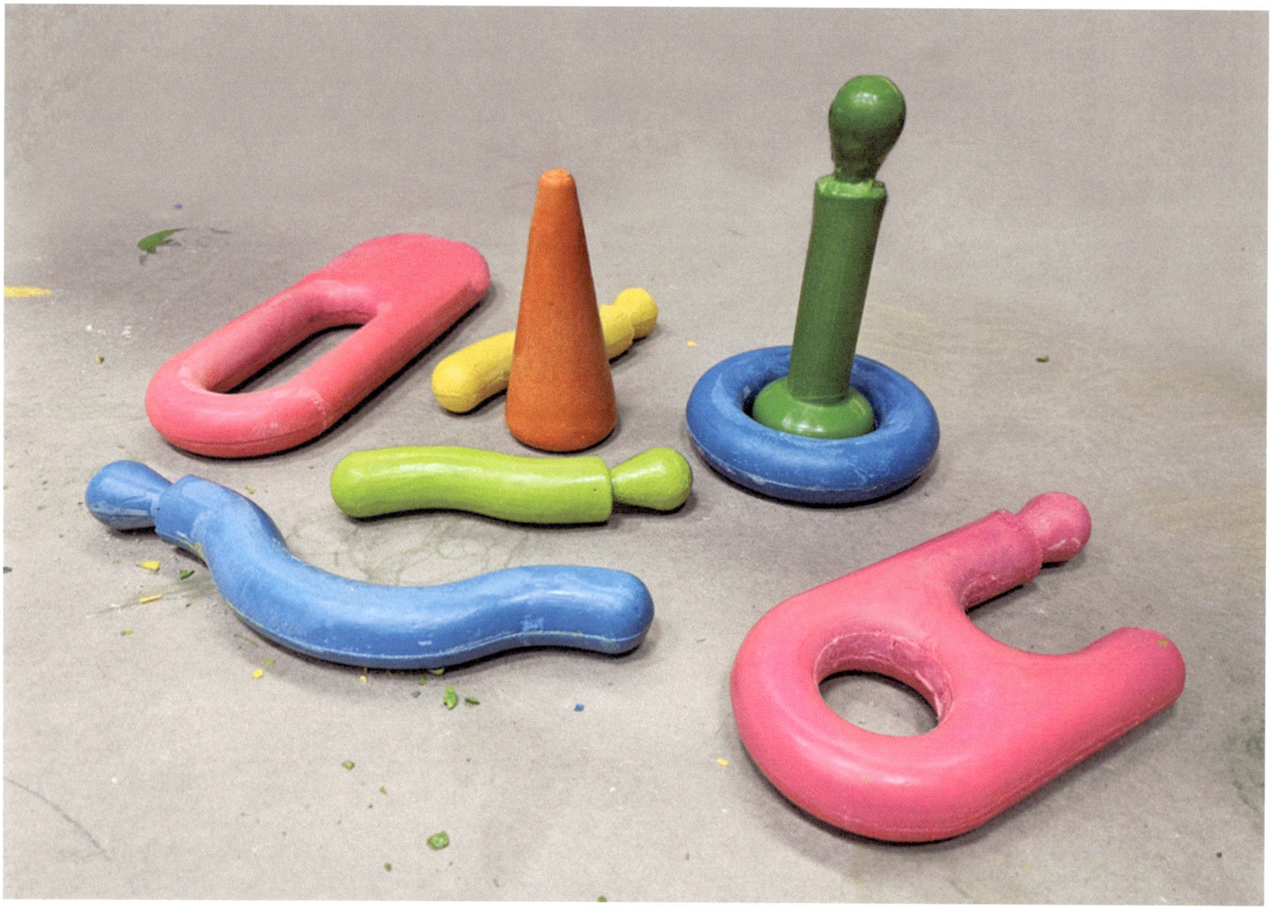

Top: Leah Wulfman, *Young Architects Program*, 2025, real-time game drawing, projection, pvc, and ripstop inflatables, installation view of *after school*, Carnegie Museum of Art, 2025; photo: Zachary Riggleman

Bottom: Leah Wulfman, Crayon detail of *Young Architects Program*, 2024; Courtesy of the artist

COURSE ACTIVITY

01 **Plan two walks.** The first should be a walk you've done before but plan to walk and see it differently this time. The second should be a walk that is completely new to you. Go on these walks with specific questions or interests in mind. For instance, maybe you're obsessed with red, so the whole tour revolves around the color. Use these questions and interests as lenses for seeing the walk and changing your relationship to it. Document your walks with photos.

02 Next, **create a map.** Draw your walks on the map and then draw them without the map on a new sheet of paper. What information is key to show, to diagram, to include? Consider sites, speeds and scales, sensory inputs, minor and major landmarks and histories. Make space for your initial research interests to be honed, challenged, extended, configured, and reconfigured. By attuning to your own unique practices and awarenesses, you will begin to transform your relationship to time, space, and story.

03 Now, **create an itinerary and invite someone on a tour of your two walks.** Allow your invitee to photograph them. What is their method and guiding interest? Do they have a theme or agenda? Is it fact or fiction or something in between? Does it pull from major or minor stories? What about time, distance, and scale? Did you go on foot, by bike, by car, or a combination? How fast or slow did you go? What was the pace of the walks, and at which points did it change? Consider how physical, how digital, or how hybrid these walks are. What about Google Maps—did you leave reviews in random places? For an ultra-digital experience, take a walking tour through your favorite video game.

04 Finally, **design a presentation** of your walks using the artifacts, stories, maps, drawings, diagrams, and other documentation you have accumulated. Consider your drawing utensil. Consider even making your own. This exercise is meant to develop research skills in the service of framing and identifying design interests and opportunities, specifically through questions around site diagramming, observational mapping, scale, story, and citation. One long-standing tactic for thinking about design research is to position design as a problem-solving endeavor—in order to design an effective solution, we must properly frame the problem or symptom. We know design is much more complex than just solving problems, so we can widen our lens to define framing as an activity that identifies design intervention hungers and opportunities based on research conversations, interests, and outcomes.

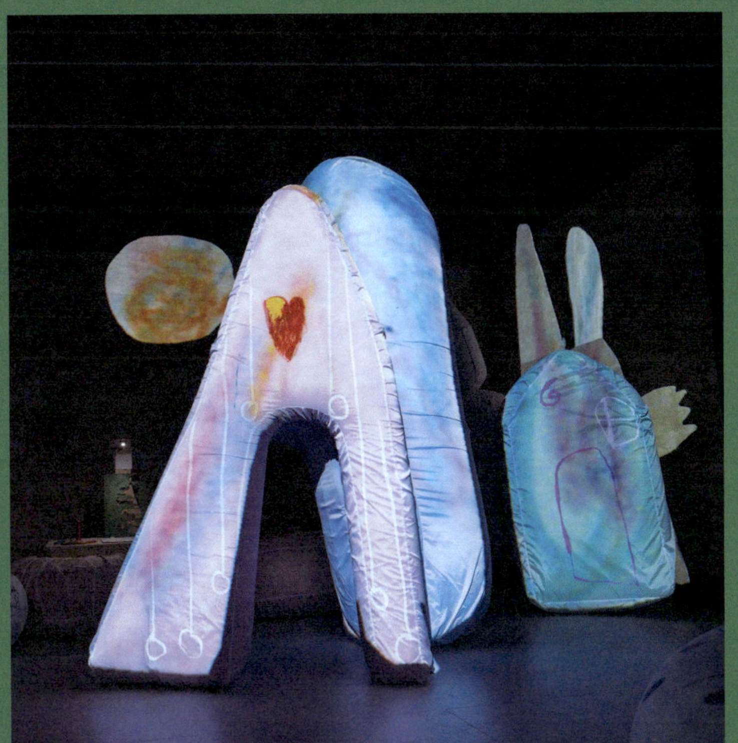

Leah Wulfman, *Young Architects Program*, 2025, installation view of *after school*, Carnegie Museum of Art, 2025; photo: Zachary Riggleman

224

THREAD ARTISTS' RESIDENCIY & CULTURAL CENTER

TOSHIKO MORI
CONSTRUCTING A MODEL

Model Design: Toshiko Mori, Charles Burke, and Olivia Champ Tremml
Model Fabrication: Olivia Champ Tremml

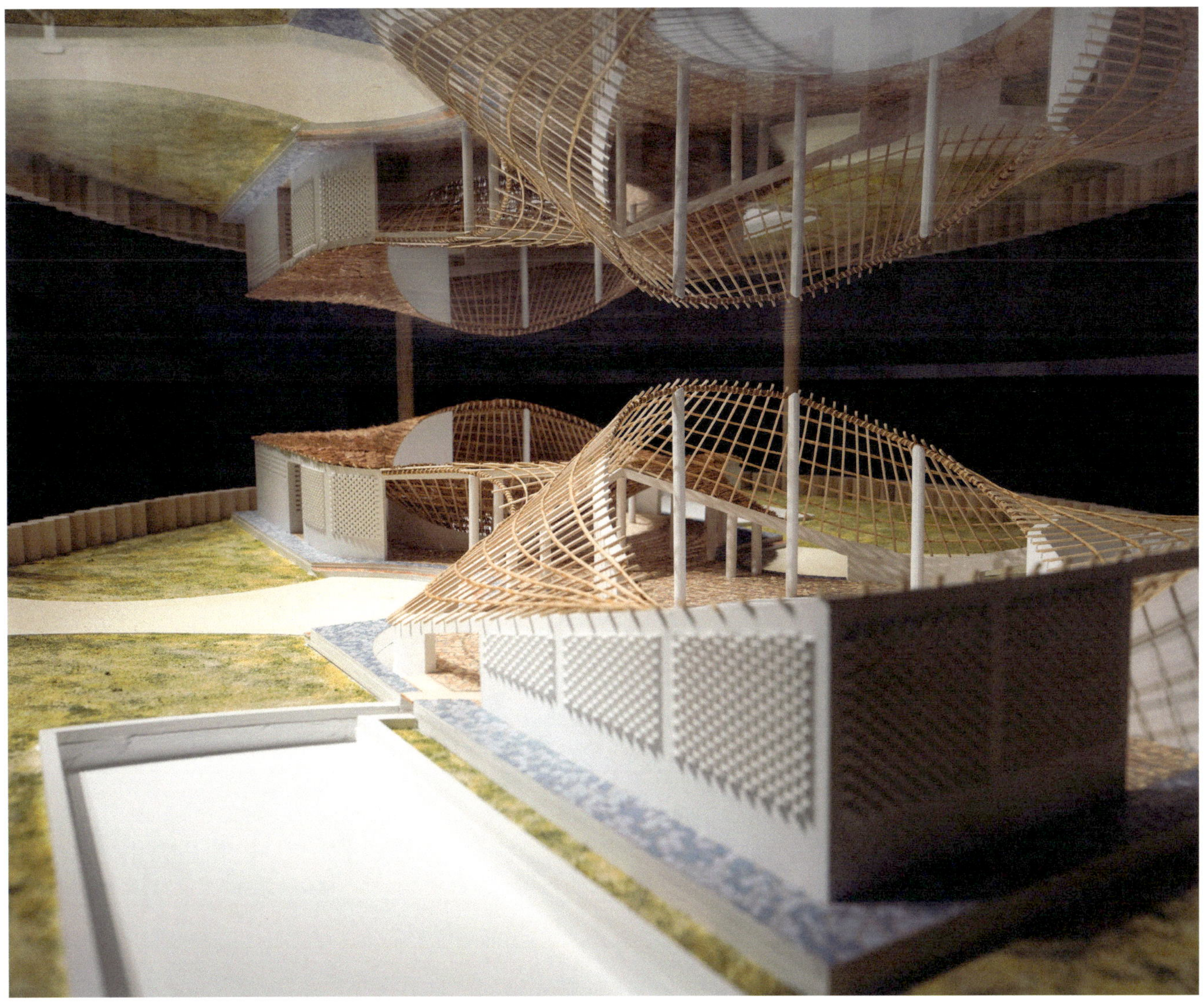

Toshiko Mori, *Thread Artists' Residency and Cultural Center Model*, 2025, jute, bamboo, coir, PCL filament, and paper, installation view of *after school*, Carnegie Museum of Art, 2025; photo: Zachary Riggleman

01 COMPLETE FOUNDATIONS, WATER CANALS, WALLS, AND COLUMNS.

Thread is an artist residency which invites both local and international artists to interact with the community of Sinthian, Senegal, sharing and promoting the culture and values of art. The project is an initiative of the Josef and Anni Albers Foundation, and the concept of weaving—represented in the name "Thread"—is a tribute to the work of Anni Albers.

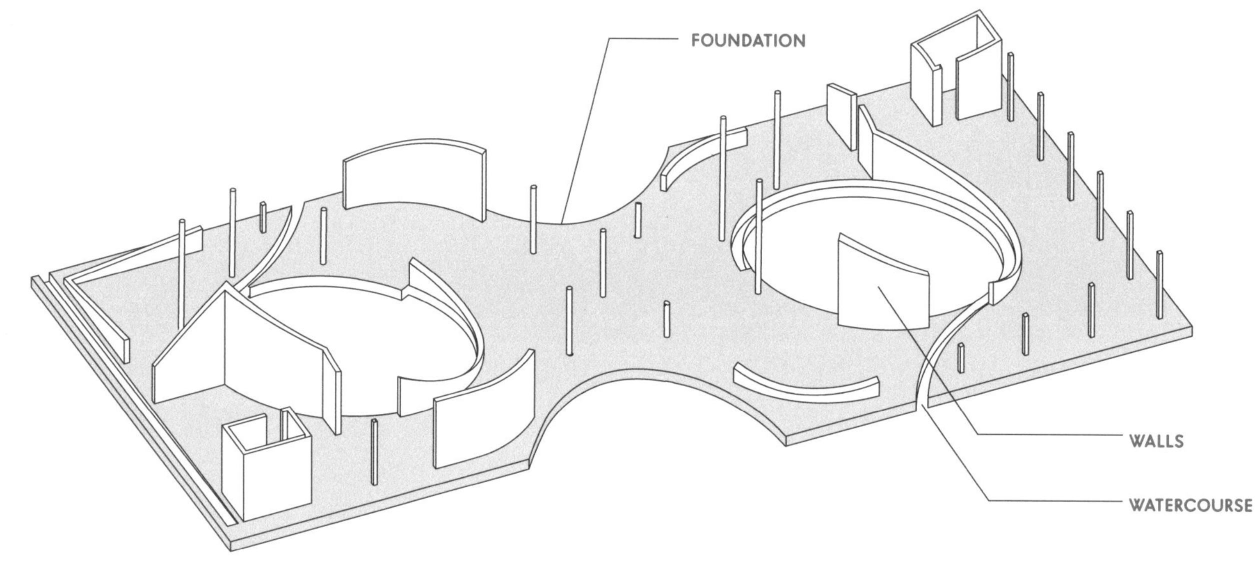

02 DRIVE STAKES INTO THE GROUND AROUND THE ELLIPSE.

There is no established architectural tradition in the Sinthian region, so a new typology was invented using the geometry and techniques of local hut buildings. Thread's assembly, which is an extension of existing craft and skill, was connected through a series of diagrams to the local construction team and craftsman.

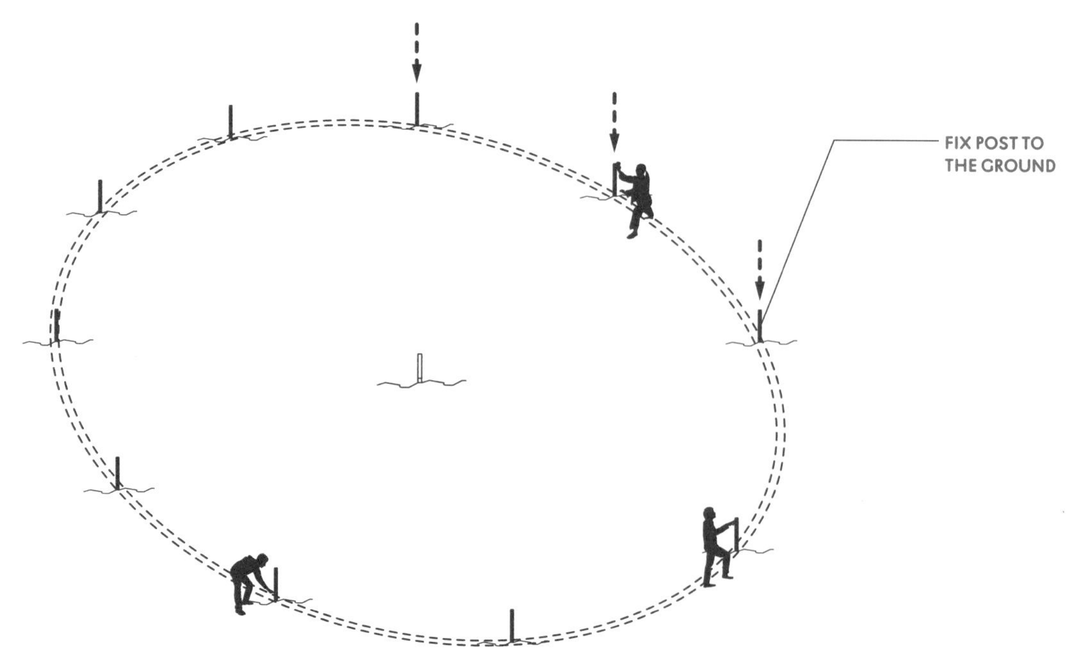

03 CURVE BAMBOO AROUND THE PERIMETER.

The roof of Thread was built by local artisans using traditional methods, as well as drawing inspiration from Anni Alber's weaving. The thatch roof is dense yet porous. It keeps out rain while allowing airflow. It also provides excellent insulation, with small air pockets blocking the relentless daytime heat.

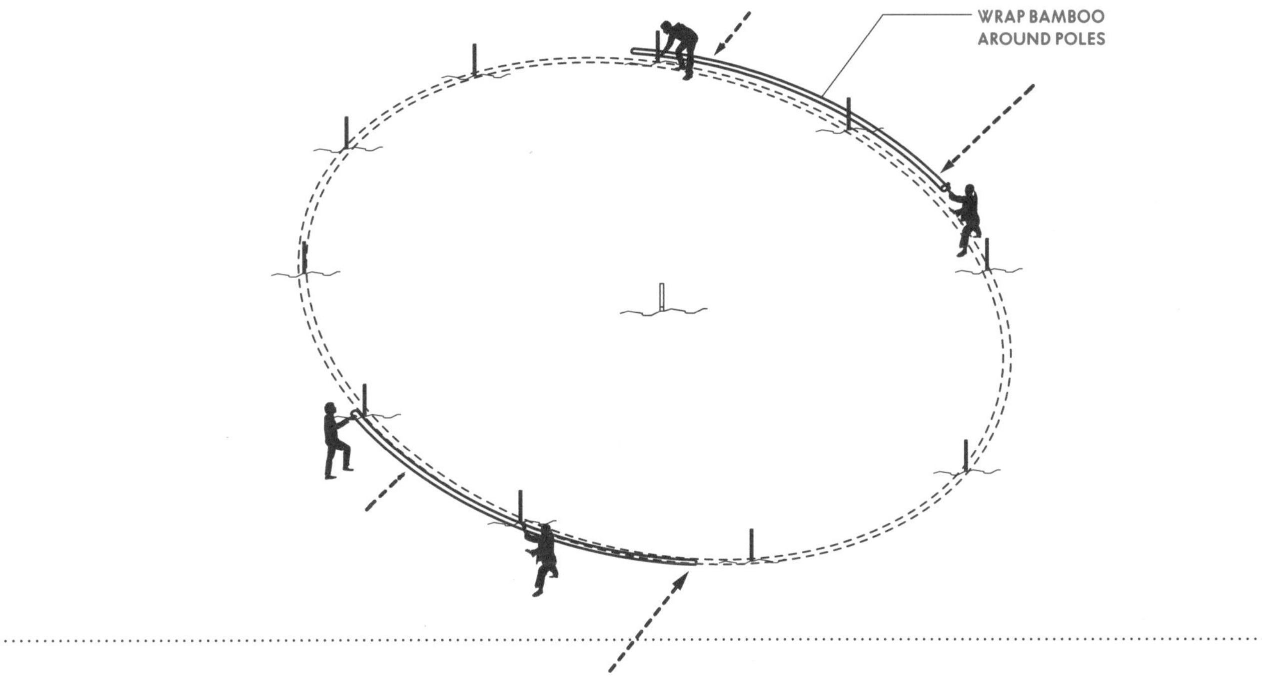

04 ONCE THE OVAL HAS BEEN COMPLETED, ADD SEVERAL LAYERS OF BAMBOO TO CREATE THE WHOLE ASSEMBLY AND TIE IT TOGETHER.

The woven plant stalks guide rainwater into a sloped canal system, feeding into cisterns for storage. The building is designed as an integral part of community life, storing water during the rainy season for use by villagers during the dry season. It is a woven vessel and depository for resources and cultural legacies from around the world.

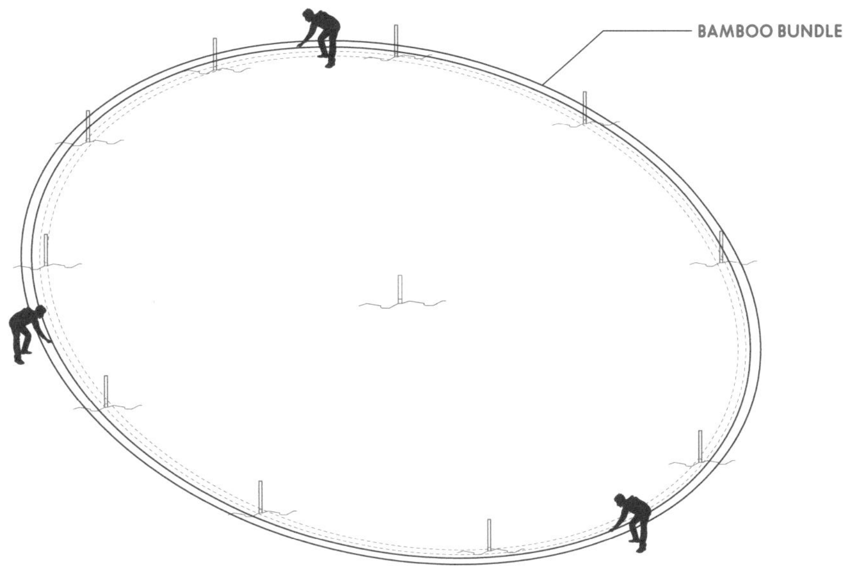

05 PLACE THE BAMBOO RING ABOVE THE WALLS AND SECURE IT IN PLACE.

The mud brick walls are crafted by villagers during the dry season, using earth on-site. The building literally rises from the land's materials and labor. The brick patterns reference the work of Josef Albers, forming walls that allow airflow while preserving privacy. Some brick shapes are hybridized with local wisdom to permit ventilation but prevent sand infiltration during sandstorms.

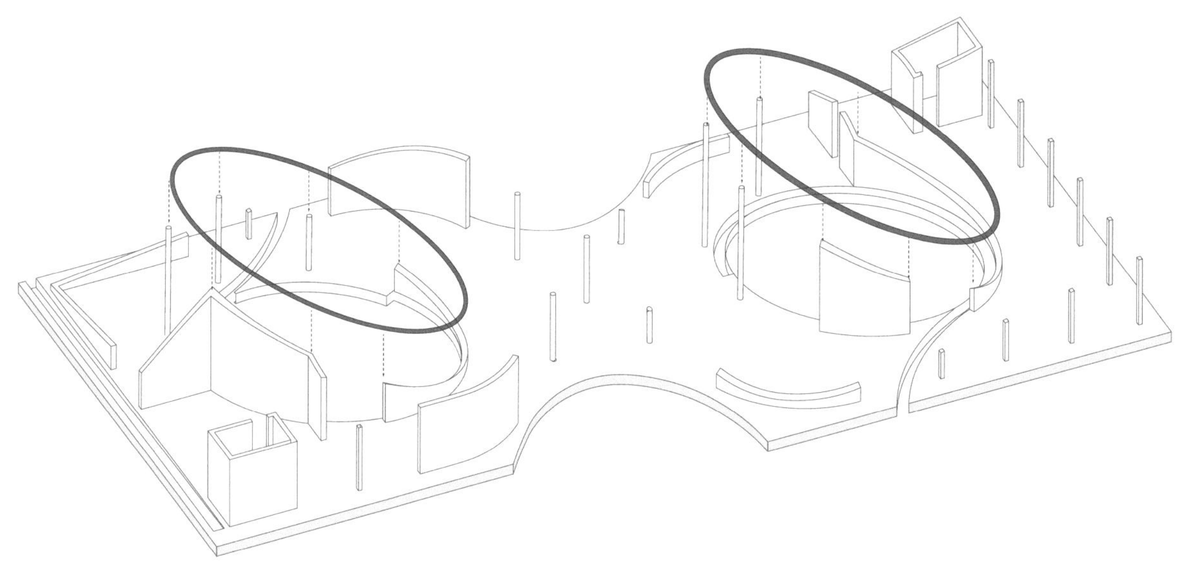

06 ADD BAMBOO FROM THE OUTSIDE OF THE STRUCTURE UP TO THE INTERIOR RING.

In the *after school* exhibition, we sought to demonstrate the vibrant and varied activities that continually redefine the residency's role and expand its mission. Many intersecting circles of influence—around music, arts, crafts, making, and design—coexist with productive agricultural initiatives, including grain and vegetable cultivation and beekeeping. These efforts improve the village's food security and nutrition while building a new economic foundation.

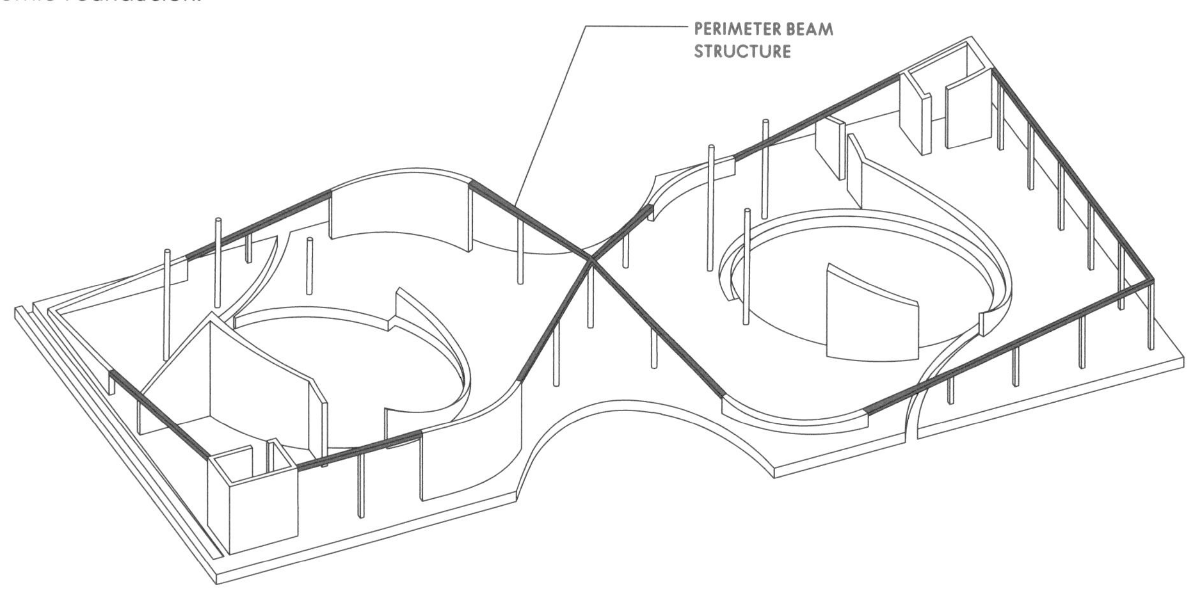

⁰⁷ POSITION AND SECURE THE PERIMETER BEAMS THAT SPAN BETWEEN THE COLUMNS AND WALLS.

Thread plays a dynamic role in the community it serves when it opens its spaces and programs to respond to everyday life. The villagers have taken an active role in the transformation and expansion of the community center, with the vital support of Le Korsa, the operating division of the Josef and Anni Albers Foundation in Senegal. As an institution dedicated to informing, engaging, and enriching its community, Thread is a unique hybrid. It is not an isolated institution or an imposition of foreign values but a gentle, intrinsic collaboration.

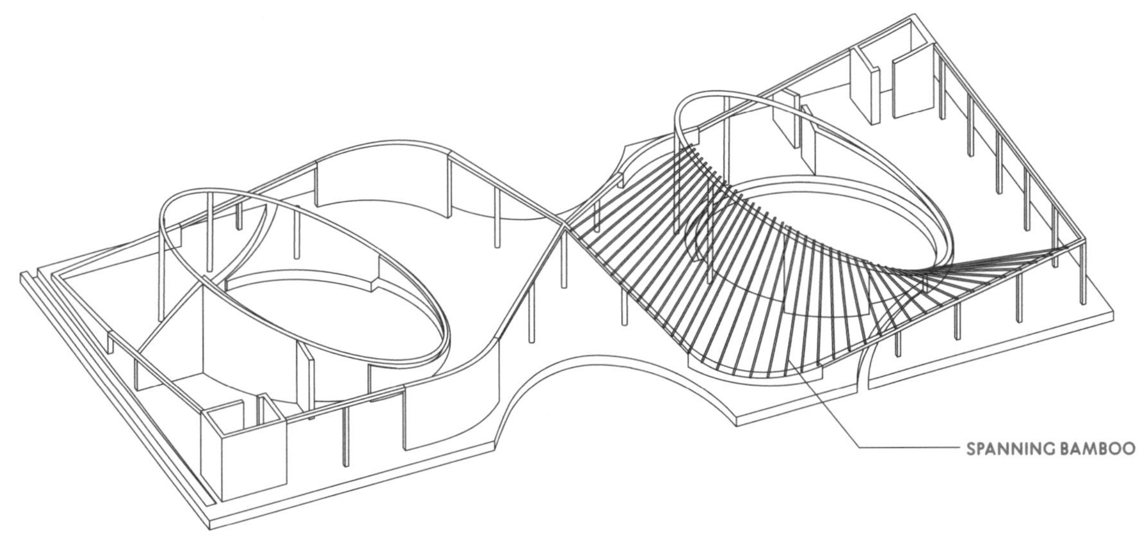

⁰⁸ ADD RADIAL LAYERS OF BAMBOO TO THE ROOF STRUCTURE. COVER WITH THATCH.

With each component, the woven experience of Thread strengthens the cultural and civic fabric of the village. The exterior spaces serve as productive gardens, with water used efficiently and crops chosen wisely to suit the local climate and economy. The outdoor areas have also become venues for regional soccer matches, attracting youth and families to popular tournaments. Lessons learned at Thread Artists' Residency reveal countless opportunities to create an ever-expanding fabric and strengthen the resilience of village life for future generations.

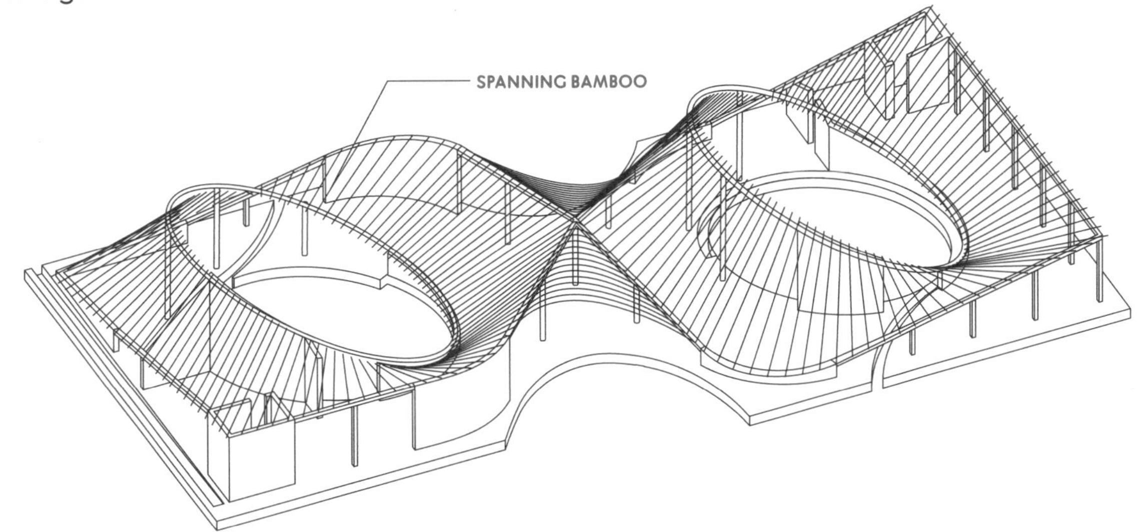

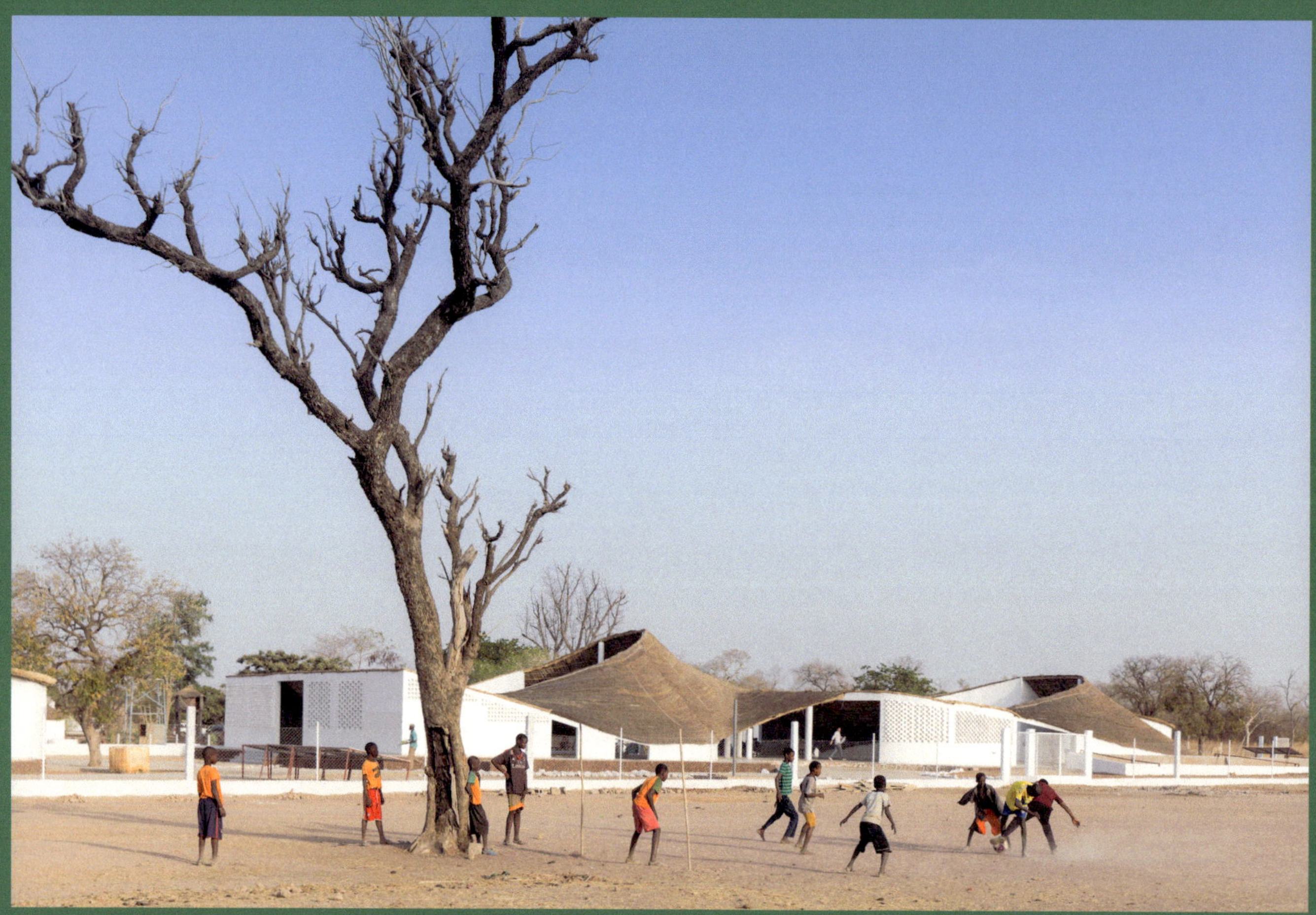

Toshiko Mori, *Thread Artists' Residency and Cultural Center*, 2015, photograph; Courtesy of Iwan Baan

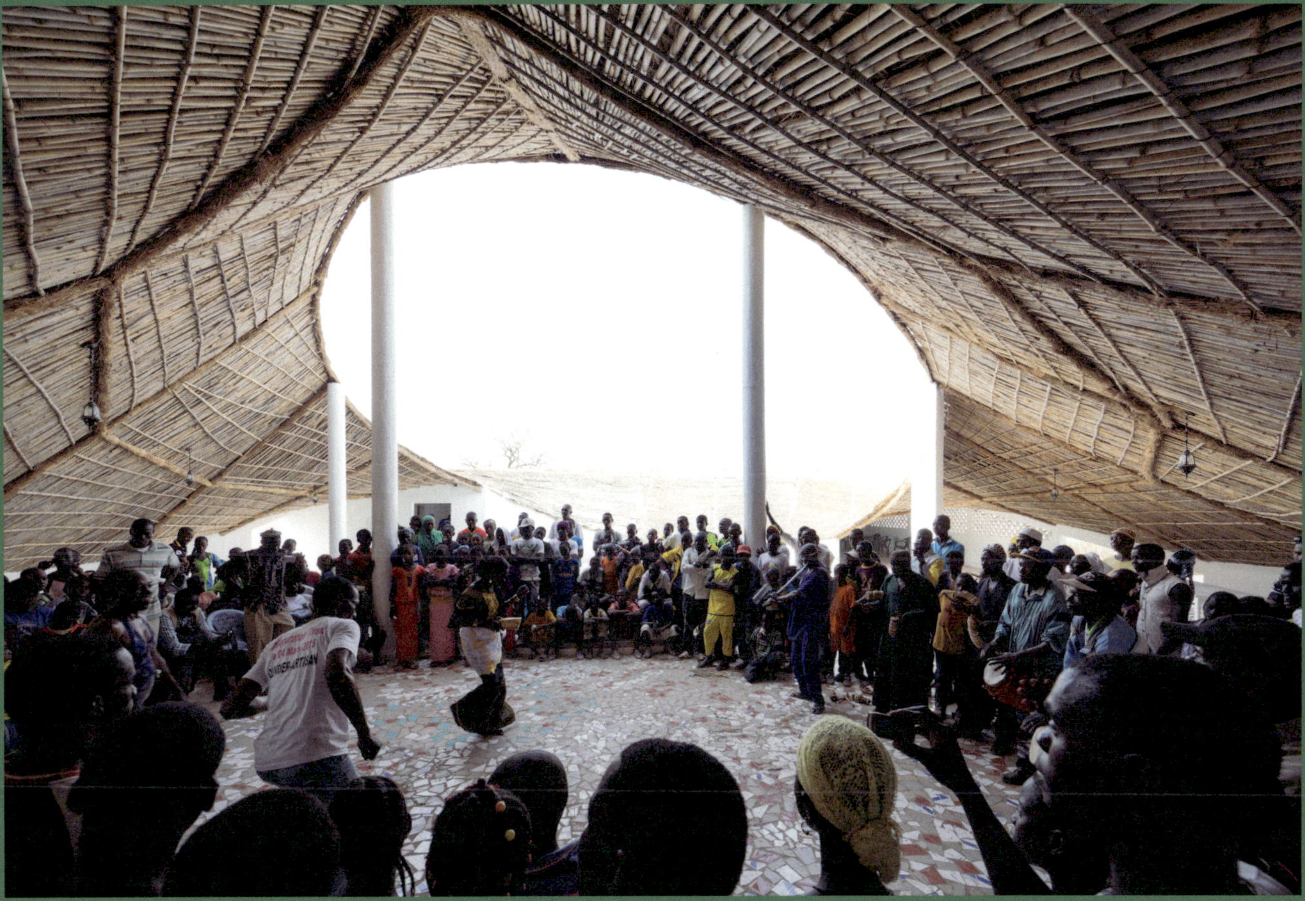

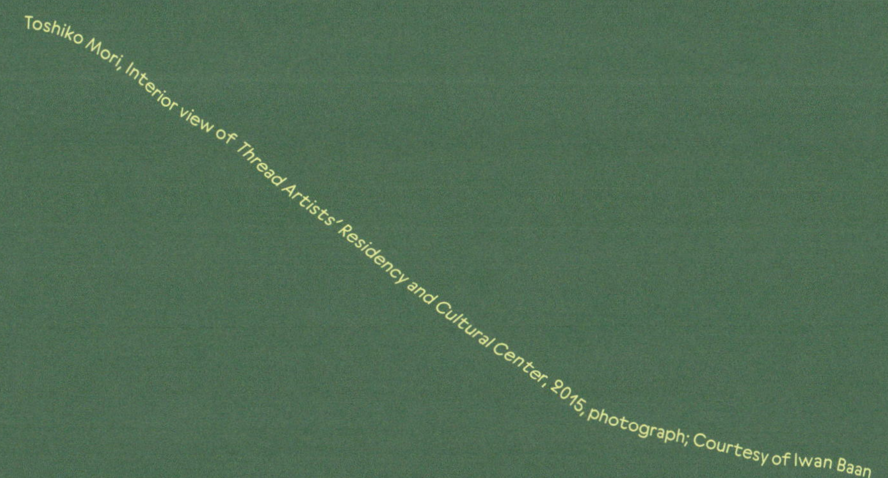

TOSHIKO MORI   Contructing A Model

CROSS-BORDER PUBLIC SPACES THAT EDUCATE

ESTUDIO TEDDY CRUZ & FONNA FORMAN

COMMUNITY STATIONS

Urban justice demands both the redistribution of resources and knowledges. This work takes place at the scale of neighborhoods. We see informal, place-based education as a civic framework, mobilizing the arts and sciences to design new experiential cultural tools. Our goal is to raise critical awareness about local impacts of climate change and histories of marginalization, summoning communities to participate in the physical transformation of their own neighborhoods—to imagine alternative futures.

We designed four Community Stations as corridors of reciprocity, to link universities and communities through a curation of new coalitions for solidaristic learning, research, and practice. Think of the Stations as a distributed university—a network of public spaces that educate— located in underrepresented neighborhoods on both sides of the border wall.

In San Diego, California, the *EARTHLAB Community Station* is situated in the southeastern San Diego neighborhood of Encanto, near the heart of the Chollas Creek Watershed: the most polluted waterway in the region. In partnership with the nonprofit Groundwork San Diego, we are developing a four-acre Climate Action Park on a vacant parcel owned by San Diego Unified School District, who granted us the parcel to increase environmental educational capacity for the six public schools located within walking distance of the site. The parcel offers community access to outdoor learning habitats, shaped by energy, water, food, community, and Indigenous knowledges, transforming the site into an open-air living laboratory. In the border town of San Ysidro, California, the *CASA Community Station* exists in one of the busiest land crossings in the Western hemisphere. In partnership with the non-profit Casa Familiar, we completed construction of *Living Rooms at the Border* project in 2020: an adaptive reuse of a historic church, transformed into a community theater that threads together ten units of affordable housing into public space on a small parcel of land that also includes an outdoor space, a civic classroom, social service pavilions, and educational spaces—a unique demonstration of small-scale urban development at the neighborhood scale.

Across the border, on the outskirts of Tijuana, Mexico, near the Laureles Canyon, the *DIVINA Community Station* functions as an informal settlement for over 100,000 people. In partnership with the nonprofit Colonos de la Divina Providencia, we are co-developing a large structural system and building made from prefabricated scaffolds that doubles as a pedagogical tool to support informal environmental education as well as economic and social programming. Additionally, we have implemented an environmental-based curriculum to help young people recognize zones of vulnerability in their own neighborhoods, emphasizing the importance of conservation, wildlife protection, and habitat restoration. In the Alacrán Canyon, the most rugged and polluted sub-basin of Laurels Canyon, the *ALACRÁN Community Station* welcomes thousands of global refugees at their point of arrival. In partnership with Embajadores de Jesús, we began construction of the Santuario Frontera refugee shelter in 2020, which has now become the largest refugee shelter in the U.S.-Mexico border region. Our Community Station here seeded the development of an entire sanctuary neighborhood, made of integrated services, including a collective kitchen and food hub, orchards, educational spaces, a library, and economic incubators.

Each of our Community Stations is activated through educational, cultural, and eco-social research activities. Some offer vocational training and small-scale economic development, while others are more focused on longer-term habitation and ecological restoration, transforming refugee shelters and integrative and inclusive ecosystems. We are committed to supporting and elevating the cross-border citizens of our future. It's never too early to begin.

DESIGNING A PLACE-BASED INFORMAL EDUCATION

REASON: **Technology and science**
Improving scientific literacy to learn like scientists and to reason using evidence

EMPATHY: **Ecology and conservation**
Improving conservation literacy to learn like ecologists and to experience the knowledge of nature

EXPRESSION: **Arts and Culture**
Improving cultural literacy to learn like artists and to visualize-perform creative processes

WELL-BEING: **Socio-emotional**
Improving restorative practice to learn through compassion and to dialogue with others

Estudio Teddy Cruz + Fonna Forman, *UCSD–CASA Community Station, San Diego, California, 2020*, photograph; Courtesy of the artist

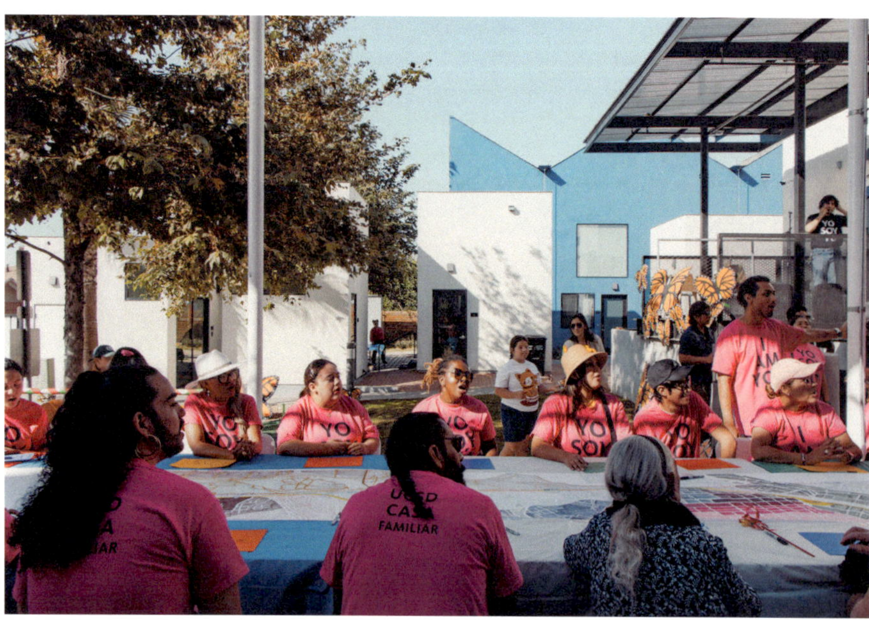

after school   lesson plans

CONNECTING FORMAL AND INFORMAL LEARNING

Extending learning time for low-income students

School-day and after-school programs

Linking socio-emotional wellbeing and environmental empathy

Integrating Indigenous cultural practices to tackle climate challenges

Enhancing Science Standards with a hands-on climate curriculum

Urban-ecological learning stations and environmental design labs

Linkages between academic and vocational knowledges

Participatory community-based climate action

Access to higher education and career pathways

Enhancing conventional STEM with multiple literacies

Opening doors for our children to see themselves reflected in our environment, understanding that the care for nature resembles the care for each other

New interfaces between indoor and outdoor, academic and experiential education, to advance creative interfaces between science, arts, humanities and socio-emotional learning, all mobilized through restorative practices

Motivating family and teacher engagement to accompany these processes

Mobilizing community voice to increase collective capacity for climate action

Constructing a new integral person, across multiple literacies, through which social and environmental empathy, moral and ethical standards are reinforced

Nurturing a new cross-sector learning coalition of school and civic partners

Advancing place-based climate action and neighborhood-based solutions

Children are the climate stewards of the future

The healthy, social and emotional life of our youth should be the catalyst for a new ecological imagination, defined by interdependence, empathy and coexistence

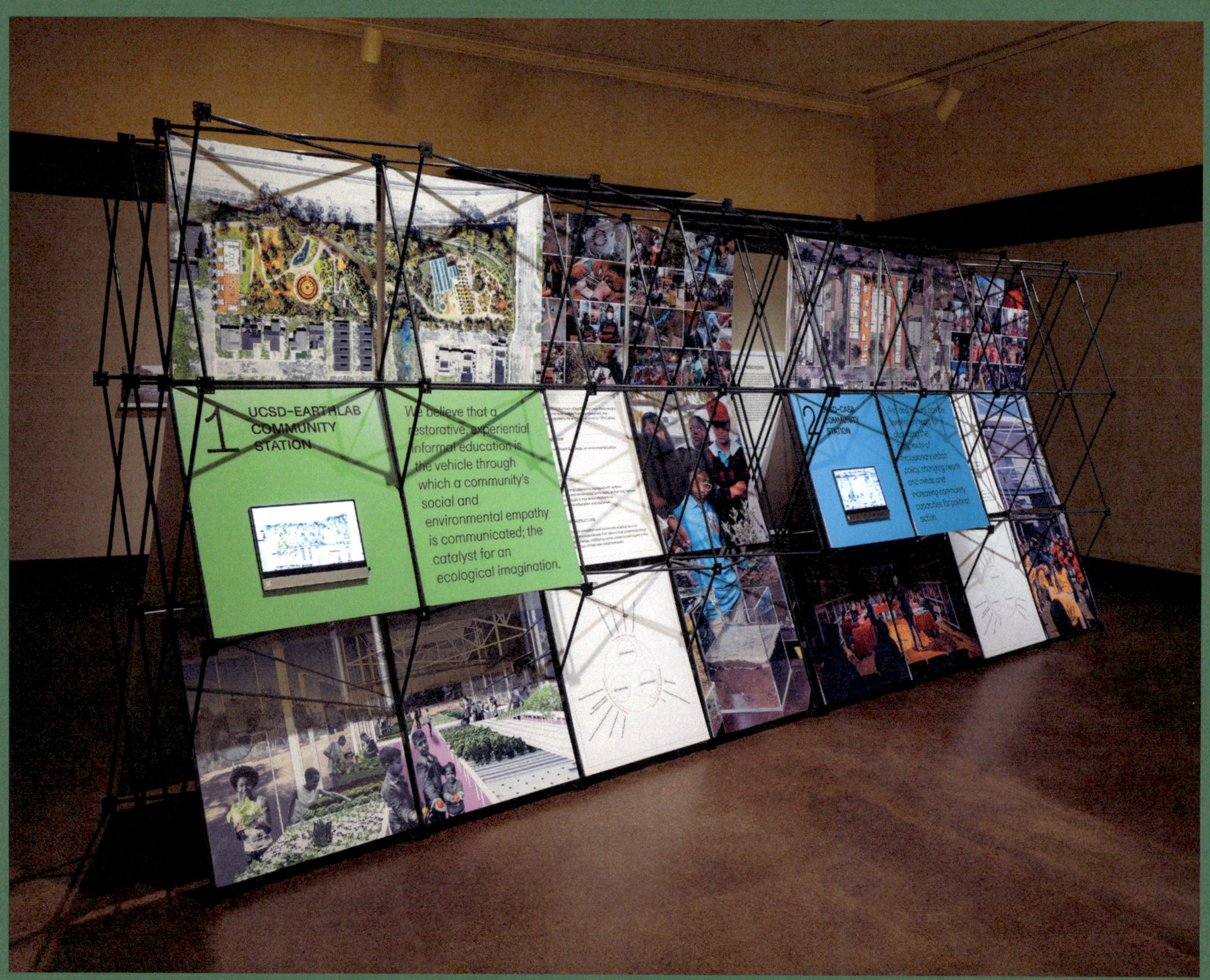

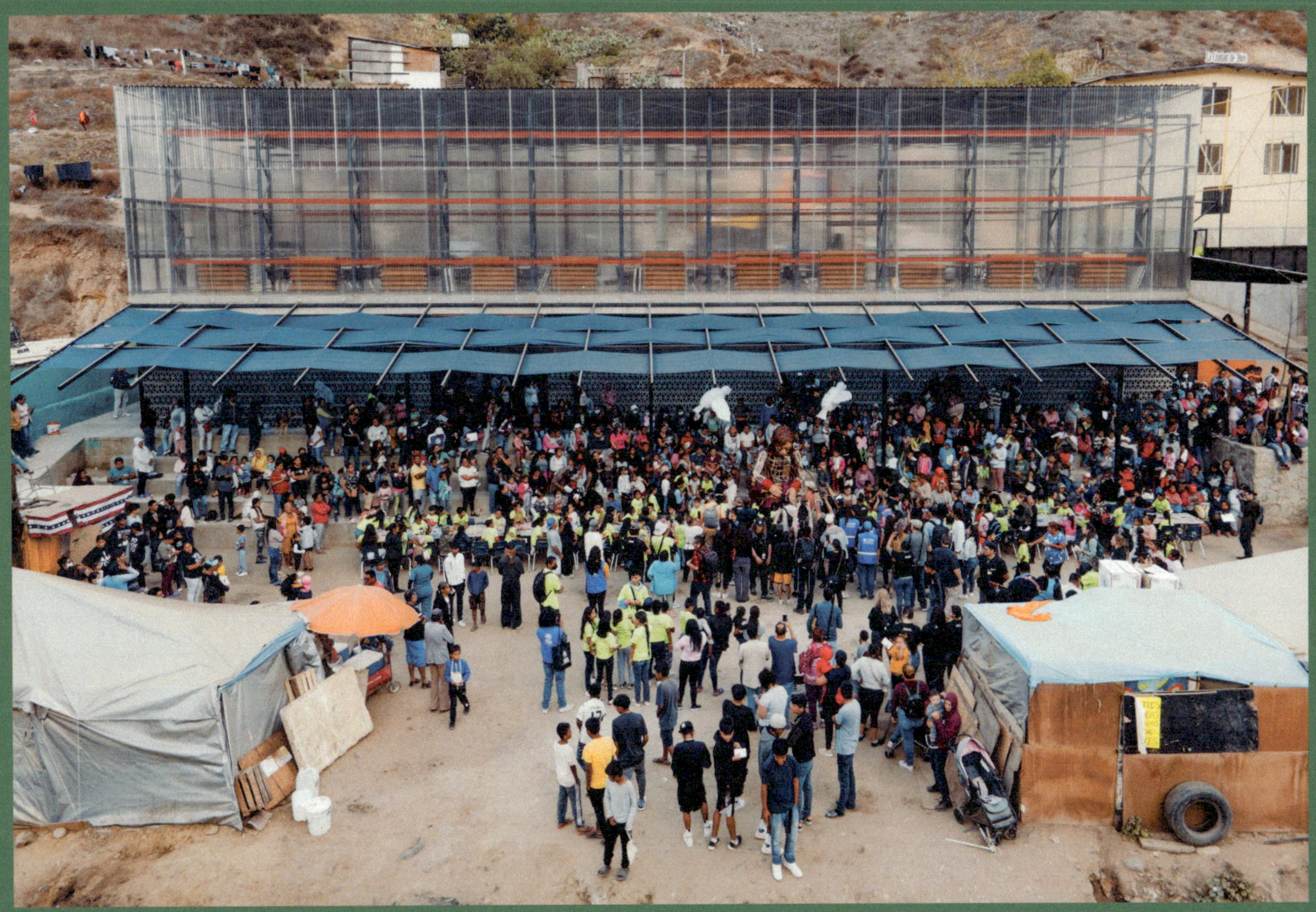

ESTUDIO TEDDY CRUZ &
FONNA FORMAN

Cross Border Public Spaces

TIMELINE OF BLACK, LATINX, INDIGENOUS SOLIDARITY IN LAND & FOOD SOVEREIGNTY

ALL REVOLUTION IS BASED ON LAND

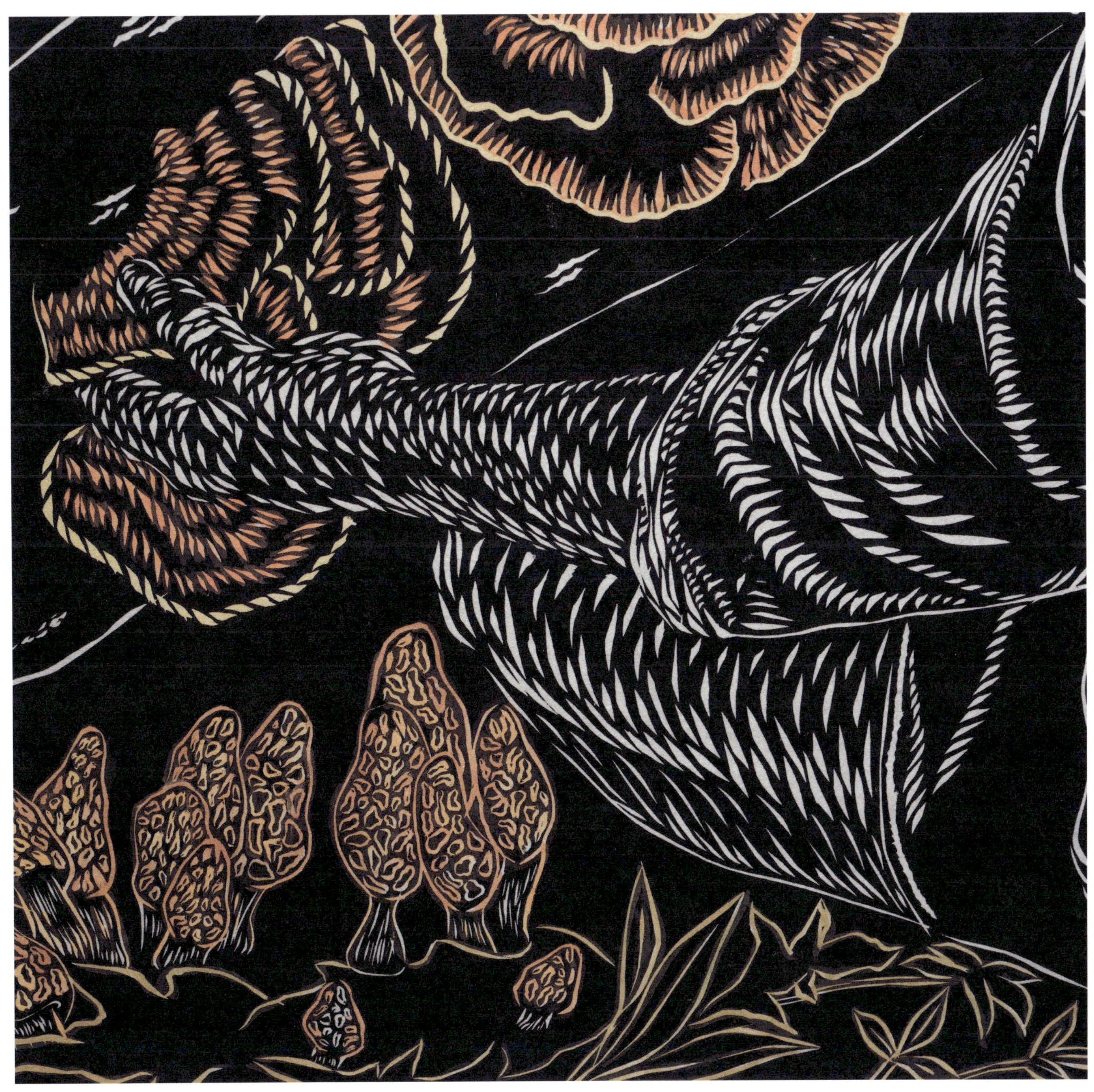

Laura Montoya, *Antonia with Mushrooms, Detail*, 2025, silkscreen print on parachute paper, installation view of *after school*, Carnegie Museum of Art, 2025; photo: Zachary Riggleman

10,000 YEARS AGO– THE 1800s Indigenous peoples of Turtle Island sustainably used fire, prayer, and natural fertility to clear grazing lands for buffalo and wild game, manage edges for fruiting brambles, and maintain intercrops of sacred maize, beans, squash, and other crops.

1600s –1800s Maroon communities, formed by Indigenous peoples and Africans who escaped the plantations, fiercely resisted slavery by establishing autonomous settlements in remote areas like forests and swamps. They carried seeds, grew their own food, and engaged in strategic attacks against plantations, liberating others and disrupting the colonial order.

1700s –1800s African women in the Dahomey region of West Africa selected and saved seeds of sorghum, rice, millet, watermelon, okra, cowpeas, barley, and hibiscus, and braided those seeds into each other's hair before boarding transatlantic slave ships.

1715 Warriors from virtually all Indigenous communities in the south, including the Catawbas, Piedmont, Choctaws, and Yamasee, took up arms against the British and ended the Native slave trade. The Yamasee began providing refuge for Africans who escaped from slavery.

1739 The Stono Rebellion was the largest revolt of enslaved people to ever occur in the thirteen colonies. There were at least two hundred and fifty such revolts before slavery was abolished, including the 1522 Hispaniola Revolt, the 1811 German Coast Uprising, the 1831 Nat Turner Rebellion, the 1839 Amistad Revolt at sea, and the successful 1841 Creole Slave Ship Rebellion.

1776-1865 Enslaved Africans in the United States resisted the dehumanizing effects of slavery through subtle, everyday acts of defiance. They maintained their cultural identity through language, songs, and religious practices. After long days working in the plantation fields, many cultivated their own gardens to supplement their meager rations and innovated soulful recipes with the "waste foods" made available to them.

1815 Alexandre Pétion, first President of the Republic of Haiti, offered sanctuary, and later military support, to Simón Bolívar, a key leader in the Central/South American fight for independence from Spain. Sanctuary was offered on the condition that Bolívar outlaw slavery in the newly liberated territories.

1836 Black people who escaped slavery in the United States took up arms alongside Indigenous Mexicans to defend Mexican Texas from the United States at the Battle of the Alamo.

1846 The first three thousand African American farmers moved to rural land in the Adirondacks of New York, calling their community "Timbucto." In 1859, Harriet Tubman and her family moved to rural Auburn, New York.

1855 Four thousand Black people escaping slavery, and en route to the Mexican border, received assistance from Mexicans in Texas—the southern Underground Railroad.

1868 After the forty acres allotments were reversed, Tunis Campbell purchased 1250 acres and formed an association of two hundred Black farmers to share the land, known as St. Catherine's Island Community. A militia of three hundred was also formed for protection from the Klu Klux Klan.

1860-1920 Black farmers established independent towns such as Africatown, AL; Kingdom of Happy Land, NC; Nicodemus, KS; Pembroke, IL; Mound Bayou, MI; Eatonville, FL; Hobson City, AL; Allensworth, CA; Rentiesville, Clearview, Boley and Langston, OK; North Brentwood, MD; Greenwood, OK, also known was "Black Wall Street"; Boley, Creek Nation, Indian Territory, OK; and Blackdom, NM.

1881 Booker T. Washington founded Tuskegee University, training generations of Black farmers, including George Washington Carver and Booker T. Whatley, who brought us "regenerative agriculture," Community Supported Agriculture (CSA), and "pick your own."

1910 Despite racial violence and the broken promise of "forty acres and a mule," Black people had purchased 120,738 farms by 1890. By 1910, Black farmers had accumulated 218,972 farms and nearly fifteen million acres, fourteen percent of the nation's farmland.

1934 After decades of nonviolent self-organization, thousands of poor whites and Blacks formed the Southern Tenant Farmers' Union to resist oppression by plantation owners and discrimination by the government.

1962 Larry Itliong organized 1500 Filipino American workers to strike as a coalition with Cesar Chavez, Dolores Huerta, and other Mexican American workers. This farmworker uprising, known as the Delano Grape Strike, brought the grape industry to its knees. In response, California was the first state to change its labor laws. This was the beginning of the United Farm Workers Union.

1964 Southern Black Farmers used their land to feed, house, and protect Civil Rights organizers. They also leveraged it as collateral for bail money.

1967 The Federation of Southern Cooperatives and the Land Assistance Fund, a collective of dozens of Black-owned cooperative businesses, was organized to save Black land and to build economic power. The Black Panthers, Young Lords, Young Patriots, Student Nonviolent Coordinating Committee, Mexican American Youth Organization, Crusade for Justice, and Hopi Nation collectively agree to fight against divisive state tactics and sign a treaty of cooperation—the Treaty of Peace, Harmony, and Mutual Assistance.

1968   The Black Panthers provided free breakfast to over twenty thousand children every day. They also provided free groceries, drove elders to doctor's appointments, and gave rides to those visiting incarcerated loved ones.

1969   Shirley and Charles Sherrod started New Communities Farm Cooperative in Albany, Georgia—the first land trust in the United States, owning 5700 acres shared by twelve Black families. Around the same time, the Honorable Elijah Muhammad purchased 4500 acres of land in Georgia as a collective farm for the Nation of Islam. Fannie Lou Hamer's Freedom Farm Cooperative, which provided land, food, scholarships, and a "pig bank" to distribute thousands of livestock animals to Black farmers in Mississippi, was founded.

1970–2013   The Oneida Nation sues local, state, and federal authorities for land theft in the seventeenth and eighteenth centuries, eventually purchasing land on the open market and putting it into trust.

1993   A coalition of 148 peasant farmer organizations from Asia, Africa, and the Americas defend seeds, protect farmer rights, advocate for agrarian reform, and work for food sovereignty as part of the Via Campesina.

1998   The state of Florida pays reparations to Black victims of the Rosewood Massacre.

1998   The Coalition of Immokalee Workers (CIW), a worker-based rights organization, ended human trafficking in their industry and won wage increases for tomato pickers in Florida.

1999   Black farmers sued the United States Department of Agriculture and won over one billion dollars for 13,300 farmers who lost their land due to government discrimination. Known as the Pigford Class Action Lawsuit, it was the largest civil rights settlement in US history at the time.

2006   At the Detroit Black Community Food Security Network and D-Town Farm, Black people run a cooperative seven-acre farm and grocery store—a national model for Black food and land sovereignty.

2010   Farmers burn Monsanto seed donations and protest the corporation's presence in Haiti as part of the Haitian Peasant Movement.

2015   Fresh Future Farm grows on 0.8 acres in the Chicora neighborhood in North Charleston, South Carolina and runs a full-service grocery store right on site.

The Dakota and Lakota peoples of the Standing Rock Sioux Reservation, together with thousands of other water protectors, (many First Nations, Black, and Latinx) resist the Dakota Access Pipeline which threatens Native land and water.

2019 The White Earth Band of the Ojibwe Nation legally recognized the rights of wild rice, furthering the international "rights of nature" movement.

2020 The Justice for Black Farmers Act is an opportunity to reverse and correct millions of acres of land loss within the Black farming community and to fortify the next generation of Black farmers. The bill includes the return of land to dispossessed Black farmers, a conservation corps for farmer training, funding for Historically Black Colleges and Universities, USDA civil rights reforms, expanded farm credit, contract protections, and legal assistance to prevent further land loss for Black farmers.

PRESENT Despite dislocation, land theft, and genocidal intentions on the part of European colonizers, 1500 registered Stockbridge-Munsee Mohican people survive and have a strong reservation community with pow wow, lodge ceremony, elder care, and ecological conservation. They are repatriating stolen artifacts and the remains of their relatives and fighting the E37 pipeline. The Eastern Woodlands Rematriation Collective sustains "the spiritual foundation of traditional livelihoods through sustainable food and agroecological systems" in the New England area.

2010–PRESENT Black Farmers and Urban Gardeners (BUGs) nurtures collective Black agrarian leadership and reimagines Black futures. The BUGs conference has grown from a small gathering to over six hundred participants.

2015–PRESENT The National Black Food and Justice Alliance (NBFJA) represents hundreds of Black urban and rural farmers, organizers, and land stewards. They work together towards an intergenerational urban/rural movement to map, assess, train, and deepen the organizing, institution-building, and advocacy work which protects Black land and works towards food sovereignty.

2018–PRESENT The Reparations Map from the Northeast Farmers of Color Land Trust (NEFOC) is created, with the goal of connecting people looking to dismantle white supremacy through reparations.

2021–PRESENT UJAMAA and Sistah Seeds are independently formed to regenerate culturally-important varieties and seed-keeping traditions from the African Diaspora, while uplifting Black seed stories and empowering aspiring Black seed stewards.

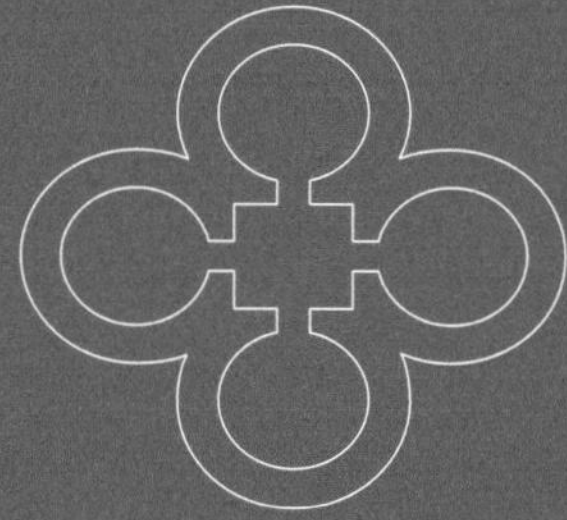 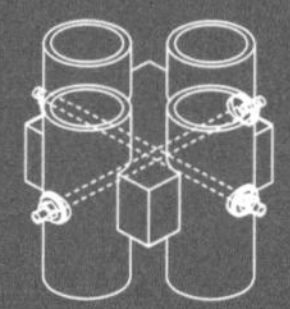

 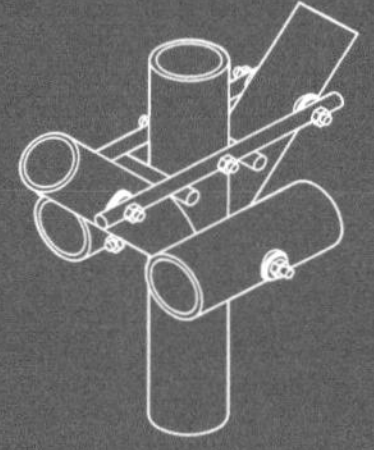

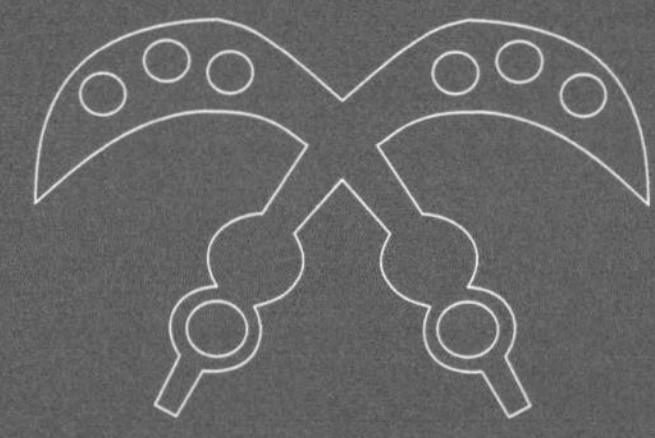 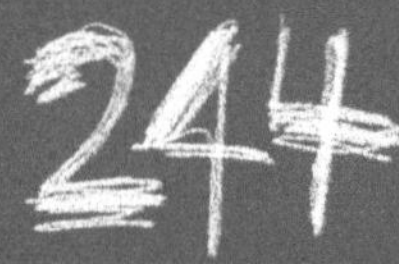

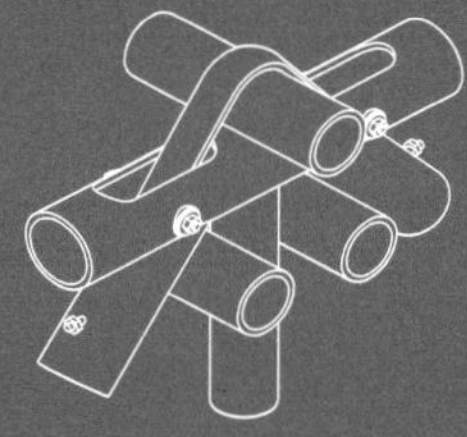

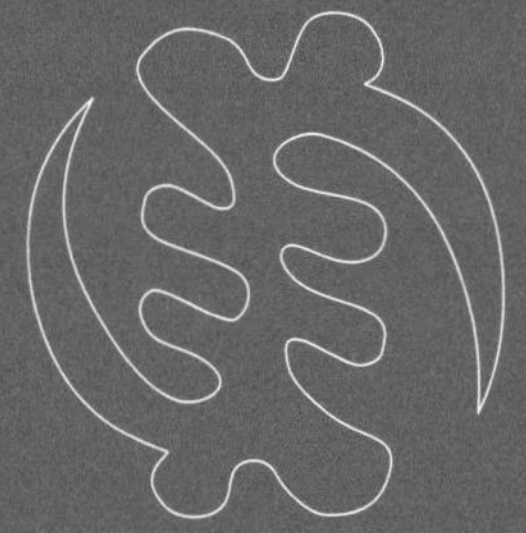 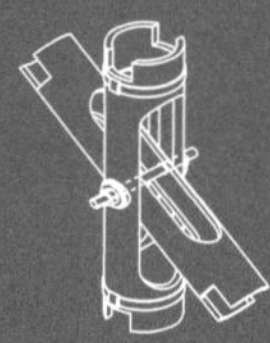

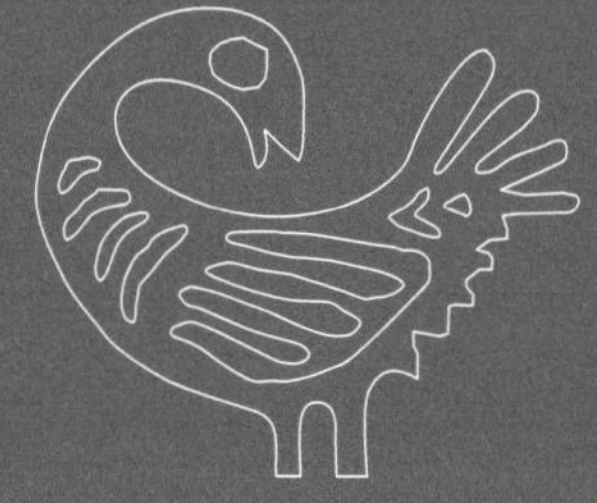 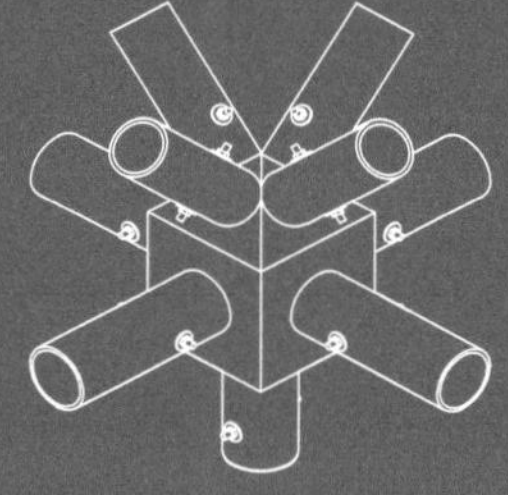

THE URBAN CLASSROOM

AYANNA JONES

FROM PANTHERS TO PLANTING: A LEGACY OF RESISTANCE THROUGH FOOD JUSTICE

IN COLLABORATION WITH VICKY ACHNANI

SANKOFA VILLAGE COMMUNITY GARDEN AND FARM

The Panthers had love for our people—not just in a romantic context but community love, revolutionary love. The kind of love that led the Panthers to feed our children before school, to gift groceries to grandmothers, to build gardens and clinics in places the system had left behind. I was there. I lived it. I saw the way the Black Panther Party moved: bold, organized, and strategic. It was not just about protest; it was about feeding the people. The Black Panther's Free Breakfast Program was power on a plate. It said to every Black child, **"YOU MATTER!"**

We're not calling Homewood South a food desert. That language hides the truth. This is food apartheid—a system that intentionally keeps fresh food, nutrition, and wellness out of Black and underserved areas. It's political. It's historical, and it's deadly.

At Sankofa Village Community Garden and Farms we've picked up the torch. We teach young people how to grow food, how to feed each other, how to organize—just like the Panthers taught us. This is not charity but a strategy. This is survival. This is love calling out across generations.

The Black Panthers gave the blueprint, and now we're passing it on to you.

Left: Vicky Achnani, Sankofa Symbols, 2025; Courtesy of the artist

FROM COMMUNITY DEFENSE TO COMMUNITY CULTIVATION

The Panthers taught us how to defend ourselves with food. At Sankofa Village, we teach how to protect our people through soil, seeds, and self-reliance. Here, we don't just build gardens, we build a living classroom, a healing space, and a command post in the fight against food apartheid.

We teach young folks how to grow what they eat, not just for the sake of gardening, but for the sake of sovereignty. When our students dig into the earth, they're digging into identity. When they harvest, they reclaim what was stolen. The food grown at Sankofa is shared, cooked, preserved, and celebrated—not sold to the highest bidder but returned to the people. It's about relationships, not transactions.

In our spaces, knowledge moves intergenerationally from elder to child, and from child to elder.

We bring together farmers, students, aunties, and activists. Sankofa isn't just about food, though. It's about symbols, rituals, music, and memory. From Sankofa's circuit-spiral to our greenhouse built by young hands, every element holds power.

We move in response to what's needed: growing when possible, distributing when necessary, and teaching always. Sankofa Village Community Garden and Farms is our new breakfast program. The soil is our strategy. Our students are future organizers, growers, healers, and defenders. No matter the city, the town, or the community, the need is the same. Our people are being kept for the very thing that sustains them. But you don't need a big grant or a title to start something. You need heart, vision, and community.

Now pick up the torch and feed your people.

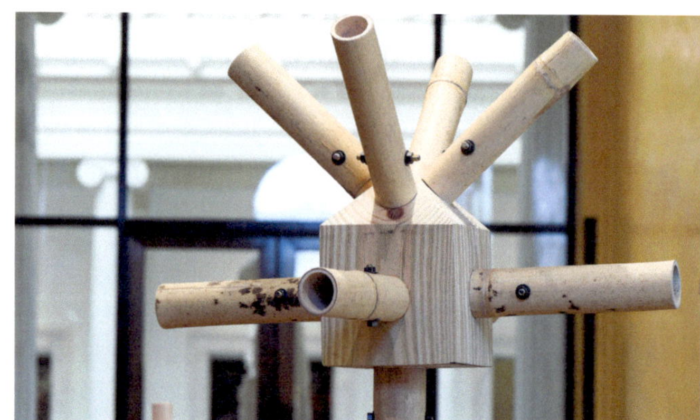

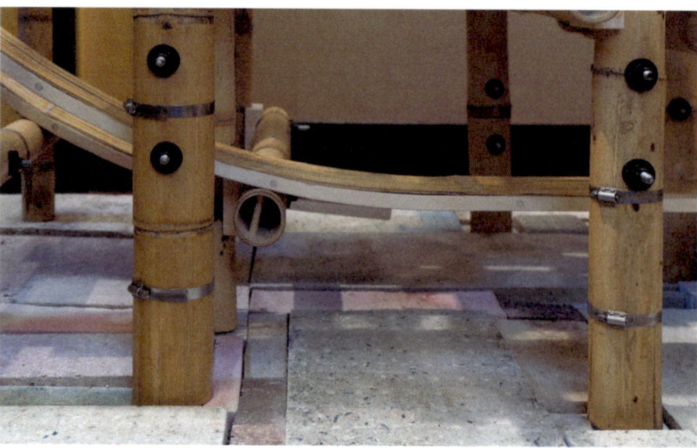

Top & Bottom: Vicky Achnani, Details of *The Urban Classroom*, 2025, repurposed bamboo, birch plywood, and recycled paper, installation views of *after school*, Carnegie Museum of Art, 2025; photo: Zachary Riggleman

FIVE WAYS TO START A MOVEMENT LIKE SANKOFA

01 Start small, start sacred. Identify one plot of land, one school, or one neighborhood. Let it be holy ground. Grow anything, even herbs on a windowsill.

02 Center the people and not the product. Don't chase scales, chase impact. Feed one family deeply before you try to serve hundreds.

03 Connect to legacy and know your local history. Honor the elders by studying Panther Fannie Lou Hamer and the farmers who came before. This work isn't new. It's inherited.

04 Build coalitions when possible. Partner with churches, mutual aid networks, youth groups, veterans, or artists—whoever's aligned. SANKOFA IS A FAMILY, NOT A SILO!

05 Keep love for our people at the center. Let it be your strategy. Let it move through your curriculum, your planning, your planting. This ain't just about kale, collards, and carrots.

This is about reclaiming the right to live

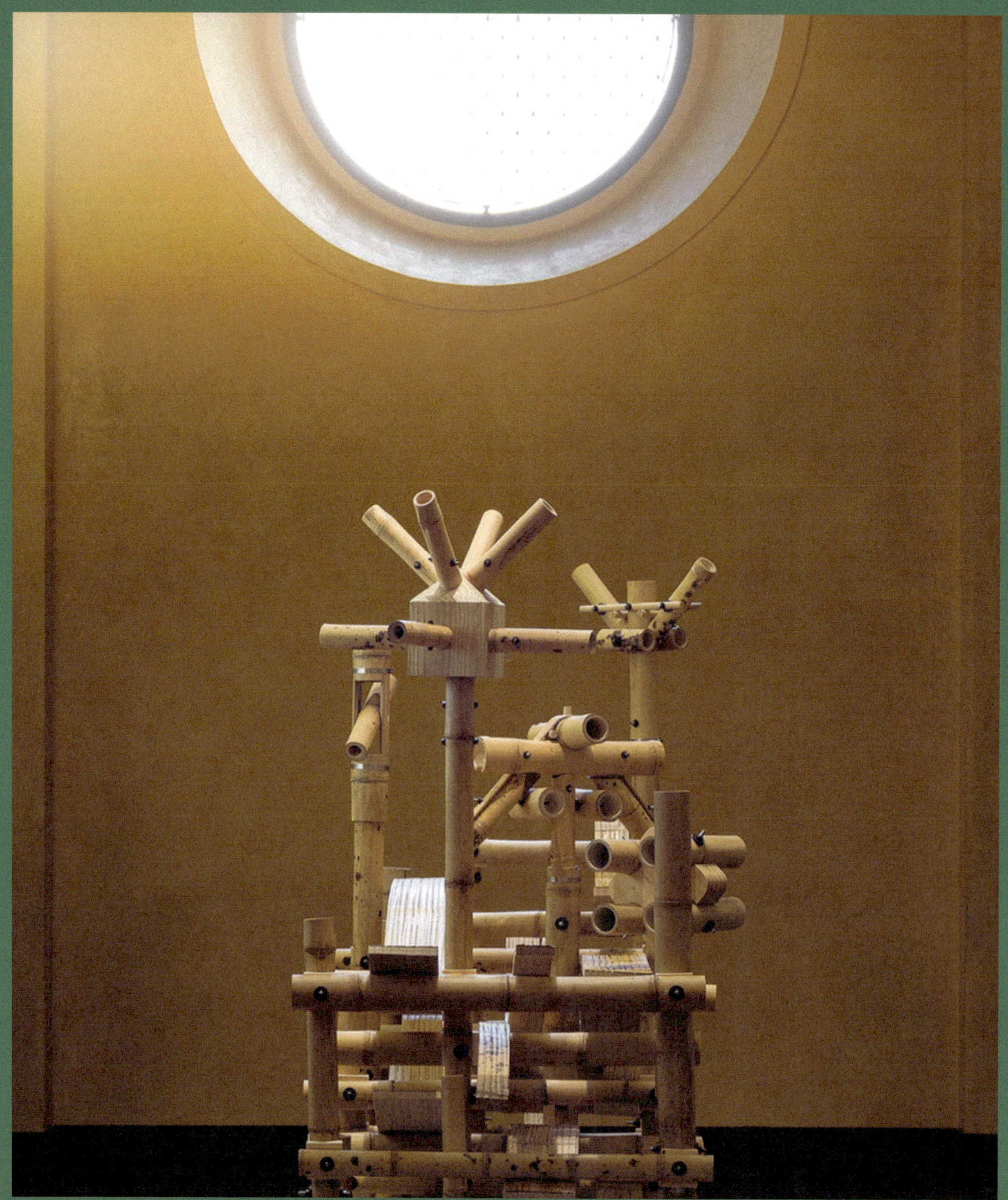

Vicky Achnani, Detail of The Urban Classroom, 2025, installation view of after school, Carnegie Museum of Art, 2025; photo: Zachary Riggleman

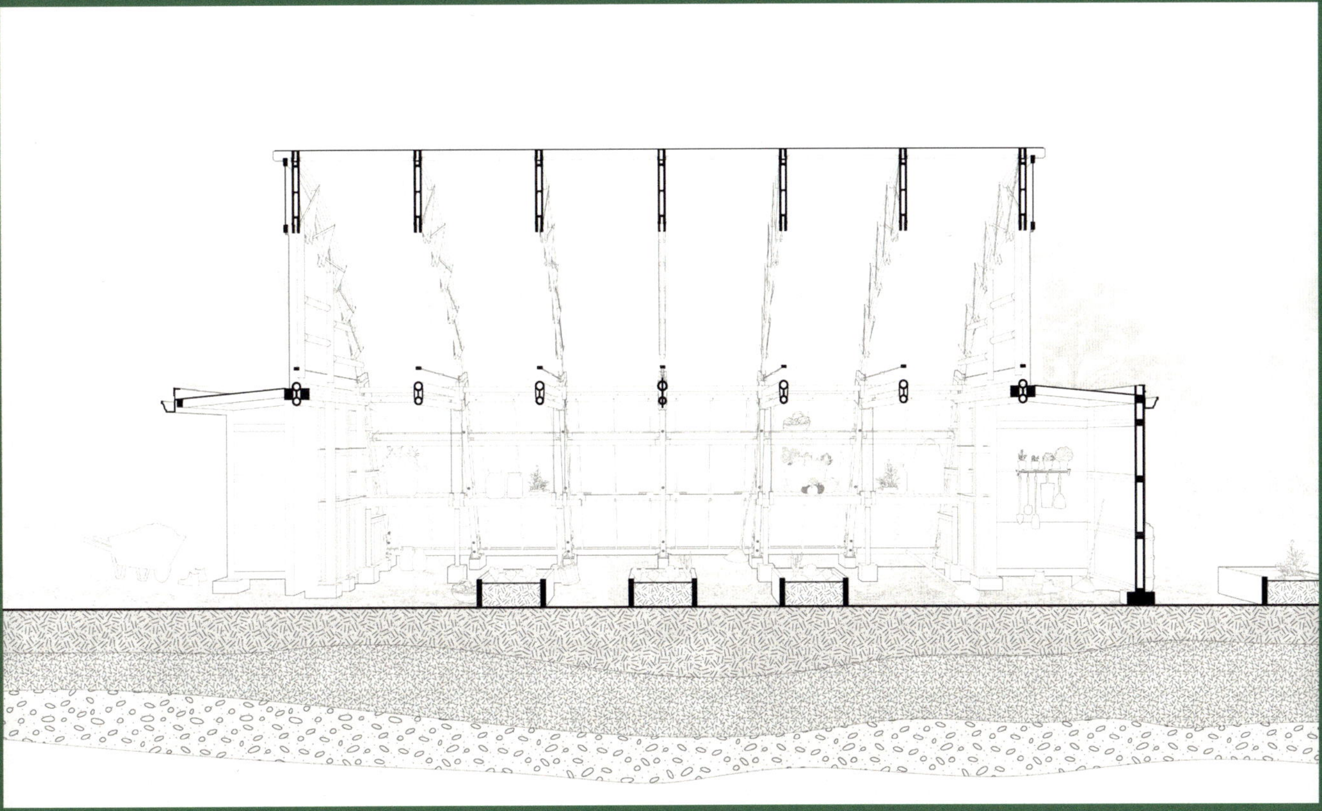

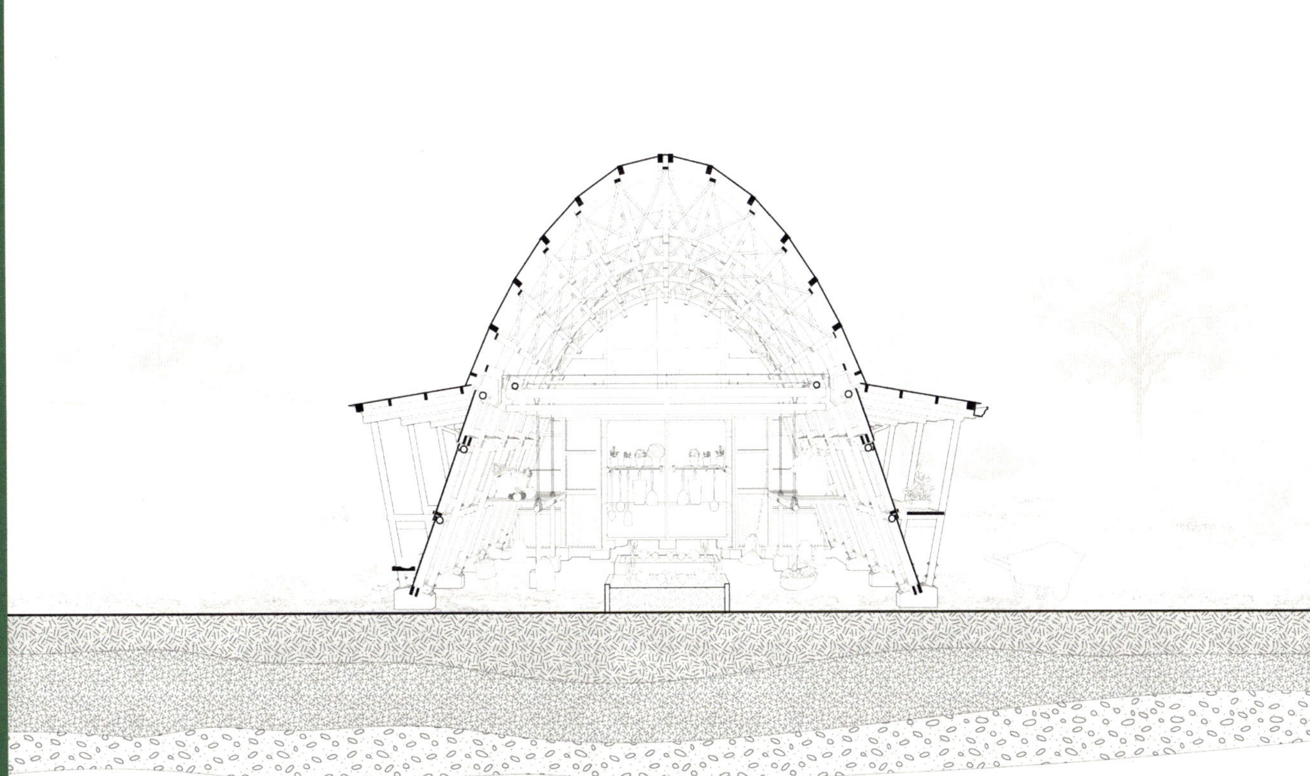

Vicky Achnani, *Sankofa Village Community Garden and Farm Greenhouse, Elevation* (top) and *Section* (bottom), 2025, architectural drawing; Courtesy of the artist

ABBREVIATIONS

CLP: CARNEGIE LIBRARY OF PITTSBURGH

CMUAA: CARNEGIE MELLON UNIVERSITY ARCHITECTURE ARCHIVES

HFF: HEINZ FAMILY FUND

HHC: SENATOR JOHN HEINZ HISTORY CENTER

JPLL: J. PAUL LEONARD LIBRARY, SAN FRANCISCO STATE UNIVERSITY

PH AND MCP STATE ARCHIVES: PENNSYLVANIA HISTORICAL AND MUSEUM COMMISSION PENNSYLVANIA STATE ARCHIVES

PPBF: PITTSBURGH PUBLIC BUILDINGS FACILITY

PPS: PITTSBURGH PUBLIC SCHOOLS

AUTHOR'S BIOS

VICKY ACHNANI is an architectural designer, educator, and maker based in Pittsburgh, serving as full-time special faculty at Carnegie Mellon School of Architecture. His design-build practice—rooted in material experimentation and social engagement, employs unconventional, sustainable methods in underserved communities. A licensed architect in India, he earned his B.Arch from CEPT University and M.Arch from Yale, supported by the India2EU II and J.N. Tata scholarships. Vicky privileges models over drawings, emphasizing making and materiality as generative design tools.

UJJU AGGARWAL has worked for over two decades to build organizing for educational justice, immigrants' rights, and abolition as well as projects at the intersection of arts and social justice, popular education, and adult literacy. She is author of *Unsettling Choice: Race, Rights, and the Partitioning of Public Education* (University of Minnesota Press, 2024). Her current project, *Education Against Enclosure*, tracks education as a practice of freedom and as a site of containment. She is currently an Assistant Professor at The New School.

SAROSH ANKLESARIA is Associate Teaching Professor and Track Chair of the M.Arch program at Carnegie Mellon University. He has practiced architecture in India, Switzerland, and the U.S. His work locates architectural agency across varied scales, temporalities, and geographies, and has been supported by the Richard Rogers Fellowship, Art Omi Residency, Taliesin Fellowship, and the PJ Dick Innovation Fund. Recent projects investigate aging modernism in South Asia, infrastructural systems, and architectures for just transitions.

MIGUEL BRACELI is an interdisciplinary artist working at the intersection of art, architecture, and social practices. Braceli has developed large-scale works across Latin America, Europe, the Middle East, and the U.S., in collaboration with institutions such as Documenta Fifteen and The Bronx Museum. He is co-founder of LA ESCUELA___, a platform for collective learning and making in public spaces.

GABO CAMNITZER is an artist and educator working across experimental pedagogy, installation, and video. Camnitzer's work revolves around questions of knowledge exchange, often focusing on childhood to examine the societal structures that surround and shape subjectivity. Camnitzer is Associate Professor of Art Education and Director of the Saturday Studios Program for children at MASSART in Boston, Massachusetts. He has presented projects at venues such as Pivô, São Paulo; PPOW, New York; Queens Museum, New York; Konsthall C, Stockholm; Momentum Biennale, Moss, Norway.

TEDDY CRUZ (MDes Harvard University) is a Professor of Public Culture and Urbanization in the Department of Visual Arts at the University of California, San Diego. He is known internationally for his urban research of the Tijuana/San Diego border, advancing border neighborhoods as sites of cultural production from which to rethink urban policy, affordable housing, and public space.

DANIELLE DEAN works with archives, video, performance, social practice, sculpture, and drawing to investigate the recursive loops between the circulation of ideas and the material reproduction of global capitalism. Operating across media and with a variety of collaborators and participants, her work examines the fault lines within this seemingly closed circuit. Dean received an MFA from California Institute of the Arts and is an alumna of the Whitney Independent Study Program. Recently completed projects include new commissions for Mercer Union, Toronto (2024), a solo show at Tate Britain, London (2022), and Performa, New York (2021).

RACHEL DELPHIA is the Alan G. and Jane A. Lehman Curator at Carnegie Museum of Art, where she is a specialist in modern and contemporary design and craft. She holds degrees from Carnegie Mellon University and the Winterthur Museum / University of Delaware.

FONNA FORMAN (PhD University of Chicago) is a Professor of Political Theory at the University of California, San Diego and Founding Director of the UCSD Center on Global Justice. Her work focuses on climate justice, borders and migration, and participatory urbanization. She serves as Co-Chair of the University of California's Global Climate Leadership Council.

JILLIAN FORSTADT is the education reporter at 90.5 WESA, Pittsburgh's NPR News station. Her work focuses on the intersection of education, equity and social justice, shedding light on Pennsylvania's school systems. Jillian's award-winning reporting includes investigations into suburban book ban debates, student discipline and misused public health funds in communities facing air pollution.

NOAH FRITSCH is a junior architect at NO ARCHITECTURE. His primary interests are novel shapes and good stories. He earned his professional degree from the Syracuse University School of Architecture, where he received a Citation for Excellence in Design Research and the Undergraduate Award for Significant Contributions to the Program.

STEFAN GRUBER is an Associate Professor at Carnegie Mellon University, where he chairs the Master of Urban Design and directs the Remaking Cities Institute, the School of Architecture's research center for urbanism, participatory action, and community design. His teaching, research, design, and curatorial practice focus on spatial justice, with a particular interest in the commons and the negotiation between top-down planning and bottom-up urban transformation.

JAMES HILL is a life-long Pittsburgher. He is a proud graduate of Pittsburgh public Schools' Miller Elementary School, Pittsburgh Classical Academy, Schenley High School, and later Point Park University. Professionally, he began his career in the administration of Mayor William Peduto. In 2019, the City Council confirmed his nomination as a member of the City's Historic Review Commission. Hill is presently the Director of Government Affairs for the Pittsburgh Cultural Trust.

THEODOSSIS ISSAIAS is an architect and educator. He serves as curator of the Heinz Architectural Center at Carnegie Museum of Art and Special Faculty at Carnegie Mellon University. His research investigates architecture's entanglement with human rights, conflict, and shelter, articulated in his Yale PhD *Architectures of the Humanitarian Front* (2021). As co-founder of FATURA Collaborative, an architecture and research collective, Issaias develops projects on ecology and the domestic.

VIKKI AYANNA JONES, at 78, continues to be a driving force with her lifelong journey of activism and service to the Black community. As a Black Panther, she helped to start one of the first free breakfast programs in Washington DC. While she champions self-sufficiency in Black communities, her profile includes: the mother of five SUNS, grandmother, and great grandmother. She now serves as CEO and founder of Sankofa Village Community Garden, which has flourished for 10 years.

LYNN KAWARATANI is an arts and humanities librarian and manager of the Architecture Archives at Carnegie Mellon University. Prior to moving to Pittsburgh, she had served as the chief of design and editing at the Exhibits Central division of the Smithsonian Institution. She is currently exploring new ways to archive architecture, including conducting oral histories and expanding representation to the inhabitants of places.

JUSTIN LAING has worked in out of school education with young people and adults since 1992 and is particularly excited about interventions informed by socialism, Pan-Afrikanism, and Black nationalism. Justin is a member of the Black Socialist Formation, and Black Alliance for Peace and initiated as a priest of Oshun in the Lukumi tradition through Ile Asho Funfun. Justin is the husband of Ebony Ross and father of Kufere, Etana and Adeyemi.

JIN KETEVAN GEORGIA MEISENBERG is an artist whose practice unfolds through play, imagination, and collaboration. Despite her young age, Jin has already participated in several notable exhibitions that merge her innate creativity with contemporary artistic frameworks. Her practice is characterized by imaginative visual storytelling and playful yet thoughtful engagement with space and material. Jin's work invites others into a collaborative process, transforming personal drawings and gestures into collective experiences.

LAJJA MISTRY is a reporter for Pittsburgh's Public Source, a new source that informs and inspires the Pittsburgh region through the power of deep, independent journalism. In her role, she writes about how school systems, classroom practices and policies impact students and families, with a focus on equity in education. Lajja is originally from India and holds a graduate degree from the University of Southern California.

TOSHIKO MORI is the founder and principal of Toshiko Mori Architect in New York City. She is the Robert P. Hubbard Professor in the Practice of Architecture at Harvard Graduate School of Design and was previously chair of the Department of Architecture (2002–2008). Mori currently serves as the vice president of architecture for the American Academy of Arts and Letters and she is also a member of the American Academy of Arts and Sciences.

LAURA NELSON researches radical pedagogies and co-organizes experiments in learning in cities. Her current book project, *After School: Collective Experiments in Art, Study, and Education*, looks at different formations of study outside of traditional schools and universities from the 1920s to the 1980s. She is an Assistant Professor of English at Princeton University.

LEIGH PATEL's work is based in the knowledge that as long as oppression has existed so have freedom struggles. She is a community-based researcher as well as an eldercare provider, educator, and writer. Prior to being a Professor, she was a middle school language arts teacher, a journalist, and a state-level policymaker. Her work has been featured in outlets including NPR, The Atlantic, and Ms. Magazine.

DAVID SERLIN is Professor of Communication and Science Studies at UC San Diego, His most recent book is *Window Shopping with Helen Keller: Architecture and Disability in Modern Culture* (University of Chicago Press, 2025). He is a Fellow of the American Academy in Rome, which awarded him the 2021 Rome Prize in Architecture.

ANA SERRANO earned her BFA from Art Center College of Design (2008). Serrano was born and raised in Los Angeles and is a first generation Mexican American. She is inspired by the intersection of her dual cultural identities. She is best known for creating work that references the built environment using brightly-colored cardboard and paper. Serrano currently lives and works in Portland, Oregon.

SISTER IASIA THOMAS has been involved with activism for educational justice and a more inclusive cultural educational state in public education for over twenty years. She leads Children's Windows to Africa. She is a consultant for institutions committed to elevating community education. *Kindezi: The Kongo Art of Babysitting* guides her praxis around Black learning, written by Kimbwandende Kia Bunseki Fu-Kiau and A.M. Lukondo-Wamba, as well as Dr. Asa Hilliard's *To Be an African Teacher*.

PETE VITTI grew up in the Stanton Heights neighborhood of Pittsburgh and attended Peabody High School 1979-1983. In 1993 he accepted a position at Pittsburgh's Schenley High School as a social studies teacher where he taught until its closure. In 2000 he transferred to the newly created Obama Academy where he taught until his retirement in 2024. He has two children, Anna and Rosa, who graduated with IB diplomas from Obama Academy in 2013 and 2015.

LEAH WULFMAN is a Carrier Bag architect, educator, game designer, digital puppeteer, and occasional writer. Trained as an architect, Wulfman assembles hybrid virtual and physical spaces in order to prototype new relationships to technology and nature, as well as challenge normative ideologies so often reinforced by technology and architecture. In addition to mixed reality installations that play with and emphasize the physical, material basis of everything digital, their research focuses on gamified environments, interactions and materials.

SOUL FIRE FARM is an Afro-Indigenous centered community farm and training center dedicated to uprooting racism and seeding sovereignty in the food system. With deep reverence for the Earth and wisdom of our ancestors, we practice regenerative agroecology, raise and distribute life-giving food, equip the rising generation of BIPOC farmers, and mobilize communities to work toward food and land sovereignty.

LALA MONTOYA currently rooted in the Hudson Valley, was born and raised in Medellín, Colombia. She draws inspiration from abundant nature, recognizing inherent individual richness, which manifests in her compelling earthy art across ceramics, wood carving, painting, and printing blocks. Through these mediums, Montoya seeks to illuminate the beauty of time and age, making transparent small details often missed. Working with youth in her partnerships keeps this work vibrant and alive.

CRYSTAL CLARITY is an artist, illustrator, printmaker, dream weaver, and visual strategist for movement moments. She brings 15+ years experience directing community mural projects and mentoring young people in using art for activism. In 2020 she launched Medicine Walls, partnering with organizers to promote social transformations through public art. She supports activists in visual resistance, strengthening strategies for direct actions and protests, aiming to magnify collective imagination for a better world through mentorship and skill-sharing.

NAIMA PENNIMAN is a multidimensional artist and visionary poet rooted in land stewardship and community organizing as Co-Founder of WILDSEED Community Farm & Healing Village and Curator of Programs at SOUL FIRE FARM. Through the groundbreaking work of Climbing PoeTree, Naima has performed poetry and music, created murals, and facilitated arts activism workshops globally. Naima's writing is published in numerous works, and her art has been featured in the Museum of the City of New York, The African American Museum in Philadelphia, The Museum of Contemporary African Diasporic Art, and Museo Del Barrio.

SHARVI SHAH is a second year Master of Architecture student at Carnegie Mellon University. She completed her Bachelor of Architecture from CEPT University, India.

She has practiced Architecture in India across various typologies including residential, commercial, and memorial design. Recent projects explore the tangible relationships in design between materiality and material practices across various regions.

TIM SMITH, a life-long Pittsburgh resident and Center of Life's CEO, is affectionately known as "PT" (short for Pastor Tim). Though Center of Life was founded in an official capacity in 2001, his roots in Hazelwood run deep, and he's worked and volunteered in the community since the 1980s. His passion for connecting with kids and families led him to create Center of Life as a nonprofit and community empowerment organization, one founded on his personal philosophies and that guides the organization's direction and impact to this day. When asked his favorite thing about Hazelwood, PT says, "The people… Because everything is about people. The people [in Hazelwood] are my professors and Hazelwood is the university."

MCKENZIE STUPICA is a curatorial fellow at the Carnegie Museum of Art and a PhD Candidate in the Department of Art History at Northwestern University, specializing in comparative and non-Western modernisms with a particular interest in design, architecture, and transnational networks of pedagogical exchange. McKenzie's dissertation project bridges historical research on the Hochschule für Gestaltung in Ulm with a theoretical questioning of the agency of education and its institutions in shaping the emerging contours of twentieth century industrial design in Latin America.

NICHOLAS THIES is a second year Master of Architecture student at Carnegie Mellon University. He graduated with his Bachelor of Architectural Design from the University of Florida and studied abroad in Vicenza, Italy in 2024. Recent projects explore fabrication, design for disassembly, and complex relationships between wastewater and civic infrastructure in Pittsburgh.

ALYSSA VELAZQUEZ is an assistant curator at Carnegie Museum of Art. Her work has been featured or is forthcoming in *S/He Speaks 2: Voices of Women, Trans & Nonbinary Folx*, *Burnaway*, and *AutoStraddle*. Residences include Storyknife and as a Freshworks Artist at Kelly Strayhorn Theater. Velazquez was selected as a 2026 Center for Craft Curatorial Fellow, a 2024 Lambda Literary fellow, and was invited to join PlayPenn's 2024-25 Playwrights Cohort.

This is a space of learning—one filled with students, teachers, parents, administrators, designers, architects, faculty, advocates, and activists. This work took over three years of research to think through the state and stakes of public education. We thank everyone who contributed to that process.

We offer heartfelt thanks to our partners who guided us throughout the city, into archives, and who will continue to care for this material well *after school:* Stephen Connell, Director of Facilities at Pittsburgh Public Schools' Building Facilities; Margaret E. Hewitt, Manager of Reference Services at the Senator John Heinz History Center; Lynn Kawaratani, Arts and Humanities Librarian at Carnegie Mellon University Archives; and Amanda Ciccone, Archivist at Carnegie Library of Pittsburgh – Main. We are deeply indebted to your care and collaboration.

We offer special thanks to the twenty-six external contributors and fellow travelers who gave their time and research toward this publication: Ujju Aggarwal, Sarosh Anklesaria, Miguel Braceli, Gabo Camnitzer, Martin Chetlin, Jolene Elder, Paula Elder, Jillian Forstadt, Noah Fritsch, Stefan Gruber, Wanda Henderson, James Hill, Regina Holley, Tamanika Howze, Ayanna Jones, Justin Laing, Lajja Mistry, Anthony Mitchell, Laura Nelson, Leigh Patel, Christen Robl, David Serlin, James Stewart, Sister IAsia Thomas, Sala Udin, and Pete Vitti. We appreciate their pedagogical inquiries and belief in a public school unbound.

We owe the deepest gratitude to our book designer, Corinne Ang, who guided the playful vision from start to finish. We are in awe of the drawings by Sharvi Kamal Shah and Nicholas Thies, in collaboration with Sarosh Anklesaria—all of which are a testament to the creative potential of learning spaces. Dani Lamorte expertly edited a variety of text styles and voices with deftness and precision, and McKenzie Stupica kept the multivalent and complex project workflows on track. We also thank Tuliza Sindi, Director of Carnegie Mellon University School of Architecture's *in otherwards* imprint, for their commitment to this project.

To the artists—Vicky Achnani; Gabo Camnitzer; Teddy Cruz and Fonna Forman; Danielle Dean; Toshiko Mori, with Charles Burke and Olivia Champ Tremml; Ayanna Jones, founder of Sankofa Village Community Garden and Farm; Ana Serrano; Soul Fire Farm, with contributions from Crystal Clarity, Lala Montoya, and Naima Penniman; and Leah Wulfman, with Jin Ketevan Georgia Meisenberg—thank you for your insightful and inciting lessons taught to us throughout and in the form of this book.

Within the museum, there were countless individuals invested in this project. We are especially grateful to photographer Zachary Riggleman for installation photography, to Brette Richmond and Hannah Lesser for their in-gallery graphic design, and to Tasha Akemah for leading the exhibition design. Erin Barnhart and Jon Irving executed an array of intricate contracts and fee structures. Melanie Groves and her team of registrars, art handlers, and conservators were indispensable in preparing artworks for the exhibition. Registrar Reba Harmon, under the leadership of Elizabeth Tufts-Brown, coordinated countless object checklists to ensure works were in the right place at the right time to be installed within the galleries. Art preparators Will Bergman, James Nestor, and Shawn Watrous, along with Chris Michaels, Stephanie Taylor, Sophie Thompson, Bill Kindelan, Aurelia Sheehan, Scout Owen, Kyp Bellinger, Timothy Green, and Dustin Perri, gave their attention to detail. In conservation, Mary Wilcop, Ana Alba, and Jessica Keister developed ingenious display strategies for much of the never-before-seen archival material.

We are also grateful to Clarissa Morales and Phoebe Irwin for financial management. As always, we appreciate the encouragement and support offered by Carnegie Museum of Art leadership, Eric Crosby, and advisory board chair, Deborah K. Dick. Finally, we thank Omar Khan, Professor and Head of the School of Architecture at Carnegie Mellon University, for championing our vision and believing in this partnership between our two institutions.

Theodossis Issaias, curator, Heinz Architectural Center

Alyssa Velazquez, assistant curator

REPRODUCTION CREDITS

All photographs of *after school* installation views are by Zachary Riggleman unless otherwise noted.

All axonometric drawings are by Sharvi Shah and Nicholas Thies, M.Arch Class of 2026, School of Architecture, Carnegie Mellon University.

Every reasonable effort has been made to identify, contact, and acknowledge rights holders. Edits or omissions will be corrected in subsequent editions.

Cover-p. 9: © Detre Library & Archives, Heinz History Center

p. 15: © Pittsburgh Public Buildings Facility

p.17: © Carnegie Museum of Art, Heinz Family Fund. Photo: Charles "Teenie" Harris

p. 19: © Detre Library & Archives, Heinz History Center

p. 20: © Carnegie Museum of Art, Heinz Family Fund. Photo: Charles "Teenie" Harris

p. 23: © Carnegie Mellon University Architecture Archives

p. 25: © Detre Library & Archives, Heinz History Center

p. 28-29: © Pittsburgh Public Buildings Facility

p. 31: © Carnegie Museum of Art, Heinz Family Fund. Photo: Charles "Teenie" Harris

p. 32: © Detre Library & Archives, Heinz History Center

p. 35: © Carnegie Museum of Art, Heinz Family Fund. Photo: Charles "Teenie" Harris

p. 36-37: © Detre Library & Archives, Heinz History Center

p. 42 and 47: © Carnegie Library of Pittsburgh

p. 49: © Detre Library & Archives, Heinz History Center

p. 50-51: © Pennsylvania Historical and Museum Commission Pennsylvania State Archives

p. 53: © Detre Library & Archives, Heinz History Center

p. 54: © National Museum of American History

p. 55: © Carnegie Museum of Art

p. 57: © Pennsylvania Historical and Museum Commission Pennsylvania State Archives

p. 59-63: © Carnegie Library of Pittsburgh

p. 69 and 72: © Carnegie Museum of Art, Heinz Family Fund. Photo: Charles "Teenie" Harris

p. 75: © Detre Library & Archives, Heinz History Center

p. 77: Courtesy of David Serlin

p. 78 and 81: © Detre Library & Archives, Heinz History Center

p. 83-91: © Labor Archives and Research Center, J. Paul Leonard Library, San Francisco State University

p. 93: © Miguel Braceli. Courtesy of Miguel Braceli

p. 94: © Stefan Gruber. Courtesy of Stefan Gruber. Photo: Tom Little; © Miguel Braceli. Courtesy of Miguel Braceli

p. 96: © Stefan Gruber. Courtesy of Stefan Gruber. Photo: Stefan Gruber

p. 99: © Miguel Braceli. Courtesy of Miguel Braceli

p. 102: © Pittsburgh Public Buildings Facility

p. 105-107: © Carnegie Museum of Art

p. 110-111: © Pittsburgh Public Buildings Facility

p. 113-114: © Detre Library & Archives, Heinz History Center

p. 115: © Carnegie Museum of Art, Heinz Family Fund. Photo: Charles "Teenie" Harris

p. 116: © Carnegie Museum of Art, Gift of Pittsburgh Public Schools

p. 117: © Carnegie Library of Pittsburgh; © Deter Library & Archives, Heinz History Center

p. 118-119: © Pittsburgh Public Buildings Facility

p. 121: © Deter Library & Archives, Heinz History Center

p. 122: © Carnegie Library of Pittsburgh

This book is published on the occasion of the exhibition *after school*, curated by Theodossis Issaias, curator, Heinz Architectural Center, and Alyssa Velazquez, assistant curator, with McKenzie Stupica, curatorial fellow, and organized by the Carnegie Museum of Art, Pittsburgh, August 23, 2025–January 11, 2026.

The programs of the Heinz Architectural Center are made possible by the generosity of the Drue Heinz Trust.

Carnegie Museum of Art's exhibition program is supported by the Carnegie Museum of Art Exhibition Fund and The Fellows of Carnegie Museum of Art.

Carnegie Museum of Art is supported by The Heinz Endowments and Allegheny Regional Asset District. Carnegie Museum of Art receives state arts funding support through a grant from the Pennsylvania Council on the Arts, a state agency funded by the Commonwealth of Pennsylvania.

This publication is made possible by the generosity of the Drue Heinz Trust and in part through Carnegie Mellon University's Jill Watson Endowment for Innovation at the Intersection of the Arts, honoring our BArch 1987 alumna and faculty member from 1989-1995.

With thanks to Carnegie Mellon University School of Architecture's *in otherwards* Imprint team for 2025: Tuliza Sindi (director), Corinne Ang, Narayan Ashanahalli, Jason Asiedu, Trijya Bhardwaj, Pausha Bovornthamajak, Melika Davarkhah, Lilianne Kouyaté, Keng Pu Li, Ananya Shrimali, and Aakash Vipparla

Copyright © 2025, Carnegie Museum of Art, Carnegie Institute and Carnegie Mellon University School of Architecture

CO-PUBLISHED BY:
Carnegie Museum of Art
4400 Forbes Avenue
Pittsburgh, PA 15213
carnegieart.org

in otherwards, the imprint of Carnegie Mellon University School of Architecture
4919 Frew St,
Pittsburgh, PA 15213
architecture.cmu.edu

Editor: Dani Lamorte
Associate Editor: McKenzie Stupica, Carnegie Museum of Art
Designer: Corinne Ang
Installation Photography: Zachary Riggleman, Carnegie Museum of Art
Printer: Thomas Group Printing, New York
Paper: Accent Opaque Text & Cover
Typeface: ABYME Axo, Champion Sans Condensed LL, Monobloc Mono & OHno Forevs

AVAILABLE THROUGH D.A.P./ DISTRIBUTED ART PUBLISHERS
75 Broad Street
Suite 630
New York, New York 10004
(212) 627-1999
artbook.com
orders@artbook.com

ISBN-13: 978-0-88039-077-4

LIBRARY OF CONGRESS CONTROL NUMBER: 2025947327